PHIGS AND PHIGS PLUS

PHIGS AND PHIGS PLUS

John W. Blake

ACADEMIC PRESS

Harcourt Brace Jovanovich, Publishers

London · San Diego · New York · Boston · Sydney · Tokyo · Toronto

ACADEMIC PRESS LIMITED
24/28 Oval Road,
London NW1 7DX

United States Edition published by
ACADEMIC PRESS, INC.
San Diego, CA 92101

This book is printed on acid free paper

A catalogue record for this book is available from the British Library

ISBN 0–12–103515–8

Printed and bound in Great Britain by Hartnolls Limited, Bodmin, Cornwall

Table of Contents

Preface

The goal of PHIGS is to provide the applications programmer with a means to define, display and modify both 2D and 3D graphical data. PHIGS has been standardized by ISO (the International Organization for Standardization), which have produced a functional specification of PHIGS as well as defined the language bindings for C, FORTRAN and ADA. The functionality of PHIGS has been defined independently of a particular programming language and the binding determines how one is to access this functionality from a particular language, such as FORTRAN. PHIGS PLUS is a set of PHIGS-compatible extensions which provide additional functionality needed for drawing primitives such as curves and surfaces as well as advanced rendering techniques such as lighting, shading and depth cueing. Although PHIGS PLUS is a draft international standard, it needs to be covered, because most PHIGS implementations include many PHIGS PLUS components and it is expected to become an international standard shortly.

The goal of this text is to provide a comprehensive introduction to both PHIGS and PHIGS PLUS as well as the underlying graphics technology. PHIGS PLUS has been covered in two seperate chapters so that one can differentiate between it and PHIGS. The PHIGS functions have been introduced independently of a particular programming language, but numerous examples are provided in C illustrating how to use the C language binding. There is both a Section dedicated to the ISO FORTRAN binding as well as an Appendix with an extensively documented example PHIGS program in FORTRAN.

PHIGS is available on numerous of platforms supporting a wide variety of windowing systems. As a consequence PHIGS has been treated here independently of any given windowing system. The PHIGS suppliers provide a means to integrate the application into the platform's windowing environment. This is unfortunately beyond the scope of both the ISO PHIGS standard and this text.

The example programs have all been written using DEC-PHIGS Version 2.3 and have subsequently been ported to SUN-PHIGS 2.0. The porting effort took one day for all example programs. The sample C code uses the ISO language bindings, currently not available for all PHIGS libraries. The ISO C binding has been available since December 1991 and is expected to be adopted by most, if not all, PHIGS suppliers in the near future.

The example programs and functions in the text have been written with a focus on using PHIGS in a real applications environment. They cover using PHIGS hierarchy and modelling transformations to define articulated objects, using viewing transformation to create a camera viewing model and the structure of an input device processing loop. The Appendix contains a PHIGS PLUS program which uses many of these example functions.

This text has been written over a period of two years and has been influenced by feedback from numerous people. First of all, I would like to thank my wife, Friederike, for her support and keeping me motivated the entire time. I would especially like to acknowledge Michael Wise for the lengthy discussions on 3D graphics and PHIGS in particular; as well as for providing the code which the structure hierarchy example was derived from. I also want to thank William Clifford for his constructive input. Finally, I would like to thank Sun Microsystems GmbH for their professional cooperation and support while porting the example code to the ISO C binding.

John Blake
Digital Equipment GmbH
email: blake@nasaxp.enet.dec.com

CHAPTER 1

The Anatomy of a PHIGS Program

Software developers access system utilities and resources through an applications programming interface (API), consisting of a set of function calls, data types and parameter values. PHIGS is an international computer graphics standard, which defines the functionality of an API addressing the needs of developers of both 2D and 3D computer graphics software. By using a standard interface for programming graphics applications, the software developer is able to write programs with a high level of portability and interoperability. PHIGS provides a large amount of functionality needed by most graphics applications, so that the programmer can focus on adding the benefit particular to his software. This saves the developer from having to write code to draw output primitives, create viewing transformations, maintain a graphical database, etc. Computer manufacturers can use PHIGS as a high-level interface to proprietary hardware accelerators, insulating the applications developer from the peculiarities of a given platform. This allows the hardware developer to supply a consistent programming interface to a range of physical devices.

1.1 Introduction

PHIGS stands for Programmer's Hierarchical Interactive Graphics System, whose functional description is defined in the document ISO/IEC 9592:1988, from the International Organization for Standardization (ISO). The functionality is defined independent of any programming language, with the actual API for a particular language being specified in supplementary documents. At this time bindings for FORTRAN, Ada and C have been standardized [ISOf, ISOg, ISOh] with a Pascal binding still under development. The API specification is also referred to as a *language binding*. Here we shall only consider the FORTRAN and C API's. All example programs in this text use the ISO language bindings and were tested on SUN-PHIGS 2.0. There are a number of issues regarding language bindings, and they will be discussed in greater detail later on in Section 11.3.

PHIGS is a graphics system supporting both output of graphical data to a drawing surface, as well as graphical input. The output primitives' appearance can be controlled by setting attributes, and their position is determined by a set of transformations. A major component of PHIGS is that graphical data are not directly sent to the drawing surface for display, but rather are stored within structures in a Central Structure Store, CSS. This is referred to as structure mode as opposed to immediate mode. Structures contain groups of primitives and their attributes, as well as references to other structures, allowing one to define hierarchical structure networks. This hierarchy, as well as having the ability to edit structures, is one of several features that distinguishes PHIGS from other graphics standards, such as GKS or GKS-3D [ISOa] and [ISOc].

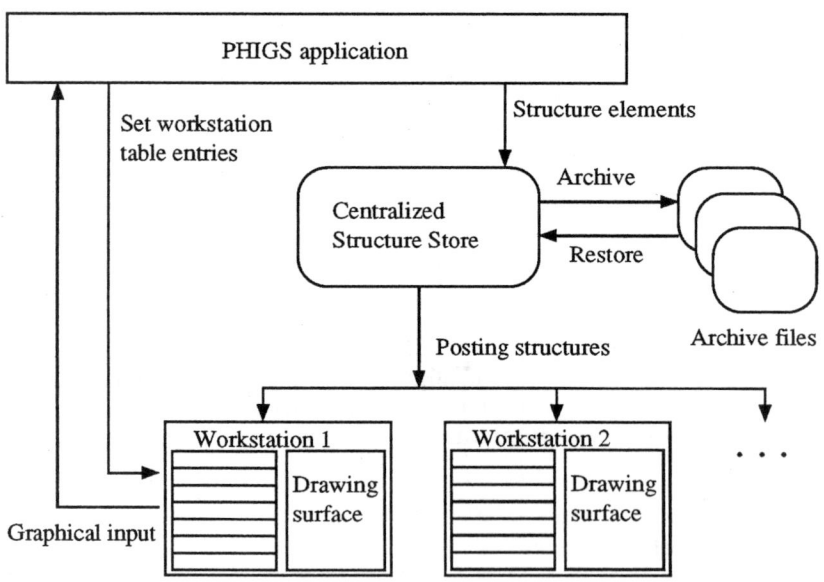

Figure 1.1 Components of the PHIGS architecture.

Pictures defined in PHIGS are displayed on a workstation, consisting of a drawing surface as well as tables defining both the workstation's capabilities and its current state. A workstation is also capable of supporting a number of input devices providing graphical input. Before a workstation can be used, it must be opened. The PHIGS workstation is not to be confused with the common term referring to a multi-tasking desktop computer with a screen, keyboard and mouse. A PHIGS workstation could also be a laser printer or a plotter. The term *physical workstation* will be used when referring to the desktop computer.

In order to draw a picture defined by a structure network, one must post the structure to an open workstation and update the workstation. Several workstations can be used simultaneously. For example one might need two workstations, one a window on a physical workstation for interactive work, the other a plotter for hardcopies. This is achieved by opening a workstation corresponding to each physical device, posting the same structures to both workstations and updating each workstation when necessary. The structures in the CSS are available to all workstations in the system. Storing and retrieving structures on a mass storage device is supported through defining archive files and a mechanism for accessing these files. Figure 1.1 illustrates how these PHIGS components are related.

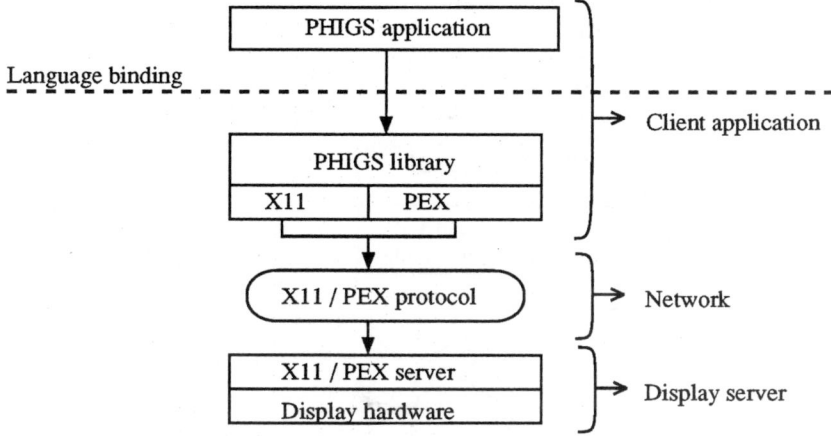

Figure 1.2 PHIGS PLUS application using PEX.

Although still in a draft stage, PHIGS PLUS also needs to be addressed when discussing PHIGS. It is an extension to PHIGS, covering advanced primitives such as curves and surfaces, as well as rendering, such as lighting, shading and depth cueing. Features of PHIGS PLUS have already been implemented in most PHIGS libraries on systems ranging from IBM compatible personal computers to multi-processor visualization systems. It is expected that PHIGS PLUS will become a standard by the end of 1992. It has already achieved the status of a de facto standard, especially with its endorsement by the MIT X consortium with the PEX extensions to the X11 Release 5 windowing system. PEX allows an application using PHIGS or PHIGS PLUS running on one computer system to display its output either locally or on a separate terminal or physical workstation connected by a local area network. The two systems do not necessarily have to come from the same manufacturer, as long as both are PEX compliant. PEX extends the MIT X11 protocol with high-level 3D primitives, allowing the application to take advantage of hardware resources on the display device (see Figure 1.2). All of this is transparent to the PHIGS PLUS application developer, who simply needs to identify the PEX display device when opening the workstation.

PEX also provides its own API, PEXlib, which complements the X11 APIs with 3D primitives and rendering operations, as well as features not found in PHIGS or PHIGS PLUS, such as immediate mode. Since PEXlib is an API that is closely integrated with the X11 windowing system, one cannot achieve the same degree of device independence as with PHIGS and PHIGS PLUS.

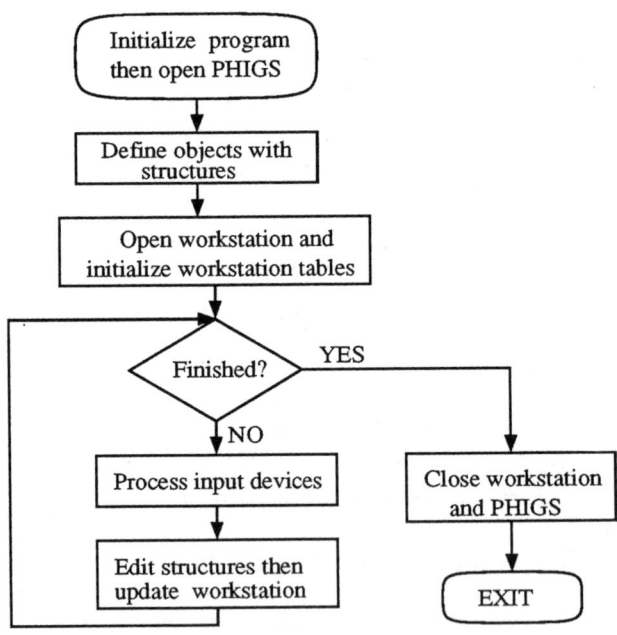

Figure 1.3 Structure of the example program.

1.2 A sample PHIGS program

A straightforward means to become familiar with PHIGS, is to look at an simple example program and see how each component of the PHIGS architecture relates to portions of the program. This example uses PHIGS both for output as well as for input. It defines a structure containing a pyramid and a text string, and then rotates the two objects around a vertical axis until the user chooses to exit (see Figure 1.3). A transformation matrix in the structure is edited to cause the objects to rotate. The example uses a PHIGS input device to let the user choose when to leave the program. This device appears as a menu with one entry: 'Exit'. This C program contains components common to most PHIGS applications:

```c
#include <stdio.h>
#include <phigs.h>
#define RootStruct   1
#define WSID         1
#define YellowInd    1
#define LghtBlueInd  2
#define MENU         1
#define TRUE   (1==1)
#define FALSE  (1==0)
#define PI     3.141592635
#define DEGRAD (PI/180.0)


void main( int argc, char *argv[] )
{

/***************************************************/
/* Main program. First define a number of variables */
/* needed in the main program and their values.      */
/***************************************************/
int Done;
Pint err;
Pint  wstype;
Pconnid  conid;
Pdisp_space_size dsize;
Pfloat           xmaxDC, ymaxDC;

/* Transformation variables */
/* ------------------------ */
Pmatrix3 mat, ident;
static Ppoint3 cor = { 0.5,0.5,0.5 };
static Pvec3   zero = { 0, 0, 0 };
static Pfloat xang = 5.0*DEGRAD;
```

5

```
static Pfloat yang = -5.0*DEGRAD;
static Pfloat zang = 0.0;
static Pvec3 scale = { 1.0, 1.0, 1.0 };

/* Choice menu variables */
/* --------------------- */
static IniCh        = 1;      /* initial choice */
static Pint ChPET = 3;        /* prompt & echo type */
static char    *mmenstr[1] = { "Exit" };
static Plimit ChSize       = { 0.0,0.25, 0.0,0.25 };
Pint           EvWsid, EvDevnum;
Pin_class      EvClass;
Pint           Cho;
Pin_status     Chstat;
Pchoice_data chrec;

/* ------------------------------------------------------- */
/* Variables used to define the objects and attributes */
/* ------------------------------------------------------- */
static Ppoint3 tp      = { 0.4,0.45, 0.5 };
static Pvec3 dir[2]    = { {1,0,0}, { 0,1,0}};

Ppoint_list3 pyr_list;
static Ppoint3 pyramid[10] = { 0.75,0.5,0.75,
          0.75,0.5,0.25,  0.25,0.5,0.25,  0.25,0.5,0.75,
          0.75,0.5,0.75,  0.5,1.0,0.5,    0.25,0.5,0.25,
          0.75,0.5,0.25,  0.5,1.0,0.5,    0.25,0.5,0.75 };

Pcolr_rep Yell;
Pcolr_rep LBlue;

/********************************************************/

    /* =================================== */
    /* Before using PHIGS, it must be opened */
    /* =================================== */
    popen_phigs( PDEF_ERR_FILE, PDEF_MEM_SIZE );

    /* --------------------------------------------------- */
    /* Initialize variables: vertex list, and initial */
    /* transformation matrix                          */
    /* --------------------------------------------------- */
    pyr_list.num_points = 10;
    pyr_list.points     = pyramid;
    pbuild_tran_matrix3( &cor, &zero, xang,yang,zang,
                         &scale, &err, mat );
```

```
/* =================================== */
/* Define the objects in a structure */
/* =================================== */
  popen_struct( RootStruct );
    pset_global_tran3( mat );         /* will be edited */
    pset_line_colr_ind( YellowInd );
    ppolyline3( &pyr_list );
    pset_text_colr_ind( LghtBlueInd );
    pset_char_ht( 0.04 );
    ptext3( &tp, dir, "Hello World" );
  pclose_struct();

  /* ========================================== */
  /* Open a workstation to display the structure */
  /* on. In SUN-PHIGS one must use a proprietary */
  /* function to generate the workstation type   */
  /* ========================================== */
  wstype = phigs_ws_type_create( phigs_ws_type_x_tool,
          PHIGS_TOOL_LABEL, "SunPHIGS X Tool Workstation",
          PHIGS_WS_CATEGORY, PCAT_OUTIN,
          PHIGS_X_BUF_MODE, PHIGS_BUF_DOUBLE, 0);
  if ( !wstype ) {
    pclose_phigs();
    exit(1);
  }

  /* ========================================== */
  /* Before opening the workstation, get the    */
  /* dimensions of the device coordinate space. */
  /* ========================================== */
  pinq_disp_space_size( wstype, &err, &dsize );
  xmaxDC = dsize.size_dc.size_x;
  ymaxDC = dsize.size_dc.size_y;
  popen_ws( WSID, (void *)NULL, wstype );

  /* ------------------------------- */
  /* Define some colours on workstation */
  /* ------------------------------- */
  Yell.rgb.red    = 0.9;
  Yell.rgb.green  = 0.9;
  Yell.rgb.blue   = 0.4;

  LBlue.rgb.red   = 0.2;
  LBlue.rgb.green = 0.7;
  LBlue.rgb.blue  = 0.9;
  pset_colr_rep( WSID, YellowInd, &Yell );
```

```
pset_colr_rep( WSID, LghtBlueInd, &LBlue );

/* --------------------------- */
/* Initialize choice input device */
/* --------------------------- */
ChSize.x_min *= xmaxDC; ChSize.x_max *= xmaxDC;
ChSize.y_min *= ymaxDC; ChSize.y_max *= ymaxDC;
chrec.pets.pet_r3.num_strings  = 1;
chrec.pets.pet_r3.strings      = mmenstr;
pinit_choice( WSID, MENU, PIN_STATUS_OK, IniCh,
              ChPET, &ChSize, &chrec );
pset_choice_mode( WSID, MENU,
                  POP_EVENT, PSWITCH_ECHO );

/* ==================================== */
/* Now post structure to workstation and update */
/* ==================================== */
ppost_struct( WSID, RootStruct, 1.0 );
pupd_ws( WSID, PFLAG_PERFORM );

/* --------------------------------------------- */
/* Now the structure has been drawn for the first time*/
/* Prepare structure for animation by opening it,   */
/* and setting the element pointer to point at the  */
/* transformation matrix.                           */
/* --------------------------------------------- */
popen_struct( RootStruct );
pset_elem_ptr( 1 );
pset_edit_mode( PEDIT_REPLACE );

/* --------------------------------------------- */
/* Now rotate the pyramid and text about the y-axis, */
/* updating the workstation each step until done.    */
/* --------------------------------------------- */
Done = FALSE;
while( !Done ){
  pawait_event( 0.0, &EvWsid, &EvClass, &EvDevnum );
  if( EvWsid == WSID && EvDevnum == MENU &&
      EvClass == PIN_CHOICE ){
    pget_choice( &Chstat, &Cho );
    if( Chstat == PIN_STATUS_OK && Cho == 1)
    Done = TRUE;
  }
  yang += DEGRAD*5;
  pbuild_tran_matrix3( &cor, &zero, xang, yang, zang,
                       &scale, &err, mat );
```

```
    pset_global_tran3 ( mat );
    pupd_ws ( WSID, PFLAG_PERFORM );
}


/* ========================================= */
/* We're done, so close everything and exit */
/* ========================================= */
pclose_struct();
pclose_ws ( WSID );
pclose_phigs();
}
```

The program starts by opening PHIGS with the function OPEN PHIGS. Once PHIGS is opened, a structure is defined containing primitives describing the shape of the objects to be drawn and their attributes. The primitives and their attributes create structure elements. In this example one structure is defined containing the following elements.

Root structure	0
SET GLOBAL TRANSFORMATION 3 (mat)	1
SET LINE COLOUR INDEX(YellowInd)	2
POLYLINE 3(pyramid)	3
SET TEXT COLOUR INDEX(LghtBlueInd)	4
SET CHARACTER HEIGHT(0.04)	5
TEXT 3(position, xdir, ydir, "Hello World")	6

The transformation matrix is used to tilt the pyramid slightly and will be edited later on in the program to cause the objects in the structure to rotate. This structure contains two objects: a pyramid and a text string saying 'Hello World'. The pyramid will be drawn with yellow lines and the text string is light blue. We have, additionally, set the height of the characters to such a value that can be read easily. Defining this structure causes nothing to be drawn. The structure and its elements have simply been created in the CSS. The functions to create the output primitives and to set the attributes can only be called when a structure is open. Once the structure is defined, it should be closed. These steps can be repeated until all structures needed to define the scene have been created.

Different workstation types have different resources; for example, the number of colours supported or the device coordinate range. Before opening a workstation of a given type, one can determine what these resources are by using inquiry functions. Here we need to know the device coordinate range of the display in order to position the input menu. This is done with the function `pinq_display_space_size`. This information can be determined even before the workstation is opened.

Now we can open a workstation where the structure will be displayed. Since several workstations may be open at the same time, we need to pass a workstation identifier to the function OPEN WORKSTATION. A PHIGS implementation can support several different types of workstation which may be accessed in a variety of different ways, so one also needs to specify a workstation type and a connection identifier. One should look at the PHIGS supplier's documentation to see what workstation types and connection identifiers are supported. Every function that requires a workstation will need to be passed the workstation identifier, for example, the function to define colours in the workstation's colour table `pset_colr_rep`. These colours are used by the attribute setting routines in the structure.

In addition to setting the colours, an input device still needs to be initialized. This device is called a choice device and will cause a menu to appear at the lower right corner of the screen containing one entry 'Exit'. The parameter `ChSize` that is passed to the choice initialization routine `pinit_choice` is known as the device's echo area and determines where the menu appears on the display. The echo area needs to be converted to device coordinates before it can be used by `pinitchoice`. This is done by scaling it with the device coordinate range that was returned by `pinq_display_space_size`. Initializing an input device also requires specifying a PET (prompt and echo type). This determines how the menu will appear on the screen. The PET has an associated data record containing data needed to define the appearance and properties of the device. In this example we used the PET 3, whose data record contains the number of menu entries and the entries. In our case there is one menu entry `'Exit'`. Once the device is initialized, it needs to be put in event mode. This will cause input to be placed into an event queue which can be checked to see if the user has chosen to exit.

Now it is time to start drawing. The structure is defined, the workstation is open, but still nothing has appeared on the screen. One needs to let PHIGS know which structures are to be drawn on which workstation. This is done by posting the structure to the workstation. To post a structure one needs a structure identifier, a workstation identifier and a priority. The priority is only used when more than one structure is posted to a workstation. Finally, the workstation can be updated with the function `pupd_ws`. This causes the pyramid and the text string to be drawn on the workstation.

PHIGS is capable of much more than just displaying static pictures. Since we have come so far, we might as well look at a very simple animation loop to get some motion on the screen. This loop will simply rotate the objects in the structure around a vertical axis in the centre of the screen until the user decides to exit the program. In order to get the objects to rotate, the transformation in the structure RootStruct needs to be edited. To prepare for editing we must first open the structure and then move the element pointer to the transformation element. The element pointer is an integer identifying the postion of an element in the opened structure. Since the transformation is the first element in the structure, the element pointer needs to be set to one. The transformation should be overwritten with a new matrix each cycle in the loop. This is achieved by setting the edit mode to REPLACE. This will cause subsequent calls to pset_global_tran3 to overwrite the transformation already in the structure.

Now the animation loop can be started. It will only be exited when the user selects the 'Exit' menu entry. Inside the loop an angle is incremented, a new transformation matrix calculated and the structure element SET GLOBAL TRANSFORMATION3 is overwritten with a new matrix. After the structure is edited, the workstation is updated causing the structure to be redrawn.

One can find out if the user has chosen to exit by waiting for an event from the choice device MENU. This is done with the function pawait_event. It can be given a timeout, but here it is set to zero to minimize any delay. Once the user has selected the menu entry 'Exit', we will get an event from the choice device MENU. The function pget_choice reads this event into the program. After checking the event to see whether the entry 'Exit' was selected, the variable Done will be set to TRUE. This causes the animation loop to be exited, the structure closed, the workstation and, finally, PHIGS closed. This is the clean way to finish a PHIGS program.

This example illustrates a number of features all PHIGS programs have in common. Most important of all is that there is a clean separation between defining objects with output primitives and drawing them. A primitive such as POLYLINE 3 is only drawn after the structure is posted to a workstation and the workstation is updated. In general, a structure network will be defined, containing many hierarchically related structures. One will often need to use inquiry functions to determine a workstation's resource limits, defaults and properties (such as the device coordinate range). Using inquiry functions makes it possible to take advantage of workstation specific resources when present, while still maintaining a degree of device independence. Once this information is known a workstation can be opened and a number of workstation specific table entries initialized. They can contain colours, input device specifications or viewing transformations. When using PHIGS PLUS, one can also define light sources, by setting entries in workstation tables.

Finally the structures to be drawn are posted to an open workstation and a loop is entered where input devices are interrogated, structures are edited and the workstation updated. Editing is a very powerful facility allowing one to insert or overwrite any element in a structure. Structure editing will be treated in detail in Chapter 2. Obviously a real application will contain a more complicated main loop with several input devices.

1.3 PHIGS operating states

The example in the previous section illustrates a number of factors that are fundamental to understanding the structure of a PHIGS program. One factor that is a key to comprehending all PHIGS programs is the *operating state* of a function. There are four state variables in PHIGS which can assume one of two values: opened or closed. They are:

	State	
Variable	*Open*	*Closed*
PHIGS	PHOP	PHCL
Workstation	WSOP	WSCL
Structure	STOP	STCL
Archive file	AROP	ARCL

Each PHIGS function requires specific values for certain state variables. For example, a structure element can only be defined if a structure is open, in other words the structure state variable must be STOP. Because more than one workstation or archive file can be open at the same time, their state variables are associated with an identifier selecting a specific workstation or archive file. Every routine that requires WSOP or AROP, will have this identifier as the first argument in the function call.

If a PHIGS function is used with the wrong operating state, an error is generated. This is a common source of error, so each function listed here is accompanied by a field identifying which operating state is necessary. This field also identifies whether the function creates a structure element or not. It contains the following entries:

For example the state:

$$(PHOP,*,STOP,*)El$$

requires both PHIGS and a structure to be open and it creates a structure element. If an asterisk is present in a field its corresponding state does not matter, so a workstation or an archive file can be either opened or closed.

As an example we can look at the first PHIGS function specification:

OPEN PHIGS		(PHCL,WSCL,STCL,ARCL)

Arguments:

in	error file	file indicator
in	size of buffer area	integer

Before PHIGS can be used it must be opened, so all four state variables must be closed when calling OPEN PHIGS. It is passed parameters that identify an error file for error messages and the size of buffers internal to PHIGS. This function initializes a number of internal tables, allocates resources and most importantly for the programmer, it will change the state from PHCL to PHOP. Now a large number of PHIGS functions can be used.

At the end of the program when PHIGS is no longer needed, one should close PHIGS to free up allocated resources. This is done with the function:

CLOSE PHIGS   (PHOP,WSCL,STCL,ARCL)
Arguments:
     none

This function also assures that all files opened by PHIGS have been properly closed. Once this function is called all buffers are released, so all structures in the CSS are lost. If one needs to save the contents of the CSS, one should save the structures to an archive file before leaving PHIGS.

Looking at the example program again, we can see a structure that most PHIGS programs have in common. This can be done by looking at what operating state each component of the program requires. Figure 1.4 shows the operating state needed by each section of code in the example.

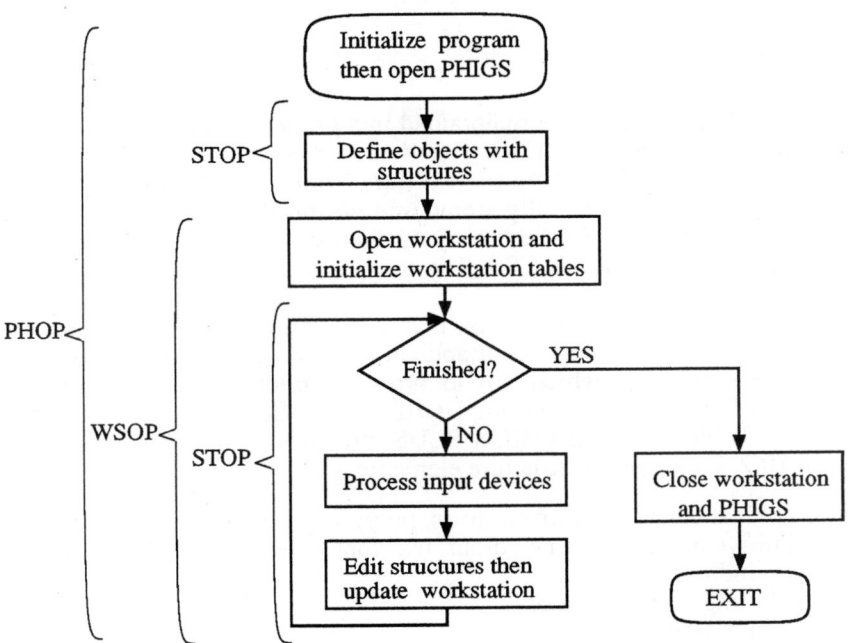

Figure 1.4 Operating states used in example program.

CHAPTER 2

The Central Structure Store

In PHIGS graphics data are maintained in a graphics database, known as the central structure store, CSS. This database is similar to a display list found in many graphics devices. It differs from a display list due to the fact that the data are centrally stored and not necessarily on a particular graphics device. PHIGS offers many mechanisms to edit, manipulate and interrogate the data in the CSS. The terms: CSS and graphics database refer to the same entity.

The CSS is central in the sense that it is available to all workstations that are in a given system. The graphical data in the CSS are grouped together in structures, which are in turn collections of atomic entities called structure elements. A complete list of PHIGS structure elements is given in Table 10.1 and PHIGS PLUS structure elements are listed in Table 10.2. Examples of structure elements are:

- graphical output primitives (lines, polygons, text, ...)
- primitive attributes (line colour, text font, interior style, ...)
- view indices
- modelling transformations
- model clipping volumes
- structure invocations
- labels
- pick identifiers and nameset commands for classifying sets of structure elements.

Most PHIGS routines which require the operating state (PHOP,*,STOP,*) create structure elements. Exceptions to this rule are structure editing and inquiry functions. Conversely, all functions which create structure elements require the operating state (PHOP,*,STOP,*).

2.1 Defining objects with structures

Before data can be written to the CSS a structure must be opened with the routine OPEN STRUCTURE. This command takes one argument, an integer supplied by the application, which identifies the structure to be opened. This identifier is the only way to refer to the structure, so it must be unique. Since only one structure can be open at a time, calling OPEN STRUCTURE when a structure is already open will generate an error message.

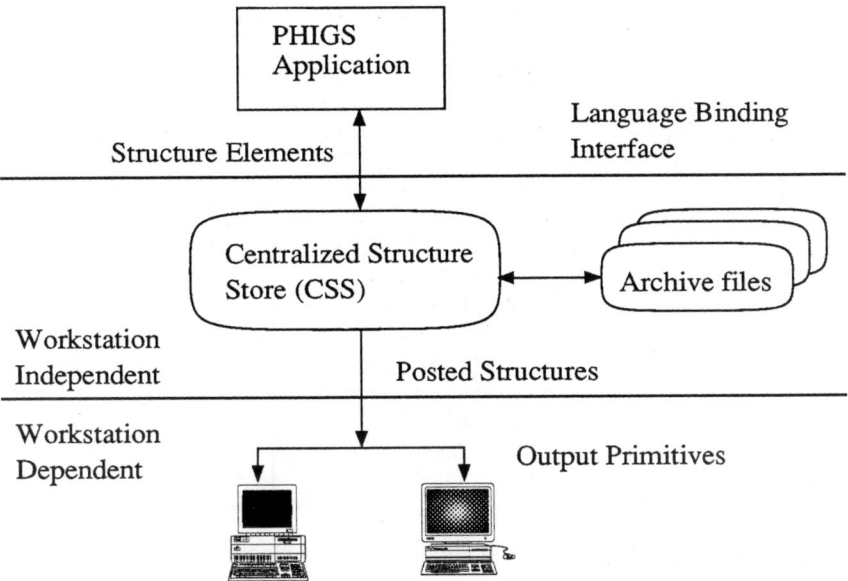

Figure 2.1 PHIGS architecture and the CSS.

A structure must be open when calling a PHIGS routine which creates a structure element. When finished entering elements into a structure the program should use the command CLOSE STRUCTURE to close the structure. In summary these routines are:

OPEN STRUCTURE   (PHOP,*,STCL,*)
Arguments:
       in   structure identifier   integer

CLOSE STRUCTURE   (PHOP,*,STOP,*)
Arguments:
         none

Once a structure has been opened, all PHIGS routines which create structure elements will be sequentially written to the structure (see Figure 2.2). The position of each element in a structure can be identified by a positive integer. This integer is known as the *element pointer*, EP and is used when editing structures. When a structure is empty, the element pointer is zero. Each element which is inserted in a structure causes the element pointer to be incremented.

In order to define an object that is to be displayed by PHIGS, a structure needs to be created which describes the object's shape. This structure will contain output primitives defining the geometry of the object and attribute primitives describing how the object is to be drawn (colours, line width scale factor, interior patterns, text fonts, etc.).

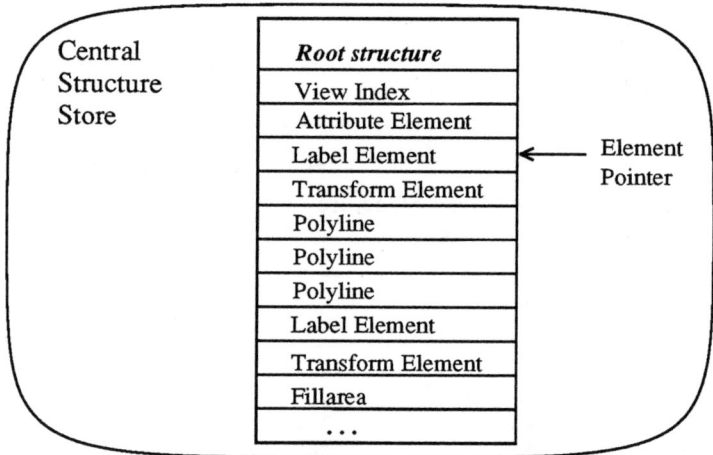

Figure 2.2 *Diagram of a structure and its element pointer.*

The following C program illustrates creating and displaying a structure.

```
#include <phigs.h>
#define Root    1
#define ViewInd 1
#define WSID    1
#define RedInd  1
#define BlueInd 2
```

```
void main(){

Pmatrix mat;
Pint error;
Pint wstype;
static Pvec offset = { 0.5, 0.5 };
static Ppoint tpos = { 0.0, 0.0 };
Ppoint_list triang;
static Ppoint tpoints[4] = { 0.1,0.1, 0.35,0.1,
                             0.35,0.35, 0.1,0.1 };
Pcolr_rep Red;
Pcolr_rep Blue;

  /* Open PHIGS and a workstation */
  popen_phigs( PDEF_ERR_FILE, PDEF_MEM_SIZE );
  wstype = phigs_ws_type_create( phigs_ws_type_x_tool,
          PHIGS_TOOL_LABEL, "SunPHIGS X Tool Workstation",
          PHIGS_WS_CATEGORY, PCAT_OUTIN, 0);
  if ( !wstype ) {
    pclose_phigs();
    exit(1);
  }
  popen_ws( WSID, (void *)NULL, wstype );

  /* Load desired colours into workstation */
  Red.rgb.red    = 1.0;
  Red.rgb.green  = 0.0;
  Red.rgb.blue   = 0.0;
  Blue.rgb.red   = 0.0;
  Blue.rgb.green = 0.0;
  Blue.rgb.blue  = 1.0;
  pset_colr_rep( WSID, RedInd, &Red );
  pset_colr_rep( WSID, BlueInd, &Blue );

  /* Define a structure containing two triangles */
  popen_struct( Root );
    pset_line_colr_ind( RedInd );
    pset_int_colr_ind( BlueInd );
    pset_int_style( PSTYLE_SOLID );
    triang.num_points = 4;
    triang.points = tpoints;
    ppolyline( &triang );
    ptext( &tpos, "Triangle drawn with polyline");
    ptranslate( &offset, &error, mat );
    pset_global_tran( mat );
    triang.num_points = 3;
```

```
    pfill_area( &triang );
    ptext( &tpos, "Triangle drawn with fill area");
  pclose_struct();   /* end of structure definition */

  /* Post the structure to the workstation and redraw */
  ppost_struct( WSID, Root, 1.0 );
  predraw_all_structs( WSID, PFLAG_ALWAYS );
  getchar();            /* wait till anything is typed*/
  pclose_ws( WSID );  /* before terminating */
  pclose_phigs();
}
```

This program starts by opening PHIGS and a workstation. Then the structure Root is created which contains:

- attribute information
- a triangle defined by a polyline
- a text string
- a transformation
- a filled triangle defined by a polygon
- a text string.

This structure is then posted to the workstation and the workstation is updated. Once a character is entered from the keyboard, the workstation and PHIGS are closed and the program ends.

In this example it is important to notice that the functions ppolyline, ptext and pfill_area do not generate any output when called, they just define elements in the structure Root. In order to see the output on the screen, the structure must be posted to an open workstation, and then the workstation must be updated. This separation of defining and displaying graphics data is a fundamental characteristic of PHIGS.

When the structure is displayed, one triangle will be drawn with red lines in the lower right corner of the workstation, and the second drawn in the centre as a solid blue triangle. It contains the following elements:

Root structure	0
SET LINE COLOUR INDEX(RedInd)	1
SET INTERIOR COLOUR INDEX(BlueInd)	2
SET INTERIOR STYLE(PSOLID)	3
POLYLINE(triang)	4
TEXT("Triangle drawn with polyline")	5
SET GLOBAL TRANSFORMATION(mat)	6
FILL AREA(triang)	7
TEXT("Triangle drawn with fill area")	8

The function `pset_colr_rep` is used to define a colour in the workstation's colour table. It is generally good programming practice not to put functions which set workstation table entries in the middle of a structure definition. The PHIGS routine `ptranslate` does not create a structure element, so it is not in the CSS. It is a utility routine which creates a transformation matrix from an offset vector. All transformation utility routines require the operating state (PHOP,*,*,*) and are often seen in the middle of a structure definition in order to simplify creating modelling transformations. In order to make a program easy to read, PHIGS routines which do not need to be called during a structure definition should be kept to a minimum.

There are many occasions when a structure which already exists needs to be opened. This is the case when editing structures (see Section 2.5) or with certain inquiry functions (see Section 10.1). If an already existing structure is opened, then the element pointer will be positioned at the last element in the structure. This will cause all further elements to be appended to the existing structure.

2.2 Structure display

Once a structure, or a structure network, has been defined, it needs to be posted to an open workstation in order to be displayed. A structure can be posted to several workstations, as long as they are all open. Any workstation can have many structures posted to it. A structure is posted to a workstation using the routine:

POST STRUCTURE   (PHOP,WSOP,*,*)
Arguments:

in	workstation identifier	integer
in	structure identifier	integer
in	display priority	real

The arguments identify which structure is being posted to which workstation. A posted structure is known as a *root structure*. If several structures are posted to a single workstation, the display priority is used to determine which order to draw the structures in (starting from the lowest priority to the highest). If two structures with the same priority have been posted to a workstation, the most recently posted structure has the higher priority.

Posting a structure to a workstation does not necessarily cause that structure to be displayed. It just adds the structure identifier and its priority to the workstation state list and the workstation identifier to the structure state list. Whether or not a structure is displayed or not depends on the workstation's deferral and modification modes. The deferral mode determines when a structure is to be redrawn and the modification mode determines how the workstation is to redraw the structure. One can force the structure to be displayed by updating the workstation. This will be discussed in detail in Section 3.3.

Of course PHIGS also provides a means to disassociate a structure network from a workstation. There are two routines to do this: UNPOST STRUCTURE and UNPOST ALL STRUCTURES. The former unposts a single structure and the latter unposts all structures posted to a given workstation. An unposted structure will not be drawn when the workstation is updated, but it still exists in the CSS. The routines to unpost structures are as follows:

UNPOST STRUCTURE   (PHOP,WSOP,*,*)
Arguments:

in	workstation identifier	integer
in	structure identifier	integer

UNPOST ALL STRUCTURES   (PHOP,WSOP,*,*)
Arguments:

in	workstation identifier	integer

Posting and unposting structures is a means to identify whether a structure network should be displayed or not when a workstation is updated. The mechanism of displaying a structure is known as *structure traversal*. Once structure networks have been covered, we can discuss traversal in detail.

2.3 Structure networks

Structures can reference other structures through the function, EXECUTE STRUCTURE, to form hierarchical networks. It should be clear that this function creates a structure element. A structure can be referenced any number of times so that objects which are to be drawn multiple times need only be defined once in the CSS.

When a structure X contains references to other structures it is called a parent of those structures. The structures which are referenced by X are called X's children. In general, all structures which either directly or indirectly cause a structure Y to be executed are called Y's ancestors; and all child structures and children of children are called descendants. For example, in Figure 2.3 structure E is a descendant of structures A,B, and C, but not of D or F and structure D is an ancestor only of structure F.

The only restriction in the complexity of a structure network is that no structure can invoke one of its ancestors, which implies that one cannot use recursion when defining objects with structures. The allowable structure networks are known as acyclical graphs (see Figure 2.3).

There is only one PHIGS routine with which structure hierarchy is defined, namely EXECUTE STRUCTURE. It is called as follows:

EXECUTE STRUCTURE (PHOP,*,STOP,*) El
Arguments:
in   structure identifier   integer

Calling this function simply writes an EXECUTE STRUCTURE element to the currently open structure. The identifier passed as an argument to EXECUTE STRUCTURE specifies which structure should be
executed at traversal time. The referenced structure does not necessarily
have to exist before EXECUTE STRUCTURE is called; if it does not an
empty structure will be created. Obviously this structure should be defined before traversal, since executing an empty structure has no effect.
Only when the posted structures are traversed, does the element EXE-
CUTE STRUCTURE get interpreted.

2.4 Structure traversal

When a workstation is updated, each posted structure is traversed in the
order specified by its priority. When a structure network is traversed,
each element in the network is sequentially interpreted until the last element of the root structure is reached. The primary mechanism available
in PHIGS to create graphics output is to traverse entire structure networks that have been posted to a workstation. Additional ways to
change the displayed image are determined by the modification modes
of a workstation. They are workstation specific facilities, which will be

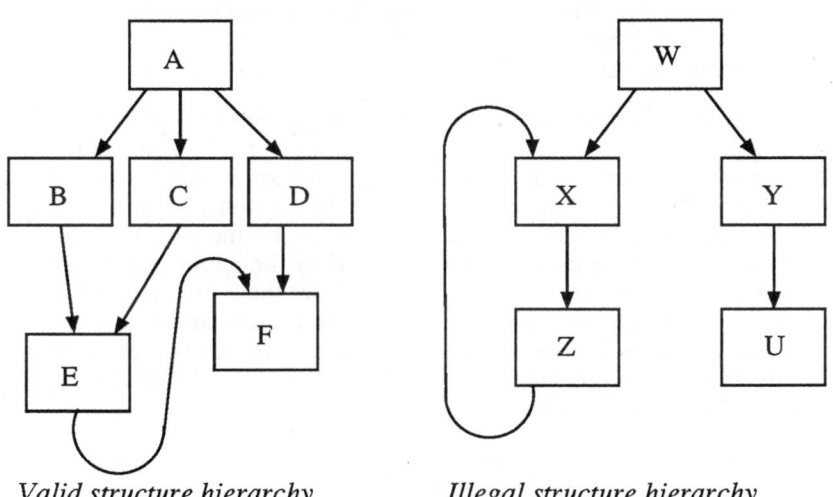

Valid structure hierarchy   *Illegal structure hierarchy*

Figure 2.3 Correct and incorrect structure hierarchies.

covered in Section 3.3. There are PHIGS implementations available which provide extensions such as an immediate mode, or non-retained structures which allow output primitives to be sent directly to the workstation for rendering. These non-standard extensions are beyond the scope of this book and, if present, are documented by your supplier.

Before traversal starts, the Traversal State List, *TSL* is initialized with default values from the PHIGS Description Table, *PDT*. The TSL contains a large amount of data (often several kilobytes). It contains information describing the current state of all attributes and transformations used to draw output primitives and can be summarized by the following list:

- current attributes used by PHIGS primitives
  — line colour index
  — line width scale factor
  — text font
  — etc.
- current attributes used by PHIGS PLUS primitives
  — surface properties
  — light source state list
  — shading and lighting methods
  — etc.
- current global and local transformations
- current modelling clipping volume and indicator
- current view index
- current hlhsr (hidden line hidden surface) identifier
- current pick identifier
- current name set.

The contents of the PDT cannot be changed by the application. There are inquiry functions which read the PDT, so that it is possible to determine what the default values are. The TSL is continually being updated at traversal time; for example, by structure elements setting attributes. Both the PDT and the TSL are used internally by the PHIGS implementation and are not meant to be directly used by the application program.

During traversal, each element is read from the structure, and is interpreted. An attribute element will update the current attribute element in the TSL, and an output primitive will be drawn by the workstation using the attributes found in the TSL. The EXECUTE STRUCTURE element causes several things to happen at traversal time:

- traversal of the current structure is suspended
- a copy of the current TSL is saved
- the global modelling transformation is set to the current composite transformation (see Section 6.3)
- the local modelling transformation matrix is set to the identity (see Section 6.3)

- the structure referenced by EXECUTE STRUCTURE is traversed
- the saved TSL is restored
- traversal of the current structure is resumed.

It is not expected that each of these steps is completely understood at this stage. What is important to notice is that the child structure inherits its parent's TSL containing the attributes, etc. Once traversal of the child structure has been completed, the original state list is restored. This implies that a child structure cannot affect the attributes, transformation matrices, name set, etc. of its ancestors. An example of using structure networks with transformation matrices is covered in Section 6.3.

It should also be mentioned that there is an overhead involved in executing structures. The TSL must be pushed onto a stack and restored, not to mention other implementation specific bookkeeping. The applications programmer must be aware of the tradeoffs between performance and hierarchy. Highly performance-sensitive applications might need to minimize the amount of hierarchy used.

An application has no mechanism to control the structure traversal once it has started. In the PHIGS standard there is no way to single step a structure network, or to set breakpoints to interrupt the traversal at a certain point. This functionality can be provided by non-standard extensions to PHIGS. It is the responsibility of the applications programmer to maintain correct structure networks. This can be difficult, especially if the structures are being interactively edited. In the section on structure editing, functions which help maintain structure integrity will be discussed.

2.5 Editing structures

So far we have seen how to create and display structure networks. One powerful feature of PHIGS is the ability to edit the structures. This makes it possible to make incremental changes to an existing structure network, without having to redefine the entire network. These changes can either be triggered through user interaction, or through program control, such as in a simulation.

In order to edit a structure, it must be open. Actually, creating a structure is a special case of structure editing. Structure editing consists of modifying the contents of the structures. This can consist of adding elements, deleting elements, or overwriting existing elements. In order to do this, the following mechanisms are provided:

- creating structure elements
- positioning the element pointer
- changing the edit mode to insert or replace
- deleting elements or element ranges

- copying structures.

Many editing routines require the state (PHOP,*,STOP,*), even though they do not create structure elements. Every element in a structure can be identified by its *element pointer, EP,* which specifies its position in the structure. The valid range for the element pointer in a structure with *n* elements is:

$$1 \leq EP \leq n$$

When elements are inserted into an open structure, the element pointer is automatically incremented. There are several ways to explicitly position the element pointer. Two routines to position the element pointer are SET ELEMENT POINTER and OFFSET ELEMENT POINTER. The first routine sets the element pointer at an absolute position in the structure:

SET ELEMENT POINTER   (PHOP,*,STOP,*)
Arguments:
        in   element pointer   integer

This function takes one argument, the value the element pointer should be set to. The argument should be between zero and the number of elements in the structure, *n*. If it is outside the valid range, the element pointer will be set to zero or *n*, depending on whether SET ELEMENT POINTER was passed a negative integer or a value greater than *n*. Passing a value outside the valid range should not cause an error condition.

In order to position the element pointer relative to its current position, we can use the function:

OFFSET ELEMENT POINTER   (PHOP,*,STOP,*)
Arguments:
        in   element pointer offset   integer

The argument is the element pointer's relative offset which can be either a positive or a negative integer. Once again, if the resulting element pointer is outside the valid range, it will be set to either zero or the maximum value.

We will modify the example from page 16 in order to illustrate structure editing. After displaying the original structure, we will edit Root to change the size of the characters in the second text string: 'Triangle drawn with fill area'. Before we can start editing, we need to open the structure and will do so immediately after the call to `getch()`. This is done by adding the routine:

```
popen_struct ( Root );
```

which results in the structure being opened with the element pointer positioned at the last element:

Root structure	
Root structure	0
SET LINE COLOUR INDEX(RedInd)	1
SET INTERIOR COLOUR INDEX(BlueInd)	2
SET INTERIOR STYLE(PSOLID)	3
POLYLINE(triang)	4
TEXT("Triangle drawn with polyline")	5
SET GLOBAL TRANSFORMATION(mat)	6
FILL AREA(triang)	7
TEXT("Triangle drawn with fill area")	8

8 ◄── Element pointer

In this case we want to add the function SET CHARACTER HEIGHT immediately before the call to FILL AREA. One way would be to re-member that the call to FILL AREA was the seventh element in the structure, Root. In this case the following two functions could be used to add the required text attribute routine:

```
pset_elemptr( 6 );  /* put the EP before FILL AREA */
pset_char_ht(0.02); /* change the text height */
```

The second way to change character height of the last text string is to use a relative offset. This would require knowing that the call to FILL AREA was the second to last element in the structure and would require the following two functions:

```
poffset_elemptr( -2 );  /* back up EP two elements */
pset_char_ht(0.02);     /* change the text height */
```

Both methods would result in the following structure:

Root structure	0
SET LINE COLOUR INDEX(RedInd)	1
SET INTERIOR COLOUR INDEX(BlueInd)	2
SET INTERIOR STYLE(PSTYLE_SOLID)	3
POLYLINE(triang)	4
TEXT("Triangle drawn with polyline")	5
SET GLOBAL TRANSFORMATION(mat)	6
SET CHARACTER HEIGHT(0.02)	7
FILL AREA(triang)	8
TEXT("Triangle drawn with fill area")	9

7 ◄── Element pointer

Note that the call to SET CHARACTER HEIGHT inserted a new ele-ment after the current element pointer and then incremented the EP. If another structure element were created, it would be inserted between SET CHARACTER HEIGHT and FILL AREA. In summary the changes to the C example to edit the structure as described are:

```
...  getch(); /* from original C example */

popen_struct( Root );      /* Open structure to edit */
poffset_elem_ptr(-2);      /* back up EP two elements */
pset_char_ht(0.02);        /* change the char. height */
predraw_all_structs( WSID, PFLAG_ALWAYS );


getch();                   /* wait for a character */
... /* terminate as in original program */
```

This example should have pointed out an aspect of structure editing which can quickly lead to complications in a large application. Namely, before we could add the call to SET CHARACTER HEIGHT, we needed to know where to place the element pointer. This is further complicated because editing the structure changes the number of elements and their numbering. It would be very difficult to keep track of the contents of a structure which is being constantly edited without the structure element LABEL.

2.5.1 Labels

In order to simplify structure editing, a label element is provided. Its only use is to mark a position in the structure. At traversal time the label has no effect. The function to create a label is:

LABEL   (PHOP,*,STOP,*) El
Arguments:
        in   label identifier   integer

This routine has one argument, an integer, which is the label identifier. Label identifiers do not need to be unique within a structure, but it is generally good practice not to duplicate label identifiers. The label would be of no use without the routine:

SET ELEMENT POINTER AT LABEL   (PHOP,*,STOP,*)
Arguments:
        in   label identifier   integer

This function starts searching at the current element, or the next element if the current element is a label, for an occurrence of a label with a matching identifier. If the end of the structure is reached without finding a match, an error is generated and the EP is not moved. It is important to note that searching for labels only looks in the open structure. It does not traverse the hierarchy to look inside referenced structures.

Since SET ELEMENT POINTER AT LABEL begins its search at the next element if the EP is positioned at a label, it is possible to use the same label identifier several times in a structure. This should be avoided, because it is an easy source for programming errors. The program must be sure that the label occurs between the EP and the end of the structure. One way to be sure is to set the EP to zero before positioning it at a label.

In the previous example labels could have been inserted while creating the structure with the C routine:

```
plabel( LabelId );
```

where LabelId is an integer. Without having to repeat the code to create the structure, we shall assume that Root was created with two labels so that it looks like the following structure:

Root structure	0
SET LINE COLOUR INDEX(RedInd)	1
SET INTERIOR COLOUR INDEX(BlueInd)	2
SET INTERIOR STYLE(PSTYLE_SOLID)	3
POLYLINE(triang)	4
TEXT("Triangle drawn with polyline")	5
LABEL(TRANSFORM)	6
SET GLOBAL TRANSFORMATION(mat)	7
LABEL(TRIANGLE2)	8
FILL AREA(triang)	9
TEXT("Triangle drawn with fill area")	10

Labels create reference points, so using labels will simplify finding a location in the structure. In our previous example we can insert SET CHARACTER HEIGHT immediately before the fill area, with the following routines:

```
pset_elem_ptr( 0 );                /* set EP at the top */
pset_elem_ptr_label(TRIANGLE2);/* EP now at label    */
pset_char_ht(0.02);                /* new char. height   */
```

Now we can be assured that the call to SET CHARACTER HEIGHT is placed at the correct position.

2.5.2 The edit mode

So far we have been assuming that structure elements are inserted into structures. This is not entirely correct. The default condition is that structure elements are inserted. This can be changed with the command:

SET EDIT MODE   (PHOP,*,*,*)
Arguments:
        in   edit mode   (INSERT,REPLACE)

This routine has one argument which can have one of two values: IN-SERT or REPLACE. In insert mode, all routines which create structure elements insert the element immediately after the EP and then the EP is incremented. In replace mode the element which the EP is pointing to is replaced by the new structure element and the EP remains unchanged.

The edit mode REPLACE is commonly used when a modelling transformation needs to be modified either due to user interaction or due to simulation data. We can further modify the example on page 16 to illustrate using the edit mode REPLACE. The changes we shall make are:

1. Insert a local transformation to rotate the fill area immediately after the global transformation.
2. Change edit mode to REPLACE.
3. Rotate the second triangle a total of 90 degrees in 10 degree steps, displaying the results after each step.

If we take the original program and make the following changes immediately after the call to `getch()`:

```
getch(); /* from original program */

/* The next four lines could be at the program's top */
#define PI 3.141592635
int i;
Pfloat angle;
static Pmatrix id2 = { 1,0,0, 0,1,0, 0,0,1 };

popen_struct( Root );                    /* Open to edit */
pset_elem_ptr( 0 );                      /* Move to the top */
pset_elemptr_label( TRANSFORM );         /* "   label */
poffset_elem_ptr(1);                     /* " psetglobaltran */
pset_local_tran( id2,PTYPE_REPLACE);
pset_edit_mode( PEDIT_REPLACE );         /* now replacing */
for( i=1; i<=10; i++ ){
   angle = (Pfloat_arg)i*PI/20.0;        /* get the angle */
   protate( angle, &error, mat );        /* create matrix */
   pset_local_tran( mat, PTYPE_REPLACE ); /*replace xform*/
   predraw_all_structs( WSID, PFLAG_ALWAYS ); /* redraw */
```

```
}
pclose_struct();                    /* finished, so close */
```

The first part of these changes should be clear. The structure is opened with the EP pointing to the last element. To get to the element SET GLOBAL TRANSFORMATION: we put the EP at the top of the structure, look for the label TRANSFORM, and then offset the EP by 1. Transformations commonly have labels, because they are edited often. The default edit mode is INSERT, so the call to `pset_local_tran` results in the structure on the following page.

Now the structure has both a global and a local transformation. The second argument to `pset_local_tran`, PTYPE_REPLACE does not refer to the edit mode. This refers to how transformations are multiplied which will be explained in Section 6.2.

Root structure	0
SET LINE COLOUR INDEX(RedInd)	1
SET INTERIOR COLOUR INDEX(BlueInd)	2
SET INTERIOR STYLE(PSTYLE_SOLID)	3
POLYLINE(triang)	4
TEXT("Triangle drawn with polyline")	5
LABEL(TRANSFORM)	6
SET GLOBAL TRANSFORMATION(mat)	7
SET LOCAL TRANSFORMATION(id2)	8
LABEL(TRIANGLE2)	9
FILL AREA(triang)	10
TEXT("Triangle drawn with fill area")	11

← Element pointer

At this stage the structure and the EP are ready for the animation loop. We start by placing structure editing in REPLACE mode and enter the loop. The routine ROTATE is a transformation utility and only generates a matrix from an angle which is derived from the loop index. It does not create a structure element. The matrix produced by ROTATE is used by SET LOCAL TRANSFORMATION, a structure element. Because editing is in REPLACE mode, all calls to structure elements overwrite the element EP is pointing to, namely SET LOCAL TRANSFORMATION. This was initialized with the identity matrix and is overwritten with a new transformation each pass through the loop. The call to REDRAW ALL STRUCTURES initiates clearing the display and retraversing the structure in order to display each angle increment.

If the edit mode had been INSERT, ten separate calls to SET LOCAL TRANSFORMATION would have been inserted. A common source of error in developing PHIGS programs is not knowing what the current edit mode is. If a program attempts to create a structure while the edit mode is REPLACE, only one element will be inserted, namely the last one. All previous elements were replaced.

2.5.3 Deleting elements

So far we have only been inserting or replacing elements. Once an element is no longer needed, it can be deleted from the structure. There are several routines to do this:

DELETE ELEMENT   (PHOP,*,STOP,*)
Arguments:
        none

    This routine deletes the element pointed to by the EP. The EP is then decremented by one to point to the element preceding the deleted element. If EP is zero when DELETE ELEMENT is called, nothing changes.
    The next routine is useful for deleting a number of elements.

DELETE ELEMENT RANGE   (PHOP,*,STOP,*)
Arguments:
in	position 1	integer
in	position 2	integer

    This routine deletes all elements between and including the lower element position and the higher element position. The EP is then set to point to the element preceding the lower position. Another routine to delete an element range is:

DELETE ELEMENTS BETWEEN LABELS   (PHOP,*,STOP,*)
Arguments:
in	label identifier 1	integer
in	label identifier 2	integer

    This will delete all elements between label identifier 1 and 2 without deleting the labels. The first label identifier must occur between the EP and the end of the structure, and the second label identifier must occur between the first label and the end or an error will be generated.
    To illustrate deleting an element range, we could add to the original example from page 16 the command:

```
pdel_elem_range( 4,6 );
```

This command would delete the elements between and including POLYLINE and SET GLOBAL TRANSFORMATION. This would result in the fill area triangle being positioned where the polyline triangle originally was. The structure would then look like:

Root structure	0
SET LINE COLOUR INDEX(RedInd)	1
SET INTERIOR COLOUR INDEX(BlueInd)	2
SET INTERIOR STYLE(PSTYLE_SOLID)	3
FILL AREA(triang)	4
TEXT("Triangle drawn with fill area")	5

This concludes the discussion of structure editing through inserting or replacing elements, manipulating the element pointer, using labels, and deleting elements. It should now be clear that a PHIGS programmer should decide on how to organize the structure network before starting to write code. It is good programming practice to use fixed rules in placing elements such as attributes, transformations and output primitives and labels should be used to simplify positioning the EP. In addition to editing the contents of structures, the CSS can be edited through manipulating entire structures.

2.6 Manipulating structures

Entire structures can also be manipulated in the CSS. The following routine can be used to make two copies of a structure:

```
COPY ALL ELEMENTS FROM STRUCTURE          (PHOP,*,STOP,*)
Arguments:
          in    structure identifier        integer
```

This routine requires a structure to be open. It causes the entire contents of the specified structure to be copied into the open structure immediately following the EP. The EP is then updated to point to the last element copied. If the specified structure is the open structure, its entire contents will be duplicated following the EP. If the specified structure is empty or does not exist, nothing happens.

2.6.1 Deleting structures

In addition to copying structures, there are several routines to delete structures from the CSS. The first routine is:

```
EMPTY STRUCTURE                           (PHOP,*,*,*)
Arguments:
          in    structure identifier        integer
```

This routine deletes all elements in the specified structure. Note that the structure does not have to be open. If it is, then all elements are deleted and the EP is set to zero. If the specified structure does not exist, an empty structure is created.

If the structure itself is to be deleted, then the following routine should be used:

DELETE STRUCTURE   (PHOP,*,*,*)
Arguments:
        in   structure identifier   integer

The specified structure is deleted. This implies it is unposted from all workstations to which it is posted, its contents and identifier are deleted. If the structure was referenced from another structure in the CSS, this reference is also deleted. This implies that the parents of the deleted structure are also modified. If this is not desired, then EMPTY STRUCTURE should most likely be used.

Deleting an open structure is equivalent to the following sequence:

> CLOSE STRUCTURE
> DELETE STRUCTURE(Structure id)
> OPEN STRUCTURE(Structure id)

After deleting an open structure the specified structure is open, empty, unposted, with no ancestors.

The following function deletes an entire structure network:

DELETE STRUCTURE NETWORK   (PHOP,*,*,*)
Arguments:
        in   structure identifier   integer
        in   reference flag   (DELETE,KEEP)

This routine is used to delete the specified structure and its descendants. Figure 2.4 illustrates a complication in deleting a structure network. This is addressed by the second argument, the reference flag. The problem is, what should happen to structures which are referenced from outside the specified network. If the reference flag is DELETE, then all structures in the network are deleted regardless of whether they are executed from outside the network. This will also delete references to the deleted structures in the entire CSS. If the reference flag is KEEP, then only the descendants which are not executed from structures outside the specified network are deleted.

Finally one can delete all structures in the CSS with the routine:

DELETE ALL STRUCTURES   (PHOP,*,*,*)
Arguments:
        none

This is equivalent to executing DELETE STRUCTURE for all struc-

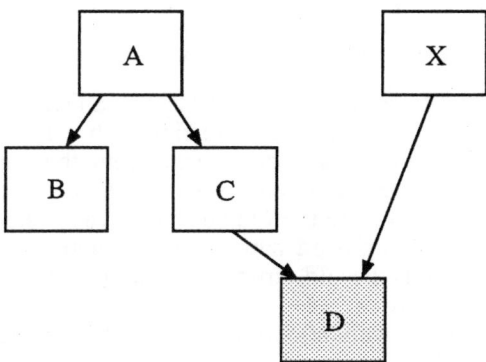

Figure 2.4 Delete network conflict.

tures in the CSS. After this call, the CSS is empty and no structures are posted. If the structure state is STOP when DELETE ALL STRUC-TURES is called, it will be changed to STCL.

2.6.2 Changing structure identifiers and references

There are times when it is desired to rename structures. Structure hierarchy and posting lead to special cases, which must be addressed. In order to rename a structure, one can use:

CHANGE STRUCTURE IDENTIFIER   (PHOP,*,*,*)
Arguments:

	in	old structure identifier	integer
	in	new structure identifier	integer

This routine creates a structure with the old structure's contents and the new structure's identifier. If the old structure was referenced, then an empty structure with the old structure's identifier is created and the references to it remain. Similarly if the old structure is open or posted to a workstation, it remains open or posted, but is empty. In the case that the old structure is open, the EP is set to zero. If it is posted, the new structure will also be posted. In summary, the old structure will continue to exist as an empty structure if:

- it is referenced by other structures
- it is posted to one or more workstations
- it is currently the open structure.

A related function changes all references to a given structure:

33

CHANGE STRUCTURE REFERENCES   (PHOP,*,*,*)
Arguments:

in	old structure identifier	integer
in	new structure identifier	integer

This routine will replace all EXECUTE STRUCTURE elements which reference the old structure identifier with elements which reference the new identifier. This occurs throughout the entire CSS. If the new structure does not exist, an empty structure is created with its identifier. On workstations where the old structure was posted, it is unposted and the new structure is posted with the old structure's priority. If both structures were posted, the old structure is unposted and the new structure remains unchanged.

Finally both routines can be combined with the function:

CHANGE STRUCTURE IDENTIFIERS AND REFERENCES   (PHOP,*,*,*)
Arguments:

in	old structure identifier	integer
in	new structure identifier	integer

This has the same effect as if CHANGE STRUCTURE REFERENCES and then CHANGE STRUCTURE IDENTIFIER were called.

A common situation where these routines could be used is to change the rendering of an object. PHIGS applications will commonly have both a wireframe representation, using polylines, and a solid representation of the same object, using polygons defined with fill area or quadrilateral mesh. The wireframe display can be drawn much faster than the polygon display, so it is used for interaction. When the user needs to see the solid representation, he could make a choice which causes the program to execute the routine

        CHANGE STRUCTURE REFERENCES(WireframeObject, SolidObject)

Both WireframeObject and SolidObject exist as structures in the CSS, but only one or the other is referenced by the posted structure network.

CHAPTER 3

Workstations

The primary goal of PHIGS is to provide a device independent programming interface to underlying graphics hardware. This interface will be used for output of graphics data, as well as user input. It needs to be general enough to support a large range of physical devices, with a broad spectrum of resources and capabilities. It must also be specific enough so that an application can take advantage of particular resources that a graphics device might offer. In PHIGS this interface is the *workstation*, which is an abstraction of a graphics device. The term workstation as used here should not be confused with the common term, referring to a single user, multi-tasking computer with a screen, keyboard and mouse. Here we will use the term *physical workstation* when we need to refer to the actual machine.

Workstations, in the PHIGS sense, can represent a broad range of physical devices. They can be for example:

- window on a physical workstation
- DIN A1 digitizer
- dials and function box
- postscript file
- X11 Terminal
- PEX Terminal
- laser printer
- plotter.

Different types of workstations can be broadly classified by their *category*. There are 5 categories of workstation, which basically identify whether it can be used for INPUT, for OUTPUT or both. The workstation categories are:

INPUT   workstations only support input, which can be due to a user manipulating a physical input device. An example of an INPUT workstation is a digitizer.

OUTPUT   workstations only generate graphics output. They have a display surface where the output primitives are drawn and have no input devices. An example of an OUTPUT workstation is a laser printer or a plotter.

OUTIN   workstations support both input and output. They have a display surface for drawing and support input from input devices. An example of an OUTIN workstation is a window on a physical workstation together with a keyboard and a mouse or digitizer.

MI   METAFILE INPUT workstations are used to read metafiles. Metafiles have a standardized format and are used for interchanging 2D graphics pictures between systems.

MO   METAFILE OUTPUT workstations are used to write metafiles.

The categories define the basic capabilities of a group of workstations. In addition to the category, workstations are classified by their types. The workstation type will specify exactly which physical device is the workstation. The workstation type is given an implementation specific value in order to identify the physical device.

This chapter will focus on using workstations for output only. The entire input model is discussed separately Chapter 8.

3.1 Using workstations

We have already seen workstations being used in the example programs. Here these routines will be formally defined. In Section 1.3 the concept of the PHIGS operating states was introduced and it was mentioned that there is an operating state corresponding to the workstation. The workstation's operating state differs from the structure's due to the fact that there can be more than one workstation open at the same time. Because of this, all routines which require a workstation to be open, have as their first argument a workstation identifier. This identifier is an integer supplied by the application to the routine:

OPEN WORKSTATION   (PHOP,*,*,*)
Arguments:

in	workstation identifier	integer
in	connection identifier	string
in	workstation type	workstation type

The workstation type identifies which physical device type is to be used and its data type is implementation dependent. A given workstation type could be accessed in several ways. The connection identifier determines how to access the specific workstation. Some examples of workstation types and connection identifiers are:

Workstation	Type	Category	Connection id
A0 digitizer	24	INPUT	"/dev/tty3"
Plotter	67	OUTPUT	"/dev/tty4"
X11 Terminal	211	OUTIN	"mynode:0.0"
MS-DOS PC	"EGA"	OUTIN	NULL
Postscript file	72	OUTPUT	"myfile.ps"

It is important to realize that both the workstation type and connection identifier are implementation dependent. Your PHIGS supplier has defined and documented the supported workstation types and their connection identifiers. For example, in SUN-PHIGS the workstation type is generated by a proprietary function, whereas in DEC-PHIGS it is an integer constant.

OPEN WORKSTATION sets the state of the workstation, which is specified by the workstation identifier, to WSOP. This involves initializing some internal tables and clearing the display surface (for OUTPUT or OUTIN workstations).

Since several workstations can be open at the same time, each open workstation must have a unique identifier. Calling OPEN WORKSTATION with an identifier of an already open workstation generates an error. Keeping a workstation open uses system resources, so each PHIGS implementation specifies a maximum allowable number of simultaneously open workstations. When you are finished using a workstation these resources can be freed up by closing the workstation. This is done with the routine:

CLOSE WORKSTATION   (PHOP,WSOP,*,*)
Arguments:
        in   workstation identifier   integer

The workstation associated with the identifier is closed. If no other workstation is open then the workstation state becomes WSCL. For those workstations belonging to the appropriate category, this call will implicitly update the display surface and flush the input queue. The connection to the workstation is released and allocated system resources are freed.

3.2 Workstation tables

Each workstation type has its own table, the workstation description table WDT, which defines what the workstation is capable of. This table contains default values for workstation dependent attributes and entries identifying available resources. Since the WDT defines capabilities of a specific device, it contains implementation dependent values. Entries in the WDT can be read with inquiry functions even before the workstation is opened. This enables an application to configure itself to take advantage of a workstation's available resources. The complete WDT is too large to list here, but the following should outline what sort of data is kept in the WDT:

- workstation type and category
- workstation classification (RASTER,VECTOR,OTHER)
- maximum display surface size
- number of available colours
- predefined viewing matrices
- predefined bundled attributes (polyline, polymarker, text, fillarea ...)
- attribute limits (number of polymarkers, maximum linewidth, maximum character height, number of interior hatching styles...)
- number of input devices of class: LOCATOR, STROKE, VALUATOR, CHOICE, PICK, STRING
- Input device defaults and limits: number of prompt and echo types, echo volume, etc. ... .

When a workstation is opened, the WDT is used to initialize the workstation state list (WSL) to its default state. Each open workstation has its own WSL. The WSL contains the actual state of workstation specific attributes and tables. The following is a summary of the data kept in the WSL:

- workstation ID, connection ID and type, (Section 3.1)
- table of defined viewing transformations, (Section 7.3)
- list of posted structures, (Section 2.2)
- deferral and modification modes, (Section 3.3)
- state of visual representation, (Section 3.3)
- bundled attribute tables for: polyline, polymarker, text, fillarea, edges, (Section 5.1)
- colour table entries, (Section 5.2)
- highlighting and invisibilty filters, (Section 9.2)
- input device state and parameters, (Chapter 8).

At this stage it is not expected that the reader is familiar with all entries in the workstation tables, so the Section in which an entry is described has also been provided. Entries in the WSL are modified by an application when it posts and unposts structures, defines tables or initializes input devices. The tables are accessed at traversal time by structure elements which require bundled attributes.

38

3.3 Updating workstations

In the Section 2.2 we introduced the command POST STRUCTURE. This was used to associate a structure network to an open workstation, so that it would be drawn when the workstation was updated. Updating the workstation initiates traversing the posted structure networks. PHIGS allows the application to control flexibly how and when a workstation is to be updated. Some workstations might not have to traverse an entire structure network to display a change in state. For example, deleting a structure element could be simulated on a graphics screen by drawing the object in the background colour. This would not work if the workstation were a laser printer. Here we want to look at the details of how to control updating workstations.

Table 3.1   Categories of actions which affect display correctness.

Structure changes
        structure content
        structure posted
        structure unposted
        structure deleted
        changing structure references (EXECUTE STRUCTURE)

Changing WSL entries
        view representation
        polyline bundle representation
        polymarker bundle representation
        text bundle representation
        interior bundle representation
        edge bundle representation
        pattern representation
        colour representation
        workstation transformation
        highlighting filter
        invisibility filter
        HLHSR mode
        data mapping representation (+)
        reflectance representation (+)
        parametric surface representation (+)
        light source representation (+)
        depth cue representation (+)
        colour mapping representation (+)

The categories followed by a (+) correspond to WSL entries defined by PHIGS PLUS. The picture that is displayed on a workstation depends on the contents of the WSL and its posted structure network. If any structures are edited or if any workstation tables are modified, then the picture on the workstation does not necessarily correspond to contents of the CSS and WSL. The WDT contains entries which define how a workstation is to respond if a change occurs in one of the categories listed in Table 3.1.

There are three ways a workstation can respond to a change in one the categories in Table 3.1:

IMM   The workstation can IMMediately update the display to reflect the change. For example, a change in the colour representation could modify a colour lookup table entry which can be performed immediately.

IRG   Some modifications to this category require Implicit ReGeneration. This means that all posted structures must be traversed to update the picture. An example would be the editing of a structure which is posted to a laser printer workstation. In this case the entire image has to be redrawn to reflect the change correctly.

CBS   The workstation can use a quick update method so that the change Can Be Simulated. A simulated update may not be entirely correct, but it is much faster than redrawing the entire image. It is provided to give the user immediate feedback. An example of a quick update method would be to draw the structure network, which has been unposted, in the background colour.

There are inquiry functions which read the WDT in order to find out how a particular type of workstation will respond to a change in one of the categories in Table 3.1 (see Section 3.6.2).

PHIGS keeps track of whether the displayed image represents what the correct picture should look like, which in turn depends on the posted structures and the contents of the WSL. This information is maintained in a WSL entry, the *state of visual representation*, SVR. The SVR can be read with the inquiry function INQUIRE DISPLAY UPDATE STATE and can assume one of the following states:

CORRECT   The display shows the correct picture.

DEFERRED   The display does not represent the correct picture. Changes are necessary to update the display.

SIMULATED   The display does not represent the correct picture. One or more necessary changes have been simulated using a quick update method. There are no deferred changes pending.

When and how a workstation is updated is governed by its display update state. This consists of its deferral mode, which determines when the display should be updated, and its modification mode, which determines how the display should be updated. The WDT contains the default value of the display update state, but it can be changed by the application with the routine:

SET DISPLAY UPDATE STATE   (PHOP,WSOP,*,*)
Arguments:

in	workstation identifier	integer
in	deferral mode	(ASAP,BNIG,BNIL,ASTI,WAIT)
in	modification mode	(NIVE,UWOR,UQUM)

The deferral mode will govern when the display should be updated. If an update is necessary depends on whether changes have been made to any of the items in Table 3.1. The deferral mode can have one of the 5 following values:

ASAP   The SVR will be CORRECT As Soon As Possible.

BNIG   The SVR will be CORRECT Before the Next Interaction Globally.

BNIL   The SVR will be CORRECT Before the Next Interaction Locally.

ASTI   The SVR will be CORRECT At Some TIme, which depends on the particular PHIGS implementation. When the update occurs, is not necessarily predictable.

WAIT   The SVR will be CORRECT only When the Application explicitly requests IT with the functions: REDRAW ALL STRUCTURES or UPDATE WORKSTATION.

These deferral modes require some explanation. In ASAP mode the picture will be updated every time a change is made to any one of the categories in Table 3.1. This update state should be avoided if several changes need to be made before the display is ready to be redrawn, since each change would trigger a retraversal of the posted structures.

The mode BNIG will update the display before an input device is used on any open workstation. This will behave like ASAP if any input devices is in SAMPLE or EVENT modes, or it will update the display, if necessary, before accepting input from a device in REQUEST mode (see Section 8.3 on input device modes). BNIL is similar to BNIG, except that only input devices belonging to the specified workstation are considered.

ASTI is an implementation specific deferral mode. There are no guarantees that an ASTI mode in one PHIGS implementation is available in another. An example of how ASTI could be used is to defer traversing a structure network, which is being edited, until it is closed. The mode WAIT is the simplest. In order for the picture to be correct, the application must explicitly ask for the workstation to be updated.

Sometimes it is not necessary for a workstation to retraverse all posted structures to update the display. Some updates can be simulated or even performed without redrawing everything. The modification mode will determine how to update the display:

41

Workstations

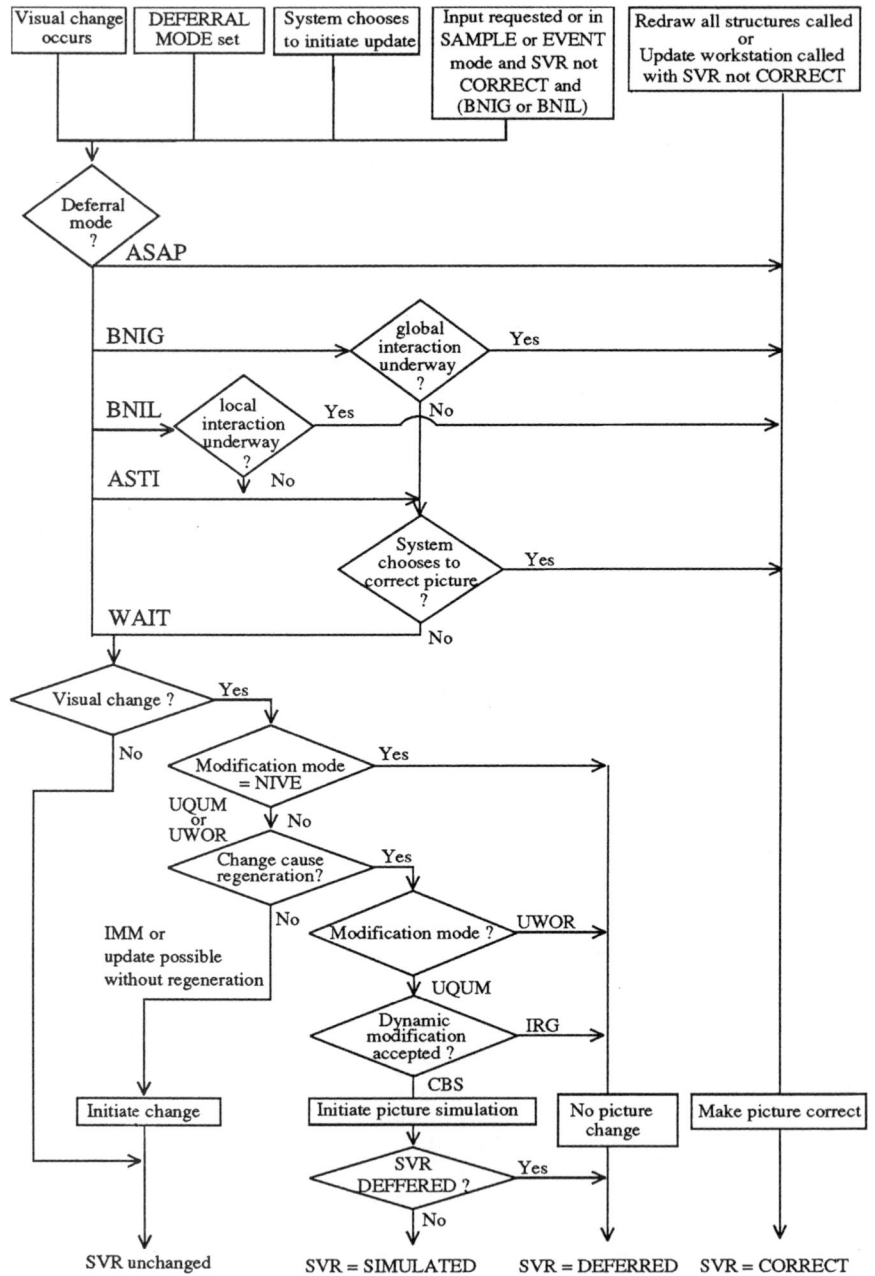

Figure 3.1 Display update flow diagram.

The modification mode can have one of the following values:

NIVE   No Immediate Visual Effects mandated. When the modification mode is NIVE, the display can only be updated by completely retraversing all posted structures.

UWOR   Update WithOut Regeneration. All updates that can be made without simulation or regenerating the entire image should be performed.

UQUM   Use Quick Update Method. The image update can be simulated with a workstation specific quick update method.

It is important to be aware that a given quick update method depends on both the workstation type and the particular PHIGS implementation. Quick update methods are provided to take advantage of mechanisms a workstation might offer to update the display without having to retraverse all structures. There are no standard quick update methods. Quick update methods only simulate the necessary changes, so the display may not be completely correct. Some examples of quick update methods which have been implemented are:

- draw deleted output primitives or unposted structures in the background colour
- only traverse structures posted since the last update.

The relationship between the deferral and modification modes is rather complicated. How these modes are interrelated and how they affect the SVR is summarized in Figure 3.1.

There are two functions to force updating a workstation. The first function is appropriately named:

UPDATE WORKSTATION   (PHOP,WSOP,*,*)
Arguments:
      in   workstation identifier   integer
      in   regeneration flag   (PERFORM,POSTPONE)

This can be used to force updating the specified workstation. If the regeneration flag is set to POSTPONE any queued data will be transmitted to the workstation, so that the WSL will be updated. If the regeneration flag is set to PERFORM, then the WSL will be updated and all posted structures will be redrawn, resulting in the state of visual representation being CORRECT once the update completes.

The next routine also forces updating the workstation:

REDRAW ALL STRUCTURES   (PHOP,WSOP,*,*)
Arguments:
      in   workstation identifier   integer
      in   control flag   (CONDITIONALLY,ALWAYS)

All structures posted to the specified workstation are redisplayed

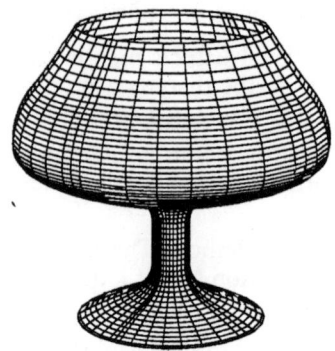

Figure 3.2 Object drawn with hidden surface removal.

using the latest WSL. This will result in the picture being completely up to date and the SVR being CORRECT. The control flag determines whether to clear the display surface or not. If set to CONDITIONALLY, it will only clear the display surface if the display is empty. If the control flag is ALWAYS then the display surface is cleared regardless of whether it is empty or not.

3.4 Hidden line and hidden surface removal

When an object is drawn in 3D, the position in space of the viewer must be defined. Some objects in a scene may obscure others when viewed from a given vantage point. Hidden line/hidden surface removal, *HLHSR* refers to techniques to make sure that only those objects which are not obscured by others are drawn. PHIGS is a 3D graphics standard, so it must address HLHSR. Since there are a number of techniques, some of which require specific hardware resources in the workstation, PHIGS provides both a workstation dependent and a workstation independent means to control which HLHSR method to use. Some examples of HLHSR methods are:

- none
- Z buffer algorithm
- depth sort (Painter's algorithm)
- binary space partitioning
- scan line algorithms.

For example the Z buffer algorithm assumes the workstation is a raster device, which has a horizontal and vertical pixel resolution. A PHIGS workstation does not need to be a raster device (e.g., a plotter). As a result, the HLHSR techniques must be workstation specific. Details of the individual HLHSR methods are beyond the scope of this book and the reader is advised to look at standard texts on 3D graphics [Foley et al.].

PHIGS uses two functions to control hidden line/hidden surface removal. The first function sets the HLHSR mode in the WSL:

SET HLHSR MODE   (PHOP,WSOP,*,*)
Arguments:

      in workstation identifier   workstation identifier
      in hlhsr mode   integer

This will set the HLHSR mode on the specified workstation. The mode is an integer, whose value depends on the PHIGS implementation and on the workstation type. This allows the user to choose which HLHSR technique to use. What HLHSR modes are available on a given workstation can be determined with the function INQUIRE HLHSR FACILITIES.

The second function to control hidden line/hidden surface removal creates a structure element. By using a structure element to select a HLHSR identifier, one can limit using HLHSR only to those portions of the posted structure networks which require it. If certain structure elements do not need HLHSR, for example, text in some situations, then the display update will generally be speeded up by disabling HLHSR for those primitives. This can be done with the structure element:

SET HLHSR IDENTIFIER   (PHOP,*,STOP,*)
Arguments:
      in   HLHSR identifier   integer

This routine will write an element to the currently open structure that will specify which HLHSR identifier to use when drawing output primitives at traversal time. The identifier is an implementation dependent integer parameter which selects which HLHSR to use. If the HLHSR identifier indicates a method which is not available on the workstation to which the structure is posted, then an implementation dependent default will be used.

Both routines can be used concurrently and are generally seen such that SET HLHSR IDENTIFIER is used to enable and disable HLHSR for specific portions of a structure, and SET HLHSR MODE selects the HLHSR technique to use.

3.5 Sending messages to a workstation

PHIGS provides a means to send a message to a workstation. Where and how it is displayed is up to the PHIGS implementation. The routine is:

MESSAGE   (PHOP,WSOP,*,*)
Arguments:
      in workstation identifier   integer

in message	character string

It displays the message string on the specified workstation or a device which is associated with the workstation. It can be used to inform the user that an action is needed, for example, to put paper in a plotter.

3.6 Workstation inquiries

The contents of the workstation description table and the workstation state list can be read with inquiry functions. An application can determine what resources a specific workstation has and how to best use them by reading the WDT. The WDT contains information which describes the workstation (e.g., number of available colours, device coordinate range, etc.) and its defaults. Reading the WDT makes it possible for an application to configure itself in order to use the workstation's resources most effectively. For example, one can read the WDT to determine whether the workstation supports colour or not. If it is a black and white workstation, then it would be more effective to fill polygons with hatch patterns instead of using colour.

The WSL is initialized with the WDT once the workstation is opened. It contains the current viewing transformations, attribute bundle tables, etc. (see Section 3.2). The contents of these tables can be read, enabling a program to react to the current state of the workstation. For example, after processing a number of user requests which caused the CSS to be edited, it might be necessary to update the workstation. Whether a given workstation needs to be updated might not be clear, especially if there are several structure networks, and several open workstations. One can avoid a costly workstation update by inquiring the workstation's SVR and only redrawing if it is not CORRECT.

The workstation tables are extensive and there are a large number of inquiry functions to read their contents. A complete list of all inquiry functions can be found in Appendix D. Here only a few functions will be briefly described. Using inquiry functions is straightforward, so an in depth discussion of each function is not necessary.

3.6.1 General workstation inquiries

These functions return information contained in the PHIGS descriptor table and state list. These functions require no input parameters and their names indicate what information is returned. All functions except INQUIRE WORKSTATION STATE VALUE return an error indicator in addition to the requested information.

INQUIRE WORKSTATION STATE VALUE	(*,*,*,*)
INQUIRE LIST OF AVAILABLE WORKSTATION TYPES	(PHOP,*,*,*)

INQUIRE SET OF OPEN WORKSTATIONS   (PHOP,*,*,*)

3.6.2 Workstation description table inquiries

All workstation description table inquiry functions need to be given a workstation type. It is important to note that it is the workstation type that must be provided, not a workstation identifier. The type identifies which WDT table to read. The required operating state for all WDT inquiries is (PHOP,*,*,*) since a workstation need not be open to read its WDT.

All functions return an error indicator and the requested information. An error can occur if the requested information is not available on the workstation. For example, one cannot inquire about input devices from an OUTPUT only workstation type.

The routines INQUIRE DISPLAY SPACE SIZE 3 and INQUIRE DISPLAY SPACE SIZE are often used, because they return size of the display space in both device coordinates and raster units. This information is needed to position input devices such as choice menus on the display surface.

The two routines INQUIRE DYNAMICS OF WORKSTATION ATTRIBUTES and INQUIRE DYNAMICS OF STRUCTURES can be called to find out what resources a workstation has to simulate or immediately regenerate the display. These functions return how a workstation can respond when the state of one of the categories of picture changes in Table 3.1 has been modified. It will return for each category (e.g. changing the colour representation) either IMM, CBS or IRG, depending on whether the workstation can immediately update the display, simulate the change, or require the picture to be regenerated. This was discussed in more detail in Section 3.3.

In order to determine what resources a workstation has when drawing output primitives one can use the routines INQUIRE XXX FACILITIES, where XXX is one of: POLYLINE, POLYMARKER, TEXT, ANNOTATION, INTERIOR, EDGE, PATTERN and COLOUR. For example, INQUIRE COLOUR FACILITIES can be called to find out if a workstation is monochrome, or how many colours it supports. The routine INQUIRE POLYLINE FACILITIES returns a list of available line types (e.g. solid, dotted, dashed, etc.), the number of available line widths, the nominal linewidth, the range of line widths supported and a list of predefined polyline indices. These indices point to table entries which contain the polyline attributes: colour index, linetype, and linewidth scale factor bundled together. An entry in a bundle table is called a representation. See Section 5.1 for more information on bundled attributes.

In order to read the contents of the predefined bundle tables, one can use the routines INQUIRE PREDEFINED XXX REPRESENTATION,

47

where XXX is one of: VIEW, POLYLINE, POLYMARKER, TEXT, INTERIOR, EDGE, PATTERN, and COLOUR. These routines must be called with an index into the table as well as a workstation type. The indices are supplied by the routines INQUIRE XXX FACILITIES.

In order to find out how big these tables are, the routine INQUIRE WORKSTATION STATE TABLE LENGTHS is provided. A common use for this function is to determine how many colour table entries can be defined.

When posting a structure to a workstation, one needs to specify a display priority. The number of display priorities supported is implementation dependent and can be determined with the function INQUIRE NUMBER OF DISPLAY PRIORITIES SUPPORTED.

Each input device has data associated with it, whose default values can be read from the WDT with: INQUIRE DEFAULT XXX DATA where XXX can be one of: CHOICE, LOCATOR, STRING, STROKE VALUATOR or PICK. These data are used to determine how an input device appears, its initial value, etc. For example, a valuator device (e.g., a slider bar or dial) has an initial value, an echo area, a data record, and a prompt and echo type. The echo area is the area on the workstation where the slider bar or dial is displayed. The prompt and echo type determines how the valuator appears to the user (e.g., whether it is a slider bar or not). The data record is provided to contain additional data associated with the input device (a title for the valuator) and is implementation dependent. The input device data will be discussed in further detail in Chapter 8.

3.6.3 Workstation state list inquiries

When a workstation is opened, a workstation state list is allocated, which is initialized with the contents of the WDT belonging to the corresponding workstation type. During a PHIGS session the contents of the WSL are modified through posting structures, defining bundled attributes, defining viewing transformations, initializing input devices, etc. The actual contents of the WSL can be read at any time while the workstation is open with inquiry functions.

All WSL inquiry functions require a workstation index as an input parameter, which specifies which WSL to read. These functions return an error indicator and the requested data. An error can occur if the data is not available, for example, trying to read the WSL of a workstation which is closed. A complete listing of the WSL inquiry functions can be found in Appendix D. The following is a brief summary of several WSL inquiry functions.

INQUIRE WORKSTATION CONNECTION AND TYPE is used to find out what connection id and workstation type were used when the workstation was opened.

INQUIRE POSTED STRUCTURES will return a list of all structure identifiers which have been posted to the workstation.

In order to read back the viewing transformation in a workstation, one can use the routines: INQUIRE LIST OF VIEW INDICES and IN-QUIRE VIEW REPRESENTATION. A workstation's WSL can have more than one viewing transformation, which is selected with an index. Once the transformation's index is known through calling the first function, the actual transformation can be read back by calling the second function.

In order to determine what bundled attributes have been defined, one can use the routines INQUIRE LIST OF XXX INDICES and INQUIRE XXX REPRESENTATION, where XXX can be one of: POLYLINE, POLYMARKER, TEXT, INTERIOR, EDGE, PATTERN. INQUIRE LIST OF XXX INDICES returns the number of entries in the bundle table for a given output primitive and the indices pointing to these bundled attributes. The routines INQUIRE XXX REPRESENTATION read the actual contents of the bundle table for a given index.

In order to find out what state an input devices is in, the routines IN-QUIRE XXX DEVICE STATE, where XXX is one of LOCATOR, STROKE, VALUATOR, CHOICE, PICK or STRING are provided. The state can be modified by initializing the input device or by changing its operating mode. For more detail see Chapter 8.

3.7 Metafile workstation types

Two workstation categories which have not yet been covered are metafile in, MI, and metafile out, MO, workstations. These workstation types are provided as an interface to a metafile, which is defined in a separate standard [ISOb]. There are a number of texts written on metafiles that should be consulted for more information, for example, [Henderson and Mumford]. These files are also known as Computer Graphics Metafiles or CGM. The file format has been standardized, so that metafiles can be used to exchange graphics data between applications, which do not necessarily use the same programming interface. For example, a metafile could be created by a program using PHIGS and read by a GKS program. This would not be possible using archive files which only store structures from the CSS (see Section 10.2).

There is no one-to-one mapping between PHIGS and metafiles. Metafiles only support two dimensional primitives and are organized as a sequence of items. These items are grouped together to define independent static pictures. Metafiles can contain primitives which have no counterpart in PHIGS, for example, circles or ellipses. Conversely, there are a number of concepts in PHIGS, which have no counterpart in CGM, such as workstation update control, or workstation transformations. The PHIGS standard defines a set of routines, with which an implementation

49

can define an interface to metafiles. It does not define exactly how this interface should behave, so there may be differences between different PHIGS implementations.

3.7.1 Writing metafiles

The metafile workstation will usually behave just like an OUTPUT workstation, but since it has no update control, any changes which cause the SVR not to be CORRECT requires an implicit regeneration. A metafile workstation will generally be in the deferral mode WAIT and needs to be updated either with REDRAW ALL STRUCTURES or with UPDATE WORKSTATION. This will initiate the traversal process, which creates a picture and writes all items to the metafile needed to define the picture. The items in a metafile have been standardized, so it is up to the PHIGS implementation to interpret the contents of the posted structure network and the workstation state list in order to create the appropriate CGM items.

Another way to write to a metafile, besides updating an MO workstation, is to explicitly write to the metafile with the command:

WRITE ITEM TO METAFILE   (PHOP,WSOP,*,*)
Arguments:

in	workstation identifier	integer
in	item type	integer
in	item data record	data record

This routine will write an item to the metafile corresponding to the workstation identifier. The item type and the data record define the item which is to be written and are specified in the CGM standard. The format of the data record is implementation dependent. It is up to the PHIGS programmer to make sure that item is correctly defined. This allows the PHIGS program to write items to a metafile in addition to those written by the PHIGS traversal procedure.

After a metafile has been written through updating the MO workstation and by calling the procedure WRITE ITEM TO METAFILE, the workstation should be closed, so that the file is closed correctly.

3.7.2 Reading from metafiles

Reading a metafile is more complicated than writing one. This is partially due to the fact that metafiles can contain items which cannot be uniquely mapped onto PHIGS functions. Another reason is that the PHIGS standard does not explicitly define the relationship between metafiles and PHIGS. A method to read metafiles that is consistent with the standard is discussed here.

A metafile consists of items which are read one at a time. In order to read a metafile, a workstation with the category MI must first be opened. Once the MI workstation is opened, the first item in the file is the current item. In order to process the metafile, the items need to be interpreted by PHIGS. Before they can be interpreted, they need to be read from the file. Reading metafile items is done in two stages. First the item type and the size of the data record are read, then the item itself. This allows the application to make sure that a buffer which is big enough to contain the data record is available before reading the item.

The item type and data record size are read from the metafile with the command:

GET ITEM TYPE FROM METAFILE   (PHOP,WSOP,*,*)
Arguments:

	in	workstation identifier	integer
	out	item type	integer
	out	size of data record	integer

This function returns the type and data record size for the current item in the open MI workstation, which is indicated by the workstation identifier. The current item remains current after calling this routine.

In order to read the item one needs to call the function:

READ ITEM FROM METAFILE   (PHOP,WSOP,*,*)
Arguments:

	in	workstation identifier	integer
	in	maximum buffer size	integer
	out	item data record	data record

This routine reads the current item from the metafile and updates the current item to be the next item in the file. An error will be generated if the maximum buffer size is too small to contain the item. If the maximum buffer size is zero, then the current item will be skipped and nothing is read.

The record returned by READ ITEM FROM METAFILE is not meant to be interpreted by the applications programmer. PHIGS provides the following routine to do this:

INTERPRET ITEM   (PHOP,*,*,*)
Arguments:

	in	item type	integer
	in	item data record	data record

The effect of this routine depends on the PHIGS implementation. Its purpose is to interpret the item, in order to display the picture defined in the metafile accurately. If the item cannot be interpreted, an error is generated. This can be possible, since there are numerous items in metafiles, such as named fonts, which a PHIGS implementation might not be able to interpret.

Some items might require an operating state other than (PHOP,*,*,*).

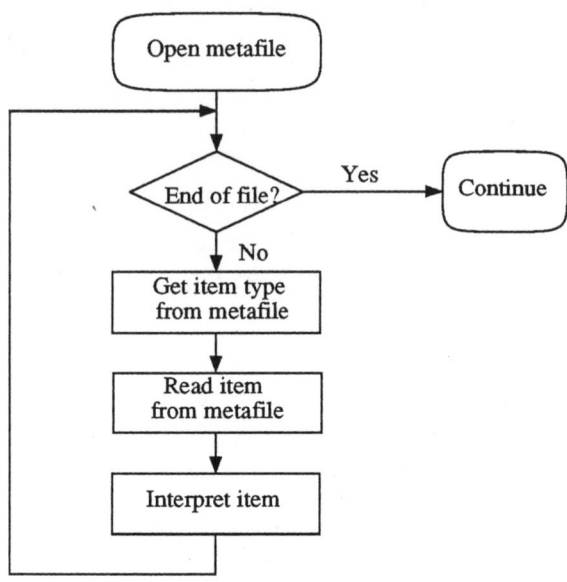

Figure 3.3 Flowchart to read metafiles from PHIGS .

For example, interpreting the item POLYLINE might require a structure to be open. Other metafile items, such as BACKGROUND COLOUR, might require an OUTPUT or OUTIN workstation to be open in order to modify the colour table in the WSL. Other items can change the operating state. For example, the item BEGIN PICTURE might open a structure with the name given by the picture identifier. This would set the correct operating state for subsequent items, such as output primitives, which would require a structure to be open.

The effect of INTERPRET ITEM as described here is not mandated by the PHIGS standard, but rather is consistent with it. Only your supplier's PHIGS documentation can accurately describe how INTERPRET ITEM has been implemented. In general a metafile can be read by code structured as in Figure 3.3.

This can only serve as a guideline on how to use metafile workstations. The behaviour when interpreting metafile items will vary from one PHIGS implementation to another. Sections of code which require metafiles should be modularly written, with restricted influence on the main application, in order to limit difficulties when porting from one PHIGS implementation to another.

CHAPTER 4

PHIGS Output Primitives

In order to draw an object with a graphics system, one has to define its shape. This is done with output primitives or drawing primitives. One cannot discuss output primitives without mentioning attributes, which determine how the output primitive is to be drawn. For example, a line has the attributes, colour index, linewidth scale factor, linetype (e.g., solid, dashed, dotted, ...). In PHIGS the attributes are defined independently of the output primitives. So, for example, to draw a dotted line, one must first define the linetype to be dotted and then draw the line. In this chapter, the individual attributes will be used to illustrate the different styles of output each drawing primitive has. Using attributes is not quite as simple as is implied here, so they will be discussed in more detail in Chapter 5.

The object's shape is defined by specifying the coordinates of its vertices. If an object contains curved surfaces, for example, an ellipsoid, then its true shape can only be approximated by defining a grid of vertices on its surface. This procedure is known as tessellation, which is in general a complicated task. PHIGS PLUS contains additional primitives (NURB's), which can be used to define curved lines and surfaces (see Section 12.3).

The drawing primitives are the building blocks with which an object is defined. All output primitives are structure elements, so a structure must be open when calling these routines. PHIGS has defined the following drawing primitives:

- polyline   : a set of connected line segments
- polymarker   : a set of discrete symbols

- text   : a text string
- annotation text   : a text string used in labeling
- fill area   : a polygon, bound by a set of vertices
- fill area set   : a set of polygons
- cell array   : a grid of coloured cells
- generalized drawing : non-standard drawing primitive
  primitive

All PHIGS primitives exist in both a 2D and a 3D form. All coordinates used in PHIGS are Cartesian coordinates. A 2D point consists of two floating point numbers, namely the x and y coordinates defining its position; and a 3D point requires a floating point triplet to define its x, y, and z coordinates. The 3D primitives are denoted by the number 3 appended to their name. For example, the function FILL AREA is used for 2D polygons and FILL AREA 3 for 3D polygons.

The coordinates are defined in what is known as modelling space. The 3D modelling space used in PHIGS is right-handed. There is no notion of handedness in 2D space. As a result the origin of the 3D modelling space is at the lower left of the drawing surface, with x increasing towards the right and y increasing towards the top of the surface. The z-axis points out of the surface. There are a number of transformations which are performed to map the coordinates used to define the object onto the drawing surface. In general if no transformation is specified, each component of the coordinates should be between 0.0 and 1.0. Chapter 6 is devoted to discussing these transformations and how to use them.

The rest of this chapter will treat each of the eight different types of PHIGS output primitive in detail. The primitives defined by PHIGS PLUS will be discussed separately in Chapter 12.

4.1 Polylines

Lines are drawn in PHIGS with the primitive POLYLINE. A polyline is defined by a list of vertices, which will be connected with straight line segments. A three dimensional object which has been drawn with polylines is called a wireframe object.

The routine to draw a 3D polyline simply needs to know the coordinates of its vertices. This is done with the routine:

POLYLINE 3   (PHOP,*,STOP,*)El
Arguments:
        in   point list   array of 3D points in MC

This routine will write to the open structure a POLYLINE 3 primitive with the vertices specified in the point list. At traversal time the polyline is drawn by connecting the vertices with straight line segments. The vertices are specified in modelling coordinates, MC.

There is also a 2D version of POLYLINE 3, called POLYLINE. The only difference between these two routines is that POLYLINE requires an array of 2D points in modelling coordinates.

In the C binding, the following program would draw two triangles on the screen.

```c
#include <phigs.h>
#define RootStruct          1
#define WSID                1

void main()
{
Pint wstype;
Ppoint_list t2;
static Ppoint triang2[4] = { 0.1,   0.1,
                             0.35,  0.1,
                             0.35,  0.35,
                             0.1,   0.1 };
Ppoint_list3 t3;
static Ppoint3 triang3[4] = { 0.5,  0.1,  0.25,
                              0.75, 0.1,  0.25,
                              0.75, 0.35, 0.25,
                              0.5,  0.1,  0.25 };

    popen_phigs( PDEF_ERR_FILE, PDEF_MEM_SIZE );
    /***************************************************
     * SUN-PHIGS specific function to create a workstation
     * type. Implementation dependent.
     ***************************************************/
    wstype = phigs_ws_type_create( phigs_ws_type_x_tool,
      PHIGS_TOOL_LABEL, "SunPHIGS X Tool Workstation",
      PHIGS_WS_CATEGORY, PCAT_OUTIN,
      PHIGS_X_BUF_MODE,  PHIGS_BUF_DOUBLE,  0);
    if ( !wstype ) {
      pclose_phigs();
      exit(1);
    }
    popen_ws( WSID, (void *)NULL, wstype );

    /* Define the geometry */
    t2.num_points = 4;
    t2.points = triang2;
    t3.num_points = 4;
    t3.points = triang3;
    /* Now create the structure using both triangles */
```

```
popen_struct( RootStruct );
  ppolyline( &t2 );
  ppolyline3( &t3 );
pclose_struct();

/* Draw the geometry defined in the structure */
ppost_struct( WSID, RootStruct, 1.0 );
predraw_all_structs( WSID, PFLAG_ALWAYS );
getchar();

/* Now finished, so close everything and exit */
pclose_ws( WSID );
pclose_phigs();
}
```

In the example above the triangle on the right was drawn with a 2D polyline and the triangle on the left with a 3D polyline. Also note that four vertices must be specified to draw a closed triangle. No transformations are needed, because the coordinates of the polyline are transformed onto the unit cube with the default transformations. The routine ppolyline3 requires a floating point triplet for each vertex since it operates in 3D. In this case a constant z coordinate of 0.25 was used.

It is important to realize that although hidden line/hidden surface removal is defined in PHIGS, it is not possible to have hidden line removal when using only the routine POLYLINE 3. This is because even with HLHSR enabled the primitive POLYLINE 3 does not contain enough information to identify which lines are being obscured. In order to have hidden line removal, one needs the concept of an area filling primitive which is obscuring the lines. This is possible with the primitive FILL AREA SET 3 by enabling drawing the polygon's edges (see Figure 3.2). Section 4.4 deals with FILL AREA SET 3 in detail.

4.1.1 Polyline attributes

There are three attributes which determine how the polyline will appear on the screen. They are:

- line colour index
- linewidth
- line type.

Colours in PHIGS are selected by choosing an index into a colour table. This is done with the function:

SET POLYLINE COLOUR INDEX   (PHOP,*,STOP,*)El
Arguments:
               in   colour index   integer

When this element is traversed, it selects a colour from a table of colours defined in the workstation state list. The actual colour this index points to can be defined with the routine SET COLOUR REPRESENTATION, as we shall see in Section 5.2 on colour. Usually the workstation contains predefined colours. The chosen colour will be used when drawing all 2D and 3D polylines.

In order to determine the width of the line segments drawn, one can use the routine:

SET LINEWIDTH SCALE FACTOR   (PHOP,*,STOP,*)El
Arguments:
        in   linewidth scale factor   real

This element determines the width of subsequently drawn polylines. The width of the lines will be set to the *linewidth scale factor* multiplied by the nominal line width. For example, if a workstation draws lines on a raster screen with a nominal width of one pixel, specifying a linewidth scale factor of three will result in lines being drawn three pixels wide.

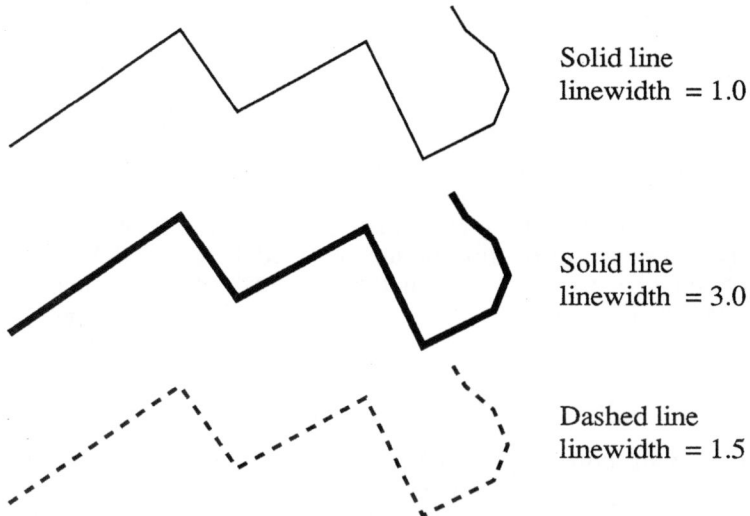

Solid line
linewidth = 1.0

Solid line
linewidth = 3.0

Dashed line
linewidth = 1.5

Figure 4.1 Polylines with different attributes.

The final polyline attribute determines what style to use when drawing polylines:

SET LINETYPE   (PHOP,*,STOP,*)El
Arguments:
        in   line type   integer

57

This will select the style to be one of:

≤ 0	implementation dependent
1	solid line
2	dashed line
3	dotted line
4	dashed-dotted line

It is important to note that all of these routines create structure elements, which are either inserted after or replace the current element. Their function is only apparent once the structure has been executed. Figure 4.1 illustrates a number of polylines which have been drawn with various widths and linetypes.

4.2 Polymarkers

Polymarkers are used to draw a set of symbols on the screen. This is done with the routine:

POLYMARKER 3   (PHOP,*,STOP,*)El
Arguments:
        in   point list   array of 3D points in MC

This function is called with a point list that determines where the symbols should be drawn. In the 3D routine, POLYMARKER 3, the points are in 3D modelling coordinate space, so are floating point triplets. The 2D version of this routine is called POLYMARKER and its vertices only have x and y coordinates. The attributes determine what the symbols look like.

4.2.1 Polymarker attributes

When drawing both 2D and 3D polymarkers, the attributes specify the following three properties of the marker used:

- polymarker colour index
- marker size scale factor
- marker type.

The first routine governs the colour used to draw polymarkers with, similarly to how SET LINE COLOUR INDEX determined the colour of polylines:

SET POLYMARKER COLOUR INDEX   (PHOP,*,STOP,*)El
Arguments:
          in   colour index   integer

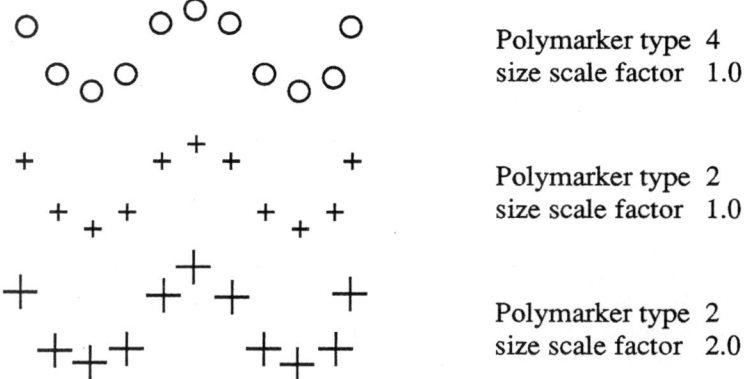

Polymarker type 4
size scale factor 1.0

Polymarker type 2
size scale factor 1.0

Polymarker type 2
size scale factor 2.0

Figure 4.2 Polymarkers with various attributes.

To change the size of the markers drawn, one should use:

SET MARKER SIZE SCALE FACTOR   (PHOP,*,STOP,*)El
Arguments:
      in   marker size scale factor   real

This element scales the size of polymarkers. Each type of symbol used in POLYMARKER is drawn with a default size, which depends on the workstation used. The *marker size scale factor* is multiplied by this default size resulting in the size actually used in drawing markers. For example, specifying a marker size scale factor of 2.5 will result in markers drawn 2 1/2 times the default size. To select what markers to use, one should call:

SET MARKER TYPE   (PHOP,*,STOP,*)El
Arguments:
      in   marker type   integer

This aspect determines what symbol to use when drawing polymarkers. At this time the following marker types have been defined:

    ≤ 0 implementation dependent
      1   · dot
      2   + plus sign
      3   * asterisk
      4   ○ circle
      5   × diagonal cross

The marker type *dot* is defined as the smallest displayable dot on the workstation. For example, on a raster device this would be a single pixel. The dot is the only marker type which is not scaled by the marker size scale factor.

Figure 4.2 shows several different polymarkers drawn with different attributes.

4.3 Fill area

The drawing primitive FILL AREA 3 is provided to draw 3D polygons in PHIGS. Here a polygon can be simple, such as a triangle, or complicated and self intersecting (see Figure 4.3). To define a fill area, one just needs to define the points which make up its boundary. The inside will be filled either with a colour or pattern, depending on what attributes are specified. The routine is:

FILL AREA 3   (PHOP,*,STOP,*)El
Arguments:
       in   point list   array of 3D points in MC

All that is needed to define the fill area is a list of points, which make up its boundary. The last point in the boundary list does not need to be the same as the first, since PHIGS will close the figure. The 2D version of this function is called FILL AREA and it obviously needs a 2D point list.

Simple polygon   *Self intersecting polygon*

Figure 4.3 Different types of fill areas.

These routines are area filling, so we need to be very precise in distinguishing the inside, which should be filled, from the outside. This becomes especially important when defining self-intersecting polygons. In order to determine whether any given point is inside or outside a fill area, PHIGS uses a simple technique, known as the even-odd counting rule. To determine whether a point is inside or outside of a polygon, one draws an infinite ray starting at the point and counts the number of crossings the ray makes with the boundary of the fill area. If the number of intersections is odd, then the point is inside the fill area, otherwise it is outside. This line has to cross the boundary, it does not count if it only touches it without crossing. This technique is the basis for a commonly used polygon filling algorithm as well as a simple method to visualize whether a point is inside a complex polygon or not. Figure 4.4 illustrates this rule.

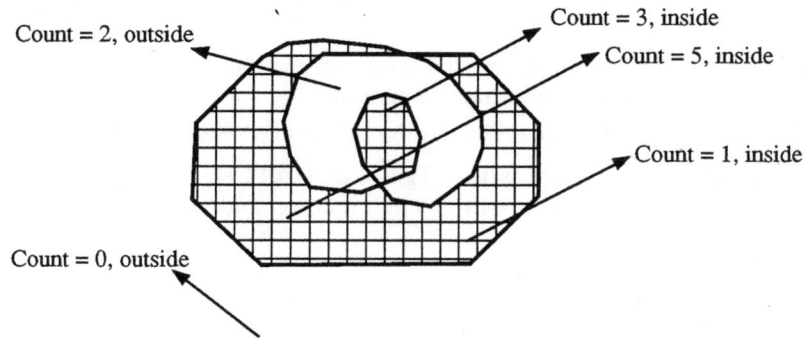

Figure 4.4 Polygon interiors with the even-odd counting rule.

4.3.1 Fill area attributes

The following attributes control how the fill area is drawn, but are also relevant for fill area set:

- interior colour index
- interior style
- interior style index.

The attribute interior colour index determines the colour with which the interior of the fill area will be filled. It is set with the function:

SET INTERIOR COLOUR INDEX   (PHOP,*,STOP,*)El
Arguments:
        in   colour index   integer

The style used to fill the polygons with is set with the function:

SET INTERIOR STYLE   (PHOP,*,STOP,*)El
Arguments:
        in   interior style   (HOLLOW,SOLID,PATTERN,
                                   HATCH,EMPTY)

The interior style establishes the method used to fill the interior of the fill area and can have one of the following values:

HOLLOW This style does not fill the polygon, but rather draws a polyline around the border with the colour selected by the INTERIOR COLOUR INDEX.

SOLID The interior of the polygon is filled with the colour selected by the INTERIOR COLOUR INDEX.

PATTERN This style fills the interior of the polygon with a pattern. The pattern can be defined by the application (see Section 5.3).

HATCH This style fills the polygon with hatching, which is selected from a table of hatch methods.

EMPTY This style does not fill the polygon's interior.

When the interior style is PATTERN or HATCH, then an additional function is needed to select which hatch method and which pattern. This is done with:

SET INTERIOR STYLE INDEX   (PHOP,*,STOP,*)El
Arguments:
      in   interior style index   integer

This routine determines which hatching method or pattern to use when filling areas. It is only relevant when one of these two interior styles is used.

The INTERIOR STYLE INDEX selects the hatching technique to use from a table of predefined hatching styles in the WDT. Hatching is a method to fill polygons with evenly spaced lines (see Figure 4.5). The supported hatching methods depend on the workstation, but in general a

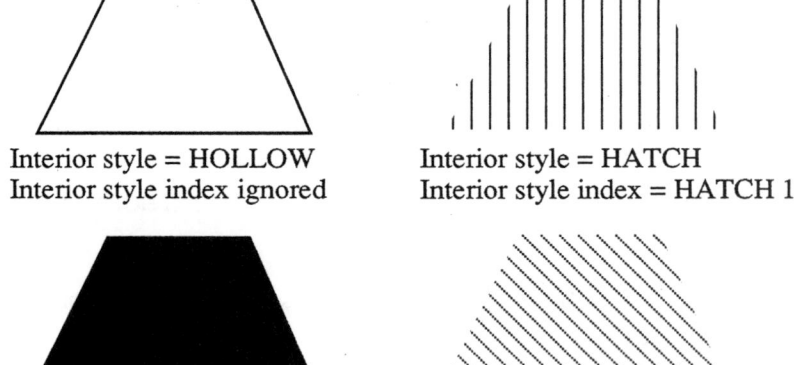

Interior style = HOLLOW
Interior style index ignored

Interior style = HATCH
Interior style index = HATCH 1

Interior style = SOLID
Interior style index ignored

Interior style = HATCH
Interior style index = HATCH 2

Figure 4.5 Fill area with different attributes.

positive INTERIOR STYLE INDEX selects a registered hatching method, whereas a negative index is implementation dependent.

When the interior style is PATTERN, then an application defined pattern can be selected with the INTERIOR STYLE INDEX. This pattern is defined as an array of colour indices, and is replicated over interior of the polygon (see Figure 5.10). The interior colour index is not used with patterns. To define the pattern one needs to use the following functions which are dealt with in greater detail in Section 5.3:

SET PATTERN REPRESENTATION - defines the pattern cell

SET PATTERN SIZE - scales the size of the pattern

SET PATTERN REFERENCE POINT - point to position the pattern array, used in 2D fill areas.

SET PATTERN REFERENCE POINT AND VECTORS - point and reference vectors to position the pattern cell in 3D fill areas.

4.4 Fill area set

The routine fill area set is more general than fill area because it allows one to define several polygons with one primitive. It can also be used to define polygons with holes in them. The fill area set also has additional attributes in order to draw the edges of polygons.

The fill area set needs a list of vertices for each of its polygons and is defined with the function:

FILL AREA SET 3   (PHOP,*,STOP,*)El

Arguments:
        in   list of point lists   array of 3D points in MC

The 2D version of fill area set is called FILL AREA SET and is passed a list of 2D point lists. The list of point lists will specify how many polygons belong to the fill area set and how many vertices each polygon has. The following example should illustrate how this routine is used.

```
Ppoint_list_list3 bounds;
Ppoint_list3      plists[2];
Ppoint3 square[4] = { 0.25,0.25,0.0,  0.75,0.25,0.0,
                      0.75,0.75,0.0,  0.25,0.75,0.0 };
Ppoint3 triang[3] = { 0.33,0.33,0.0,  0.66,0.33,0.0,
                      0.5,0.5,0.0 };
```

```
// This structure contains a fillarea which defines a
// square containing a triangle. The area between the
// square and the triangle is the interior of the fill
// area set.
    plists[0].num_points   = 4;
    plists[0].points       = square;
    plists[1].num_points   = 3;
    plists[1].points       = triang;
    bounds.num_point_lists = 2;
    bounds.point_lists     = plists;
    popen_struct( 1 );
        pfill_area_set3( &bounds );
    pclose_struct();
```

The interior of the polygon is filled according to the interior style, but now there are several disjoint boundaries (see Figure 4.6A). Once again we need to use the even-odd rule to determine what is inside and what is not (see Figure 4.4). This lets us put holes in the polygons. One just has to count the number of times a line starting at a point intersects any boundary in the fill area set. If this number is odd, then the point is in the interior, otherwise it is outside and should not be filled.

In Figure 4.6 we have drawn 3 separate fill area sets, each consisting of a square and a triangle. Each fill area in the set is an independently positioned polygon. In this figure the triangle is successively shifted downward by changing the last three points in the fill area set's vertex

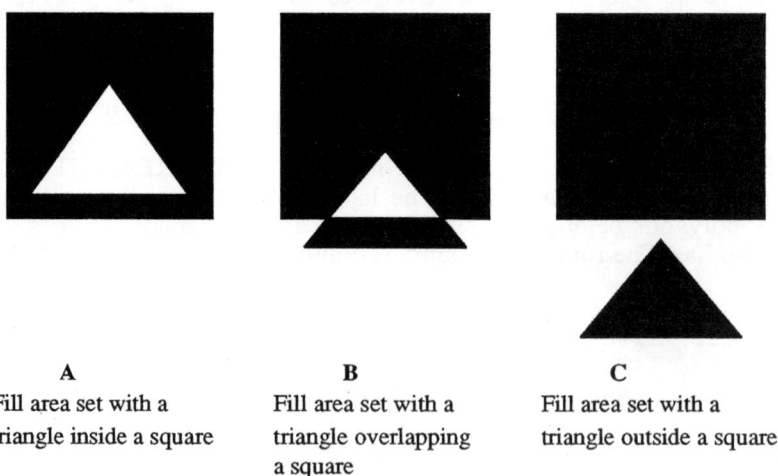

A	**B**	**C**
Fill area set with a triangle inside a square	Fill area set with a triangle overlapping a square	Fill area set with a triangle outside a square

Figure 4.6 Three fill area sets.

list. In 4.6A the triangle defines a border between the square and its exterior, forming a triangular hole. In 4.6B the triangle has been shifted downward so that it is overlapping the square. In this case, only the upper portion of the triangle, which is inside the square, defines an area exterior to the fill area set. In 4.6C the two polygons are disjoint, so their interiors are completely filled. This shows that the borders can be considered as a whole when determining the interior with the even-odd rule.

4.4.1 Fill area set attributes

In addition to the attributes used in drawing fill areas, fill area set has edge attributes. The edge attributes make it possible to draw the borders of each fill area in the primitive in addition to filling its interior. The other attributes treat the interior of the fill area set exactly as they did with the fill area. In summary the attributes governing how the fill area set is drawn are:

- interior colour index
- interior style
- interior style index
- edge flag
- edge colour index
- edge type
- edgewidth scale factor.

The first three attributes have already been described in Section 4.3.1. The edge flag is used to determine whether to draw edges or not. It is set with the function:

```
SET EDGE FLAG                                    (PHOP,*,STOP,*)El
Arguments:
          in    edge flag                        (OFF,ON)
```

If the edge flag is ON then all the borders of the fill areas will be drawn, otherwise they will not. If the edges are to be drawn, then one needs to specify how to draw the edges. They have three attributes:

- edge colour index
- edge type
- edgewidth scale factor.

The edges are drawn as lines around the polygons' borders, so have the same sort of attributes as polylines. These attributes are maintained separately for the edges, so they are set with distinct functions. Because of their similarity, these functions are only briefly listed here. The reader is referred to Section 4.1.1 on line attributes for further detail. These functions are:

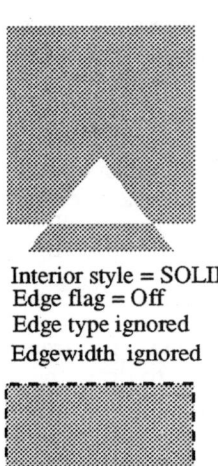

Interior style = SOLID
Edge flag = Off
Edge type ignored
Edgewidth ignored

Interior style = Hatch
Edge flag = On
Edge type = SOLID
Edgewidth = 2.0

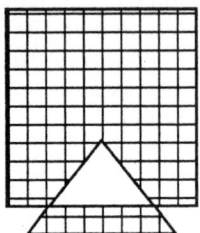

Interior style = SOLID
Edge flag = On
Edge type = DASHED
Edgewidth = 1.0

Interior style = Hatch
Edge flag = On
Edge type = SOLID
Edgewidth = 1.0

Figure 4.7 Effect of fill area set attributes.

SET EDGE COLOUR INDEX   (PHOP,*,STOP,*)El
Arguments:
       in   colour index   integer

SET EDGEWIDTH SCALE FACTOR   (PHOP,*,STOP,*)El
Arguments:
       in   edgewidth scale factor   real

SET EDGETYPE   (PHOP,*,STOP,*)El
Arguments:
       in   edge type   integer

The effect of various fill area set attributes is illustrated in Figure 4.7.

4.5 Text

An important component of any graphics system is the ability to draw text. PHIGS has several routines to do this. The model used to define text and its attributes is essentially the same as that used in GKS. There are additional routines and parameters to support text in a 3D environment. PHIGS provides four different routines to write text to a workstation:

- TEXT writes a 2D text string
- TEXT 3 writes a 3D text string
- ANNOTATION TEXT RELATIVE 2D text annotation
- ANNOTATION TEXT RELATIVE 3 3D text annotation

The routines TEXT and ANNOTATION TEXT RELATIVE are the 2D variants of their corresponding 3D routines. The functions TEXT 3 and ANNOTATION TEXT RELATIVE 3 differ in that the latter is used to annotate a drawing, so it is always drawn in a legible manner. The function TEXT 3 can be rotated so that it cannot be read. For example, a character string will become a vertical line after being rotated so that the text is viewed from one end. Annotation text is drawn relative to a point which is transformed with the current modelling and viewing transformations, but it will be drawn 'flat' on the screen, so that it is always readable.

Figure 4.8 Text in three dimensions.

If one wants to draw a text string that is fully transformed, then the function TEXT 3 should be used:

TEXT 3 (PHOP,*,STOP,*)El
Arguments:

in	text position	3D point in MC
in	text direction vectors	two 3D vectors in MC
in	character string	string

This will cause a character string to be drawn starting at the text position. How the string is positioned relative to this point depends on the TEXT ALIGNMENT, an attribute (see Section 4.5.1). Drawing text in

3D is complicated by having to define a plane to draw the text on. The two direction vectors specify this plane. One vector, specifies the horizontal path of the text and the other a vertical axis. The text position, direction vectors and the string itself are fully transformed. This causes text to be drawn which appears three dimensional (see Figure 4.8), but it has the disadvantage that there will be times when a text string can become unreadable.

The two dimensional version of this primitive is:

TEXT   (PHOP,*,STOP,*)El
Arguments:

in	text position	2D point in MC
in	character string	character string

This is a short cut version for drawing 2D text in the X-Y plane. The position is transformed in the 2D transformation pipeline as well as the text.

When annotating a drawing one does not want to have the text string sheared or transformed. This is achieved in 3D with the routine:

ANNOTATION TEXT RELATIVE 3   (PHOP,*,STOP,*)El
Arguments:

in	reference point	3D point in MC
in	annotation offset	3D vector in NPC
in	character string	character string

This routine draws the text string in a plane which is parallel to the display surface. As a result, the character string appears 'flat' on the screen. so it is always readable. The text is positioned relative to a reference point which is defined in modelling coordinates. In addition one can specify an offset between the reference point and the start of the string. This offset makes it possible to adjust the starting point of the text relative to its reference point, so that the text does not obscure the object it is annotating.

4.5.1 Text attributes

The attributes for both text and annotation text are described here. Since the model used to define text and its attributes is based on GKS, there are many parallels between the text attributes in GKS and PHIGS.

Some attributes are shared by both text and annotation text. Other attributes are set for text and annotation text with distinct functions, but have the same effect on the text's appearance. Finally, annotation text has a style for which there is no corresponding text attribute.

In order to limit the amount of redundancy in describing the attributes, '(Annotation text)' will be added to the function's name if the attribute can be set separately for annotation text. For example, the height of characters used to draw text with is set with the attribute, SET

CHARACTER HEIGHT; the corresponding function for annotation text is SET ANNOTATION TEXT CHARACTER HEIGHT. Both functions will be referred to as SET (ANNOTATION TEXT) CHARACTER HEIGHT. The appearance of text can be modified with the following attributes:

- text font
- text colour index (Annotation text)
- text path (Annotation text)
- text alignment (Annotation text)
- character height (Annotation text)
- character up vector
- character expansion factor
- character spacing
- text precision
- annotation style.

Because it is a complicated primitive text requires a large number of attributes to define its appearance. A complete set of characters, with similar characteristics, is called a font. Several different fonts are shown in Figure 4.9. Fonts are designed according to a set of rules to maintain a consistency in the character's visual features and to position each character in its cell. Figure 4.11 shows an example of the character cell and the reference lines, which are used to position the character. There are three vertical reference lines: left, centreline, and right; and five vertical lines: topline, capline, halfline, baseline, and bottomline.

A text font is selected using:

SET TEXT FONT   (PHOP,*,STOP,*)El
Arguments:
        in   text font   integer

This function creates a structure element, which selects the font to use for both text and annotation text. Fonts are workstation-dependent, so one must be sure that a font is available on the workstation, which is being updated. A list of the available fonts is kept in the WDT for each workstation. This list can be read with the function INQUIRE TEXT FACILITIES. Each workstation should support at least two different fonts, namely font number 1 and 2, which should be visually distinct from one another. Font numbers which are positive have been registered, negative font numbers are purely implementation dependent. Your PHIGS supplier should document the fonts that are available for each workstation type.

The colour of both text and annotation text is set with the function:

SET TEXT COLOUR INDEX   (PHOP,*,STOP,*)El
Arguments:
        in   colour index   integer

Вшсиллив еону

(Serman font

English font

Italic font

Roman font

Figure 4.9 Different text fonts.

One can specify how to position the characters in a string relative to each other with the command:

SET (ANNOTATION) TEXT PATH   (PHOP,*,STOP,*)El
Arguments:
   in text path ·   (LEFT,RIGHT,UP,DOWN)

The text path determines the position of the first character in the string relative to the text starting point and the position of each subsequent character relative to its predecessor. For example, the text path LEFT writes the string from left to right, whereas DOWN positions each character below its predecessor. Text and annotation text have their own paths. Figure 4.10 illustrates the effect of each of the four text paths.

The text string's position relative to its starting point is determined by the function:

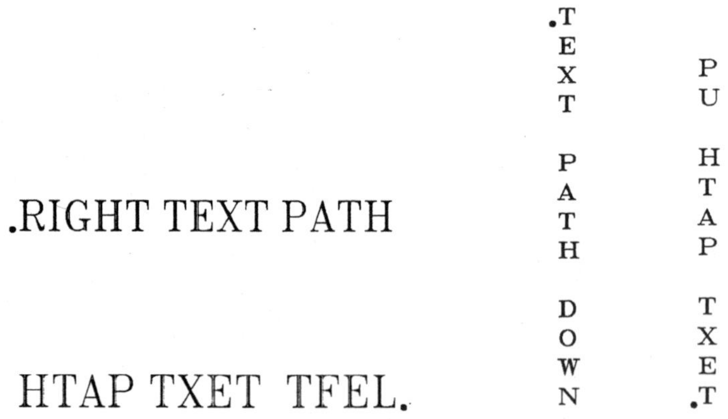

```
                                        .T                  P
                                         E                  U
                                         X
                                         T
                                         P                  H
                                         A                  T
    .RIGHT TEXT PATH                     T                  A
                                         H                  P

                                         D                  T
                                         O                  X
                                         W                  E
    HTAP TXET TFEL.                      N                  .T
```

Figure 4.10 Effect of text path.

SET (ANNOTATION) TEXT ALIGNMENT   (PHOP,*,STOP,*)El
Arguments:

| in horizontal alignment | (NORMAL,LEFT,CENTRE,RIGHT) |
| in vertical alignment | (NORMAL,TOP,CAP,HALF, BASE,BOTTOM) |

A text string is bound by an extent parallelogram. The text alignment determines how to position this parallelogram relative to the text's starting point. The NORMAL alignment depends on the text path

text path	*NORMAL alignment*
RIGHT	(LEFT, BASE)
LEFT	(RIGHT, BASE)
UP	(CENTRE, BASE)
DOWN	(CENTRE, TOP)

The vertical alignment parameters refer to the reference lines of the text font (see Figure 4.11). So, for example, an alignment of (CENTRE,CAP) would cause the text's capline to pass through the text's starting point; and the string would be centred on this point.

The following functions set the sizes of text and annotation text:

SET (ANNOTATION TEXT) CHARACTER HEIGHT   (PHOP,*,STOP,*)El
Arguments:

     in   character height   real

These functions scale the size of characters in the string drawn. The character height is a real number whose default is 0.01.

In order to control the orientation of the characters on the screen, one can use the functions:

SET (ANNOTATION TEXT) CHARACTER UP VECTOR   (PHOP,*,STOP,*)El
Arguments:

     in   character up vector   x and y components in TLC

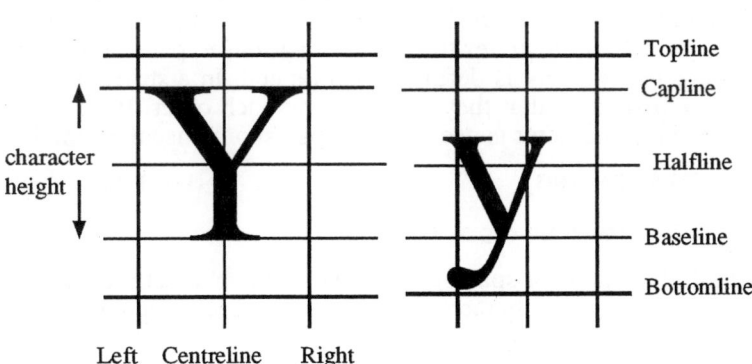

Figure 4.11 Character reference lines.

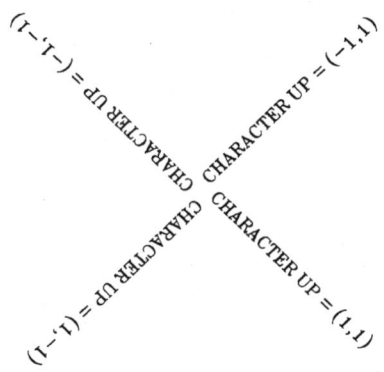

Figure 4.12   Effect of the character up vector on text.

These two functions let one specify the orientation of text and annotation text. The character up vector determines the direction of a vertical line in text local coordinates and is used to rotate each individual character in the string. It is only used to specify an angle, so its magnitude is unimportant. The character up vector is used to rotate the entire string. For example, a character up vector of (1.0, 1.0) will rotate the string -45 degrees (see Figure 4.12).

To make characters wider, one can use the function:

SET CHARACTER EXPANSION FACTOR   (PHOP,*,STOP,*)El
Arguments:
        in   expansion factor   real

Each character in a font has a default width-to-height ratio, which is specified by the font designer. The ratio can be scaled by the character expansion factor. To make characters wider than normal, factors greater than 1.0 should be used; otherwise use factors less than one but greater than zero. Figure 4.13 illustrates the effect of various expansion factors.

Each character in a font is defined within a cell. In a string the character cells are placed so that they are touching each other. If additional space between the character is needed, then one should use the function:

SET CHARACTER SPACING   (PHOP,*,STOP,*)El
Arguments:
        in   character spacing   real

By default the character spacing is 0.0, since the character cells touch each other. By setting the character spacing to 1.0, each character will be separated from the next by an additional distance equal to its own height. If it is negative, then the character cells will overlap (see Figure 4.13).

Character expansion factors:

1.5 Expansion factor

1.0 Expansion factor

0.5 Expansion factor

Character spacing:

0.25 Text spacing

0.0 Text spacing

-0.25 Textspacing

Character height:

0.2 Character height
0.1 Character height
0.05 Character height

Figure 4.13 Affect of character expansion factor height and spacing aspects.

The accuracy with which a workstation draws a text string can be controlled with the function:

SET TEXT PRECISION   (PHOP,*,STOP,*)El
Arguments:
        in   text precision   (STRING,CHAR,STROKE)

Text precision governs how closely the text drawn represents what it should look like; after applying the attributes, transformations, and clipping. The text precision can have one of three values: STRING, CHAR, or STROKE. Not all fonts need to have all precisions, but the two required fonts, 1 and 2, must be supported with all three precisions.
The text precision values are defined as follows:

STRING   This text precision is the least accurate, but should be the quickest to draw. The text should be drawn with the requested font, at the text starting point, and with the correct colour. The character height, width, and expansion factor are approximated as well as possible; but no other text attribute need be considered. It is left to the PHIGS implementor whether to clip a text string which passes through a clipping boundary

CHAR   This precision draws each character separately and the attributes: character height, expansion factor, and up vector are applied as accurately as possible. The character spacing is evaluated exactly and each character is clipped individually.

STROKE   This is the most accurate precision. Its name stems from stroke fonts, where characters are drawn as a series of short vectors. It should not be mistaken to imply that stroke fonts must be used. With this precision all attributes are evaluated exactly; and clipping occurs exactly at the clip boundary, even if that is within a character.

Annotation text is primarily used for labelling, so it has an additional attribute to specify the appearance of the label. This is set with the function:

SET ANNOTATION STYLE   (PHOP,*,STOP,*)El
Arguments:
           in   annotation style   integer

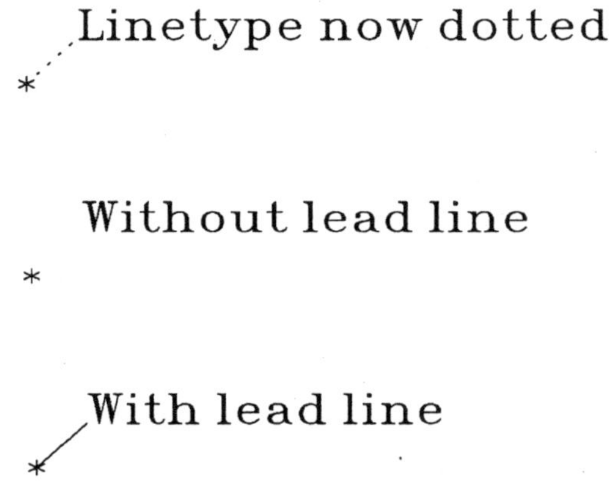

.Linetype now dotted

*

Without lead line

*

With lead line

*

Figure 4.14 Annotation text styles.

PHIGS requires that two styles be supported with the values:

1. Annotation text is not connected to its reference point.

2. A straight line is drawn between the text starting point and the reference point. This line is known as the lead line, which is drawn using the current polyline attributes.

Implementation specific annotation styles are possible, for example using an arrow instead of a lead line. They will be selected with an annotation style less than one. Annotation text drawn with different attributes is shown in Figure 4.14. In this figure the reference points are marked with an asterisk and the annotation offset is (0.05, 0.05. 0.0).

4.5.2 Text extent

The actual size of the text drawn depends on the text string and the attributes. The minimum rectangle which completely encloses the text string is known as the text extent rectangle. An application needs to know the size of this rectangle in order to position text so that it does not obscure other parts of the picture.

PHIGS provides an inquiry function which will return the size of this rectangle:

INQUIRE TEXT EXTENT   (PHOP,*,*,*)
Arguments:

	in	workstation type	workstation type
	in	text font	integer
	in	expansion factor	real
	in	character spacing	real
	in	character height	real
	in	text path	(LEFT,RIGHT,UP,DOWN)
	in	horizontal alignment	(NORMAL,LEFT,CENTRE,RIGHT)
	in	vertical alignment	(NORMAL,TOP,CAP,HALF, BASE,BOTTOM)
	in	character string	string
	out	error indicator	integer
	out	text extent	(xmin,xmax, ymin,ymax) in TLC
	out	concatenation offset	2 vectors in TLC

This function returns the text extent rectangle surrounding a string in text local coordinates TLC. Here the text starting position is the origin of the TLC. In order to calculate this rectangle, one needs to know the workstation type, since several attributes are workstation dependent. Then one needs to specify the text attributes which determine the text size and spacing and the string itself. If a non zero error indicator is returned, the information is not available (for example, the text font might not be available on the specified workstation type).

The text extent rectangle is returned in text local coordinates. In order to find the text extent in modelling coordinates, one still needs to offset the rectangle by the text starting point and to rotate it by an angle derived from the character up vector.

A concatenation offset is also returned. This is a pair of vectors in TLC that can be used to append a second string to the string. This offset is relative to the text starting point, but it might need to be rotated due to a character up vector which is not vertical. The offset takes the character spacing after the last character into account so that another string can be drawn immediately after the original string.

4.6 Cell array

PHIGS was designed to be a graphics system, not an imaging system with which one can display images as pixel arrays. Although the cell array primitives are not specifically designed for image display, they come close. The major difference is that cell arrays are geometric objects, which live in modelling coordinates and can be fully transformed. It consists of a parallelogram which is filled with a grid of colour cells. Because cell arrays are geometric entities, they will not be displayed with the same performance as images would be with a library such as the MIT X11 library. In spite of this, the cell array has a number of interesting features, such as being able to rotate, scale and translate it.

DX rows
DY columns

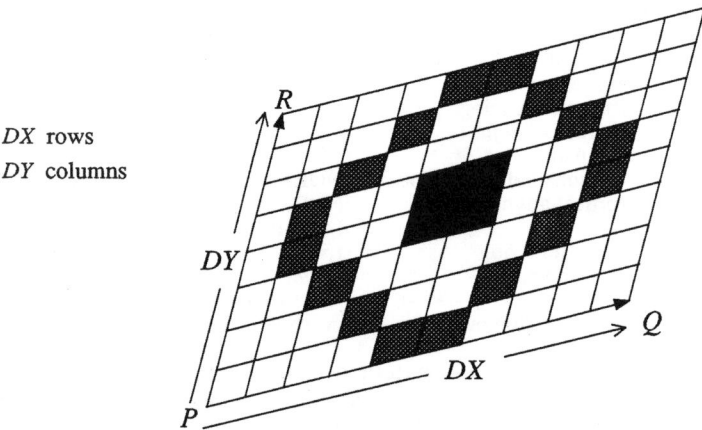

Figure 4.15 Cell array primitive.

The three dimensional version of cell array requires the following arguments:

CELL ARRAY 3   (PHOP,*,STOP,*)El
Arguments:

in	cell parallelogram	three 3D points in MC
in	rows	integer
in	columns	integer
in	array of colour indices	array of integers

The parallelogram is defined by three points in modelling coordinates, (P,Q,R). Two sides of the parallelogram are defined by the lines PQ and PR, (see Figure 4.15). The rows are evenly spaced along the edge PQ and the columns evenly spaced along the edge PR. The array of colour indices contains rows x columns elements. Each index points to an entry in the colour table (see Section 5.2 on colour).

Each colour index defines a cell which is filled with a solid colour. In the simplest case the cells are squares, but they can be transformed to look like quadrilaterals. On a raster display the criteria used to determine what colour to set a pixel to is known as point sampling. This will set the pixel to the colour index of the cell containing the pixel's centre.

In two dimensions the primitive is:

CELL ARRAY   (PHOP,*,STOP,*)El
Arguments:

in	cell rectangle	two 2D points in MC
in	rows	integer
in	columns	integer
in	array of colour indices	array of integers

The 2D cell array primitive is a rectangle, defined by two points *(P,Q)* which are at diagonally opposite points. Otherwise the primitive is similar to its 3D counterpart.

4.7 Generalized drawing primitive

There are a number of additional output primitives which are not defined by PHIGS, such as spheres, ellipsoids, circles, arcs, etc. Sometimes these are primitives for which there is special hardware support in the workstation. Since PHIGS can not incorporate all possible forms of output, there is a generalized drawing primitive, (GDP) with which additional implementation specific primitives can be defined. The GDP has two properties in common with all other drawing primitives: (1) it has coordinate data which are transformed through modelling and viewing transformations and (2) the GDP will be clipped by the clipping volume.

A three dimensional GDP is created with:

GENERALIZED DRAWING PRIMITIVE 3   (PHOP,*,STOP,*)El
Arguments:

in	point list	list of 3D points in MC
in	GDP 3 identifier	integer
in	GDP 3 data record	data record

The GDP is a drawing primitive, whose coordinate data is kept in the point list; for example, a sphere might be defined by its centre and a point on its surface. The identifier will specify which GDP 3 to use. It may have additional data; for example, if the GDP were a sphere, a tessellation parameter could be passed in the data record which would specify how exactly the sphere should be rendered.

The reader should consult the documentation of their PHIGS supplier to see what GDP's, if any, are defined. A program can also determine what GDP's are available on a given workstation with the command INQUIRE LIST OF AVAILABLE DRAWING PRIMITIVES 3.

PHIGS does not assume that a GDP has any specific set of attributes.

The implementation is free to choose what attributes best suit a particular GDP. For example, a primitive which defines a surface will probably have the same attributes as fill area. PHIGS does require that an implementation maintain a list of the attribute types which affect a given GDP in the WDT. These attributes could be one or more of: POLYLINE, POLYMARKER, TEXT, INTERIOR, EDGE. One can find out what attributes are used by a given GDP with the function INQUIRE GENERALIZED DRAWING PRIMITIVE 3.

Care must be taken when using GDP's. A GDP used on one workstation might not be available on another. One PHIGS implementation might not have the same GDP's as another.

CHAPTER 5

PHIGS Attributes

The previous chapter dealt with attributes in an overly simplistic manner. Its goal was to introduce the attributes belonging to each primitive to illustrate the various styles of output. This chapter will focus on how to use attributes, colour, and interior patterns.

5.1 Attributes in PHIGS

Attributes control how to draw an output primitive. The term *aspect* is also used to refer to the properties that affect how an output primitive is drawn. There are two different types of aspects: global and workstation dependent. Global aspects are also called geometric aspects, such as character height. Workstation dependent aspects are non-geometric, such as the interior colour index. For example, the polyline has the three non-geometric aspects: linetype, linewidth scale factor, and polyline colour index.

Non-geometric aspects have one additional level of complexity, which has not been mentioned yet. There are two ways to define these aspects, individually as was discussed in the previous chapter, or bundled in tables which are kept in the workstation.

5.1.1 Attribute binding

The key to understanding how to use attributes, is to notice that they are bound to the primitive at traversal time. For example, when a polyline structure element is created, its colour, width, and linetype are undefined. The attributes that are used to draw the polyline depend on where the polyline lies in the structure network. The attributes will be 'bound' to the primitive once the polyline element is executed at traversal time.

When attribute elements are encountered, they will update entries in the PHIGS traversal state list TSL. This state list will be copied onto a stack when traversing from one hierarchy level to the next through the EXECUTE STRUCTURE element. Once the called structure is completed, this traversal state list will be restored from the stack. This is the mechanism with which attributes are inherited by child structures. If the child structure modifies the traversal state list through setting attributes, it will not affect its parent's, whose TSL is sitting on a stack waiting for the child to finish.

The attributes are read from the TSL when an output primitive is encountered during structure traversal. These attributes define the style, or aspects, used when drawing the primitive. It is important to note that certain attributes set an index, e.g., SET POLYLINE COLOUR INDEX, which points to an entry in a bundle table in the workstation. The attribute selection mechanism determines which aspect is used. Figure 5.1 illustrates attribute binding for the output primitive polyline.

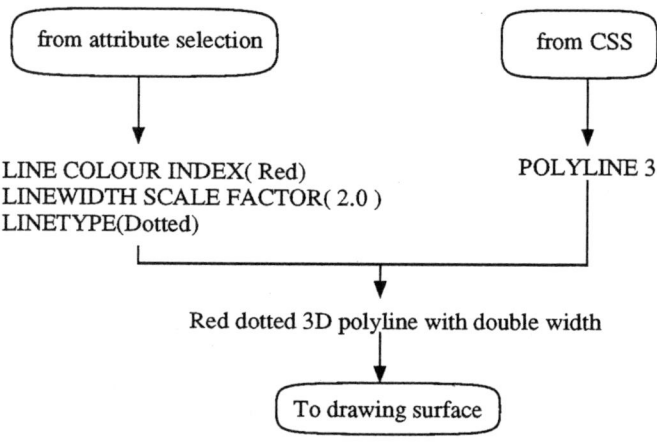

Figure 5.1 Attribute binding at traversal time.

5.1.2 Bundled attributes

The model for defining and selecting attributes in PHIGS is comparable to that in GKS. Individual attributes can be directly set, e.g. SET INTERIOR STYLE. An alternative method to select an attribute, is to define a table entry containing the desired attributes, and to select the attributes from the table by setting an index pointing to that entry. There is a bundle table containing the workstation dependent aspects for each type of output primitive. For example, the bundle table for polylines consists of entries containing the linetype, the linewidth scale factor, and the polyline colour index.

Bundle tables are kept in the WSL. Each workstation has predefined bundle tables, whose contents can be inquired with the function INQUIRE PREDEFINED XXXXXX REPRESENTATION, where XXXXXX is one of the following primitive types:

- POLYLINE
- POLYMARKER
- INTERIOR
- EDGE
- . TEXT.

In order to load the bundle tables with attributes other than the defaults, one should use the functions:

SET XXXXXX REPRESENTATION(WSID, INDEX, DATA, ...)

where:

XXXXXX = POLYLINE, POLYMARKER, TEXT, INTERIOR, or EDGE

Since these tables are kept in the WSL, the first argument is always the workstation identifier. The second argument is the table index, and the remaining arguments are the attributes that are to be loaded. These five routines are all similar, differing only in the type and number of attributes that are loaded. In summary, these routines are:

SET POLYLINE REPRESENTATION   (PHOP,WSOP,*,*)
Arguments:

in workstation identifier	integer
in polyline index	integer
in linetype	integer
in linewidth scale factor	real
in polyline colour index	integer

SET POLYMARKER REPRESENTATION   (PHOP,WSOP,*,*)
Arguments:

in workstation identifier	integer
in polymarker index	integer
in marker type	integer
in marker size scale factor	real
in polymarker colour index	integer

SET TEXT REPRESENTATION   (PHOP,WSOP,*,*)
Arguments:

81

```
            in workstation identifier        integer
            in text index                    integer
            in text font                     integer
            in text precision                (STRING,CHAR,STROKE)
            in character expansion factor    real
            in character spacing             real
            in text colour index             integer
```

SET INTERIOR REPRESENTATION   (PHOP,WSOP,*,*)
Arguments:
```
            in workstation identifier        integer
            in interior index                integer
            in interior style                (HOLLOW,SOLID,PATTERN,
                                             HATCH,EMPTY)
            in interior style index          integer
            in interior colour index         integer
```

SET EDGE REPRESENTATION   (PHOP,WSOP,*,*)
Arguments:
```
            in workstation identifier        integer
            in edge index                    integer
            in edge flag                     (ON,OFF)
            in edgetype                      integer
            in edgewidth scale factor        real
            in edge colour index             integer
```

Workstation state list

Polyline bundle table

Index	Line type	Linewidth scale factor	Line colour index
1	Solid	1.0	Red Index
2	Solid	2.0	Blue Index
3	Dashed	1.5	Green Index
4	Dotted	1.0	Black Index

Polymarker bundle table
Text bundle table   • • •
Interior bundle table

Edge bundle table

Index	Edge flag	Edge type	Edgewidth scale factor	Edge colour index
1	ON	Solid	1.0	Black Index
2	ON	Dotted	1.0	Yellow Index
3	OFF	Dashed	2.0	Purple Index

Figure 5.2 PHIGS bundle tables.

The attributes these tables are being loaded with, have been discussed in Chapter 4. The reader is referred to these sections for details on how the attributes affect the style of output.

Using bundle tables allows one to select a group of non-geometric aspects by setting one index. It also simplifies changing these aspects globally, since changing a table entry will affect all primitives using it throughout the CSS. Figure 5.2 illustrates bundle tables in the WSL.

5.1.3 The Aspect Source Flag

So far, we have only dealt with how to load the bundle tables. There are two stages to using bundled attributes. First of all, one must let PHIGS know that one wants to use bundled attributes instead of individual ones. Then one must select a specific table entry by setting an index.

The source for the aspects can be either a bundle table or a routine setting an individual attribute. If one wants to use bundled attributes, PHIGS needs to be informed of this for each attribute. This is done with

Table 5.1 Aspect Identifiers

Primitive	Aspect identifier
POLYLINE	LINETYPE ASF LINEWIDTH SCALE FACTOR ASF POLYLINE COLOUR INDEX ASF
POLYMARKER	MARKER TYPE ASF MARKER SIZE FACTOR ASF POLYMARKER COLOUR INDEX ASF
TEXT	TEXT FONT ASF TEXT PRECISION ASF CHARACTER EXPANSION FACTOR ASF CHARACTER SPACING ASF TEXT COLOUR INDEX ASF
ANNOTATION TEXT RELATIVE	TEXT FONT ASF TEXT PRECISION ASF CHARACTER EXPANSION FACTOR ASF CHARACTER SPACING ASF TEXT COLOUR INDEX ASF
FILL AREA	INTERIOR STYLE ASF INTERIOR STYLE INDEX ASF INTERIOR COLOUR INDEX ASF
FILL AREA SET	INTERIOR STYLE ASF INTERIOR STYLE INDEX ASF INTERIOR COLOUR INDEX ASF EDGE FLAG ASF EDGETYPE ASF EDGEWIDTH SCALE FACTOR ASF EDGE COLOUR INDEX ASF

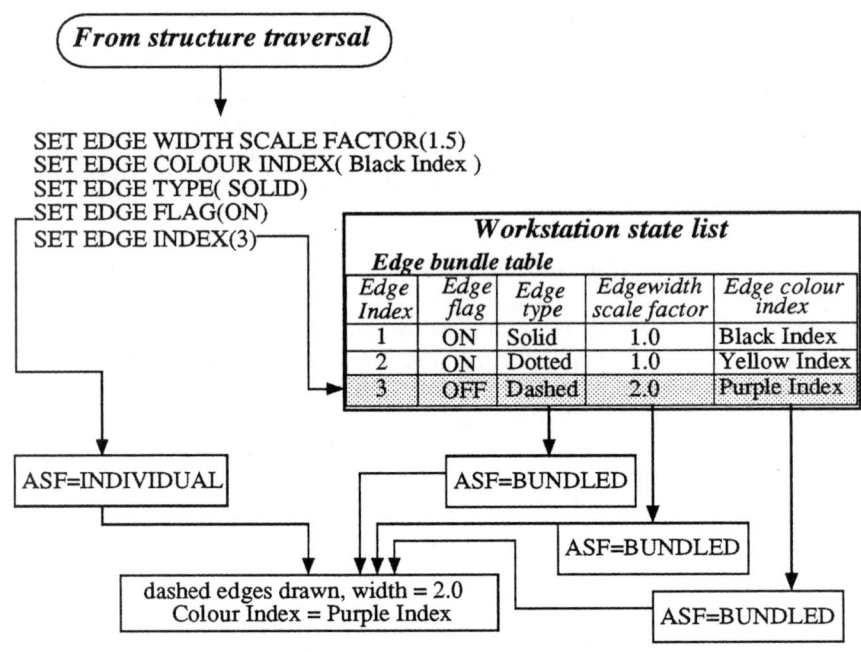

Figure 5.3 Diagram on using ASF's for attribute selection.

the aspect source flag *ASF,* which can have one of two values: INDI-VIDUAL or BUNDLED. The aspect source flag is set with a structure element, so that only at traversal time is it clear where the attributes are coming from. The default ASF is INDIVIDUAL. To change the ASF for each aspect one should use the function:

```
SET INDIVIDUAL ASF                                    (PHOP,*,STOP,*)El
Arguments:
            in aspect identifier            see Table 5.1
            in aspect source                (BUNDLED,INDIVIDUAL)
```

This routine determines source for each aspect. Table 5.1 lists the aspect identifiers and their corresponding output primitive.

Once the ASF has been set to use bundled attributes, then the actual table entry is selected by setting an index. There are five routines to set bundle table indices, one for each table:

```
SET POLYLINE INDEX(LineIndex)             (PHOP,*,STOP,*)El
SET POLYMARKER INDEX(MarkerIndex)         (PHOP,*,STOP,*)El
SET TEXT INDEX(TextIndex)                 (PHOP,*,STOP,*)El
SET INTERIOR INDEX(InteriorIndex)         (PHOP,*,STOP,*)El
SET EDGE INDEX(EdgeIndex)                 (PHOP,*,STOP,*)El
```

For these routines to affect the style of output, the ASF must be set to bundled for at least one aspect in the table. The index points to a table entry containing a number of attributes. Only those aspects whose ASF is set to BUNDLED will be taken from the table. Figure 5.3 illustrates using ASF's for edges. In this example the ASF is set to bundled for: EDGETYPE, EDGEWIDTH SCALE FACTOR and EDGE COLOUR INDEX. The ASF for the EDGE FLAG remains INDIVIDUAL. As a result the edge index selects all edge aspects except for the edge flag. This causes edges to be drawn with the edge type, edgewidth scale factor and colour index as specified in the bundle table.

Bundled attributes provide a level of indirection when specifying aspects, allowing one to define all workstation dependent aspects in one location in the program. This makes it possible to organize the use of attributes to enhance the program's portability. It is easier to change the bundle table initialization routines than to change every attribute setting in a structure definition. The use of aspects might have to change from one workstation to another, such as a program that has to run on both a colour and a monochrome workstation. In this situation it is not enough to use colour to distinguish between two different types of objects; one needs to use the other aspects. The structures do not need to be changed, since they are using the bundle tables. Only the table entries need to be loaded with aspects that best suit the workstation.

An example is an architectural drawing of a floor plan containing the following basic components: structural bodies (walls, etc.), electrical wiring, hot water, cold water, gas. In this example there are five basic types of objects to draw. We will limit the discussion to using only polylines. The polyline bundle table contains the aspects used to draw the floor plan. Table 5.2 shows the contents of this bundle table. These entries are loaded by calling SET POLYLINE REPRESENTATION. When drawing the floor plan, a call to SET POLYLINE INDEX will select all aspects needed for a given object. Figure 5.4 shows how the structure network could appear to draw this floor plan.

Table 5.2 Example polyline bundle table entries.

Workstation state list

Polyline bundle table

Object	Index	Line type	Linewidth scale factor	Line colour index
Wall	1	Solid	2.0	Black Index
Wiring	2	Solid	1.0	Yellow Index
Hot Water	3	Dashed	1.0	Red Index
Cold Water	4	Dashed	1.0	Blue Index
Gas	5	Dotted	1.0	Green Index

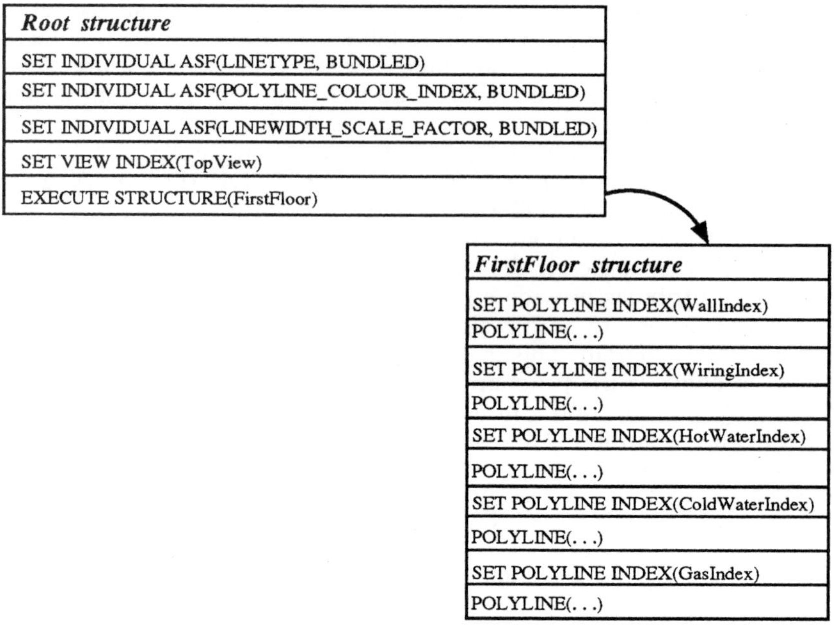

Root structure
SET INDIVIDUAL ASF(LINETYPE, BUNDLED)
SET INDIVIDUAL ASF(POLYLINE_COLOUR_INDEX, BUNDLED)
SET INDIVIDUAL ASF(LINEWIDTH_SCALE_FACTOR, BUNDLED)
SET VIEW INDEX(TopView)
EXECUTE STRUCTURE(FirstFloor)

FirstFloor structure
SET POLYLINE INDEX(WallIndex)
POLYLINE(. . .)
SET POLYLINE INDEX(WiringIndex)
POLYLINE(. . .)
SET POLYLINE INDEX(HotWaterIndex)
POLYLINE(. . .)
SET POLYLINE INDEX(ColdWaterIndex)
POLYLINE(. . .)
SET POLYLINE INDEX(GasIndex)
POLYLINE(. . .)

Figure 5.4 Structure network using bundled aspects.

A point that is sometimes overlooked is that the bundle tables, like all workstation tables, will not be saved if the structures are archived. If a structure that uses bundled aspects is read from an archive file, then the application needs to load the bundle tables with aspects which best suit the workstation's capabilities.

5.2 Colour in PHIGS

Now it is time to look at how PHIGS uses colour. So far we have taken for granted that colour is available and is selected by setting an index, such as SET POLYLINE COLOUR INDEX. Colour is a workstation-specific resource. Some workstations might be monochrome, or support only a limited number of colours. A PHIGS program can determine what colour resources a workstation has by calling the routine INQUIRE COLOUR FACILITIES.

PHIGS PLUS extends the colour capabilities by allowing one to set the colour directly. Direct colour allows one to avoid having to use indices to specify a colour. This will be covered in greater detail in Chapter 12.

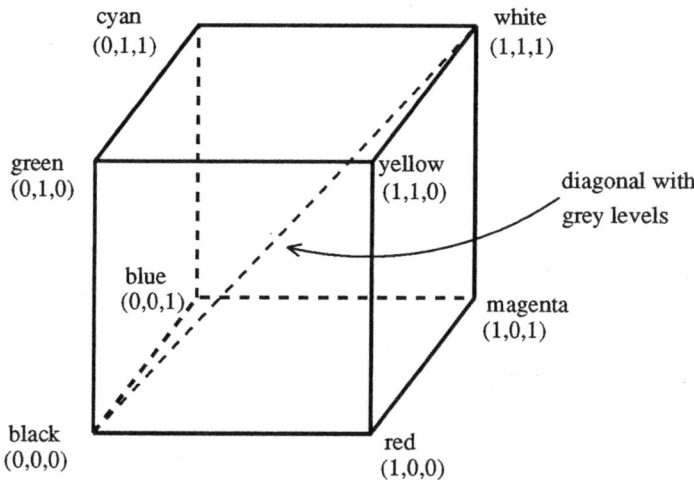

Figure 5.5 The RGB cube.

5.2.1 Colour models

The colour index, which is used to select a primitive's colour attributes is simply a pointer into a table of colours maintained by the workstation. The actual colour is stored in this table as a set of colour coordinates. Before the colour tables can be introduced, we need to understand colour models.

Colours are based on a model, which establishes how they should be defined. PHIGS uses four models: RGB, CIE LUV, HLS, and HSV. An implementation is only required to support the models RGB and CIE LUV. These models define a colour space, in which a colour is a point in this space with three coordinates as a rule. Models with a different number of coordinates do exist and are allowable as an implementation specific colour model. For example, CYMK (cyan, yellow, magenta, black) has four components and is used in the printing industry. Although physical devices can only display an integral number of colours, PHIGS achieves device independence through expressing colour coordinates as floating point triplets. For example, a colour in the RGB model is defined by three coordinates: its red, green, and blue component. In this model the colour yellow has the coordinates: red = 1.0, green = 1.0, and blue = 0.

One can choose the colour model with the command:

SET COLOUR MODEL   (PHOP,WSOP,*,*)

Arguments:

in workstation identifier   integer
in colour model   integer

This sets the colour model used to interpret colour-tuples on the specified workstation. PHIGS allows for four different models:

1. RGB   : Red, Green, Blue
2. CIE LUV   : Commission Internationale de l'Eclairage
3. HSV   : Hue, Saturation, Value
4. HLS   : Hue, Lightness, Saturation

An implementation specific colour model would be selected by a negative integer. The default colour model is generally RGB, but to be sure that colours are correctly interpreted this command should be used. The reader should consult the following texts [Foley et al.; Rogers] for more detail, since an in depth discussion of the various colour models is beyond the scope of this book. Nevertheless, it is necessary to give a brief introduction to the various colour models.

Of the four colour models, the RGB is the simplest. Here the red, green, and blue component of the colour are specified. This is an additive model, so white is defined by red = 1, green = 1, and blue = 1. In this model the colour space can be visualized as a unit cube with red at (1, 0, 0), green at (0, 1, 0), and blue at (0, 0, 1). Black and white are at

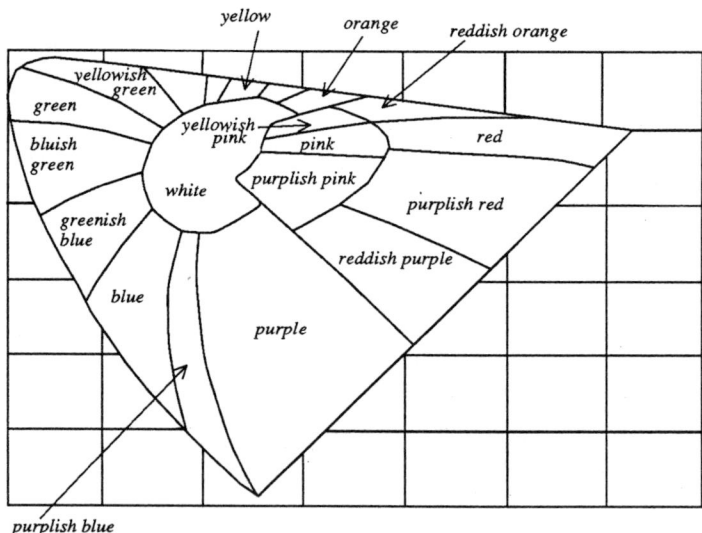

Figure 5.6 The CIE u' v' uniform chromaticity diagram.

opposite corners, connected by a diagonal where the gray levels are represented. Figure 5.5 illustrates the RGB cube.

The CIE LUV model gets its name from the Commission Internationale de l'Eclairage, which established a means to classify colours in 1931. This model is needed because it is a standard way to define colours in a device independent way. In order to implement the CIE model, one needs to measure physical properties of the output device. These parameters will differ even among different types of monitors. This provides the PHIGS programmer with a method to generate colours on different devices that match. The original CIE model is not uniform. That means a fixed distance separating a given pair of colours in CIE space, does not appear to be the same for all pairs of colours. This was modified in 1976 with the CIE LUV model. In spite of the advantage that it is device independent, this model has the drawback that it is not particularly intuitive to use. Colours in this model have the coordinates (L,U,V), where L is the luminance component, ranging from black for L=0, to the maximum brightness for L = 1. The components U and V are chromaticity components, which define colours such as red, yellow, or purple. Figure 5.6 shows a slice of the CIE space for a fixed value of L. Standard texts on computer graphics such as [Foley et al.; Rogers] provide more information on the CIE colour model.

The HSV (Hue, Saturation, Value) model is more intuitive than the CIE. This colour space can be represented by a colour cone (see Figure 5.7). The value coordinate corresponds to the central axis of the cone.

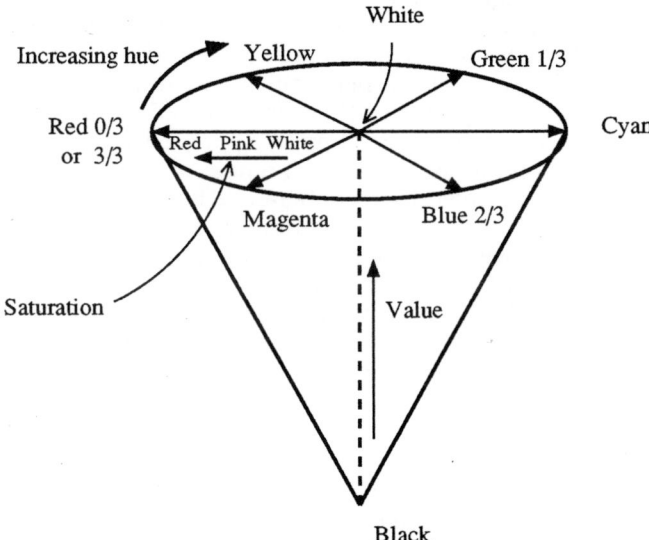

Figure 5.7 The HSV colour cone.

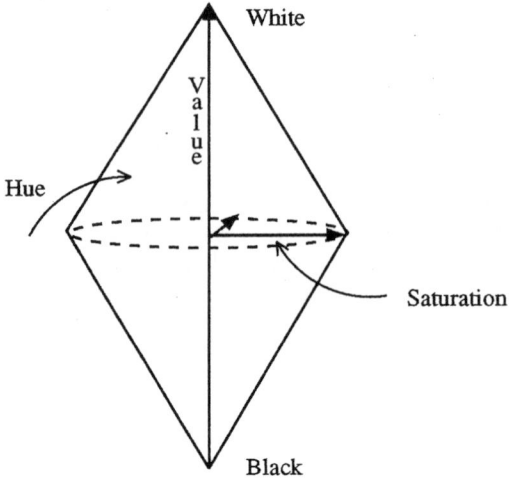

Figure 5.8 The HLS double cone.

This determines the brightness of the colour. Shades of grey are found on the axis with black given by V = 0 and white at the centre of the base of the cone with V = 1. Hue and saturation are most easily understood by looking at the cone's base, so V = 1. The hue represents an angle around the axis of the cone ranging from red at H = 0, through yellow to green at H = 1/3 through cyan to blue at H = 2/3 through magenta back to red. Complementary colours are found at opposite ends of a diameter on the base of the HSV cone. The saturation is the given by the distance from the axis of the cone, and it determines how much the pure hue is mixed with white. For any given colour, such as red, white corresponds to S = 0 and varies through shades of pink to pure red at S = 1.

The HLS (Hue, Lightness, Saturation) model is closely related to the HSV model. It is represented by a double-ended cone. In this model the hue and saturation have the same meaning as in the HSV model, but here the value is replaced by lightness. In this case white occurs at the vertex of the upper cone and black at the vertex of the lower cone. It can be thought of as the HSV cone with white pulled upward to form a double cone. The pure hues are found on the perimeter where the two cones meet, so L = 0.5, and S = 1. Figure 5.8 shows the HLS double cone.

5.2.2 Colour tables

Once the colour model has been established, the colour coordinates have a specific meaning. Unless stated otherwise, the RGB colour model will be assumed. The following command defines a colour which can be selected with an index.

SET COLOUR REPRESENTATION   (PHOP,WSOP,*,*)
Arguments:

in	workstation identifier	integer
in	index	integer
in	colour	colour tuple

This command enters the colour specified by the colour-tuple in the workstation colour table at the location *index*. The index zero has a special meaning. This entry is used to specify the background colour. An output workstation's colour table must have at least two entries: foreground and background colours. In order to find out how many colours can be loaded in the workstation, one should use the function INQUIRE WORKSTATION STATE TABLE LENGTHS.

In order to use a colour representation for a given primitive, one needs to define the structure element SET XXXXXX COLOUR INDEX, where XXXXXX can be one of EDGE, INTERIOR, POLYLINE, POLYMARKER, or TEXT. These functions were defined in Chapter 4.

5.3 Interior patterns

In Chapter 4 attributes used by area filling primitives were introduced. The interior style determines how to fill the polygon. This primitive is called with a parameter which can be one of: HOLLOW, SOLID, PATTERN, HATCH, or EMPTY. A discussion of patterned styles has been deferred to this section. Patterns can be defined by the application and loaded into a workstation table for use at traversal time. Any given pattern in the table can be chosen with SET INTERIOR STYLE INDEX, whose index selects a pattern in this table.

Patterned interior styles are not necessarily found in all PHIGS implementations. Although its use has been standardized, an implementation is not required to support patterns. In order to determine whether an output workstation is capable of patterns, one can use the function INQUIRE WORKSTATION STATE TABLE LENGTHS. This returns the maximum number of pattern indices allowed, which could be zero.

The pattern is a two dimensional array of colour indices which is replicated over the entire interior of the polygon. This pattern is kept in the workstation state list and is defined by the function:

SET PATTERN REPRESENTATION   (PHOP,WSOP,*,*)
Arguments:

in	workstation identifier	integer
in	pattern index	integer
in	pattern colour index array	array of integers

This routine loads the specified workstation with the pattern array. The loaded pattern can be selected by setting the interior style index to be the pattern index. The colour index array consists of the x dimension DX, the y dimension DY, and DX × DY colour indices which point into the colour table.

It is not enough to define the pattern alone. One also needs to specify how to use it. The pattern is a two dimensional array which is to be mapped onto a surface in three dimensions. One needs to define how to map the pattern onto the surface. There are three structure elements to determine this mapping:

> SET PATTERN REFERENCE POINT
> SET PATTERN REFERENCE POINT AND VECTORS
> SET PATTERN SIZE

Although the pattern is replicated over the interior of the polygon, one still needs to identify where to start mapping the pattern onto the polygon. This is done with the function:

SET PATTERN REFERENCE POINT AND VECTORS   (PHOP,*,STOP,*)
Arguments:

in	pattern reference point	3D point in MC
in	pattern reference vectors	Two 3D vectors in MC

The pattern reference point and vectors are projected onto the fill area along its normal vector (see Figure 5.9). The projection of the reference point defines the origin of the pattern on the fill area. The reference vectors consist of the pattern width and height vectors, whose projection defines a parallelogram on the surface onto which the pattern is mapped. Using the notation that the pattern consists of the colour indices $p(1,1)$, $p(1,2), \dots , p(DX,DY)$, the upper left corner contains the index $p(1,1)$, and the lower right the index $p(DX,DY)$; so the colour index p(1,dy) is at the origin of the pattern. The reference vectors do not necessarily have to be orthogonal, but generally they will be.

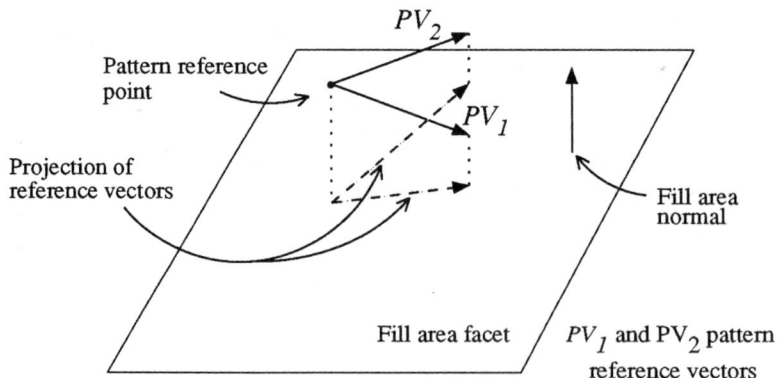

Figure 5.9 Projection of the pattern reference vectors.

92

If PHIGS is being used for 2D graphics, there is a simpler notation for defining rectangular patterns:

SET PATTERN REFERENCE POINT   (PHOP,*,STOP,*)
Arguments:
       in   pattern reference point   2D point in MC

In addition to defining the pattern box, one can scale its size. This is done with the function:

SET PATTERN SIZE   (PHOP,*,STOP,*)
Arguments:
         in   pattern width   real
         in   pattern height   real

The pattern width scales the size of the width vector, and the pattern height the size of the height vector. The pattern array is actually mapped onto this scaled parallelogram. Figure 5.10 illustrates this pattern box.

The pattern parallelogram is divided into DX x DY colour cells. If the centre of a pixel lies within a given colour cell, it is drawn with that colour index. This method of pattern mapping is known as point sampling. More sophisticated techniques, such as texture mapping are not addressed by PHIGS or PHIGS PLUS.

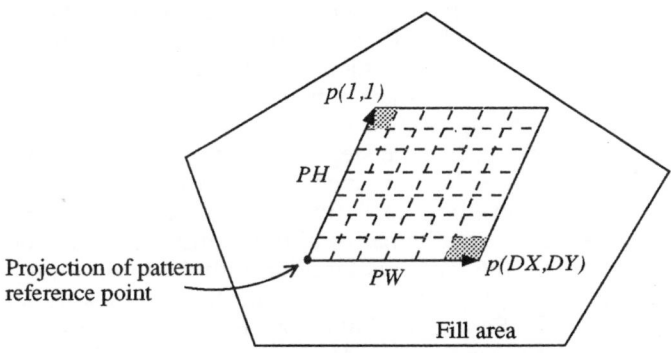

Figure 5.10 Pattern box in a fill area.

CHAPTER 6

Modelling Transformations in PHIGS

A user of a 3D graphics application generally wants to be able to view a scene from various vantage points and to move objects relative to each other. This can be achieved in PHIGS by using viewing and modelling transformations. Modelling transformations are defined with structure elements, whereas viewing transformations are defined in the workstation tables. Viewing transformations will be covered in detail in the next chapter.

Modelling transformations are used to position, orient, and scale objects relative to each other. The PHIGS programmer can define each object in a scene in its own coordinate system and then use modelling transformations to place the object where it belongs. Motion within a scene can be created by updating each body's modelling transform and redrawing the scene for each time step. This technique is useful in robot simulation or dynamic displays of kinematic processes.

Before we can discuss how to define transformations in PHIGS, we should look briefly at the mathematics of transformations and coordinate systems to ensure that the reader is familiar with the terminology. There are numerous texts on graphics that deal with these topics in depth, for example [Foley et al.; Penna and Patterson; Rogers and Adams]. If this material is familiar, the reader may move on to Section 6.2.

6.1 The mathematics of coordinate systems and transformations

The output primitives used to define objects in PHIGS all require coordinate data at the vertices to specify its shape. These coordinates are either an (x,y) pair in 2D, or an (x,y,z) triplet in 3D. Here we will focus on three-dimensional coordinates and transformations. A point in 3D will be represented by a column vector:

$$P = \begin{pmatrix} x \\ y \\ z \end{pmatrix}$$

This point is defined relative to a right-handed, Cartesian coordinate system. This coordinate system is mapped onto the screen with the origin in the lower left corner and the positive z-axis pointing out of the screen (see Figure 6.1). Now we want to rotate, scale, translate and project the primitive onto a display surface. Transformations are the means to do this, and are represented mathematically by matrices. A 3D transformation matrix does almost everything: it can rotate and scale an object, but it cannot translate or project the object onto a display surface. A particularly elegant means to get all the desired mappings into one matrix is to use homogeneous coordinates and transformations.

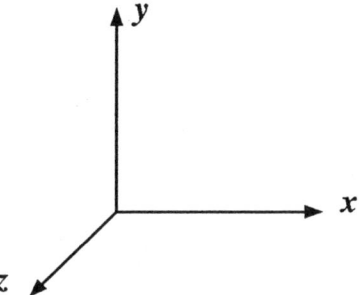

Figure 6.1 The right-handed coordinate system.

6.1.1 Homogeneous coordinates

A point in an n-dimensional Cartesian coordinate system is represented by a point in an $(n+1)$-dimensional space using homogeneous coordinates. Homogeneous coordinates are the basis for projective geometry, which is needed to draw in 3D using perspective. An added benefit of using homogeneous coordinates is that one can also represent all 3D transformations including translations in the matrix.

With the exception of rational B-splines, defined in PHIGS PLUS, the PHIGS programmer does not need to use homogeneous coordinates directly. Points are automatically converted into their homogeneous representation, transformed and then drawn. We will denote homogeneous

95

points by adding the an 'h' as a superscript. A 3D point is converted to its homogeneous coordinate by adding a fourth component:

$$P = \begin{pmatrix} x \\ y \\ z \end{pmatrix} \qquad\qquad P^h = \begin{pmatrix} x \\ y \\ z \\ 1 \end{pmatrix}$$

Homogeneous coordinates have an unusual property. Basically, two homogeneous points are considered equivalent if they lie on the same line passing through the origin (see Figure 6.2). Another way to say the same thing is the points P^h and Q^h are equivalent if for:

$$P^h = \begin{pmatrix} p_x \\ p_y \\ p_z \\ p_w \end{pmatrix} \qquad\qquad Q^h = \begin{pmatrix} q_x \\ q_y \\ q_z \\ q_w \end{pmatrix}$$

there is a non-zero constant k such that:

$$p_x = k\, q_x$$
$$p_y = k\, q_y$$
$$p_z = k\, q_z$$
$$p_w = k\, q_w$$

Our 3D coordinates were initially mapped onto the plane $w=1$. So to get a 3D point back from its homogeneous representation, we simply need to divide by the last term:

$$P^h = \begin{pmatrix} x \\ y \\ z \\ w \end{pmatrix} \curvearrowright \begin{pmatrix} x/w \\ y/w \\ z/w \\ 1 \end{pmatrix} \Rightarrow P = \begin{pmatrix} x/w \\ y/w \\ z/w \end{pmatrix}$$

We obviously have problems if $w=0$. If the points are transformed correctly, this will be avoided. Of the geometric transformations used in 3D graphics, only perspective transformations alter the fourth component. This point will be revisited later on in this section.

Now that we are transforming homogeneous coordinates, we need to represent the transformations as 4x4 matrices. A homogeneous point P is transformed with a matrix M as follows:

$$P^{h'} = M P^h$$

$$
\begin{pmatrix} x' \\ y' \\ z' \\ w' \end{pmatrix} =
\begin{pmatrix}
m_{xx} & m_{xy} & m_{xz} & m_{xw} \\
m_{yx} & m_{yy} & m_{yz} & m_{yw} \\
m_{zx} & m_{zy} & m_{zz} & m_{zw} \\
m_{wx} & m_{wy} & m_{wz} & m_{ww}
\end{pmatrix}
\begin{pmatrix} x \\ y \\ z \\ w \end{pmatrix}
$$

$$
\begin{aligned}
x' &= m_{xx} x + m_{xy} y + m_{xz} z + m_{xw} w \\
y' &= m_{yx} x + m_{yy} y + m_{yz} z + m_{yw} w \\
z' &= m_{zx} x + m_{zy} y + m_{zz} z + m_{zw} w \\
w' &= m_{wx} x + m_{wy} y + m_{wz} z + m_{ww} w
\end{aligned}
$$

All the viewing and modelling transformations used in PHIGS can be represented in this matrix form. To understand the structure of this matrix, four basic types of transformations are considered.

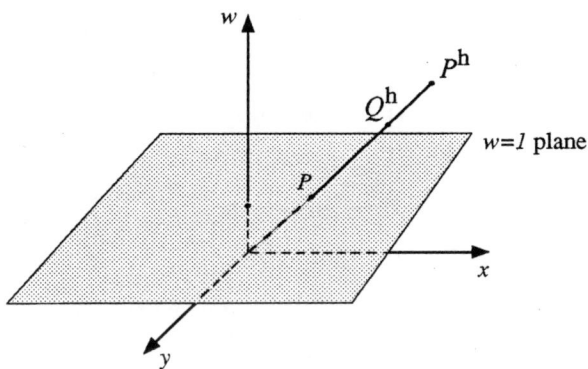

Figure 6.2 Homogeneous coordinates and projection.

6.1.2 Scaling about the origin

A general form of scaling relative to the coordinate origin is to have separate scale factors for the x, y, and z directions. To scale a point (x,y,z) by the factors (S_x, S_y, S_z), we can use the matrix:

$$\begin{pmatrix} x' \\ y' \\ z' \\ w \end{pmatrix} = \begin{pmatrix} S_x & 0 & 0 & 0 \\ 0 & S_y & 0 & 0 \\ 0 & 0 & S_z & 0 \\ 0 & 0 & 0 & 1 \end{pmatrix} \begin{pmatrix} x \\ y \\ z \\ 1 \end{pmatrix}$$

so

$$x' = S_x \ x$$
$$y' = S_y \ y$$
$$z' = S_z \ z$$

Figure 6.3 shows the effect of this transformation. One should notice that the points are scaled relative to the origin. Scaling and rotating about another point is covered later.

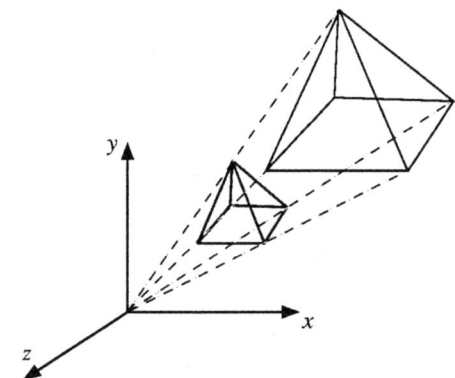

Figure 6.3 Scaling relative to the coordinate origin.

6.1.3 Rotating about the origin

In 3D there are a number of ways to define a rotation. In general, they can be broken down to rotations about each of the coordinate axes. A rotation not only requires an angle, but also a centre of rotation. This is generally the coordinate origin, although PHIGS provides utility routines where one may specify an arbitrary centre of rotatation. This will be covered in Section 6.2.2.

For example, to rotate a point about the x-axis by an angle θ:

$$\begin{pmatrix} x' \\ y' \\ z' \\ w' \end{pmatrix} = \begin{pmatrix} 1 & 0 & 0 & 0 \\ 0 & \cos\theta & -\sin\theta & 0 \\ 0 & \sin\theta & \cos\theta & 0 \\ 0 & 0 & 0 & 1 \end{pmatrix} \begin{pmatrix} x \\ y \\ z \\ 1 \end{pmatrix}$$

$x' = x$
$y' = \cos\theta \; y \; - \; \sin\theta \; z$
$z' = \sin\theta \; y \; + \cos\theta \; z$

Similarly a rotation about the y-axis by ϕ has the matrix:

$$\begin{pmatrix} \cos\phi & 0 & -\sin\phi & 0 \\ 0 & 1 & 0 & 0 \\ \sin\phi & 0 & \cos\phi & 0 \\ 0 & 0 & 0 & 1 \end{pmatrix}$$

and a rotation about the z-axis by ξ has the matrix:

$$\begin{pmatrix} \cos\xi & -\sin\xi & 0 & \\ \sin\xi & \cos\xi & 0 & 0 \\ 0 & 0 & 1 & 0 \\ 0 & 0 & 0 & 1 \end{pmatrix}$$

Figure 6.4 shows the effect of a rotation about the z-axis. These three basic rotations can be combined to form a rotation about an arbitrary axis.

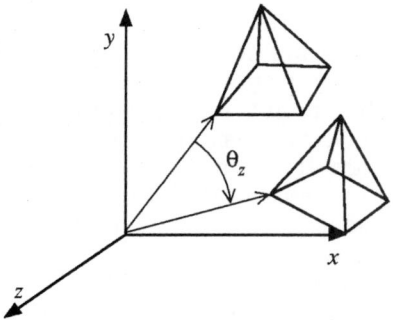

Figure 6.4 Rotation about the z-axis.

A general rotation occupies the upper left 3x3 sub-matrix in the homogeneous transformation:

99

$$\begin{pmatrix} r_{xx} & r_{xy} & r_{xz} & 0 \\ r_{yx} & r_{yy} & r_{yz} & 0 \\ r_{zx} & r_{zy} & r_{zz} & 0 \\ 0 & 0 & 0 & 1 \end{pmatrix}$$

6.1.4 Translating using homogeneous coordinates

The homogeneous transformation can also be used to represent a translation. To translate a point by an offset (T_x, T_y, T_z) we can use the matrix:

$$\begin{pmatrix} x' \\ y' \\ z' \\ w' \end{pmatrix} = \begin{pmatrix} 1 & 0 & 0 & T_x \\ 0 & 1 & 0 & T_y \\ 0 & 0 & 1 & T_z \\ 0 & 0 & 0 & 1 \end{pmatrix} \begin{pmatrix} x \\ y \\ z \\ 1 \end{pmatrix}$$

so:

$$x' = x + T_x$$
$$y' = y + T_y$$
$$z' = z + T_z$$

6.1.5 Perspective projection

A major advantage of using homogeneous coordinates is the ability to represent a perspective projection with the transformation matrix. This is essential in 3D graphics to give the viewer the impression of depth. Perspective distorts the scene, making objects which are closer appear larger than distant ones. It can map parallel lines onto lines which converge. This is what one sees when looking at the rails of a train track vanishing in the distance. The point where parallel lines converge is called a vanishing point.

This warping is caused by the transformation matrix changing the fourth, homogeneous coordinate. Until now all transformations have changed the *x, y,* and *z* components. Now the *w* component will be affected. By looking at the matrix, one should notice that we will need to change the terms in the bottom row of the transformation matrix. The term m_{ww} affects only the *w'* component of the transformed point, so it

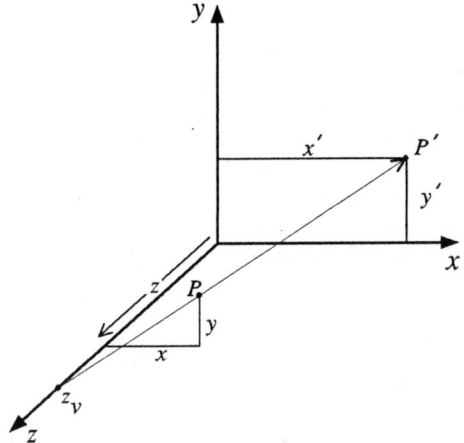

Figure 6.5 Perspective projection onto the z=0 plane.

scales *x, y,* and *z* equally. This is not exactly what we want, so we need to consider the terms m_{wx}, m_{wy}, and m_{wz}.

In the simple case where only one of these three terms in the bottom row are non-zero, we have the matrix:

$$\begin{pmatrix} x' \\ y' \\ z' \\ w' \end{pmatrix} = \begin{pmatrix} 1 & 0 & 0 & 0 \\ 0 & 1 & 0 & 0 \\ 0 & 0 & 1 & 0 \\ 0 & 0 & p_z & 1 \end{pmatrix} \begin{pmatrix} x \\ y \\ z \\ 1 \end{pmatrix}$$

After projecting the point P^h onto the plane *w=1*, we get:

$$x' = \frac{x}{(1 + p_z z)}$$

$$y' = \frac{y}{(1 + p_z z)}$$

$$z' = \frac{z}{(1 + p_z z)}$$

Now the coordinates are scaled by the *z* value in the denominator. In other words as *z* increases, the terms *x', y',* and *z'* are scaled down. The meaning of p_z becomes clear by looking at the case when the denominator vanishes. This happens when:

$$z_v = \frac{-1}{p_z}$$

The term p_z is constant for a given transformation, so the value z_v corresponds to a particular point. It is actually the z coordinate of the viewer's position, who is looking towards the origin (see Figure 6.5). This transformation will divide by zero if it is applied to any point in the plane $z = z_v$. This is what one should expect, since we can only look at points in front of the plane that the viewer is in. PHIGS actually generates an error, if the viewer's position is placed within the viewing volume.

Another point to consider, is what happens to points as z approaches infinity. In this case the point is transformed to:

$$P' = \begin{pmatrix} \dfrac{x}{(1 + p_z z_{big})} \\ \dfrac{y}{(1 + p_z z_{big})} \\ \dfrac{z_{big}}{(1 + p_z z_{big})} \end{pmatrix} \cong \begin{pmatrix} 0 \\ 0 \\ \dfrac{-1}{p_z} \end{pmatrix}$$

So, lines parallel to the z-axis converge at the point $(0,0,1/p_z)$. This is called a vanishing point. The homogeneous transformation has warped the 3D viewing space such that points at infinity are now finite, and parallel lines converge. This what one sees in a perspective view. This is most easily seen in a simple drawing of a railroad track converging in the distance.

The terms m_{wx} and m_{wy} in the transformation matrix warp the viewing volume in a similar manner. A non-zero m_{wx} term will cause lines parallel to the x-axis to converge at a vanishing point. The term m_{wy} distorts the scene similarly. Therefore, non-zero terms p_x, p_y and p_z in the transformation matrix:

$$\begin{pmatrix} 1 & 0 & 0 & 0 \\ 0 & 1 & 0 & 0 \\ 0 & 0 & 1 & 0 \\ p_x & p_y & p_z & 1 \end{pmatrix}$$

will generate three vanishing points (see Figure 6.6). Fortunately, the PHIGS programmer does not have to directly create the transformation matrices needed to view a scene. PHIGS provides utility functions to do this.

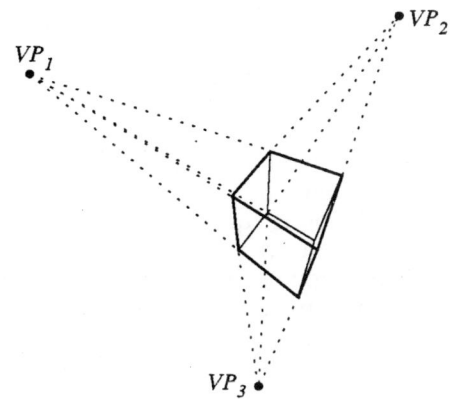

Figure 6.6 A perspective view with three vanishing points.

6.1.6 Composing transformations

The previous sections covered the four basic types of transformation used in 3D graphics. They can be considered as building blocks for more complicated transformations, such as rotating about an arbitrary axis or projecting a scene onto a viewing surface. In order to apply a series of transformations one needs to multiply the corresponding matrices to-

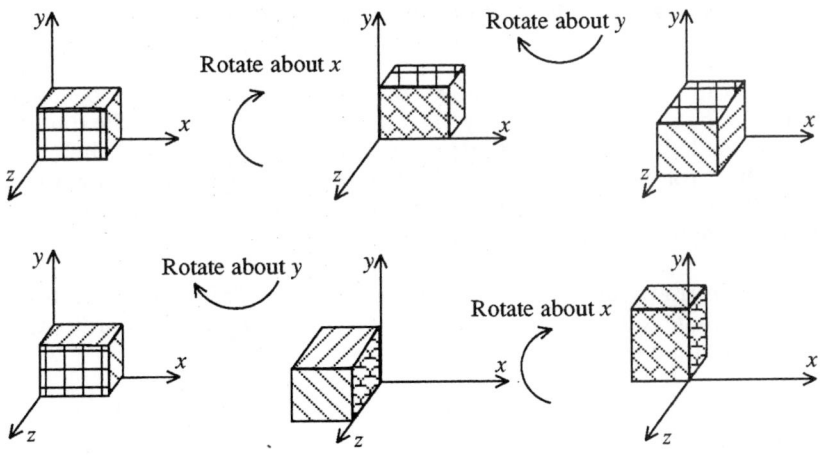

Figure 6.7 Transformations depending on the order applied.

103

gether. Multiplying transformation matrices is also referred to as con-catenating the transformations.

An interesting property of matrices is that the product of two matrices depends on the order in which they are multiplied. Geometric transfor-mations behave analogously. An object rotated first about the x-axis and then about the y-axis is oriented differently from one rotated about the y and then the x-axis, (see Figure 6.7).

Applying a transformation is equivalent to changing a point's coordi-nate system. A complicated transformation can be decomposed to a number of simple steps mapping one coordinate system to another. By multiplying the respective matrices, preserving the correct order, the composite transformation can be easily generated.

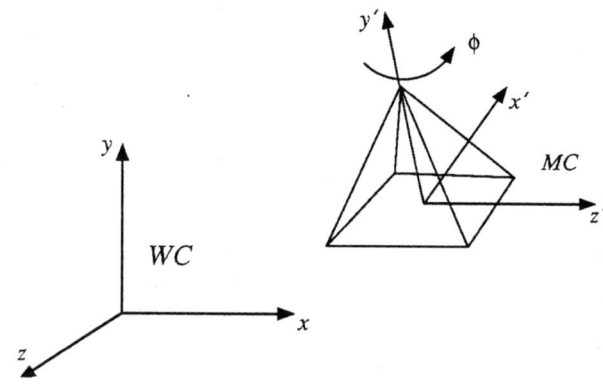

Figure 6.8 A pyramid with its own local coordinate system.

For example, Figure 6.8 shows a pyramid which should be rotated about its own local y'-axis by an angle ϕ. We have all the building blocks needed to generate the required transformation. It is helpful to break this problem down into smaller steps, keeping track of how the co-ordinate axes are transformed. In the problem with the pyramid a possi-ble set of steps would be:

Transform pyramid coordinate's y'-axis to origin's y-axis	Rotate about y	Transform back to pyramid coordinates
M	$R_y(\phi)$	M^{-1}

To transform the pyramid's coordinates to coincide with our origin we could use the following sequence of transformations:

Translate primed origin to unprimed	Rotate y' to y" in the y-z plane about z	Rotate y" to y about x
$T(-d)$	$R_z(\theta_z)$	$R_x(\theta_x)$

So the composite transformation is:

$$M\,p \;=\; R_x(\theta_x) \quad R_z(\theta_z) \quad T(-d)\;p$$

$$\begin{pmatrix} x' \\ y' \\ z' \\ w' \end{pmatrix} = \begin{pmatrix} cos\theta_x & -sin\theta_x & 0 & 0 \\ sin\theta_x & cos\theta_x & 0 & 0 \\ 0 & 0 & 1 & 0 \\ 0 & 0 & 0 & 1 \end{pmatrix} \begin{pmatrix} 1 & 0 & 0 & 0 \\ 0 & cos\theta_z & -sin\theta_z & 0 \\ 0 & sin\theta_z & cos\theta_z & 0 \\ 0 & 0 & 0 & 1 \end{pmatrix} \begin{pmatrix} 1 & 0 & 0 & T_x \\ 0 & 1 & 0 & T_y \\ 0 & 0 & 1 & T_z \\ 0 & 0 & 0 & 1 \end{pmatrix} \begin{pmatrix} x \\ y \\ z \\ 1 \end{pmatrix}$$

Since we are using the convention of representing points as column vectors, the translation is applied first, then $R_z(\theta_z)$ and finally $R_x(\theta_x)$.

In order to get back to the pyramid's coordinates one needs the inverse of the matrix M. In terms of the transformations it should be clear what we need to do. We just need to undo the transformations that we applied in the first place. Since the last building block used to create M was to rotate about the x-axis θ_x degrees, we can easily undo that by rotating by $-\theta_x$ degrees. Then we need to undo the rotation about the z-axis $-\theta_z$ degrees, and finally translate the rotated coordinate system back where it came from. The formula for the inverse is:

$$M^{-1} \;=\; T(d) \quad R_z(-\theta_z) \quad R_x(-\theta_x)$$
$$(M)^{-1} \;=\; (R_x(\theta_x) \quad R_z(\theta_z) \quad T(-d))^{-1}$$

This illustrates a more general point, which is the inverse of a product of matrices is equal to the product of the inverses in reverse order.

6.2 PHIGS coordinate systems and transformations

To provide both powerful and flexible tools for viewing and modelling scenes, PHIGS has defined several coordinate systems and transformations to move from one system to another. It is important to understand how these transformations are used in order to write a PHIGS application. A common mistake is to write a program where everything is correct, except that the transformation has the viewer looking in the wrong direction, so the screen is blank.

The PHIGS programmer has a number of functions with which transformations can be created and used to model and view a scene. These PHIGS coordinate systems and transformations are used in a fixed way, defining a viewing pipeline. The easiest way to understand this pipeline is by looking at the component coordinate systems and their purposes. The transformation pipeline in PHIGS consists of five coordinate systems (see Figure 6.9).

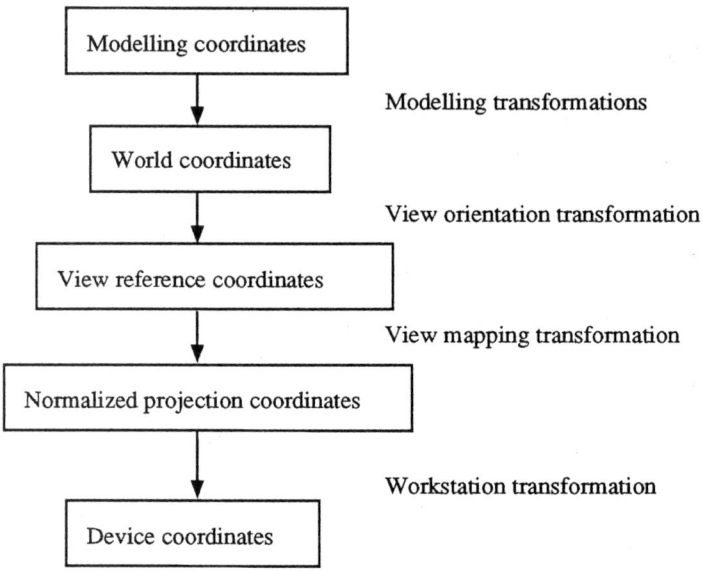

Figure 6.9 The PHIGS modelling transformation pipeline.

At first sight, the number of coordinate systems seems excessive, but, as we shall see, each system has an explicit purpose. Each body is defined in its own modelling coordinates, *MC*. It can then be positioned, rotated, and scaled with a modelling transformation so that it fits into the scene as desired. The modelling transformations place all the bodies where they belong in the world coordinate system, *WC*. The world coordinate system contains everything that the application would like to display, but so far there has been no mention of a viewer of the scene. The rest of this chapter focuses on modelling transformations, and the following chapter deals with the viewing transformations.

6.2.1 Modelling with PHIGS

When a body is defined using output primitives, one specifies the vertex data in coordinates which best suit the type of object being created. Each

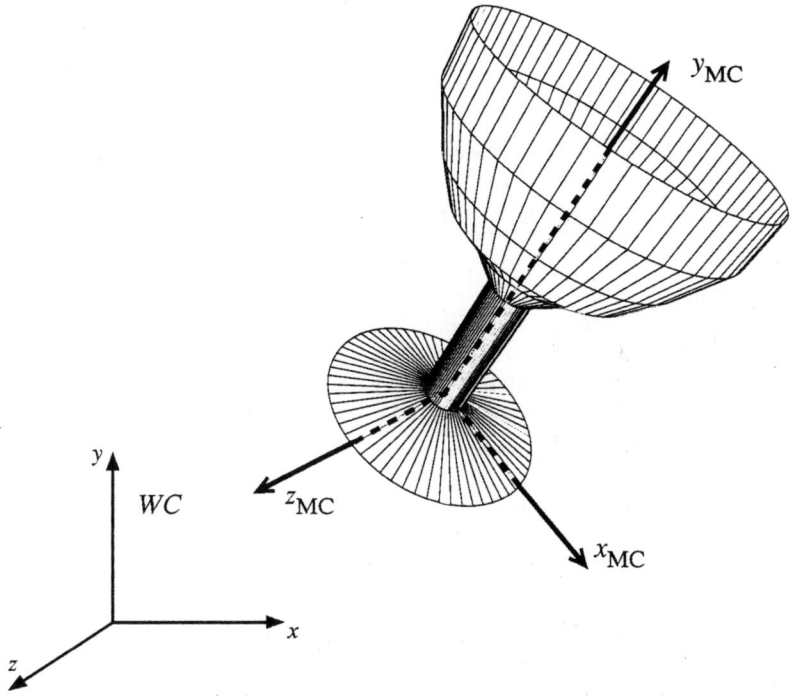

Figure 6.10 Glass in its own modelling coordinates.

body has its own origin. For example, a surface of revolution is usually defined with the axis of revolution being one of its major axes (see Figure 6.10).

Modelling transformations take these vertex data and convert them into world coordinates which all bodies in a picture have in common. There are two routines to set the modelling transformations. Since these transformations belong to the objects in a scene, they are set with structure elements. Two routines are needed because the modelling transformation has an internal structure, which consists of a global and a local component. These two components are combined to form the composite modelling transformation, *CMT* as follows:

CMT = G L

Here *G* is the global, and *L* is the local modelling transformation. Since points are represented as column vectors in homogeneous coordinates, the local transformation is applied, then the global transformation. These transformations are applied from right to left.

$$CMT\,p \;=\; G\,L\,p$$

$$= \begin{pmatrix} g_{xx} & g_{xy} & g_{xz} & g_{xw} \\ g_{yx} & g_{yy} & g_{yz} & g_{yw} \\ g_{zx} & g_{zy} & g_{zz} & g_{zw} \\ g_{wx} & g_{wy} & g_{wz} & g_{ww} \end{pmatrix} \begin{pmatrix} l_{xx} & l_{xy} & l_{xz} & l_{xw} \\ l_{yx} & l_{yy} & l_{yz} & l_{yw} \\ l_{zx} & l_{zy} & l_{zz} & l_{zw} \\ l_{wx} & l_{wy} & l_{wz} & l_{ww} \end{pmatrix} \begin{pmatrix} x \\ y \\ z \\ 1 \end{pmatrix}$$

The preceding equation shows these transformations, whose internal structure has been discussed in Section 6.1. The components will generally be created with PHIGS utility functions (see Section 6.2.2).

By default, the global transformation matrix is the identity, but it can be changed with the structure element:

SET GLOBAL TRANSFORMATION 3   (PHOP,*,STOP,*)El
Arguments:
       in   transformation matrix   4x4 transformation matrix

The argument is a 4x4 global transformation matrix which is applied to the vertices after they have been transformed by the local modelling transformation. If PHIGS is being used for 2D graphics, then the routine SET GLOBAL TRANSFORMATION should be used, which takes a 3x3 homogeneous 2D transformation matrix as an argument. There is only one global modelling transformation, so calling SET GLOBAL TRANSFORMATION(M) actually sets a 4x4 matrix as follows:

$$\begin{pmatrix} m_{xx} & m_{xy} & m_{xw} \\ m_{yx} & m_{yy} & m_{yw} \\ m_{wx} & m_{wy} & m_{ww} \end{pmatrix} \longrightarrow \begin{pmatrix} m_{xx} & m_{xy} & 0 & m_{xw} \\ m_{yx} & m_{yy} & 0 & m_{yw} \\ 0 & 0 & 1 & 0 \\ m_{wx} & m_{wy} & 0 & m_{ww} \end{pmatrix}$$

The local transformation is set with the structure element:

SET LOCAL TRANSFORMATION 3   (PHOP,*,STOP,*)El
Arguments:
       in   transformation matrix   4x4 transformation matrix
       in   composition type   (PRECONCATENATE,
                                              POSTCONCATENATE, REPLACE)

This routine is slightly more complicated than setting the global transformation. This is because one can use this routine to compose a new transformation matrix with the current local transformation. The composition type specifies how to multiply the new matrix. It selects one of the following possibilities:

PRECONCATENATE: $L * N \rightarrow L$ $CMT = G * L * N$
POSTCONCATENATE: $N * L \rightarrow L$ $CMT = G * N * L$
REPLACE: $N \rightarrow L$ $CMT = G * N$

Here N is the new matrix, passed as an argument to SET LOCAL TRANSFORMATION 3, and L is the current local modelling transformation. Being able to have PHIGS concatenate the matrix with the local transformation provides the PHIGS programmer with a flexible means to define and update complicated modelling transformations. Similar to setting a 2D global transformation matrix, there is a routine to set a 2D local transformation matrix: SET LOCAL TRANSFORMATION. This routine is passed a 3x3 homogeneous transformation to be applied to 2D primitives and a composition type.

The composition type PRECONCATENATE applies the new transformation before the current local modelling transformation. An example of using preconcatenation is to use the local transformation matrix to rotate a body in its own local coordinate system. For example, if a robot's hand is to be rotated about its y-axis, we can preconcatenate a rotation matrix just before the hand's geometry is defined. Any transforms defined higher up in the structure hierarchy will be applied to the rotated hand.

```
popen_struct( HandStruct );
pset_local_tran3( Identity, PTYPE_REPLACE );
ppolyline3( ... );
...
pclose_struct();
...


/* To rotate the body */
popen_struct( HandStruct );
pset_edit_mode( PEDIT_REPLACE );
pset_elem_ptr( 1 );
while( NotDone )
{
protate_y( ThetaY, &errind, mat );
pset_local_tran3( mat, PTYPE_PRECONCAT );
pupd_ws( WSID, PFLAG_PERFORM );
...
getangle( &ThetaY );
}
```

The code excerpt illustrates an example of how to use preconcatenation. The hand's structure is created with a local transformation followed by the output primitives. This transform initially contains the identity matrix, but it will be subsequently edited. Before entering the loop, the structure is opened, the edit mode is set to REPLACE and the EP positioned to point to the local transformation. In the loop, the rotation angle is updated and used to create a new tranformation matrix. By preconcatenating the transform, we are assured that the rotation occurs relative to the coordinate system the hand was defined in, regardless of what transforms have been used by `HandStruct`'s parents. For example, a parent of `HandStruct` could use a local transformation to position the hand relative to the robot's arm.

Using postconcatenation is similar, but in this case the new transformation is applied between the local and global transform. In our previous example we could postconcatenate a translation matrix. This would cause the body to be translated after it had been rotated, which would keep the rotation about the body's local y-axis (see Figure 6.11).

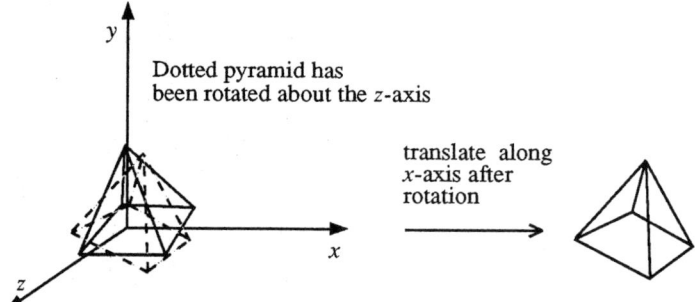

Figure 6.11 A translation postconcatenated after a rotation.

6.2.2 Modelling transformation utility routines

Fortunately PHIGS provides a number of utility routines to generate the matrices which are used by the modelling transformations. These functions just create matrices, so they only require the state (PHOP,*,*,*). All utility routines return an error indicator. This will be set to a non-zero value if an error occurs; for example, calling a utility routine before opening PHIGS.

The utility routines generate all of the commonly used transformations. The programmer can still create the matrices if special effects such as shearing or mirroring are required. An interesting effect that can be achieved by directly manipulating these transformations is to create singular transformations which can be used to simulate shadow casting onto a flat surface [Blinn]. Colour Plate 16 shows the effect of this transformation.

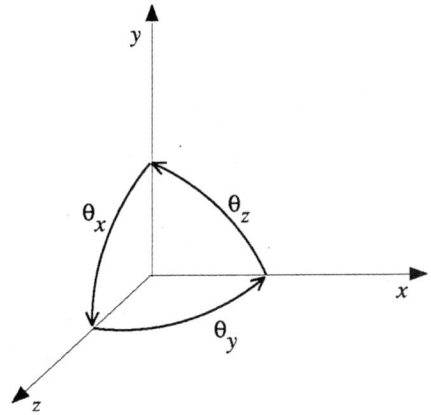

Figure 6.12 Positive rotations in a right-handed coordinate system.

There are a large number of utility routines. Many of these functions have self-explanatory names, so where there is no doubt, the function will be listed.

There are two functions to create a translation matrix, one for a translation in 3D:

TRANSLATE 3   (PHOP,*,*,*)
Arguments:

in	translation vector	3D offset vector
out	error indicator	integer
out	transformation matrix	4x4 transformation matrix

The other routine is a 2D function, called TRANSLATE, and takes a 2D offset vector and returns a 3x3 2D transformation.

Similarly, there are two routines to create a transformation matrix, which scales about the origin. The 2D version is called SCALE and is analogous to the 3D function:

SCALE 3   (PHOP,*,*,*)
Arguments:

in	scale factor vector	3 real scale factors
out	error indicator	integer
out	transformation matrix	4x4 transformation matrix

There are three utility routines to generate a 3D rotation matrix, one for each of the axes: ROTATE X, ROTATE Y and ROTATE Z. In a right-handed coordinate system a positive rotation is counter-clockwise when looking from the end of the axis towards the origin (see Figure 6.12). A general rotation in 3D can be formed by combining one or more of these transformations. All three functions take the same arguments:

ROTATE X   (PHOP,*,*,*)
Arguments:

in	angle in radians	real
out	error indicator	integer
out	transformation matrix	4x4 transformation matrix

In 2D one can rotate only about the origin, so there is only one utility routine:

ROTATE   (PHOP,*,*,*)
Arguments:

in	angle in radians	real
out	error indicator	integer
out	transformation matrix	3x3 transformation matrix

In order to build more complex transformations one often needs to compose transformation matrices. This simply involves multiplying the two matrices; PHIGS provides a routine to do this:

COMPOSE MATRIX 3   (PHOP,*,*,*)
Arguments:

in	matrix A	4x4 transformation matrix
in	matrix B	4x4 transformation matrix
out	error indicator	integer
out	composed matrix	4x4 transformation matrix

This routine returns a matrix which is the product: $A * B$. The 2D version, which composes two 3x3 homogeneous transformation matrices, is called COMPOSE MATRIX.

The next routine is particularly useful since it combines the previous functions to scale, rotate and translate. The scaling and rotation are about a given fixed point, *COR* and then translation is applied. This function has a 2D counterpart BUILD TRANSFORMATION MATRIX, whose arguments are similar to:

BUILD TRANSFORMATION MATRIX 3   (PHOP,*,*,*)
Arguments:

in	fixed point COR	3D point
in	shift vector	3D offset vector
in	x rotation angle (radians)	real
in	y rotation angle (radians)	real
in	z rotation angle (radians)	real
in	scale factor vector	3 real scale factors
out	error indicator	integer
out	transformation matrix	4x4 transformation matrix

The resulting transformation can be broken down into the following components:

$$T(sh) \; T(COR) \; R_z(\theta_z) \; R_y(\theta_y) \; R_x(\theta_x) \; S(s) \; T(-COR) \; p$$

Whereby $T(sh)$ is a translation by the shift vector and $T(COR)$ is a translation by the fixed point centre of rotation. The transformations

112

$R_x(\theta_x)$, $R_y(\theta_y)$, and $R_z(\theta_z)$ are rotations about the *x-*, *y-* and *z-*axes respectively, and *S* is the scaling transformation. It is interesting to note that the routines which are relative to the centre of rotation are first shifted by *-COR* and finally shifted by *COR*.

The following function combines the previous two routines to build a transformation and then compose it with a given matrix:

COMPOSE TRANSFORMATION MATRIX 3   (PHOP,*,*,*)
Arguments:

in	transformation matrix	4x4 transformation matrix
in	fixed point	3D point
in	shift vector	3D offset vector
in	*x* rotation angle (radians)	real
in	*y* rotation angle (radians)	real
in	*z* rotation angle (radians)	real
in	scale factor vector	3 real scale factors
out	error indicator	integer
out	transformation matrix	4x4 transformation matrix

Once again its 2D counterpart is COMPOSE TRANSFORMATION MATRIX with similar arguments.

The last utility routine in this section is used to see where a transformation maps a given 3D point (the 2D version is called TRANSFORM POINT):

TRANSFORM POINT 3   (PHOP,*,*,*)
Arguments:

in	point	3D point
in	transformation matrix	4x4 transformation matrix
out	error indicator	integer
out	transformed point	3D point

6.3 Modelling transformations in structure networks

Structure hierarchy provides PHIGS with a powerful mechanism to represent complex objects. An object can consist of many components, each of which is in its own structure. The object as a whole is created by linking the structures together and using modelling transformations to position and orient each element relative to the other. An example of this sort of object is shown in Figure 6.13.

The lamp in Figure 6.13 has been defined with the structure network illustrated in Figure 6.14. This network links the structures together to form a lamp. These elements are hierarchically related to one another. For example, the head of the lamp can only move relative to the lower arm. If the upper arm moves, we would like the lower arm and the head of the lamp to move as well. An object with hierarchically related elements is called an articulated object. Another example of such an object is a robot arm.

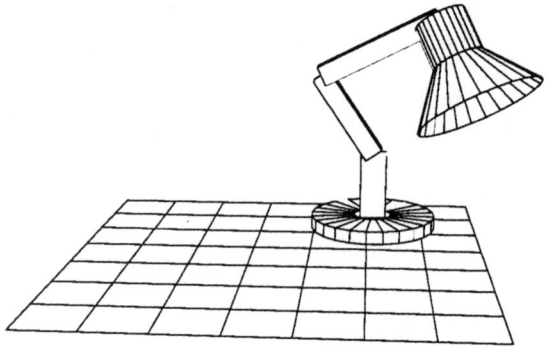

Figure 6.13 A lamp created from a structure hierarchy.

Modelling transformations and structure hierarchy are a natural means to define articulated objects. The transformations are composed to link the elements together. In this example the global modelling transformation is used to position the lamp as an entity in the scene, and the local transformations are used to define the interrelationship between its components.

When a structure network is traversed, modelling transformations follow inheritance rules. A child structure will inherit the composite transformation from its parent. Since the CMT consists of the product of

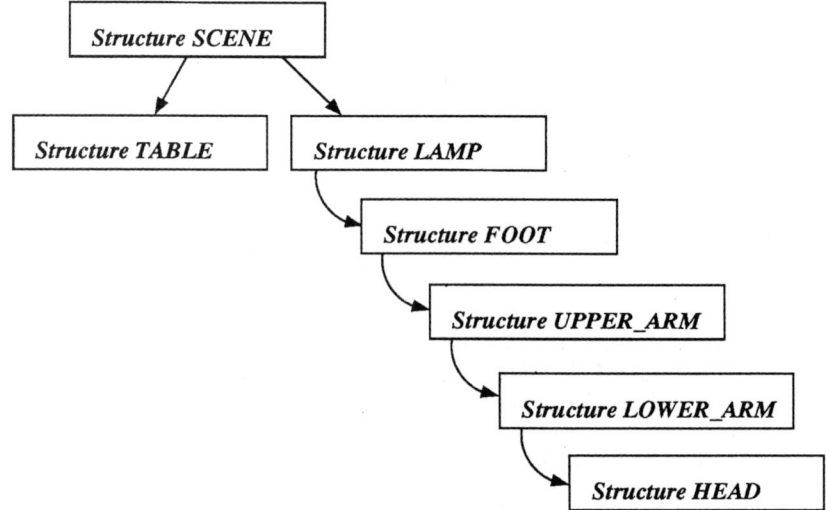

Figure 6.14 Structure network used to create a lamp.

the global and the local modelling transformation, the procedure is slightly more complicated. Structure hierarchy is realized at traversal time by executing an EXECUTE STRUCTURE element. This saves the current traversal state list, TSL, sets the global modelling transformation to the composite modelling transformation, sets the local modelling transformation to the identity, executes the child structure, and restores the TSL to its original state before continuing with the parent structure. Figure 6.15 illustrates this procedure.

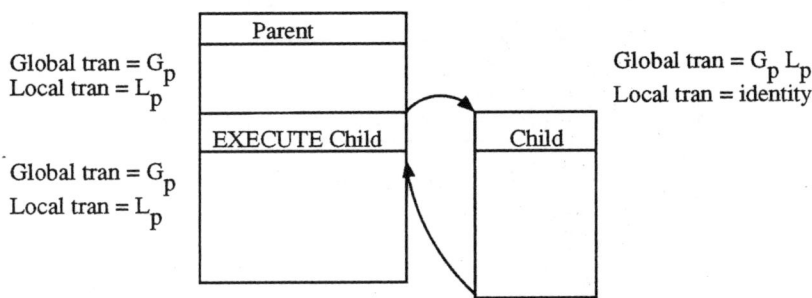

Figure 6.15 Structure networks and modelling transformations.

In the example of the lamp, only the structure SCENE sets the global transformation, which is used to position the lamp in world coordinates. The structure SCENE is the root structure, and it executes TABLE and LAMP. The child structures in the network LAMP set local transformations to position each component of the lamp. The lamp contains the children: FOOT, UPPER_ARM, LOWER_ARM, and HEAD. Figure 6.16 shows how this structure network uses local transformations to position each componen.

An interesting point to notice is that the child structures of LAMP all start by replacing the local transformation. Remember that during network traversal a child's global transformation is its parent's CMT, which is the product of the parent's global and local transformation. The local transformation that is being replaced is actually the identity. The parent's original global and local transformation will be restored once the child is finished being traversed.

In the structures FOOT, UPPER_ARM, and LOWER_ARM, a translation is preconcatenated to the local transformation prior to executing the respective child structures. This translates the modelling coordinate's origin to where the child structure should begin. For example, the lower arm begins at the end of the upper arm that is not connected to the foot. This is achieved by translating the modelling coordinate origin the length of the upper arm. Figure 6.17 shows the coordinate axes for the origin of the lower arm's modelling coordinates.

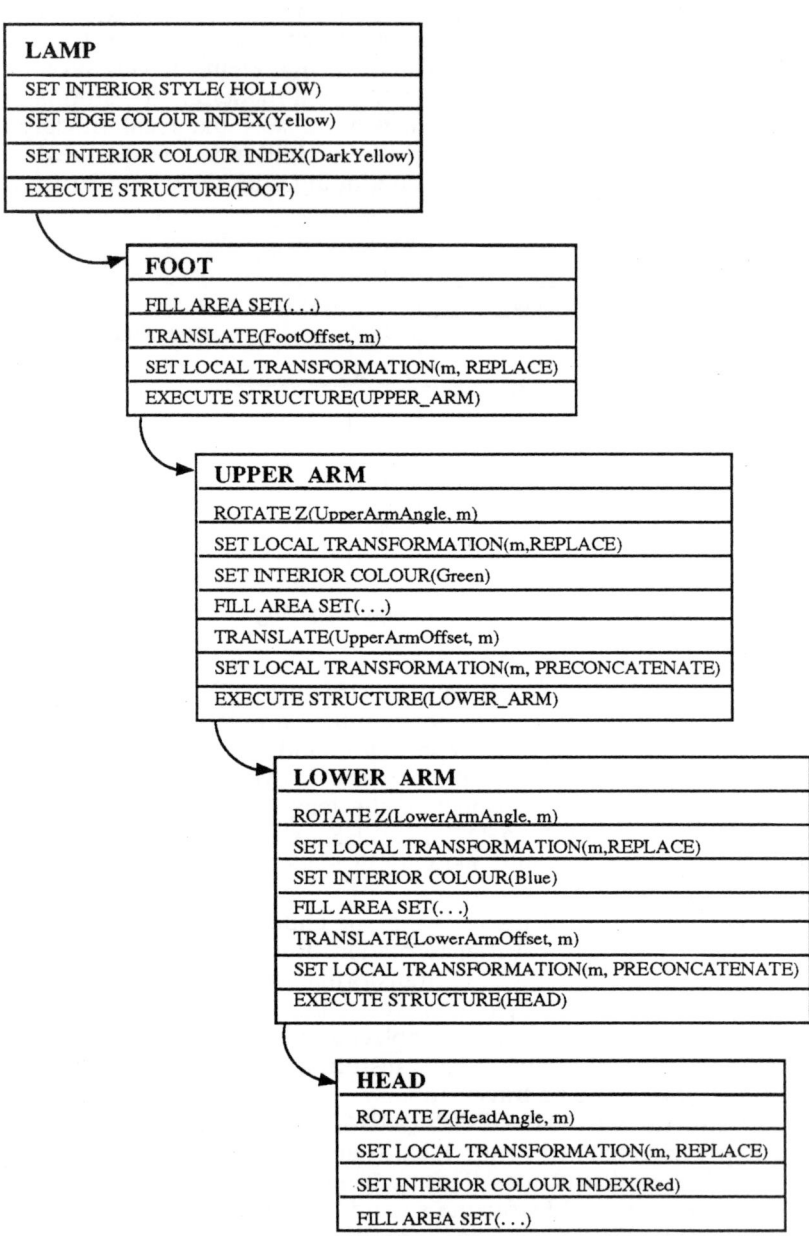

Figure 6.16 Lamp structure network contents.

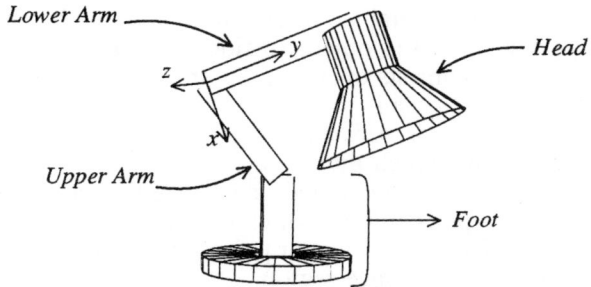

Figure 6.17 Modelling coordinate's origin for the lamp's lower arm.

Since each child inherits its parent's CMT, the child's modelling transformations and output primitives are relative to the parent's modelling coordinates. So, if we rotate the upper arm, then the lower arm and the head of the lamp will rotate as well, keeping all elements of the lamp connected. This is exactly what we need to represent articulated objects. Figure 6.18 shows three examples of editing the local transformations in the lamp's network.

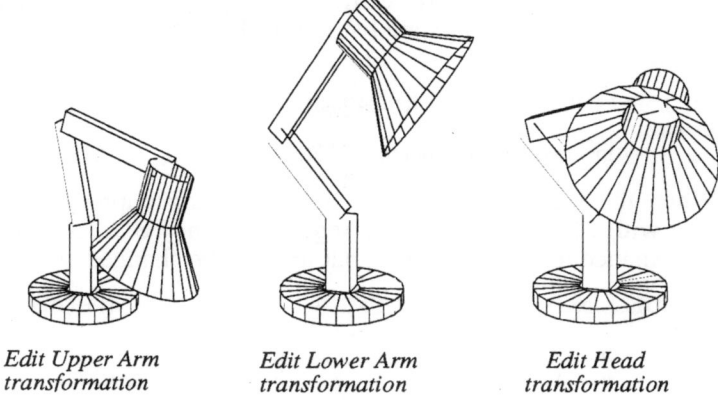

Edit Upper Arm
transformation

Edit Lower Arm
transformation

Edit Head
transformation

Figure 6.18 Editing local transformation in the lamp's network.

6.4 Model clipping

Once an object is mapped to world coordinates, it can be clipped. This is done with model clipping structure elements. Clipping is a technique to restrict output primitives from drawing outside a certain volume. The region where drawing is enabled is known as the *acceptance region* or modelling clipping volume. It can be used to remove parts of an object which are obscuring other details. For example, it would be necessary to clip a hole in a sphere to see objects inside it. This can be done with model clipping, which consists of two steps: specifying the clipping volume and telling PHIGS to use it.

The acceptance region is defined using half-spaces. A half-space is simply an infinite plane which divides the WC into two halves: one in which output primitives are drawn and one where they are clipped. This plane is specified by a point in MC, which lies on the plane, and a vector normal to the plane. The normal vector points towards the portion of the half-space which is its acceptance region.

More than one half-space can be used to define the acceptance region. This makes it possible to create complex clipping volumes. Obviously one cannot define an arbitrary number of half-spaces. A PHIGS implementation is required to support at least six half-spaces, and the maximum number depends on system resources. The number of distinct half-spaces that can be supported may be determined with the function INQUIRE MODELLING CLIPPING FACILITIES.

The intersection of the acceptance regions for each half-space defines the model clipping volume used when output primitives are drawn. Figure 6.19 shows the effect of intersecting regions defined by half-spaces.

The first function relating to model clipping is the simplest. It just sets a flag in the traversal state list telling PHIGS to use model clipping or not.

SET MODELLING CLIPPING INDICATOR   (PHOP,*,STOP,*)El
Arguments:
    in modelling clipping indicator   (CLIP,NOCLIP)

When the indicator is set to clip, modelling clipping will be performed with whatever acceptance region is in the TSL. The entire WC is the acceptance region by default, but this can be changed with:

SET MODELLING CLIPPING VOLUME 3   (PHOP,*,STOP,*)El
Arguments:
   in operator   integer
   in half-spaces   list of 3D half-spaces

The acceptance region defined by this structure element is used to update the current modelling clipping volume, which is in the TSL. The operator determines how to update the TSL's volume. PHIGS requires two operators:

REPLACE This just replaces the modelling clipping volume in the TSL with the volume defined by the half-spaces.

INTERSECT This generates a new acceptance region, which is the intersection of the current modelling clipping volume and that specified by the half spaces (see Figure 6.20).

Other modelling clipping operators were considered when PHIGS was a draft standard, but only these two are required. Operators with negative values are implementation dependent, whereas those greater than two have been registered.

There is also a 2D version of this structure element, SET MODEL-LING CLIPPING VOLUME. Its functionality and arguments are analogous to its 3D cousin, so it will not be discussed.

The half-spaces in the list consist of a 3D point in MC and the plane's normal vector. This implies that these half-spaces first need to be transformed to world coordinates before they can be intersected with the TSL's acceptance region. This should be clear, since the CMT could have changed since the current modelling clipping volume was defined.

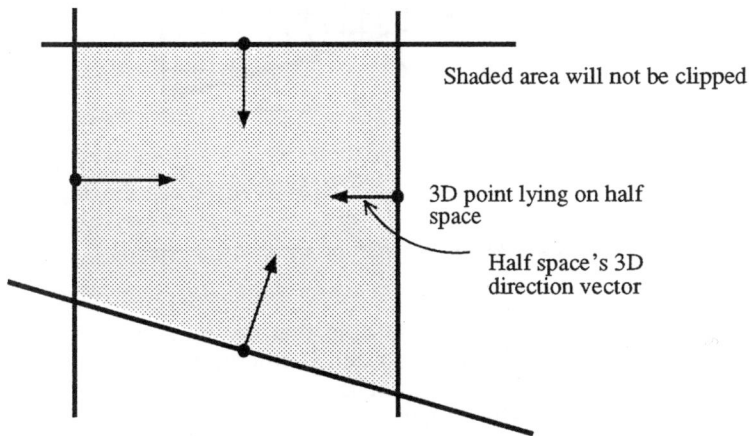

Shaded area will not be clipped

3D point lying on half space

Half space's 3D direction vector

Figure 6.19 Clipping volume define by four half spaces.

The last function is used to restore the modelling clipping volume to the state it was in when the structure was invoked. This is needed if the structure has changed the acceptance region, but requires the original clipping volume again. For example, a structure might define a modelling clipping volume for its own output primitives, and need to restore the original volume before referencing a child structure. This structure element has no arguments:

RESTORE MODELLING CLIPPING VOLUME   (PHOP,*,STOP,*)El
Arguments:
      none

Using structure elements to define modelling clipping volumes, gives PHIGS considerable flexibility. By setting different acceptance regions on separate branches of a structure network, one can independently clip

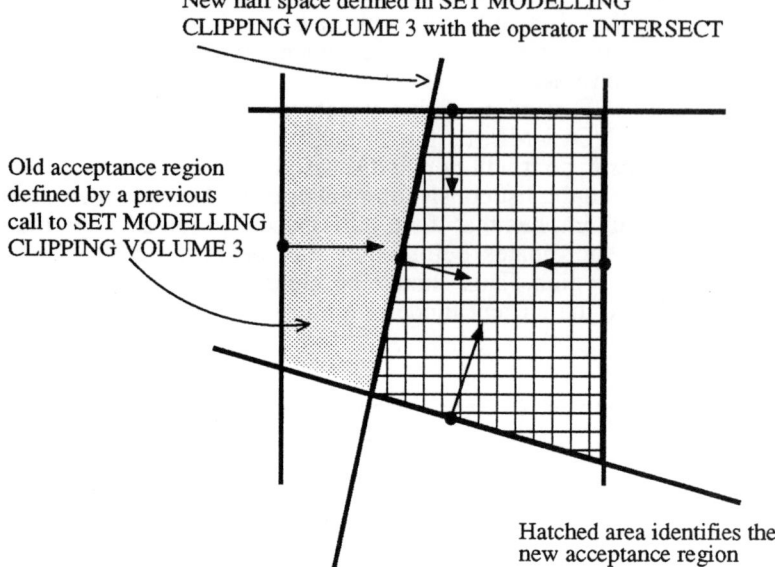

New half space defined in SET MODELLING
CLIPPING VOLUME 3 with the operator INTERSECT

Old acceptance region
defined by a previous
call to SET MODELLING
CLIPPING VOLUME 3

Hatched area identifies the
new acceptance region

Figure 6.20 Intersection of acceptance regions.

distinct objects. It is important to note that the modelling clipping volume is maintained in the TSL, so child structures inherit their parent's acceptance region and indicator. It is simple to restrict modelling clipping to those objects which need it by setting the modelling clipping indicator to CLIP only on the sub-branches of the structure network where these objects are defined.

CHAPTER 7

Viewing in PHIGS

In the previous chapter the mathematics of transformations and modelling transformations were introduced. These transformations map objects defined in the CSS to world coordinates, *WC*. So far there has been no mention of how to view the scene, which is now in *WC*. This chapter completes the discussion of the transformation pipeline with viewing transformations. Figure 7.1 shows the entire transformation pipeline in detail.

The viewing transformations determine the position from which the scene is being looked at. On workstations it is common to have user interaction continually update these transformations: for example, rotating a scene by moving the mouse. At other times the viewing transformation will be calculated by a numerical simulation, so that the viewer will appear to fly through a scene. How these transformations are used depends on the requirements of the application.

The viewing mechanism consists of the transformations which map world coordinates to normalized projection coordinates, *NPC*. The viewing transformations are needed to define where the viewer is and how to display the scene. Figure 7.1 shows that they are workstation dependent, which implies they are defined by entries in the workstation's tables. They consist of two separate transformations:

1. The *view orientation transformation* determines the direction from which the viewer is observing the scene. Its effect is to rotate the *WC* so that it appears to be observed from a given direction.

2. The *view mapping transformation* determines how far away the observer is and how to project the scene onto a fixed viewing space. This transformation determines whether a scene is to be displayed with perspective or not.

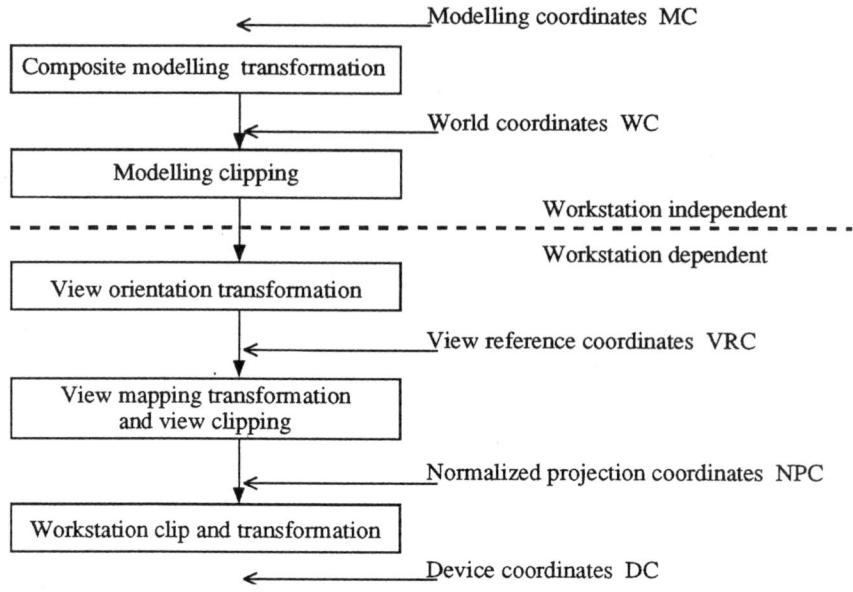

Figure 7.1 The PHIGS transformation pipeline.

The view orientation and the view mapping transformations are bundled together in the workstation view table. This allows an application to define multiple views of the same scene. Any given view may be selected by setting a view index.

The following sections will focus on 3D viewing and workstation transformations. The utility routines which generate the viewing transformations will be used to illustrate how viewing has been realized in PHIGS.

7.1 The view orientation transformation

The first stage of the viewing pipeline is the view orientation transformation. It simply rotates the scene in world coordinates so that it appears to be observed from a given direction. It maps the world coordinates to view reference coordinates, *VRC*. By changing the view orientation transformation, one can create the effect of moving around the object being looked at.

A straightforward way to define this transformation is to specify the axes of the *VRC*'s coordinate system in world coordinates. The axes of this coordinate system are labelled *U-V-N* (see Figure 7.2).

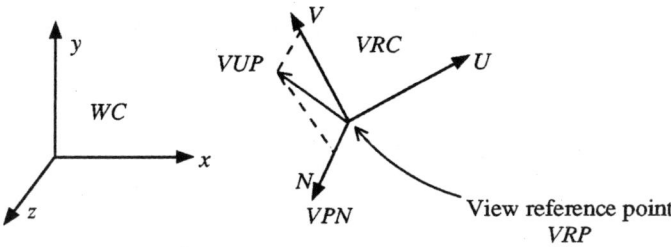

Figure 7.2 The view reference coordinates.

As a start one needs the origin of the *VRC*, which we will call the view reference point, *VRP*. The *VRP* is often, but not always, a point in the scene we want to look at. Then we need to specify the directions of just two axes, since the third axis will determined by the right-hand rule (all coordinate systems in PHIGS are right-handed).

The first axis which will be defined is called the *N*-axis and is determined by the view plane normal vector, *VPN*. A 3D scene is projected onto the view plane by the view mapping transformation. The *VPN* simply defines the orientation of this plane. It is common to choose the vector from the view reference point to the viewer as the *VPN*. Exceptions to this are when oblique projections are needed.

Once we have the *VPN*, we need one additional vector. This is called the view up vector, *VUP*. As its name implies, this vector determines which direction corresponds to the vertical axis on the workstation. The *VUP* vector does not have to be perpendicular to the *VPN*, but it certainly cannot be parallel. The projection of the *VUP* vector onto the view plane is used as the *V*-axis of the *VRC*.

These three components are all that is required to specify the view orientation transformation. PHIGS provides the following routine to convert these data into a view orientation transformation matrix:

EVALUATE VIEW ORIENTATION MATRIX 3   (PHOP,*,*,*)
Arguments:

in view reference point	3D point in WC
in view plane normal	3D vector in WC
in view up vector	3D vector in WC
out error indicator	integer
out view orientation matrix	4x4 transformation matrix

The view orientation matrix returned by this function is used when defining a view representation, which sits in the workstation state list. A view representation contains everything needed to define a view.

The 2D version of this routine is called EVALUATE VIEW ORIENTATION MATRIX. In 2D all that is needed to define the view orientation matrix is a 2D view reference point and a view up vector. This will define the centre of rotation and the rotation angle. The function returns a 2D homogeneous view orientation matrix that is used to define the 2D view.

7.2 The view mapping transformation

View mapping takes the view reference coordinates and projects them onto normalized projection coordinates. This is the stage where it is determined whether to use a perspective projection or not. A simplistic way to describe this transformation is that it maps a volume of *VRC* space onto a rectangular box in *NPC* space. The volume in *VRC* space is not always a rectangular box, because of perspective and oblique projections. As its name implies, normalized projection coordinates are all in the range 0.0 to 1.0.

In order to define a view mapping, one needs a projection reference point, *PRP*. This is used to define projectors, which are rays that pass through each object in the viewing volume and intersect the view plane. The projection onto this plane corresponds to what appears on the screen, if we neglect the workstation transformations for the time being. In perspective projections the projectors intersect each other at the *PRP*, whereas they are parallel to the line connecting the *PRP* to the centre of the view plane for parallel projections. Figure 7.3 illustrates both types of projection. The *PRP* is defined in view reference coordinates.

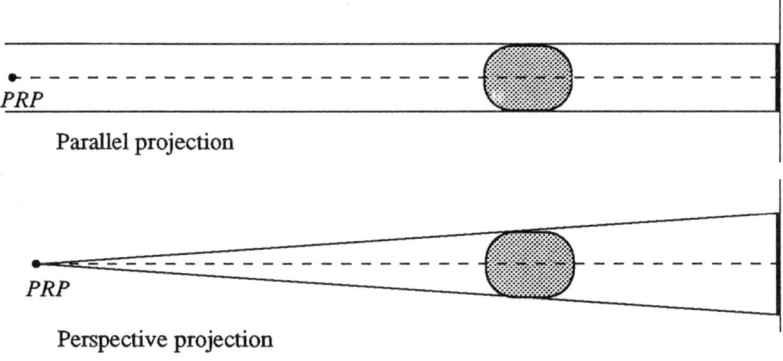

Figure 7.3 Parallel and perspective projections.

Once the *PRP* is defined, one needs to define three planes in *VRC*: the front, view and back planes. The front and back plane define the extent of the viewing volume along the *N*-axis. Remember, the *N*-axis in *VRC* is parallel to the view plane normal, *VPN*. These planes are perpendicular to the *N*-axis, so they can be defined by a distance along the *N*-

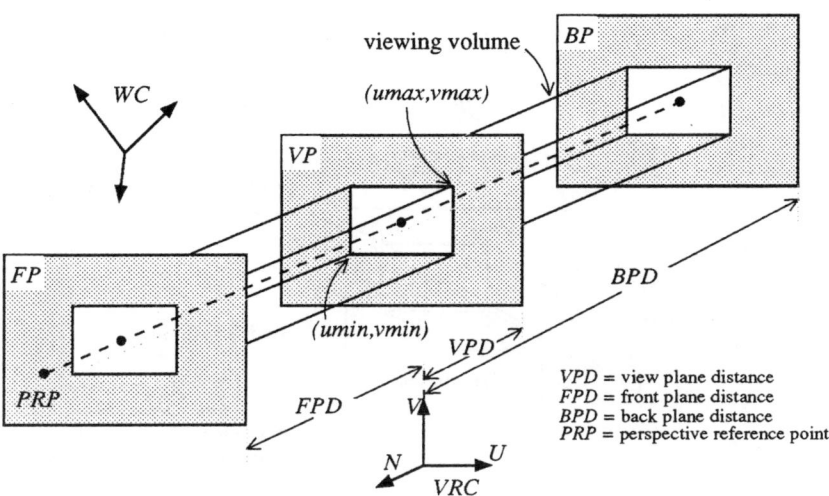

Figure 7.4 Viewing volume for a parallel projection.

axis. The view plane must lie between the front and back plane. Obviously the front plane distance cannot be less than the back plane distance. Finally, the *PRP* cannot lie between the front plane and the back plane.

The view plane is used as a reference plane on which window limits are defined. This window defines the width and height of the viewing volume. The window is defined in *VRC* by the four values UMIN, UMAX, VMIN, and VMAX. Figure 7.4 shows the viewing volume for a parallel projection.

When using a perspective projection the viewing volume is a pyramid, whose vertex is the *PRP*. This pyramid has had its top cut off by the front viewing plane (see Figure 7.5). Actually the pyramid will lean to one side if an oblique projection is used. The projection is oblique if the line connecting the centre of the projection window and the *PRP* is not parallel to the view plane normal (see Figure 7.6). If an oblique projection is not wanted, one should derive the *u* and *v* coordinates of the *PRP* from the window as follows:

```
prp.u = umin + (umax-umin)/2
prp.v = vmin + (vmax-vmin)/2
```

Remember *u*, *v* and *n* in *VRC* correspond to *x*, *y* and *z* in a general 3D space; they are just named differently in order to distinguish *VRC* from *WC*.

When perspective is used, the viewing volume is a truncated pyramid, (assuming the projections are not oblique). This volume will be

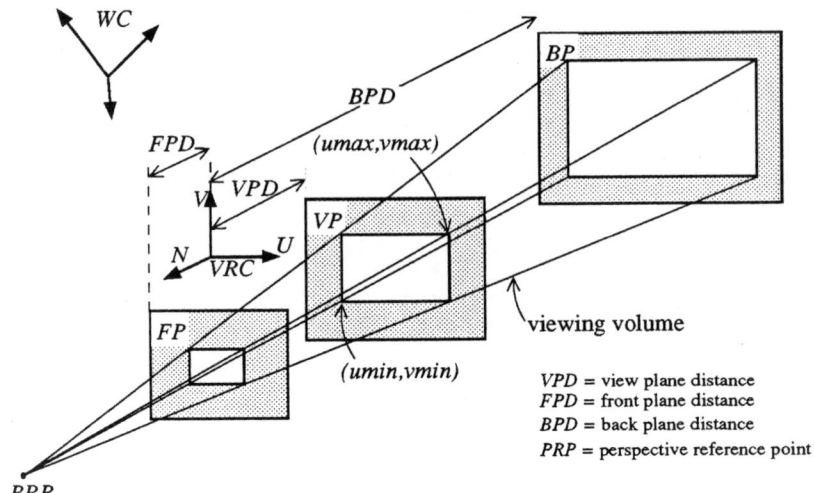

Figure 7.5 Viewing volume for a perspective projection.

mapped onto a rectangular box in *NPC*. This mapping will have to stretch objects on the front plane and squash objects on the back plane. This is exactly what we want to have happen. Objects which are closer should appear larger. This is known as perspective foreshortening. The simplest way to visualize this effect is to use projectors to see how an object is mapped onto a view plane. Figure 7.7 illustrates how the size of an object depends on its distance from the projection reference point.

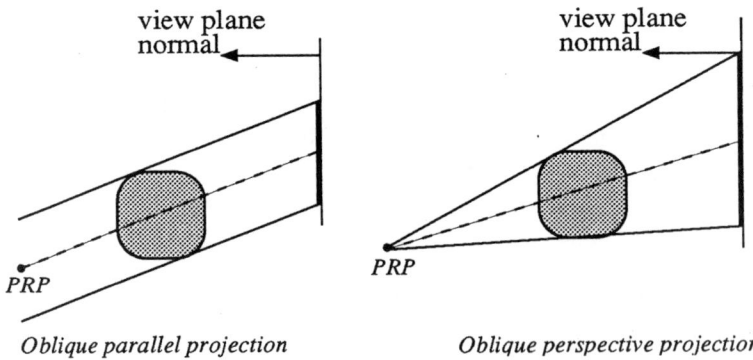

Oblique parallel projection   *Oblique perspective projection*

Figure 7.6 Oblique projections.

This viewing volume is mapped onto a rectangular box in *NPC*. This box is specified by the projection viewport limits: XMIN, XMAX, YMIN, YMAX, ZMIN, ZMAX. Since the *NPC* is normalized, all limits must be greater than or equal to 0, and less than or equal to 1.0. It should also be clear that XMAX is greater than XMIN, and YMAX is greater than YMIN. ZMAX can equal ZMIN, but only if the front, back and view planes of the viewing volume coincide. In this case only a cross-

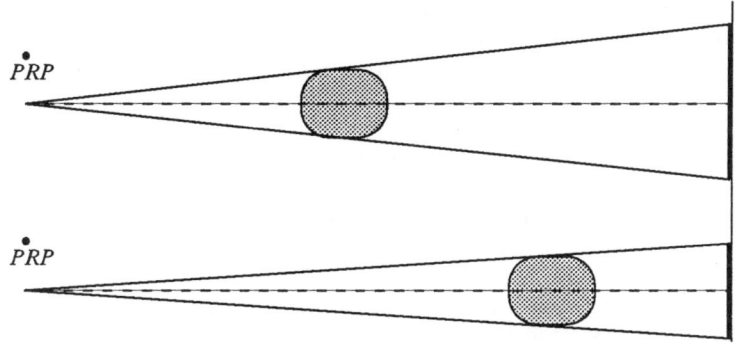

Figure 7.7 Foreshortening in a perspective projection.

section will be displayed. In actuality, a PHIGS implementation could have trouble with such a view mapping, since round-off errors could lead to gaps in drawing a cross-section.

Everything needed to define a view mapping has now been covered, so we just need to see how to use the PHIGS utility routine to create the view mapping matrix. This function is called:

EVALUATE VIEW MAPPING MATRIX 3   (PHOP,*,*,*)
Arguments:

in	window limits	UMIN,UMAX, VMIN,VMAX in VRC
in	projection viewport	XMIN,XMAX, YMIN,YMAX, ZMIN, ZMAX in NPC
in	projection type	(PARALLEL,PERSPECTIVE)
in	projection reference point	3D point in VRC.
in	view plane distance	real distance along VRC's N axis
in	back plane distance	real distance along VRC's N axis
in	front plane distance	real distance along VRC's N axis
out	error indicator	integer
out	view mapping matrix	4x4 transformation matrix

The previous discussion should have clarified the meaning of these parameters. It should be emphasized that the window limits and *PRP* are in view reference coordinates. A common mistake is to use world coordinates when defining the window limits. Remember, the mapping from *WC* to *VRC* rotates the scene and shifts the origin to the *VRP*.

Another source of error is to place the projection reference point between the front and back planes. A simple way to avoid this is to calculate the front plane to be a fixed distance in front of the *PRP* (putting the *PRP* behind the back plane is rarely done). Finally, make sure that the projection viewport limits are all in the range from 0.0 to 1.0.

In 2D the function to create the view mapping matrix is called EVALUATE VIEW MAPPING MATRIX. Two-dimensional projections are much simpler than 3D, and so is the function to create the matrix. All that is needed is to specify the window limits in *VRC* and the viewport limits in *NPC*. This mapping can be used to move a window around the 2D scene as well as to zoom in or zoom out.

7.3 Using viewing transformations

The previous sections have covered how to create the view orientation and the view mapping transformations. Now it is time to use these two transformations. This is done by defining a view in the workstation's view tables. A view in the workstation table is called a *view representation*. A workstation can contain a number of view representations. An existing view representation can be used by setting a view index in a structure. We shall start by defining a view representation.

A 3D view representation is defined in the workstation state list with the routine:

SET VIEW REPRESENTATION 3   (PHOP,WSOP,*,*)
Arguments:

in	workstation identifier	integer
in	view index	integer
in	view orientation matrix	4x4 transformation matrix
in	view mapping matrix	4x4 transformation matrix
in	view clipping limits	XMIN,XMAX, YMIN,YMAX, ZMIN,ZMAX in NPC
in	*x-y* clipping indicator	(CLIP,NOCLIP)
in	back clipping indicator	(CLIP,NOCLIP)
in	front clipping indicator	(CLIP,NOCLIP)

This defines a view representation in the specified open workstation. The view index is used to select the view, and it can be any integer greater than zero but less than or equal to the maximum number of allowable views. A workstation has finite resources, so it cannot have an arbitrary number of views. The maximum number of views a workstation can contain may be determined by calling the function INQUIRE WORKSTATION STATE TABLE LENGTHS.

The view is derived from the view orientation and the view mapping matrices. These two matrices are generated by the functions: EVALUATE VIEW ORIENTATION MAPPING MATRIX 3 and EVALUATE VIEW MAPPING MATRIX 3, which have already been covered.

The view representation also contains clipping limits and indicators. This clipping is applied in *NPC*, so the limits need to be in the range-from 0.0 to 1.0. If the indicators are set to CLIP, PHIGS will clip output primitives to lie within the corresponding limits in *NPC*. One can determine whether to clip relative to the *x-y* limits in *NPC*, ZMIN, or ZMAX, depending on whether the *x-y*, back or front clipping indicators are set to CLIP.

The 2D version of this routine is called SET VIEW REPRESENTATION, and takes similar arguments, except that the matrices are 3x3 homogeneous matrices and the clipping limits are ranges in *x* and *y*. Of course, there are no front and back clipping indicators in 2D.

In order to use a view representation once it is in the WSL one needs to set a view index in the CSS. A given structure can contain more than one view index. Actually, this is how to use multiple views of the same scene at the same time. The function to do this is:

SET VIEW INDEX   (PHOP,*,STOP,*)El
Arguments:
        in   view index   integer

This function creates a structure element to set the view index in the currently open structure. The view representation this index points to will be used to define the viewing transformations at traversal time. The view index can be an integer between zero and the maximum number of views. The view index 0 points to the default view representation which is the identity.

It is simple to use view indices to create multiple views of the same scene. If a scene is created by a structure network whose root is called SCENE, then one can create multiple views with a structure network as follows:

Root structure	0
SET VIEW INDEX(FrontViewIndex)	1
EXECUTE STRUCTURE(SCENE)	2
SET VIEW INDEX(TopViewIndex)	3
EXECUTE STRUCTURE(SCENE)	4
SET VIEW INDEX(LeftViewIndex)	5
EXECUTE STRUCTURE(SCENE)	6
SET VIEW INDEX(RightViewIndex)	7
EXECUTE STRUCTURE(SCENE)	8

Here each of the four view indices is defined to view the scene from an independent direction and project it onto a separate region of *NPC*.

7.4 Workstation transformations

The workstation transformation is the final stage of the transformation pipeline. It is simply used to position and scale the output on the workstation's physical display surface. To define the workstation transformation, a window in *NPC* and a viewport in device coordinates *DC* need to be defined.

There are certain restrictions when using workstation transformations. The window in *NPC* will be mapped onto the workstation viewport such that the aspect ratio is preserved, which means that it will scale equally in the *x* and *y* dimension. If the workstation transformation is not able to map the *NPC* window onto the entire viewport and maintain the aspect ratio, then it will be mapped onto the lower left corner of the viewport so that the aspect ratio is preserved. The remaining area in the upper right of the viewport will be left blank.

The tranformation is defined by two functions, one to set the window and one to set the viewport:

SET WORKSTATION WINDOW 3   (PHOP,WSOP,*,*)
Arguments:

in	workstation identifier	integer
in	workstation window limits	XMIN,XMAX, YMIN,YMAX, ZMIN,ZMAX in NPC

SET WORKSTATION VIEWPORT 3   (PHOP,WSOP,*,*)
Arguments:

in	workstation identifier	integer
in	workstation viewport limits	XMIN,XMAX, YMIN,YMAX, ZMIN,ZMAX in DC

The 2D versions of these functions are SET WORKSTATION WINDOW and SET WORKSTATION VIEWPORT.

7.5 A viewing example

The viewing pipeline is rather complicated, so an example of how to use it should help get the PHIGS programmer started. In the following example we will turn the viewing mechanism around and define a subroutine which is viewer-based. PHIGS provides a more general viewing model, but it can be complicated to use correctly. It is based on a simplistic camera model and is given the following arguments.

wsid	- workstation identifier.
view index	- view index to use.
viewer	- position of the viewer in *WC*.
viewee	- position of the object being viewed in *WC*.

vup	- vector identifying vertical axis of scene.
aperture	- the angle of the view aperture in degrees.
depthrat	- ratio of the distance between the front and view plane to the distance between the viewer and the view plane.

Several assumptions are being made by this subroutine. First of all the viewing transformation is not oblique and will use perspective. The view reference point is equal to the point being viewed and is in the centre of the viewing window in *VRC*. Also the view reference point is on the view plane which lies equidistant between the front and back planes. Figure 7.8 illustrates how the variables used in the subroutine correspond to the viewing volume.

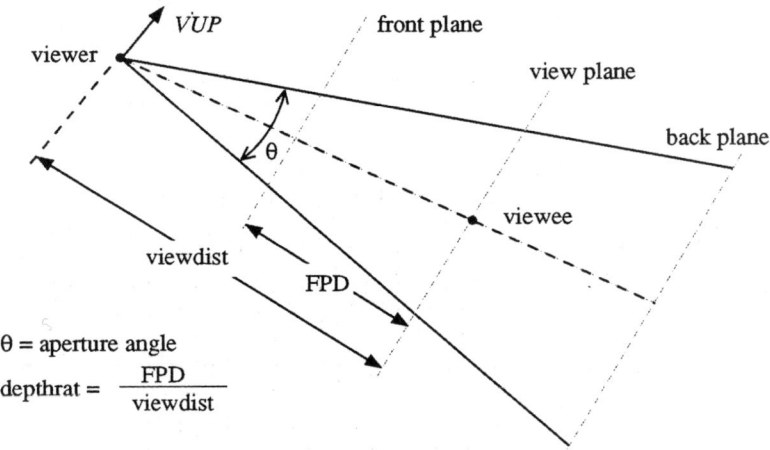

Figure 7.8 Viewing volume for example subroutine.

The following is example code in C used to create a view representation based on the input arguments. It is not tuned for efficiency, since it is meant to illustrate how to use the viewing transformations:

```
#define DEGRAD (3.141592654/180.0)


Pint
set_camera_view( Pint wsid, Pint ViewIndex,
          Ppoint3 viewer,
          Ppoint3 viewee,
          Pvec3   *vup,
          float aperture, float depthrat )
{
```

```
Pint err;
float width, viewdist;
Ppoint3 vrp;
Pvec3 vpn;
Pview_map3 vmap;
Pview_rep3 vrep;
static Plimit3 allnpc = { 0.0, 1.0, 0.0,1.0, 0.0,1.0 };

/* Initialize and check arguments*/
/*===============================*/
err = 0;
if( depthrat <= 0.0 || depthrat >= 1.0 ) return( -1 );
if( aperture <= 0.0 || aperture >= 90.0 ) return(-2);
vrp = viewee;

/* Calculate distance between viewer and viewee */
/*==============================================*/
viewdist = sqrt( (viewer.x-vrp.x)*(viewer.x-vrp.x)
         +      (viewer.y-vrp.y)*(viewer.y-vrp.y)
         +      (viewer.z-vrp.z)*(viewer.z-vrp.z) );

/************************************/
/* Create the view orientation matrix */
/************************************/

/* Now get the VPN as vector from viewee to viewer */
/*=================================================*/
vpn.delta_x = (viewer.x-vrp.x) / viewdist;
vpn.delta_y = (viewer.y-vrp.y) / viewdist;
vpn.delta_z = (viewer.z-vrp.z) / viewdist;

peval_view_ori_matrix3( &vrp, &vpn, vup, &err,
                        vrep.ori_matrix);
if( err != 0 ) return( err );

/**********************************/
/* Create the view mapping matrix */
/**********************************/

/* First derive the window from the aperture angle */
/*=================================================*/
width = viewdist*sin( DEGRAD*aperture );
vmap.win.x_min = -width/2.0;
vmap.win.x_max = width/2.0;
vmap.win.y_min = -width/2.0;
vmap.win.y_max = width/2.0;
```

```
/* Define the prp and use the whole NPC viewport */
/*================================================*/
vmap.proj_ref_point.x = 0.0;
vmap.proj_ref_point.y = 0.0;
vmap.proj_ref_point.z = viewdist;
vmap.proj_vp          = allnpc;
vmap.proj_type        = PTYPE_PERSPECT;

/* Now the viewing reference planes */
/*==================================*/
vmap.view_plane = 0.0;
vmap.front_plane = depthrat*viewdist;
vmap.back_plane = -vmap.front_plane;

peval_view_map_matrix3( &vmap, &err,
                        vrep.map_matrix);
if( err != 0 ) return( err );

/* We have our matrices, now use them */
/*====================================*/
vrep.xy_clip    = PIND_CLIP;
vrep.back_clip  = PIND_CLIP;
vrep.front_clip = PIND_CLIP;
vrep.clip_limit = allnpc;
pset_view_rep3( wsid, ViewIndex, &vrep);

return( 0 );
}
```

This subroutine returns zero if the view representation is set successfully, otherwise it returns an error indicator. Two error flags have been defined in this routine:

-1   The ratio of the front plane distance to the viewing distance is invalid. This ratio must be between 0 and 1.0, otherwise either the *PRP* will lie in the viewing volume, or the front plane will be equal to or behind the view plane.

-2   The aperture angle is not between 0 and 90 degrees, which would create an invalid window in *VRC* (see Figure 7.8).

Other possible error flags which can be returned are generated by PHIGS in the routines EVALUATE VIEW ORIENTATION MATRIX 3 and EVALUATE VIEW MAPPING MATRIX 3. They could arise, for example, if the viewer position is equal to the the viewee's or if the view up vector is parallel to the *VPN*.

The routine starts off with some basic argument checking and initializes internal variables. The viewee is set to be the view reference point. It then calculates the distance between the viewer and the *VRP*, which is needed to define the *PRP*, the window limits, and view plane distances. The *VPN* can be simply derived as the the vector difference between the viewer and the *VRP*. The user of this routine still needs to specify the view up vector, since there is no way to derive what is needed. One only has to make sure that the *VUP* vector is not parallel to the *VPN*. At this stage the view orientation matrix can be evaluated.

The next stage determines the arguments needed by the view mapping matrix. First of all the window limits are calculated from the viewer's distance and the aperture angle (see Figure 7.8). Then the *PRP* is set. Remember the *PRP* is defined in *VRC*, so the point being viewed is at the origin. Also, the viewer's position is on the *N*-axis because the window is centred on the origin, so the transformation is not oblique. The front plane distance is the depth-ratio times the viewer's distance. The entire *NPC* is used in this example, so the viewport and view clipping limits are hardwired into the code. Now the view mapping matrix can be evaluated and the view representation set.

This example subroutine does not meet the requirements for all viewing applications but is simpler to use and understand. It also illustrates that other viewing models can be based on the PHIGS model.

CHAPTER 8

Using PHIGS Input

PHIGS is an interactive graphics system, so it must support a mechanism to accept input from the user. PHIGS workstations were covered in Chapter 3, but only features relating to graphical output were treated. Now we shall focus on workstations belonging to the categories IN and OUTIN. Workstations belonging to these categories are able to accept input from the user through the PHIGS input model. This model is based on input devices, which provide a device independent programming interface to accept interaction from the user. The input model used in PHIGS has been derived from GKS (Graphical Kernel System), with which some readers may be familiar.

The most common workstation belonging to the category OUTIN is a physical workstation with a screen, keyboard and mouse. Many suppliers offer additional physical input devices, such as dials or button boxes. They are discussed later in this chapter. The PHIGS input device model is a set of subroutines which present a logical interface to a broad range of physical devices. Since there are a number of different types of data that a user could input, the PHIGS model supports six different classes of input devices: choice, locator, string, stroke, valuator and pick.

In addition to supporting different classes of input devices, there are a number of ways a user might want to use an input device. The different ways to interact with an input device are addressed by using a device in one of three different operating modes: sample, request or event.

Getting input with PHIGS can be broken down into three parts: initializing the input device, setting it in the correct operating mode, and finally using the device to get input. PHIGS provides subroutines to realize each of these three parts. Before we look at the functions PHIGS provides to use these devices, let us see what types of input device are being considered.

8.1 PHIGS input device classes

Different types of input device are represented in PHIGS by a logical device belonging to one of six different classes: *choice, locator, string, stroke, valuator* and *pick*. Although a range of physical devices can belong to a given class, each class is used to accept a specific type of data. The following list summarizes the data each class provides and identifies physical devices that could belong to each class:

CHOICE   This device returns an integer which represents a choice from one or more alternatives. This device could be function keys on the keyboard, a menu bar containing several options, an on-screen pushbutton or a button box.

LOCATOR   A locator provides the program with a point in world coordinates, and a view index identifying which view transformation was used to get from DC to WC. Examples of locator devices are arrow keys on a keyboard, mice, trackballs or digitizers. PHIGS defines both 2D and 3D locator devices. Since mice are intrinsically 2D devices, most suppliers only provide a 2D locator position and return a constant z coordinate. There are, however, PHIGS implementations available which do provide a true 3D locator using a z-buffered cursor. In this case the x-y position is updated with the mouse as usual, and the z coordinate is modified by moving the mouse with a mouse button depressed.

STRING   As its name implies, this device returns a character string. It is usually associated with the keyboard attached to the physical workstation.

STROKE   A stroke device returns a sequence of points in WC and a view index. It is generally used to accept a free-hand drawing. Stroke devices are similar to locators which are optimized to accept many points. This device is often a mouse, or a digitizer with a stylus for drawing.

VALUATOR   This device returns a real number which lies within a given range. This number can come from a slider bar or dial mapped on the workstation screen, or from a physical device such as a dial box, or a torque ball.

PICK   The pick device is used to identify an output primitive in the CSS which corresponds to part of the displayed picture. Since a structure network is hierarchical, this device returns a *pick path*, which identifies not only which primitive drew at the selected point, but an entire tree of structure identifiers, pick identifiers, and element positions. This tree uniquely identifies which instance of the structure drew at the selected position. A pick device is generally mapped to a locator type device such as a mouse or digitizer. Since pick devices are more involved to use than the other five, they are covered in detail in the next chapter.

The input device class can be any one of the following six: CHOICE, LOCATOR, STRING, STROKE, VALUATOR and PICK. Since the LOCATOR and STROKE return position data in *WC*, these devices have both 2D and 3D varieties. When it does not matter which device class is meant, we shall use <input class>.

PHIGS has standardized the classes of input devices, their operating modes and the programming interface to use them. The range of physical input devices is broad. The physical devices which actually correspond to the PHIGS devices depend on the implementation and the workstation type. A particular input device is identified by the workstation identifier, a device number and a prompt and echo type, PET. The *device number* is used to distinguish between different devices belonging to the same class. The prompt and echo type determines how the device is to interact with the user; it is covered in the next section.

8.2 The PHIGS input model and PET

The PHIGS input model is based on an abstraction of a physical input device. This model determines what properties input devices of all classes have in common. The measure and trigger processes are the basis of this model. This section discusses the model without going into detail on any particular device.

Every active input device has a current value. This value is known as the input device's *measure*. A device's measure has a default that can be initialized by the program. As the device is being used, its measure is being updated by the measure process. When the input data are validated, the measure is returned to the program as the input data.

Input devices often need to make it known that input is expected. This is done with a *prompt,* for example, a crosshair on the screen shows the position of a mouse. The prompt is output once the measure process comes into existence.

Each input device has a *trigger* which may be used to let the system know the input data are valid. An example of a trigger could be hitting RETURN when entering a string, or pressing a mouse button. Triggers are only used in the operating modes: request and event. In addition to a trigger, one needs a *break* function, which allows one to cancel the input process. This is useful if one started an input process by mistake. For example, if one accidentally chose to pick an object on the screen. The trigger and break action will depend on the PHIGS implementation and the particular device being used. One should consult the supplier's documentation for specifics.

Once the measure process has been initiated it is often necessary to give the user feedback while the input is ongoing. This is provided by the *echo*. A given class of input device might support different ways to give the user feedback. For example, a locator device could provide feedback by displaying a crosshair, a cursor, a digital display of the locator's position or a rubber line between an initial position and the current position.

The *prompt and echo type*, PET determines how the input device appears to the user. The actual PETs available for a certain device class depends on the PHIGS implementation. Since data are often required to define a PET, the device needs to be initialized with a data record specific to a given PET. For example, a menu choice device would need to be initialized with a data record containing the choice strings. The structure of the data record is different for each PET. A PET is selected with an integer when the device is initialized. Positive PETs are registered, whereas negative PETs are implementation specific.

In addition to the prompt and echo type, an *echo area* needs to be specified. This determines where in device coordinates the input device will prompt the user. This is used, for example, to position choice menus. In 3D an *echo volume* in *DC* is used, but the *z* dimension of the echo volume is rarely used.

The concepts introduced here are referred to throughout the rest of this chapter. The next section on operating modes shows how these components are related.

8.3 Operating modes of input devices

In the PHIGS input model there are three operating modes which determine how to get input from the device. There is a function to set the operating mode for each device. Each operating mode has a particular set of functions to accept input. In summary, the operating mode can be any one of the three.

REQUEST When input is requested from a device, the program will block until either the user triggers that valid data are ready or issues a break. This is the default operating mode.

SAMPLE When a device is sampled, the measure of the device is immediately returned. Sampling does not block the program.

EVENT A device in this mode puts its input events on a queue. Using a device in event mode occurs in two stages:

awaiting the event and removing an event from the queue. There are additional functions to manipulate the queue.

Before one can use a device in a given operating mode, it needs to be set to that mode. This is done with the functions:

SET <device class> MODE   (PHOP,WSOP,*,*)
Arguments:

in	workstation identifier	integer
in	device number	integer
in	operating mode	(REQUEST,SAMPLE,EVENT)
in	echo switch	(ECHO,NOECHO)

There are six different functions to set the operating mode, one for each device class: CHOICE, LOCATOR, STRING, STROKE, VALUATOR and PICK. The default operating mode is REQUEST, so this function must be called before using a device in any other mode.

The particular device is identified by the workstation identifier and the device number. The third parameter specifies which of the three operating modes to put the device in. The last parameter is a flag which determines whether the measure process should provide an echo or not. Usually an echo is desired, but at times one would like to suppress the echo. For example, an echo may not be required when using dials as a valuator device.

An example of using this function for a particular device is:

```
#define WSID     1
#define MainMenu 1

pset_choice_mode(WSID,MainMenu,POP_EVENT,PSWITCH_ECHO);
```

This sets the operating mode for the choice device `MainMenu` to EVENT. Echoing is enabled on this device. One needs to define how this device appears by initializing it. Once in event mode the input queue can be used to accept choice events from the `MainMenu`.

The next three sections cover the three operating modes in detail in a device independent manner. Each operating mode behaves the same, regardless of the device class or device number. The device class determines only what type of data is returned. The device number identifies how the device appears and its initial value. The sections on the device classes go into detail on the format of the input data returned.

8.3.1 Request mode

When in request mode, the application can get data from the user by making a request as follows:

REQUEST <input class> (WSID, DeviceNumber, Status, Data, ...)

There is a function for each input class to request input. When data are requested from an input device, the program stops executing and waits until the user provides input. This is similar to the FORTRAN function READ(...) or the C function scanf(...). An error will be generated under certain conditions. For example, if data are requested from a device that does not exist or it is not in request mode.

Once a call to this function has been made, the measure process is started, which prompts the user for input. While the measure process is active, the device state will be echoed, if echoing was enabled for the device. Figure 8.1 shows the flow diagram for a device in request mode.

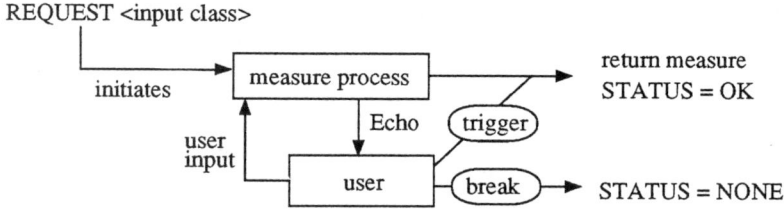

Figure 8.1 Request mode input.

There are two ways to return to the application once a request has been made. The user can either use the trigger to say the input data are valid, or a break to cancel the request. The status field will indicate whether the data was validated with a trigger or if the break was issued. A simple example of using the request mode is:

```
REQUEST CHOICE( WSID, MainMenu, Status, Choice )
```

This function will cause the MainMenu to appear on the screen, and will block until the user provides input. The Status field will indicate whether the input data are valid, and if so, the Choice field will contain the input data.

8.3.2 Sample mode

When a device is placed in sample mode, the measure process is started. This leads to the user being prompted as soon as the device is put into sample mode. This differs from request mode, where the prompt appears only after data were requested from it. This makes sense, since in request mode the application only wants input when it explicity asks for it.

Once in sample mode, the measure process is continually getting the state of the device. Only when the device is sampled will the application actually be aware of its state. There is neither a trigger nor a break in sample mode, so no confirmation from the user is needed. Figure 8.2 shows a diagram of a device in sample mode.

SAMPLE <input class>

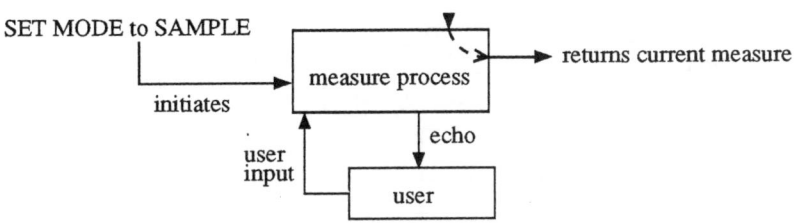

Figure 8.2 Sample mode input.

A device is sampled with a function with the following format:

SAMPLE <input class> (WSID, DeviceNumber, Data, ...)

The workstation identifier and the device number identify which device is being sampled. Sampling returns the current state of the device in the last parameters. Obviously, the device must be in sample mode otherwise an error will be generated. An example of using a particular device in sample mode is (see Section 8.5 for datails on locator devices):

SAMPLE LOCATOR(WSID, MOUSE, ViewIndex, Position)

A call to this function will immediately return a view index and a position in *WC* for the locator device MOUSE.

8.3.3 Event mode

Devices in event mode use a central queue to store all input events. Once a device is placed in event mode, the measure process and the trigger process are started. The user can manipulate the input device, and feedback is given if echoing is enabled. When the state of a device is valid, the user can trigger the device to place an input event on the queue.

Using devices in event mode consists of two stages: waiting for an

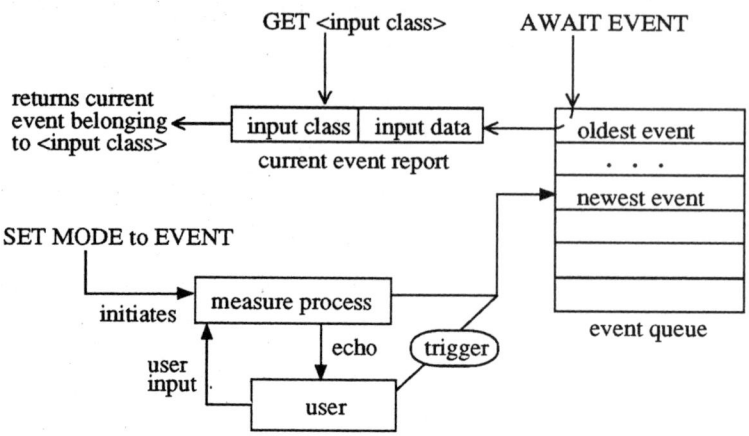

Figure 8.3 Event mode input.

event to be queued, and getting the current event. Figure 8.3 illustrates the structure of an event mode device.

While a device is in event mode, its measure process updates the input queue once the user triggers that the input data are valid. The input queue stores all events in the order that they arrived (see Figure 8.3).

The first stage in getting data out of the input queue is to wait for an event. This is done with the function:

AWAIT EVENT   (PHOP,WSOP,*,*)
Arguments:

in	timeout in seconds	non-negative real number
out	workstation identifier	integer
out	input class	(NONE,LOCATOR,STROKE,PICK, VALUATOR,CHOICE,STRING)
out	input device number	integer

This function looks at the input queue to see if there are any events. If the queue is empty, this routine will wait for *timeout* seconds. If the queue is still empty after the timeout, then the function returns with the input class set to NONE. If the queue is not empty before the timeout elapses, then this function returns the workstation identifier, input class, and device number of the oldest event in the queue. Giving AWAIT EVENT a timeout of zero will result in sampling the input queue, otherwise the function will block for the specified period of time. The corresponding event report containing the device data is removed from the input queue and placed in the PHIGS state list, where it can be retrieved.

The function AWAIT EVENT indicates that the input queue contained a valid event by returning an input class other than NONE. Now the actual device data can be retrieved by calling a function for the appropriate input class:

142

GET <input class>   (PHOP,WSOP,*,*)
Arguments:
       out device data   depends on input class

There is a separate function for each input class to get the event data. The actual data returned depend on the input class of the device. For details, see the section on the appropriate device.

The input class of the GET function must match the input class returned by AWAIT EVENT, otherwise an error will be generated. An event mode input loop will generally be headed by a call to AWAIT EVENT, and the branch on the input class to retrieve the actual data. Section 8.5 contains an example event mode loop.

The last two functions in this section are used for maintaining the input queue. The first function is used to flush events from the input queue belonging to a particular device:

FLUSH DEVICE EVENTS   (PHOP,WSOP,*,*)
Arguments:

in	workstation identifier	integer
in	input class	(NONE,LOCATOR,STROKE,PICK, VALUATOR,CHOICE,STRING)
in	input device number	integer

This function is provided with parameters to identify the input device whose events are to be flushed from the input queue. This can be useful if one needs to backtrack and remove all user input for a particular device, or if the input queue has overflowed.

All PHIGS implementations have finite resources, so it is possible that the input queue overflows. PHIGS keeps track of an overflow situation, and the program can determine which device caused the overflow with the function:

INQUIRE INPUT QUEUE OVERFLOW   (PHOP,WSOP,*,*)
Arguments:

out	error indicator	integer
out	workstation identifier	integer
out	input class	(NONE,LOCATOR,STROKE,PICK, VALUATOR,CHOICE,STRING)
out	input device number	integer

This function returns an error indicator that is set to zero if an overflow condition has occurred. If an overflow occurred, the remaining arguments identify which device caused the overflow.

It is important to note that if an overflow has occurred then no more events will be added to the input queue until it has been completely emptied. This can be done by calling FLUSH DEVICE EVENTS for each device which is in event mode.

8.4 PHIGS input devices

Each device has its own initialization routine. A device must be in request mode when it is initialized. All initialization routines have features in common, so these properties are covered here in a device independent manner. In general, the initialization routine has the following format:

INITIALIZE <device class>   (PHOP,WSOP,*,*)
Arguments:

in	workstation identifier	integer
in	device number	integer
in	<initial device value>	device dependent
in	prompt and echo type	integer
in	echo volume	XMIN,XMAX, YMIN,YMAX, ZMIN,ZMAX
in	device data record	PET specific data record

This function initializes the device belonging to the workstation identifier. The device can be one of: CHOICE, LOCATOR, PICK, STRING, STROKE or VALUATOR. There are both 2D and 3D initialization routines for each device class, whereby the 3D version will have a 3 appended to the function name. The actual device will be referred to by its device number. The PHIGS supplier will document which device numbers are available for each workstation type. This function also sets the *initial device value* of the device. The initial value depends on the device and can consist of more than one argument. Sections 8.4.1 through 8.4.5 provide details on how to initialize a device of a particular class.

The *prompt and echo type,* PET determines how the device appears to the user and how input is echoed when the device is being used. Each PET has its own *data record.* This data record will contain both device specific data and PET specific data. Your PHIGS supplier should document what PETs are available for each device and the structure of its data record.

The echo volume identifies a region in *DC* where the device will be displayed. This is used to position a device, such as a choice menu, on the screen. The 2D device will be initialized with an echo area instead of an echo volume.

8.4.1 Locator and stroke input

The locator and stroke devices are covered in the same section, because they share many similar properties. The locator returns a view index and a position in world coordinates, whereas the stroke returns a view index and a sequence of points in *WC.*

Both the locator and the stroke are generally mapped onto a pointing device such as a mouse or a digitizer, but they could also be realized with arrow keys. The trigger to indicate valid locator input data is usually pressing a mouse button, or pressing RETURN if the locator is mapped onto the arrow keys. The stroke is often realized by pressing a mouse button to initiate drawing the stroke, holding down the button and drawing the stroke, and finally releasing the mouse button to trigger that the stroke has been completed.

These devices need to return a view index, because the pointing device can only input positions on the screen, in other words in device coordinates. The view index identifies what inverse viewing transform was used to get from *DC* to *WC*. This shows that the viewing transforms must have an inverse. If the PHIGS utility functions were used to create the viewing transforms, then they will be invertible. Later in this section we will discuss the function SET VIEW TRANSFORMATION INPUT PRIORITY which addresses how to select which transformation is used to map from *DC* to *WC*.

There are both 2D and 3D locator and stroke devices. The 2D version uses a 2D *WC*, and the 3D version uses the 3D *WC*. Here only the 3D version is explicitly dealt with.

The locator is often used with default device data, but it can be initialized with the function:

INITIALIZE LOCATOR 3   (PHOP,WSOP,*,*)
Arguments:

in	workstation identifier	integer
in	locator device number	integer
in	initial view index	integer
in	initial locator position point in *WC*	
in	prompt and echo type	integer
in	echo volume	XMIN,XMAX, YMIN,YMAX, ZMIN,ZMAX
in	locator data record	PET specific data record

When the locator is initialized a PET is specified which determines how the locator appears. The following PETs have been registered:

1. Current locator position is indicated in a device dependent manner.
2. Crosshair. A vertical and a horizontal line spanning the display surface.
3. A tracking cross.
4. Rubber band line. Use a line connecting the current locator position to the initial position.
5. Rubber band box. Draw a rectangle where the current locator position and the initial position are diagonally opposite.
6. Digital. Displays a digital representation of the locator position within the echo volume.

Not all of these PETs may be supported on a given PHIGS implementation. Some PETs require additional data, for example, it may be possible to specify the attributes of the rubber band line. These data will be provided in the locator data record.

The stroke device delivers a list of points in *WC* and the corresponding view index. The sequence of points is called a stroke, and could result from the user drawing a curve. The stroke device is initialized with the function:

INITIALIZE STROKE 3   (PHOP,WSOP,*,*)
Arguments:

in	workstation identifier	integer
in	stroke device number	integer
in	initial view index	integer
in	coordinates of initial stroke	list of points in *WC*
in	prompt and echo type	integer
in	echo volume	XMIN,XMAX, YMIN,YMAX, ZMIN,ZMAX
in	stroke data record	PET specific data record

When the stroke is initialized a PET is specified which determines how the device appears. The following PETs have been registered:

1. Current stroke is indicated in a device dependent manner.
2. Display a digital representation of the latest stroke position.
3. Display a marker at each point in the stroke.
4. Join successive points in a stroke with a line.

The stroke data record will contain PET specific data. For example, if markers are used to indicate stroke positions, the data record could contain the marker attributes.

The data record might also contain data that is relevant for all PETs. For example, one can specify the size of the stroke buffer, the initial editing position, a offset threshold in *WC* and a time interval. The buffer size is the maximum number of points that the application can accept from the stroke. The editing position identifies a point in the list of *WC* points of the initial stroke. The new stroke is appended to the initial stroke following this point. The offset threshold will determine how close adjacent points in a stroke can be. Another way to specify how to get points in the stroke is with the time interval. This determines how fast the pointing device should be sampled to get points in the stroke. One needs to consult the supplier's documentation to see what PET's have been implemented and the structure of the stroke data records.

Now that these two devices have been initialized, they can be used in any one of the three operating modes. In request mode the following functions are used:

REQUEST LOCATOR 3   (PHOP,WSOP,*,*)
Arguments:

in	workstation identifier	integer
in	locator device number	integer

out	status	(OK,NONE)
out	view index	integer
out	locator position	point in *WC*

REQUEST STROKE 3   (PHOP,WSOP,*,*)
Arguments:

in	workstation identifier	integer
in	stroke device number	integer
out	status	(OK,NONE)
out	view index	integer
out	coordinates of stroke	list of points in *WC*

These two functions will block until the user has either triggered a valid input or has entered a break. A status of NONE is returned if the break was entered. These devices can be sampled with:

SAMPLE LOCATOR 3   (PHOP,WSOP,*,*)
Arguments:

in	workstation identifier	integer
in	locator device number	integer
out	view index	integer
out	locator position	point in *WC*

SAMPLE STROKE 3   (PHOP,WSOP,*,*)
Arguments:

in	workstation identifier	integer
in	stroke device number	integer
out	view index	integer
out	coordinates of stroke	list of points in *WC*

If the function AWAIT EVENT indicated that the event was from a locator or a stroke device, then one of the following functions should be called to get the actual data:

GET LOCATOR 3   (PHOP,WSOP,*,*)
Arguments:

out	status	(OK,NOCHOICE)
out	locator position	point in *WC*

GET STROKE 3   (PHOP,WSOP,*,*)
Arguments:

out	view index	integer
out	coordinates of stroke	list of points in *WC*

The actual device which generated this event was returned by the function AWAIT EVENT.

8.4.2 The view input transformation priority

Both locator and stroke devices return a view index which specifies which transformation was used to get from *DC* to *WC*. Since a workstation can have only one workstation transformation at a time, one needs to identify which inverse viewing transformation to use to get from *NPC* to *WC*. This inverse mapping happens internally to PHIGS.

An application can define a number of views which map onto overlapping parts of *NPC*. PHIGS has a default view which covers the entire *NPC* and has the index 0. View 0 is the identity transformation and cannot be changed by the program. Any user-defined view will map onto a region which is contained in the *NPC* clipping limits of view 0. A view priority is used to determine which view to use to map from *NPC* to *WC*. View 0 has the highest priority, but this can be changed with the function:

SET VIEW TRANSFORMATION INPUT PRIORITY   (PHOP,WSOP,*,*)
Arguments:

in	workstation identifier	integer
in	view index	integer
in	reference view index	integer
in	relative priority	(HIGHER,LOWER)

This will establish the relative priority between two view indices on a given workstation. The priority of the *view index* will be set relative to the *reference view index*. Even in the case of only one user-defined view, this function will have to be called. Otherwise locator and stroke data will be normalized, since view 0 is the identity and has top priority. For example, to use view 1 for the input transformation one would have to use the call:

SET VIEW TRANSFORMATION INPUT PRIORITY(WSID, 1, 0, HIGHER)

View transformation input priorities
View 1 highest
View 2 middle
View 0 lowest

View transformation used
Stroke 0 in view 0
· Stroke 1 in view 1
Stroke 2 in view 0

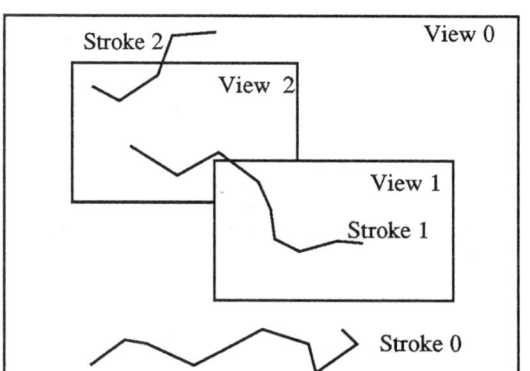

Figure 8.4 Using locator and stroke with multiple views.

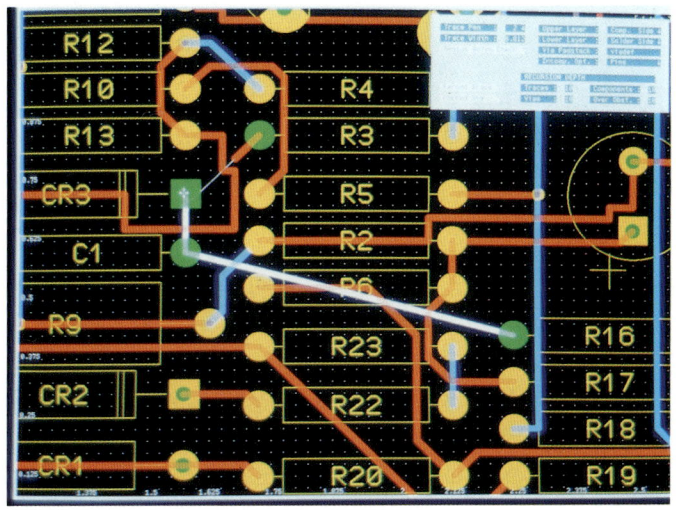

Colour Plate 1 Two dimensional image rendered with text, polylines and area filling primitives (image courtesy of Prime Computer GmbH).

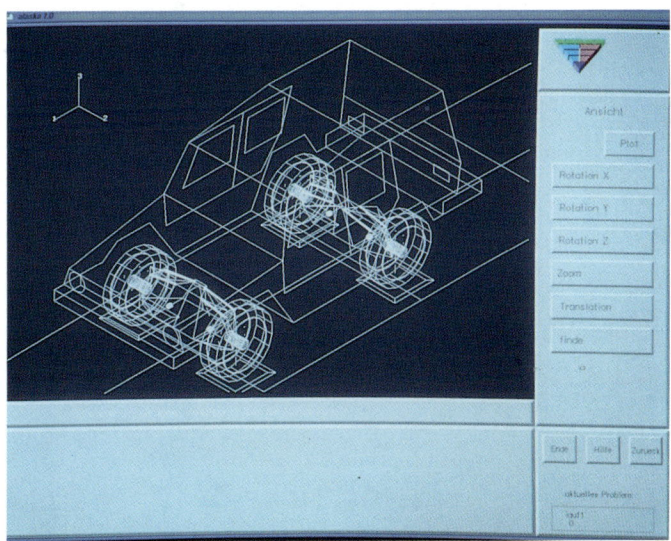

Colour Plate 2 3D wireframe rendering of an automobile (image courtesy of VW-Gedas GmbH).

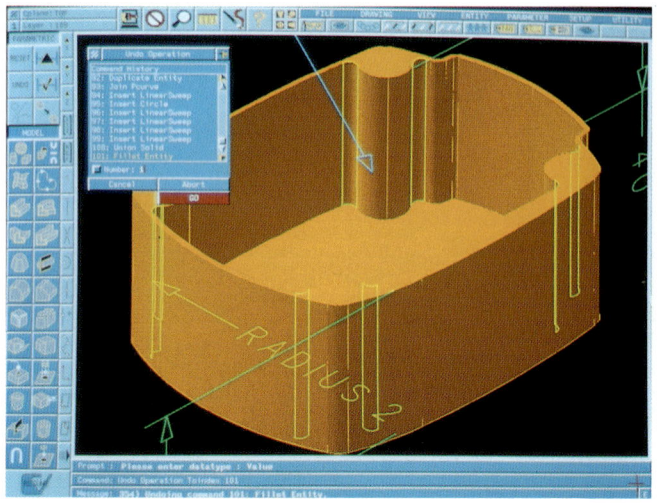

Colour Plate 3 Image rendered using 3D text, polyline and area-filling primitives (image courtesty of Prime Computer GmbH).

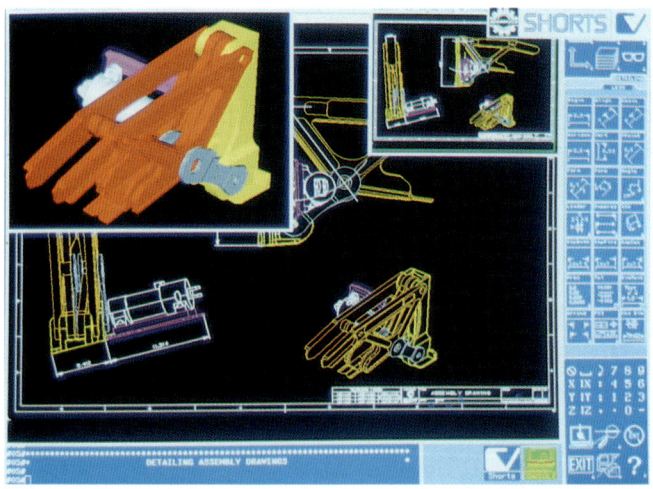

Colour Plate 4 Assembly drawn using several different viewing transformations and rendered both as a wireframe and as a shaded solid (image courtesy of Prime Computer GmbH).

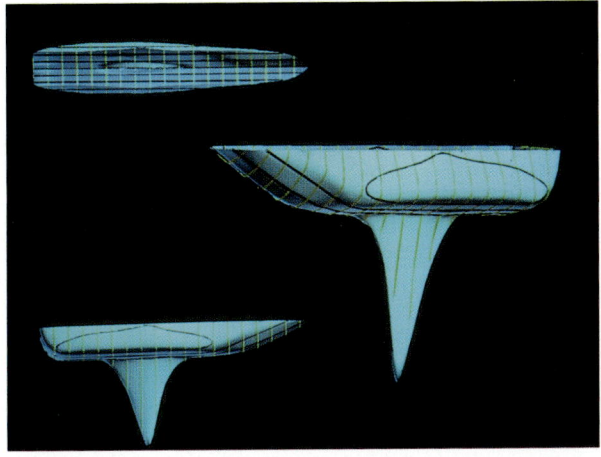

Colour Plate 5 Gouraud shaded image of a yacht's hull (image courtesy of Uniras A/S).

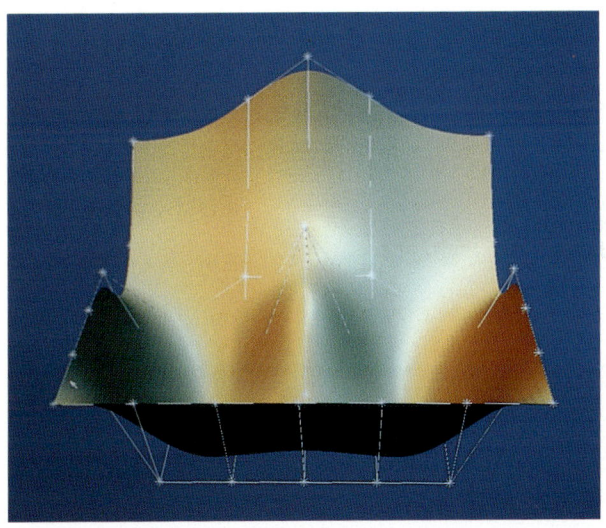

Colour Plate 6 Non-uniform rational B-spline surface and its control point mesh. All homogeneous coordinates are one. Surface illuminated by two light sources.

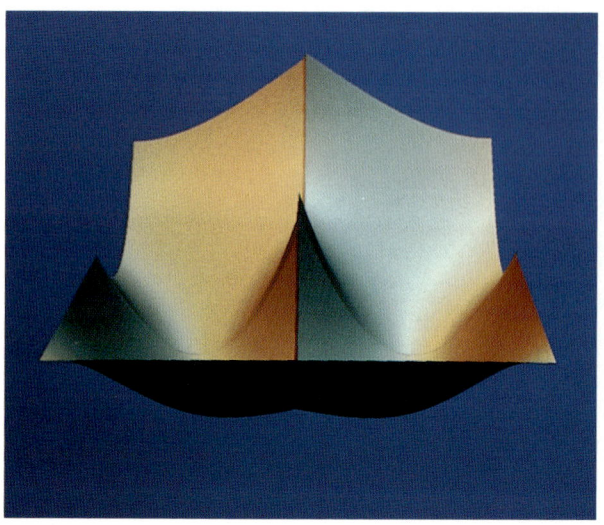

Colour Plate 7 Same surface as in Plate 6, but with a triple knot at its central control point.

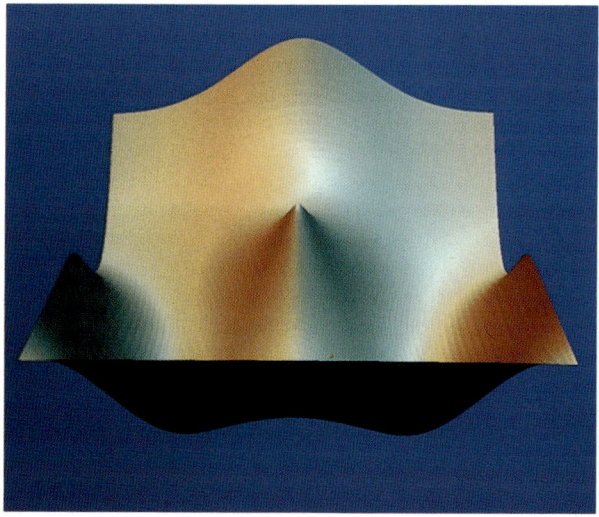

Colour Plate 8 Same surface as in Plate 6, but with the central control point weighted by a homogeneous coordinate of 10.

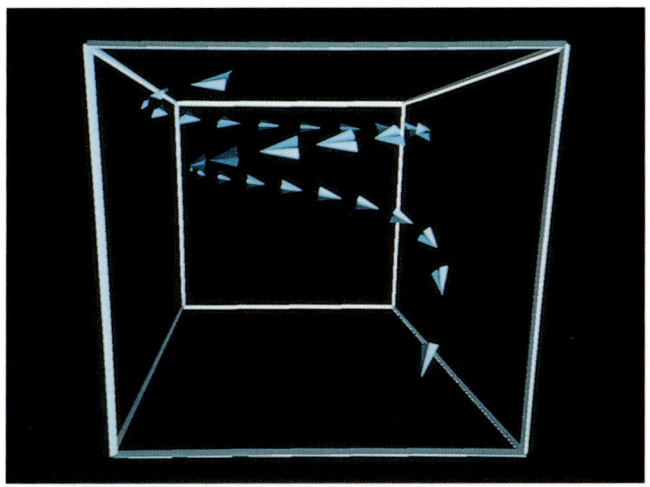

Colour Plate 9   Animation simulated by multiple structure references and modelling transformations (image courtesy of Uniras A/S).

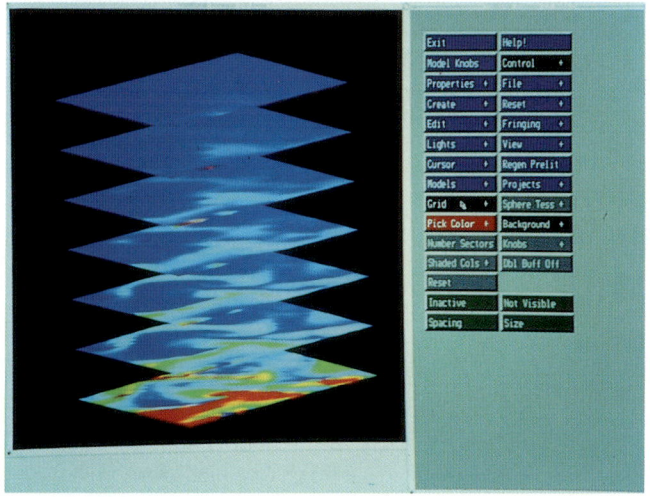

Colour Plate 10   Atmospheric humidity field rendered as a 'with data' primitive containing colour data at the vertices (image courtesy of Uniras A/S).

Colour Plate 11 Glass defined as a NURB surface with its control point mesh.

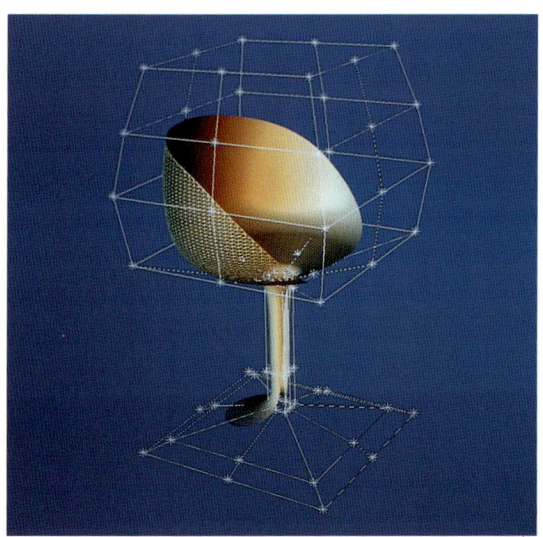

Colour Plate 12 Same glass as in Plate 11, but using the NURB surface primitive and one trimming curve loop. Front facing facets are rendered using the interior style HOLLOW.

Colour Plate 13 Torus defined as a quadrilateral mesh and rendered using flat shading and two light sources.

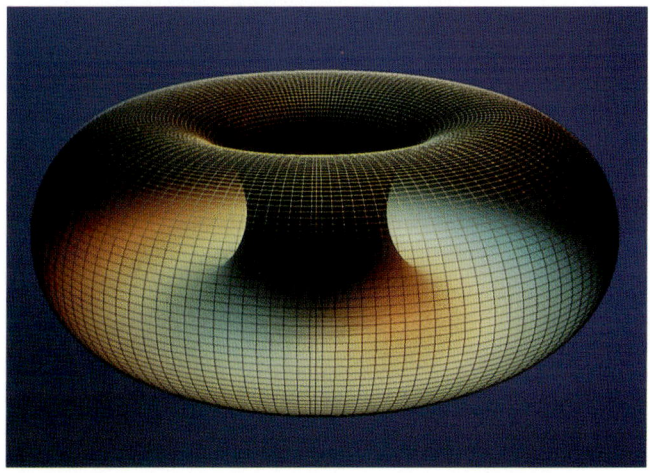

Colour Plate 14 Same torus as in Plate 13, but with front facing facets rendered using the interior style HOLLOW.

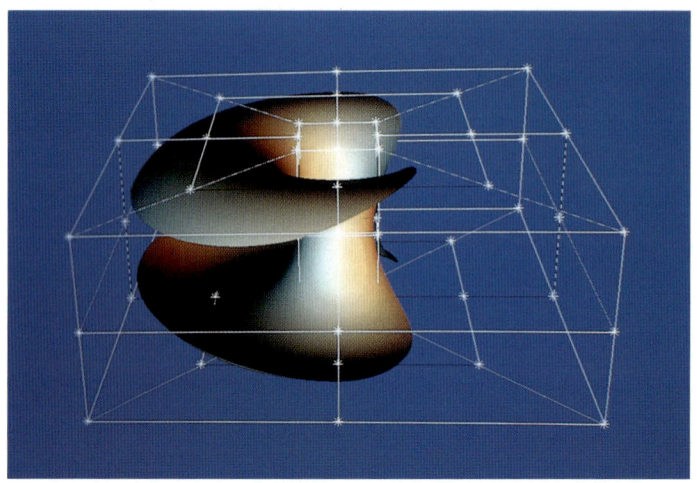

Colour Plate 15 Torus defined as a NURB surface and its control point mesh. Surface rendered with one trimming curve loop.

Colour Plate 16 Glass rendered using specular, diffuse and ambient lighting. Shadow casting rendered using Blinn's algorithm (image courtesy of Wise Software GmbH).

Before a view index is selected for the inverse transformation, locator and stroke devices initially have their coordinate mapped to *NPC*. A locator device will return the view index of the highest priority transformation containing the locator's *NPC* position within its clipping limits. A stroke device will return the view index of the highest priority transformation which contains the entire stroke in *NPC* within its clipping limits (see Figure 8.4).

8.4.3 Choice device input

A choice device presents the user with a number of alternatives that can be selected. It returns an integer that identifies which option was selected. It can be realized in a number of ways: a pushbutton, a vertical menu, a horizontal menu, the function keys or a physical button box. For example, if the choice device were a menu with six options, the device would return a number between one and six identifying which option was selected. The types of choice device that are available and their PETs is documented by your PHIGS supplier.

Although each choice device has default data, one will usually wish to initialize it. For example, one will want to define the strings used in a choice menu. It is initialized with the function:

INITIALIZE CHOICE 3   (PHOP,WSOP,*,*)
Arguments:

in	workstation identifier	integer
in	choice device number	integer
in	initial status	(OK,NOCHOICE)
in	initial choice number	integer
in	prompt and echo type	integer
in	echo volume	XMIN,XMAX, YMIN,YMAX, ZMIN,ZMAX
in	choice data record	PET specific data record

See the beginning of Section 8.4 for details on initializing devices. A choice device is initialized with both an initial status and an initial choice number. The status determines whether a choice is valid or not. The choice number is an integer identifying which alternative has been chosen.

The *choice data record* contains PET specific data such as the number of alternatives, the menu title, and the text strings of the menu entries. For example a pushbutton would display a button and could return information indicating whether it had been selected or not. In this case the PET data record could contain the title of the pushbutton, for example 'Exit'.

Once the choice device has been initialized, it can be used in one of three ways, depending on the operating mode. In request mode it is used as follows:

REQUEST CHOICE   (PHOP,WSOP,*,*)
Arguments:

in	workstation identifier	integer
in	choice device number	integer
out	status	(OK,NOCHOICE,NONE)
out	choice number	integer

This function will block until the user provides input on the specified choice device. If the user enters a break action, the *status* NONE is returned, if the status is OK then the *choice number* contains the requested data. If the status is NOCHOICE, then the choice number is not valid.

In sample mode the program only needs to specify which choice device should be sampled, and its current status and choice number will be returned:

SAMPLE CHOICE   (PHOP,WSOP,*,*)
Arguments:

in	workstation identifier	integer
in	choice device number	integer
out	status	(OK,NOCHOICE)
out	choice number	integer

If the function AWAIT EVENT indicated that the event was from a choice device, then it can be read with the function:

GET CHOICE   (PHOP,WSOP,*,*)
Arguments:

out	status	(OK,NOCHOICE)
out	choice number	integer

The actual device which generated this event was returned by the function AWAIT EVENT.

8.4.4 String device input

A string device is used to get text from the user. The input is usually from the keyboard on a physical workstation. It can be used to prompt the user to enter a text string, for example a filename. Often the string can be edited using the DELETE key before confirming the input string is valid. Usually the trigger to confirm valid data is the RETURN key. A string device will often appear as a window placed in the echo volume, with a line for entering text, and perhaps a title. How an actual device appears depends on the implementation and the PET.

A string device is initialized with the function:

INITIALIZE STRING 3   (PHOP,WSOP,*,*)
Arguments:

in	workstation identifier	integer
in	string device number	integer
in	initial string	text string

in	prompt and echo type	integer
in	echo volume	XMIN,XMAX, YMIN,YMAX, ZMIN, ZMAX
in	string data record	PET specific data record

When this device is activated the user will be prompted for input with the initial string. See the beginning of Section 8.4 for details on initializing devices. When initializing a string, one needs to specify a buffer size. This ensures that when the device is actually used that the applications string buffers are not overrun. The PET data record will contain the input buffer size and an initial editing position. This is the position of a cursor in the initial string. Usually the initial string can be edited before the input is validated.

Some implementations put additional information in the PET data record, for example a title for the string device box. This title can be used as a prompt, for example "Enter filename: ". One needs to refer to the supplier's documentation for details.

Once the string device has been initialized, it can be used in one of three ways, depending on the operating mode. It is used in request mode as follows:

REQUEST STRING   (PHOP,WSOP,*,*)
Arguments:

in	workstation identifier	integer
in	string device number	integer
out	status	(OK,NONE)
out	character string	text string

This function will prompt the user to enter a string and will block until the user provides input on the specified device. If the user enters a break action, the status NONE is returned, otherwise status is OK and the string is returned.

In sample mode the program need only specify which string device should be sampled, and its current string will be returned:

SAMPLE STRING   (PHOP,WSOP,*,*)
Arguments:

in	workstation identifier	integer
in	string device number	integer
out	character string	text string

A string device can be used in sample mode if one wants to read from the keyboard in a non-blocking manner. For example, one might assign functions to keys on the keyboard, such as typing an 'x' to rotate an object by a fixed increment about the x-axis. In this case one could sample the string device and see what characters have been entered and execute the appropriate functions. One should consult the supplier's documentation to see how a string device has been implemented in sample mode.

If the function AWAIT EVENT indicated that the event was from a string device, then the string can be read with the function:

GET STRING   (PHOP,WSOP,*,*)
Arguments:

out	status	(OK,NONE)
out	character string	text string

The actual device which generated this event was returned by the function AWAIT EVENT.

8.4.5 Valuator device input

A valuator is an input device which returns a real number within a certain range. This device can be realized in a number of ways. For example, a valuator can be an on-screen slider bar, dial or digital display of the value. It could also be a physical device such as a dial box or a torque ball. Your PHIGS supplier has documented what valuator devices have been implemented and how to set device specific data.

Each valuator has default data, but one will usually want to initialize the device. The valuator is initialized with the function:

INITIALIZE VALUATOR 3   (PHOP,WSOP,*,*)
Arguments:

in	workstation identifier	integer
in	valuator device number	integer
in	initial value	real
in	prompt and echo type	integer
in	echo volume	XMIN,XMAX, YMIN,YMAX, ZMIN,ZMAX
in	valuator data record	PET specific data record

See the beginning of Section 8.4 for details on initializing devices. The PET data record contains at least the minimum and maximum value the device can attain, which defines the valuator's range. The initial value is a real number that must lie within the device's range. The data record can also contain PET specific data. For example, if a valuator is a slider bar, one might want to label the slider with text, such as "Red Value".

Once the valuator has been initialized, it can be used in one of three ways, depending on the operating mode. The valuator is used in request mode as follows:

REQUEST VALUATOR   (PHOP,WSOP,*,*)
Arguments:

in	workstation identifier	integer
in	valuator device number	integer
out	status	(OK,NONE)
out	value	real

This function will block until the user provides input on the specified valuator. If the user enters a break action, the status NONE is returned, otherwise status is OK and the value contains the requested data.

In sample mode the program needs only specify which valuator device should be sampled, and its current value will be returned:

SAMPLE VALUATOR   (PHOP,WSOP,*,*)
Arguments:

in	workstation identifier	integer
in	valuator device number	integer
out	value	real

If the function AWAIT EVENT indicated that the event was from a valuator, then its value can be read with the function:

GET VALUATOR   (PHOP,WSOP,*,*)
Arguments:

out	value	real

The actual device which generated this event was returned by the function AWAIT EVENT.

8.5 A PHIGS input example

In is common for an application to have an input loop, where user requests are processed. This is a common way to use PHIGS input devices. The following code, uses devices in both sample and event mode. It comes from an application which was developed under DEC-PHIGS and subsequently ported to SUN-PHIGS 2.0. The main issues involved in porting the input code entail using different device numbers and PETs for some devices. This example is written in C. There is an example of using input devices in FORTRAN in Appendix A.

This code samples a locator to get the position of the mouse, and gets both choice and valuator input in event mode. There is one choice device which is selected to exit the application. Seven valuators are used in this example, which are mapped onto a physical dial box. The device numbers and PETs used are given in the SUN-PHIGS documentation. The dials are used for translating, rotating and scaling.

Before one can start, the devices need to be initialized and put in the appropriate mode. This is done with the two routines: `init_devices` and `init_knobs`. The first routine initializes the choice and locator devices and then calls `init_knobs`. The choice device is called MENU and the locator MOUSE. The choice device is put into event mode and the locator into sample mode.

The initialization routines use two globally defined variables: `xmaxDC` and `ymaxDC`. These variables are derived from a call to INQUIRE DISPLAY SPACE SIZE which returns the device coordinate range. This is needed to scale the echo area to fit in the device coordinates. The actual range of device coordinates is implementation specific. The C listing follows:

```
#define MENU  1
#define MOUSE 1

Pfloat xmaxDC, ymaxDC;

void
init_devices( Pint wsid ) {

  static char   *menstring[1] = { "EXIT" };
  static Plimit chsize = { 0.9, 1.0, 0.95, 1.0 };
  static Pint   chPET = 3;
  Pchoice_data  chrec;

  static  Plimit locsize;
  Ploc_data      locrecord;
  Ppoint         inipos;

  /*==========================================*/
  /* First initialize the choice device MENU */
  /*==========================================*/
  chsize.x_min *= xmaxDC; chsize.x_max *= xmaxDC;
  chsize.y_min *= ymaxDC; chsize.y_max *= ymaxDC;
  chrec.pets.pet_r3.num_strings = 1;
  chrec.pets.pet_r3.strings     = menstring;
  pinit_choice( wsid, MENU, PIN_STATUS_OK, 1, chPET,
              &chsize, &chrec );
  pset_choice_mode( wsid, MENU, POP_EVENT, PSWITCH_ECHO );

  /*==================================*/
  /*  Now initialize the locator MOUSE */
  /*==================================*/
  locsize.x_min = 0.0; locsize.x_max = xmaxDC;
  locsize.y_min = 0.0; locsize.y_max = ymaxDC;
  inipos.x = 0.0;
  inipos.y = 0.0;
  pinit_loc( wsid, MOUSE, 1, &inipos, 1, &locsize,
            &locrecord );
  pset_loc_mode(wsid, MOUSE, POP_SAMPLE, PSWITCH_NO_ECHO);

  /* Change the priority of view 1 to be top priority */
  /*===================================================*/
  pset_view_tran_in_pri( wsid, 1, 0, PPRI_HIGHER );

  /* Finally initialize the dials */
  init_dials( wsid );
}
```

The second initialization routine will initialize seven dials as valuators in event mode. Each dial is a separate valuator device. The device numbers are specific to SUN-PHIGS, but otherwise they are used as standard valuator devices.

```
/* Valuator device numbers for dials in SUN-PHIGS 2.0 */
#define XROT   11
#define YROT   12
#define ZROT   13
#define XTRAN 14
#define YTRAN 15
#define ZTRAN 16
#define ZOOM  17

#define DIAL_PET 1
#define PI         3.14159264

void
init_dials( Pint wsid )
{
  Pint       i, err;
  Pval_data dial_rec;
  static     Plimit dial_area = { 0.0, 10.0, 0.0, 10.0 };

  /* Initialize the dials to be used for rotation */
  /*===============================================*/
  dial_rec.low = -PI;
  dial_rec.high = PI;
  for( i=XROT; i <= ZROT ; i++ ){
    pset_val_mode( wsid, i, POP_REQ, PSWITCH_NO_ECHO );
    pinit_val( wsid, i, 0.0, DIAL_PET, &dial_area,
               &dial_rec);
    pset_val_mode(wsid, i, POP_EVENT, PSWITCH_NO_ECHO);
  }

  /* Initialize the dials to be used for translation*/
  /*===============================================*/
  dial_rec.low = -100.0;
  dial_rec.high = 100.0;
  for( i=XTRAN; i <= ZTRAN; i++ ){
    pset_val_mode( wsid, i, POP_REQ, PSWITCH_NO_ECHO );
    pinit_val( wsid, i, 0.0, DIAL_PET, &dial_area,
               &dial_rec);
    pset_val_mode( wsid, i, POP_EVENT, PSWITCH_NO_ECHO );
  }
```

```
/* Initialize the dials to be used for scaling */
/*===============================================*/
dial_rec.low = 0.0;
dial_rec.high = 10.0;
pset_val_mode( wsid, ZOOM, POP_REQ, PSWITCH_NO_ECHO );
pinit_val( wsid, ZOOM, 1.0, DIAL_PET, &dial_area,
           &dial_rec);
pset_val_mode( wsid, i, POP_EVENT, PSWITCH_NO_ECHO );
}
```

First the program opens a workstation and initializes the input devices. Then the workstation tables containing views, colours, and bundled attributes are set. A structure network is created and posted to the workstation. Finally the input loop is reached. This loop calls the function `ProcessInput` to get input from the PHIGS devices. This function sets two variables: `Done` and `knob_matrix`. When the variable `Done` is true, the program will exit. The `knob_matrix` is used to set a global transformation in the function `edit_root_struct`.

The routine `ProcessInput` first samples the mouse and uses the current mouse position. It then processes events from the input queue. If the event is from a choice device, then the choice will be used to update the variable `Done`, a global variable used by the calling routine to terminate. Otherwise the input is tested to see if it came from a valuator. If it is from a valuator, then the routine will test which dial was turned, and use the value to update the appropriate variable. A transformation matrix is created from the dial input which is used to edit a global transformation in the root structure. The variable `centre` is globally defined and is set to be the centre of rotation. The routine `ProcessInput` follows:

```
#include <phigs.h>
#define TRUE (1==1)
#define FALSE (1==0)

Pfloat xmaxDC, ymaxDC;
Pint Done;
Pvec3 centre = { 0.0, 0.0, 0.0 };

void
ProcessInput( Pint wsid )
{
Pint       err;
Pint       choices;
Pmatrix3 knob_matrix;
Pint       view_ind;
Ppoint     mousepos;
Pfloat     knob_val;
```

```
Pvec3      knob_trans;
Ppoint3    knob_rot;
Pvec3      knob_scale;

Pin_status status;
Pin_class  DevClass;

Pint wsid_in, DevNum;


/* Process all sampled devices */
/* =========================== */
psample_loc( wsid, MOUSE, &view_ind, &mousepos);
use_mouse_position( mousepos );

/* Process all event driven devices */
/* ================================= */
pawait_event( 0.01, &wsid_in, &DevClass, &DevNum );
    if( DevClass == PIN_CHOICE ) {
        pget_choice( &status, &choices);
        if( status == PIN_STATUS_OK && DevNum == MENU )
            Done = TRUE;
    }

    if( DevClass == PIN_VAL ) {
     pget_val( &knob_val );
     switch (DevNum) {
     case XTRAN:
         knob_trans.delta_x = knob_val;
         break;
     case YTRAN:
         knob_trans.delta_y = knob_val;
         break;
     case ZTRAN:
         knob_trans.delta_z = knob_val;
         break;
     case XROT:
         knob_rot.x = knob_val;
         break;
     case YROT:
         knob_rot.y = knob_val;
         break;
     case ZROT:
         knob_rot.z = knob_val;
         break;
      case ZOOM:
```

157

```
        knob_scale.delta_x = knob_val;
        knob_scale.delta_y = knob_val;
        knob_scale.delta_z = knob_val;
        break;
    default:
        break;
    }
    pbuild_tran_matrix3( &centre, &knob_trans,
                knob_rot.x,knob_rot.y,knob_rot.z,
                &knob_scale, &err, knob_matrix );
    edit_root_struct( knob_matrix );
    pupd_ws( wsid, PFLAG_PERFORM );
    }
}
```

CHAPTER 9

Using Filters and Picking

Applications that require 3D graphics often deal with large amounts of data. These data may represent complex scenes, or objects rendered with a high degree of realism. Managing large volumes of data will slow down an application's response time. PHIGS provides powerful tools to filter data in the CSS, so that only portions of structures are considered for certain actions. This chapter will focus on filtering data in the CSS and on the operations which use filters: invisibility, highlighting, picking, and incremental spatial search (ISS).

A primitive is made invisible, highlighted, or pickable depending on the results of a comparison between the corresponding filter and the current *name set*. The name set is an attribute that identifies a group of primitives in a structure. By using the name set judiciously, one is able to add context information to the CSS. For example, the name set can be used to identify components of an architectural drawing: first floor, second floor, structural beams, plumbing, wiring, etc. It is then straightforward to set a filter in order to highlight the plumbing on the second floor.

9.1 Using the name set

The name set is simply a list of names that PHIGS maintains in the traversal state list, TSL. Names are added and removed from the name set with structure elements. It is the responsibility of the PHIGS programmer to maintain the name set.

Names are integer constants supplied by the applications programmer. A PHIGS implementation must support at least 64 names (0...63). A different name should be assigned to each component of a scene that needs to be individually identified. The name set is initially empty, so it must be updated in order for it to represent the actual context of the drawing. There are two functions to update the name set: ADD NAMES TO SET and REMOVE NAMES FROM SET. They are structure elements:

ADD NAMES TO SET   (PHOP,*,STOP,*)El
Arguments:
          in   names   list of integers

and

REMOVE NAMES FROM SET   (PHOP,*,STOP,*)El
Arguments:
          in   names   list of integers

These calls are the only way to make sure that the name set represents the contents of the structure. Figure 9.1 illustrates an example set of names that could be used in an architectural application. In this example there are the names: BUILDING, WIRING, PLUMBING, FIRST-FLOOR, and SECONDFLOOR. The right hand side of Figure 9.1 illustrates how the contents of the name set are updated as the structure is being traversed. The name set is empty at the beginning of traversing any root structure. The calls to add and remove names from the name set keep it updated. In order to use the name set one needs to define filters. This is covered in the following section where this example will be revisited.

	Actual name set
Root structure	(Empty)
ADD NAMES TO SET(Building)	(Building)
ADD NAMES TO SET(Firstfloor)	(Building, Firstfloor)
... start drawing first floor ...	
ADD NAMES TO SET(Wiring)	(Building, Firstfloor, Wiring)
... start drawing first floor wiring ...	
REMOVE NAMES FROM SET(Wiring)	(Building, Firstfloor)
... finish drawing first floor ...	
REMOVE NAMES FROM SET(Firstfloor)	(Building)
ADD NAMES TO SET(Secondfloor)	(Building, Secondfloor)
... start drawing second floor ...	
ADD NAMES TO SET(Wiring)	
... start drawing second floor wiring ...	(Building, Secondfloor, Wiring)
REMOVE NAMES FROM SET(Wiring)	(Building, Secondfloor)
... finish drawing second floor ...	
REMOVE NAMES FROM SET(Secondfloor)	(Building)

Figure 9.1 Using name sets.

160

9.2 Using filters

The name set is defined only during traversal, so there is no direct way to inquire its contents. In order to use the name set, one must define a *filter*. Of the four different operations which use filters, invisibility and highlighting are the simplest. These two operations will be used to introduce the principle of data filters, and then picking and the ISS will be covered. The operations which use filters can be summarized by:

INVISIBILITY   By default all primitives are drawn at traversal time, but sometimes it is desirable not to draw certain components of a picture without deleting elements in the CSS. An example of when this filter is useful is if one wants temporarily to inhibit drawing detail that could be cluttering up the screen.

HIGHLIGHTING   Highlighting is a means to draw the user's attention to a particular object on the screen. The are a number of methods to highlight an object. It could be drawn in an emphasized colour, or made to blink on and off, or it could be drawn in a highlight colour such as red. How the highlighting is realized depends on the PHIGS implementation.

PICKING   Picking is actually an input device, but since it uses filters it is presented here. Picking is a means to point at an object on the screen and have PHIGS identify what primitive in the CSS drew it. The actual data that a pick device delivers is a structure hierarchy tree from a root structure to the actual primitive which drew the selected object. Filters are useful in picking because they limit the amount of data that has to be considered.

ISS   Incremental Spatial Search is a means to interrogate the CSS and find primitives which would draw within a given region in world coordinates. The filters are used to restrict the search only to those primitives that meet certain criteria.

Simply stated, the highlighting filter separates output primitives into two categories: those which are highlighted, and those which are not. The invisibility filter behaves analogously: it determines whether a primitive should be drawn or not. Filters have an internal structure. They consist of an *inclusion set* and an *exclusion set*. Each of these sets is a list of names that are compared with the name set at traversal time. The names used to create a filter should correspond to the names used to form the name set.

Whether an output primitive is highlighted or not, depends on the results of two tests: a comparison of the current name set with the inclusion set and with the exclusion set. If the results of both tests are true, then the primitive is highlighted. The first test compares the name set with the names in the filter's inclusion set, and if at least one name is in both then the result is true. The second test compares the name set with the exclusion set, and if they have no names in common, the result is true. Figure 9.2 illustrates these tests for the highlight filter.

The inclusion set and exclusion set simplify creating sophisticated rules for filtering data in the CSS. In the architectural example from Figure 9.1 it is simple to highlight the wiring by putting the name WIRING in the highlight filter's inclusion set. If only wiring on the first floor should be highlighted, then the name SECONDFLOOR should be put in the exclusion set. This results in all wiring to be highlighted except for that on the second floor. Figure 9.3 illustrates using this filter with the architectural example.

The invisibility and highlighting filters are kept in the WSL. Both filters are initially empty, so that the default state is everything is visible and nothing is highlighted. In order to use these filters, one needs to define the inclusion and exclusion sets on the workstation:

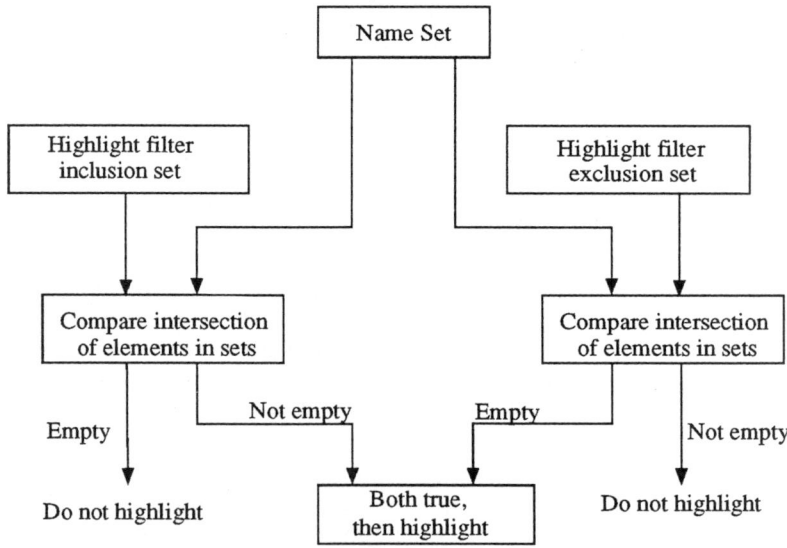

Figure 9.2 Testing the name set with a highlighting filter.

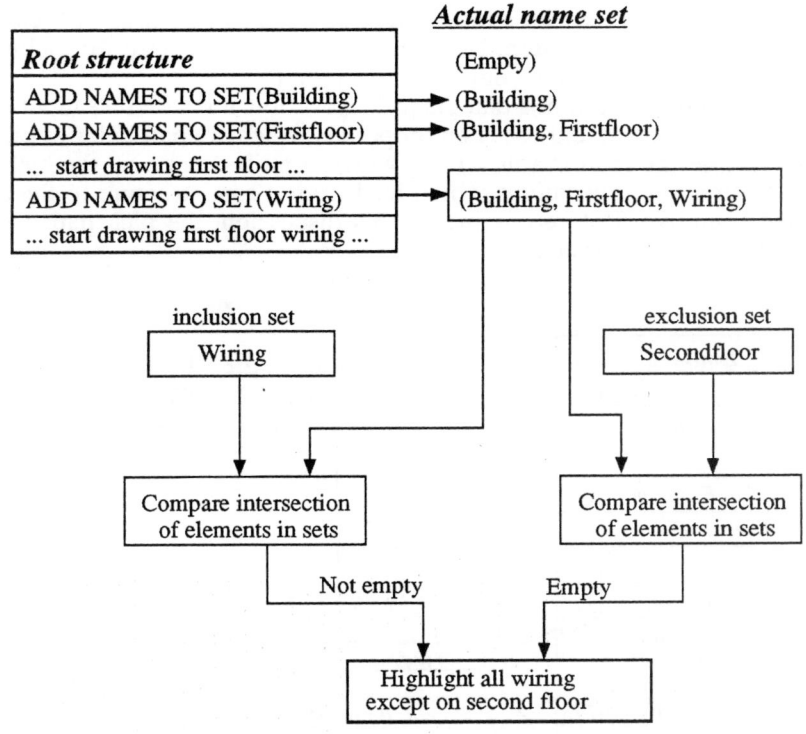

Figure 9.3 Example of a filter acting on a structure.

SET INVISIBILITY FILTER   (PHOP,WSOP,*,*)
Arguments:

in	workstation identifier	integer
in	inclusion set	list of integers
in	exclusion set	list of integers

SET HIGHLIGHTING FILTER   (PHOP,WSOP,*,*)
Arguments:

in	workstation identifier	integer
in	inclusion set	list of integers
in	exclusion set	list of integers

9.3 Picking with PHIGS

Picking lets the user point to some object on the screen, and then will traverse the CSS to identify what primitive drew at that position. The user generally points with a locator device, such as a mouse, and selects by pressing a mouse button. How physical devices are used for picking, should be documented by your PHIGS supplier.

Here it will be assumed that the principles of using a PHIGS input device are understood and focus on properties which are particular to picking. This device returns a *pick path*, which is a list describing the hierarchy of structure invocations which lead from a root structure to the selected primitive. Before continuing this discussion, the pick path must be defined and understood.

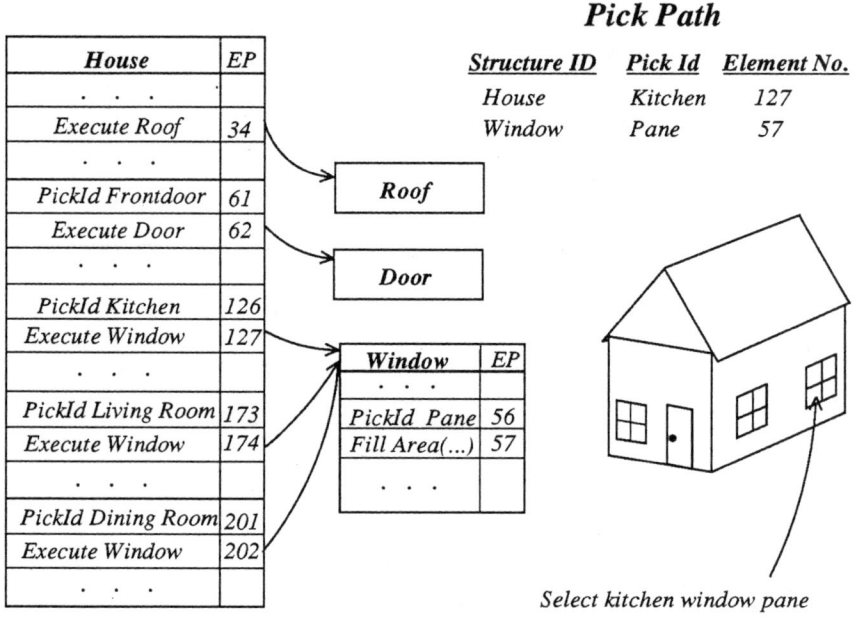

Figure 9.4 A sample pick path.

9.3.1 The pick path

Each entry in the pick path consists of: a structure identifier, a pick identifier, and an element pointer, EP. The pick identifier is an additional attribute used with a pick device to identify primitives. It is zero by default but can be set with the function:

SET PICK IDENTIFIER   (PHOP,WSOP,*,*)El
Arguments:
           in   pick identifier   integer

Pick identifiers, like all attributes, conform to the PHIGS inheritance rules. So child structures will inherit their parent's pick identifier, but not the other way around. Usually groups of primitives will be associated with a single pick identifier to simplify interpreting the pick path. Often one does not need to know the exact EP of the selected primitive. It is also difficult in many cases to interpret the exact EP, because the structure has been edited. Here the pick identifier is used to mark a section of a structure.

For example, a structure representing a house might have a large number of primitives, whereas the application might only be interested in knowing if the user selects the roof, a window, or a door. In this case one could choose an unique integer constant to represent each basic component in the structure, such as: KITCHEN, WINDOW, DOOR, ROOF, etc. Then before defining the primitives to draw each component, set the pick identifier to the appropriate value.

Figure 9.4 illustrates how a pick path uniquely identifies the primitive that was selected. There are two ways the pick path can be sorted: the root structure is either the first or the last element in the list. This depends on the *pick path order* which is defined when the device is initialized.

9.3.2 Using pick devices

Using a pick device can be broken down into three stages: initializing a pick device, defining the pick filter, and finally getting input from the device. Picking is supported in one of three operating modes: sample, request, or event. Putting a device in a given operating mode has been discussed in Section 8.3.

As is the case with all other input devices, pick must be in request mode when being initialized. Both a 2D and a 3D initialization routine exist for picking, the only difference being whether 2D or 3D device coordinates are used to define the echo area (see Section 8.4). To initialize the 3D pick one should use:

INITIALIZE PICK 3   (PHOP,WSOP,*,*)
Arguments:

in	workstation identifier	integer
in	pick device number	integer
in	initial pick status	(OK,NOPICK)
in	initial pick path	pick path
in	prompt and echo type	integer
in	echo volume	XMIN,XMAX, YMIN,YMAX, ZMIN,ZMAX
in	pick data record	PET specific data record
in	pick path order	(TOPFIRST,BOTTOMFIRST)

Obviously pick devices exist only on OUTIN workstations: one needs to draw the primitive to be picked as well as support input. The device number is used to refer to the specific pick device. One can define more than one pick device. The maximum number of allowable pick devices on a given workstation is returned by the function INQUIRE NUMBER OF AVAILABLE LOGICAL INPUT DEVICES.

The prompt and echo type determines how the pick device appears to the user. Your PHIGS supplier has documented what PETs are supported and how they are used. It is common to temporarily identify the primitives being 'pointed at' by the pick device during the measure process. This can be done either by drawing a box around the primitive, or by highlighting the primitive during the measure process. This should not be confused with highlighting associated with the highlighting filter, which is not directly related to picking.

The data record contains implementation dependent information on the pick device. Although the PHIGS standard leaves this record undefined, many implementations have used this record to define a pick aperture. A pick aperture defines a threshold that determines how close the pointing device has to be to a primitive before a successful pick is registered. One should refer to the documentation provided by the PHIGS supplier to see exactly how the data record is used.

The pointing device's position is transformed from *DC* to *NPC* before picking is initiated. Only certain primitives are eligible for picking. Factors such as clipping, HLHSR, and filters can affect whether a primitive is pickable or not. It is left to the implementor to determine whether a primitive that is obscured by another due to a HLHSR method is pickable. Few PHIGS implementations support true 3D pointing devices, which would be needed to distinguish between two primitives differing only by their z-coordinate. How picking is affected by HLHSR should be documented by your PHIGS supplier. Primitives that have been clipped from the scene, for example, through model clipping, or that are not drawn because of the invisibility filter, are not eligible for picking.

In order to establish explicitly which primitives are pickable one must use a pick filter. This filter needs to be defined for each active pick device. Similar to invisibility and highlighting, pick filters consist of inclusion and exclusion sets of names. These two sets are compared with the actual name set in the TSL as described in Section 9.2. In this situation, the filter determines whether an output primitive is eligible to be picked or not. The pick filter is set with the function:

SET PICK FILTER   (PHOP,WSOP,*,*)
Arguments:

in	workstation identifier	integer
in	pick device number	integer
in	inclusion set	list of integers
in	exclusion set	list of integers

This call differs from the functions to set the invisibility and highlighting filters in that one must identify a specific pick device.

The pick filter's inclusion and exclusion sets are initially empty, so by default nothing is pickable. In order to pick something on the screen at least one name must be defined and added to the name set at the top of the structure network. This name must also be added to the pick filter's inclusion set, so that everything is pickable.

Picking requires considerable computing power since each primitive must be transformed and compared with the position of the pointing device to see if it has been picked. In order to reduce the amount of data to consider one can define 'hot spots' for each object that needs to be picked, and use a filter to make only these spots pickable. For example, in a molecular modelling application, one might not necessarily need to pick individual primitives or atoms. Each group of atoms that needs to be individually identified by the user can have its own 'hot spot'. This 'hot spot' might consist of several polylines drawn in a reserved colour, used solely to identify the group of pickable atoms. These hot spots can be identified by a unique name in the name set that can be added to the inclusion set of the the pick device's filter. These names can be added to the invisibility filter's inclusion set when the hot spots are not needed.

Once the pick device has been initialized and a pick filter has been defined, one can start picking. First it needs to be set in the appropriate operating mode with the function SET PICK MODE, see Section 8.3. Then depending on the mode, the pick path can be returned by one of the functions: REQUEST PICK, SAMPLE PICK, and GET PICK.

These functions return a pick path, whose depth depends on how many levels of hierarchy were traversed to get to the selected object. The application does not neccesarily need to know the entire pick path, so it can specify the maximum depth to return. If this depth is not enough to return the entire path, a truncated path is returned. The pick path order that was defined when the device was initialized will determine whether the top or the bottom part of the truncated path is returned. In addition to the pick path, a status is returned, which identifies whether a successful pick occured or not. A pick is unsuccessful if the user enters a break or if something that is not pickable is selected. A user break returns the status NONE, a successful pick returns OK, otherwise NO-PICK is returned.

In request mode the user is prompted for input with the function:

REQUEST PICK   (PHOP,WSOP,*,*)
Arguments:

in	workstation identifier	integer
in	pick device number	integer
in	depth of path to return	integer
out	status	(OK,NOPICK,NONE)
out	pick path	pick path

The application will block until the user either enters a break, or attempts to pick something. A pick device is sampled with the function:

167

SAMPLE PICK   (PHOP,WSOP,*,*)
Arguments:

in	workstation identifier	integer
in	pick device number	integer
in	depth of path to return	integer
out	status	(OK,NOPICK)
out	pick path	pick path

Finally if the pick device is in event mode, and if the function AWAIT EVENT indicates the current event is from a pick device, the pick path can be retrieved with the function:

GET PICK   (PHOP,WSOP,*,*)
Arguments:

in	depth of path to return	integer
out	status	(OK,NOPICK)
out	pick path	pick path

9.4 Incremental spatial search

If one is looking for an output primitive that lies within a certain area of world coordinate *(WC)* space, the *incremental spatial search* (ISS) function can be used. This function traverses the structure hierarchy looking for an output primitive which satisfies the search criteria. It returns a path, identifying the structure hierarchy leading from a root structure to the found element. Both a 2D and a 3D variant of ISS occur, depending on whether 2D or 3D *WC* should be searched.

ISS is used to find a primitive which lies within a certain distance, the *search distance* of a reference point in *WC*. This function is provided with a *starting path* defining where the search should begin. A path consists of a list of integer pairs, containing the structure identifier and element pointer for each hierarchy level (see Figure 9.5). It is incremental in the sense that a returned structure path leading to a found element can be used as the starting path in a subsequent search.

The following function is used to start an ISS:

INCREMENTAL SPATIAL SEARCH 3   (PHOP,*,*,*)
Arguments:

in	search reference point	3D point in WC
in	search distance	real
in	starting path	structure path
in	modelling clip flag	(CLIP,NOCLIP)
in	search ceiling index	integer
in	normal filter list	list of filters
in	inverted filter list	list of filters
out	error indicator	integer
out	found path	structure path

There are a number of ways to limit the ISS. The *modelling clip flag*

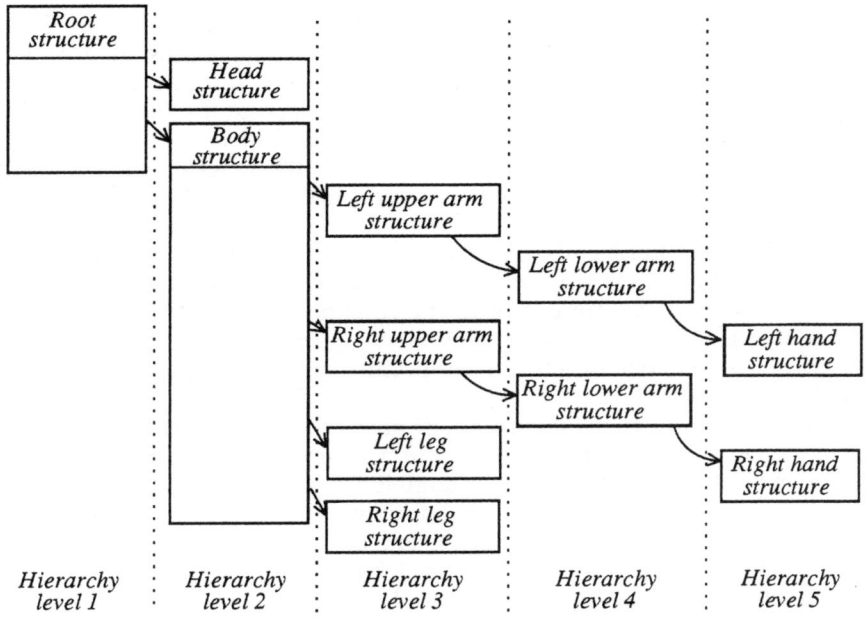

Figure 9.5 Structure path used by incremental spatial search.

determines whether the ISS should consider primitives which have been removed by modelling clipping. Setting this flag to CLIP applies modelling clipping during the ISS.

The *search ceiling* is an integer that determines when to stop the search. It specifies which hierarchy level in the starting path should be completely searched before stopping the ISS. This can be illustrated with the following path from the example in Figure 9.5:

Structure ID	EP	Hierarchy level
ROOT	8	1
BODY	12	2
RIGHT UPPER ARM	1	3

This path has three hierarchy levels and will be used as a starting path. By setting the search ceiling to 1 all elements from the starting path to the end of the root structure would be searched. If one wanted to restrict the search to the right arm, the search ceiling index should be set to 3. This would stop the search once the end of the structure at the third hierarchy level was reached. This corresponds to the structure RIGHT UPPER ARM. If the search ceiling is reached and no primitive is found meeting the search criteria a null path is returned.

Incremental spatial search can also be restricted to certain primitives by using filters. The ISS filtering is based on the mechanism described

169

in Section 9.2, and groups primitives into those that are eligible for ISS and those that are not. Up until now individual filters, consisting of an inclusion and an exclusion set, were the basis for filtering operations. ISS uses two lists of filters: the *normal filter list*, and the *inverted filter list*. A primitive is eligible for ISS if it is accepted by each filter in the normal filter list and rejected by each filter in the inverted filter list. If the normal and the inverted filter lists are empty, then all primitives are considered eligible for ISS.

An inverted filter has the same structure and operates on the name set in the same manner as a normal filter, but the result of the comparison is reversed in sense. So, for example, if a filter normally used for invisibility is used as an inverted filter, only visible primitives would be eligible for ISS. This is because the visible primitives were rejected by the invisibility filter.

The inverted filter list commonly contains the invisibility filter, if one exists. One reason inverted filters were not previously required, was because only visible primitives were eligible for picking. Using lists allows one to use individual filters as building blocks for more complex searches with ISS. For example, to search all visible primitives which are not highlighted, could be realized by putting the invisibility and highlighting filters in the inverted filter list.

CHAPTER 10

A Final Look at the CSS

There are still several topics regarding the CSS that have not yet been mentioned. They are relevant for the more experienced PHIGS programmer, so were not included in Chapter 2. These topics are structure inquiry and searching, structure archival and retrieval and finally two rarely used structure elements: GENERALIZED STRUCTURE ELEMENT GSE and APPLICATION DATA.

10.1 Using inquiry and searching the CSS

A large amount of data is maintained by the CSS. It is easy for an application to lose track of what is in it, or what state it is in. In order for the application to get this information, there are a number of inquiry functions which can return data about the contents of the CSS. It is also possible to search for certain types of structure elements.

Many of the inquiry and search functions return an error indicator. If the requested information is not available, a non-zero value is returned. Some reasons for a non-zero error indicator can be either that PHIGS is not open or the requested structure identifier does not exist. A list of PHIGS errors is given in Appendix F.

Because there are so many inquiry functions whose names are self-explanatory, the descriptions have been kept brief where possible. The first inquiry function is also the simplest. It is used if one is not sure whether a structure is open or not.

INQUIRE STRUCTURE STATE VALUE   (*,*,*,*)
Arguments:
            out   structure state value   (STCL,STOP)

171

Note that this function can be called even if PHIGS has not yet been opened. The next routine returns more information than simply whether a structure is open:

INQUIRE OPEN STRUCTURE   (PHOP,*,*,*)
Arguments:

out	error indicator	integer
out	open structure status	(NONE,OPEN)
out	structure identifier	integer

This returns not only a status saying whether a structure is open or not, but also the structure identifier of the open structure. If one needs to determine whether a specific structure exists or not, then one should use:

INQUIRE STRUCTURE STATUS   (PHOP,*,*,*)
Arguments:

in	structure identifier	integer
out	error indicator	integer
out	structure status	(NON_EXISTENT, EMPTY,NOTEMPTY)

In order to get a list of all structures in the CSS, one should use:

INQUIRE STRUCTURE IDENTIFIERS   (PHOP,*,*,*)
Arguments:

out	error	integer
out	list of structure identifiers	list of integers

The next routine returns a list of workstations, if any, to which a given structure is posted:

INQUIRE SET OF WORKSTATIONS TO WHICH POSTED   (PHOP,*,*,*)
Arguments:

in	structure identifier	integer
out	error indicator	integer
out	list of workstation identifiers	list of integers

In the process of editing a structure, it is often necessary to know what the current element pointer is, since all structure editing is relative to the current EP value. This information is returned by the function:

INQUIRE ELEMENT POINTER   (PHOP,*,STOP,*)
Arguments:

out	error indicator	integer
out	current element pointer	integer

In order to avoid unintentionally overwriting or inserting elements, one can use the next inquiry, which will return the current edit mode:

INQUIRE EDIT MODE   (PHOP,*,*,*)
Arguments:

out	error indicator	integer
out	current edit mode	(INSERT,REPLACE)

172

10.1.1 Inquiries about structure content

We will now discuss inquiry functions, which can be used to read structure elements from the CSS. The amount of data associated with each
structure element varies greatly. For example, one structure element
could be SET VIEW INDEX which has only one argument, an integer,
or it could be a POLYLINE 3 with several thousand 3D vertices. As a
consequence, the procedure to retrieve a structure element has two
stages. The first stage in getting a structure element from the CSS is to
find out what type of element it is, and how much space its contents occupy. Once this is known the second stage: retrieving the structure contents can begin. The first stage of this procedure is achieved with the
function:

INQUIRE ELEMENT TYPE AND SIZE   (PHOP,*,*,*)
Arguments:

in	structure identifier	integer
in	element position	(0,...,n)
out	error indicator	integer
out	element type	see Tables 10.1 and 10.2
out	element size	(0,...,n)

This function which can be called even if no structure is open, will
return the element type and size found at the specified element position
in the specified structure. The structure identifier must exist in the CSS,
and the element position has to be valid within the structure, otherwise
the error indicator is set to a non-zero value. If the two input parameters
are valid, then the element type will indicate one of the element types in
Tables 10.1, or 10.2. If the element pointer is zero, the returned element
type is NIL. The element size will be a non-negative integer specifying
how much space the element contents occupy. This integer can be used
to derive the size of the buffer needed to contain the element's contents.
  Once the type and size of an element are known the actual contents of
the element can be read from the CSS with the routine:

INQUIRE ELEMENT CONTENT   (PHOP,*,*,*)
Arguments:

in	structure identifier	integer
in	element position	(0,...,n)
out	error indicator	integer
out	structure element record	data record

If the structure identifier and the element position are valid, then the
contents of the specified element are returned in the data record. This
function can also generate language binding specific errors. One such
cause for error, is that the buffer provided is not large enough to contain
the element's contents. The format of the data record depends on the
language binding and the specific PHIGS implementation.

173

Table 10.1   List of PHIGS structure elements.

NIL	SET TEXT PATH
POLYLINE 3	SET TEXT ALIGNMENT
POLYLINE	SET ANNOT. TEXT CHAR. HEIGHT
POLYMARKER 3	SET ANNOT. TEXT CHAR. UP VECTOR
POLYMARKER	SET ANNOTATION TEXT PATH
TEXT 3	SET ANNOTATION TEXT ALIGNMENT
TEXT	SET ANNOTATION TEXT STYLE
ANNOTATION TEXT REL. 3	SET INTERIOR STYLE
ANNOTATION TEXT REL.	SET INTERIOR COLOUR INDEX
FILL AREA 3	SET EDGE FLAG
FILL AREA	SET EDGETYPE
FILL AREA SET 3	SET EDGEWIDTH SCALE FACTOR
FILL AREA SET	SET EDGE COLOUR INDEX
CELL ARRAY 3	SET PATTERN SIZE
CELL ARRAY	SET PATTERN REF. PT. & VECTORS
GENERAL. DRAWING PRIMITIVE 3	SET PATTERN REF. POINT
GENERAL. DRAWING PRIMITIVE	ADD NAMES TO SET
SET POLYLINE INDEX	REMOVE NAMES FROM SET
SET POLYMARKER INDEX	SET INDIVIDUAL ASF
SET TEXT INDEX	SET HLHSR IDENTIFIER
SET INTERIOR INDEX	LOCAL MODEL. TRANSFORM 3
SET EDGE INDEX	LOCAL MODEL. TRANSFORM
SET LINETYPE	GLOBAL MODEL. TRANSFORM 3
SET LINEWIDTH SCALE FACTOR	GLOBAL MODEL. TRANSFORM
SET POLYLINE COLOUR INDEX	SET MODELLING CLIP VOLUME 3
SET MARKER TYPE	SET MODELLING CLIP VOLUME
SET MARKER SIZE SCALE FACTOR	SET MODELLING CLIP INDICATOR
SET POLYMARKER COLOUR INDEX	RESTORE MODELLING CLIP VOLUME
SET TEXT FONT	SET VIEW INDEX
SET TEXT PRECISION	EXECUTE STRUCTURE
SET CHAR. EXPANSION FACTOR	LABEL
SET CHARACTER SPACING	APPLICATION DATA
SET TEXT COLOUR INDEX	GENERAL STRUCTURE IDENTIFIER
SET CHARACTER HEIGHT	SET PICK IDENTIFIER
SET CHARACTER UP VECTOR	

Two additional element inquiry functions are provided for convenience. Both functions behave exactly like INQUIRE ELEMENT TYPE AND SIZE and INQUIRE ELEMENT CONTENT, except that they require a structure to be open and will return information about the element that the EP is pointing at in the currently open structure. These functions are:

INQUIRE CURRENT ELEMENT TYPE AND SIZE   (PHOP,*,STOP,*)
Arguments:

out	error indicator	integer
out	element type	see Tables 10.1 and 10.2
out	element size	(0,...,n)

INQUIRE CURRENT ELEMENT CONTENT   (PHOP,*,STOP,*)
Arguments:

out	error indicator	integer
out	structure element record	data record

Table 10.2 List of PHIGS PLUS structure elements.

POLYLINE SET 3 WITH DATA	SET (BACK) INTERIOR COLOUR
FILL AREA SET 3 WITH DATA	SET (BACK) REFLECTANCE INDEX
SET OF FILL AREA SET 3 WITH DATA	SET (BACK) INT. SHADE METH.
TRIANGLE STRIP 3 WITH DATA	SET (BACK) DATA MAPPING INDEX
TRIANGLE SET 3 WITH DATA	SET (BACK) DATA MAP. METHOD
QUAD. MESH 3 WITH DATA	SET (BACK) REFLECTANCE PROP.
CELL ARRAY 3 PLUS	SET (BACK) REFLECTANCE MODEL
NON UNIFORM B-SPLINE CURVE	SET BACK INTERIOR STYLE
NON UNIF. B-SPL. CURVE W. DATA	SET BACK INTERIOR STYLE INDEX
NON UNIFORM B-SPLINE SURFACE	SET BACK INTERIOR INDEX
NON UNIF. B-SPLINE SURF. W. DATA	SET FACE CULLING MODE
SET CURVE APPROX. CRITERIA	SET FACE DISTINGUISH MODE
SET SURFACE APPROX. CRITERIA	SET POLYLINE COLOUR
SET PARAMETRIC SURFACE INDEX	SET POLYLINE SHADING METHOD
SET PARAMETRIC SURF. CHARACT.	SET POLYLINE SHADING METHOD
SET RENDERING COLOUR MODEL	SET TEXT COLOUR
SET DEPTH CUE INDEX	SET EDGE COLOUR
SET COLOUR MAPPING INDEX	SET LIGHT SOURCE STATE

10.1.2 Inquiries about structure hierarchy

In addition to being able to read back elements from the CSS, one can also inquire about the hierarchy of the structure networks. This will return information about the ancestors and descendants of a given structure. The information is returned as a list of paths. A path consists of a list of structure identifier and element pointer pairs. For each structure identifier in the returned path, the element pointer is the EP of the EXECUTE STRUCTURE element which invokes the next level in the hierarchy. The bottom of the path consists of a structure identifier and 0 for the EP.

Figure 10.1 shows an example structure network defining objects in a

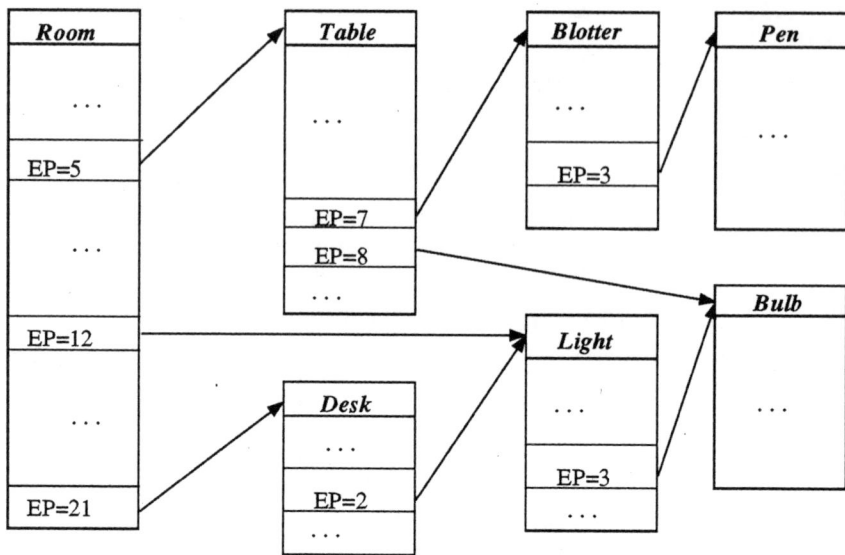

Figure 10.1 An example of a structure network.

room. In this room there is a light, a desk with an additional light on it and a table with a light bulb on it and a blotter. There is a pen on the blotter and both lights have light bulbs. This structure network contains the following paths:

Path 1	*Path 2*	*Path 3*	*Path 4*
Room,5	Room,5	Room,12	Room,21
Table,7	Table,8	Light,3	Desk,2
Blotter,3	Bulb,0	Bulb,0	Light,3
Pen,0			Bulb,0

The two inquiry functions used to get this hierarchy information from the CSS are INQUIRE PATHS TO DESCENDANTS and INQUIRE PATHS TO ANCESTORS. Both functions provide a means to specify how much data to return using the parameter *path depth*, and a means to format the returned paths with the *path order* parameter. The path depth is used to specify the maximum number of hierarchy levels in any returned path. The path order determines whether the returned path list should be started with highest structure in the hierarchy, TOPFIRST, or whether the list should start with the lowest, BOTTOMFIRST.

To get a list of all structure networks starting from a specific structure, one should use the function:

INQUIRE PATHS TO DESCENDANTS   (PHOP,*,*,*)
Arguments:
           in   structure identifier   integer

176

in	path order	(TOPFIRST, BOTTOMFIRST)
in	path depth	(0,..,n)
out	error indicator	integer
out	list of structure paths	list of paths

This routine will search the CSS for all maximal paths to descendants of the specified structure. A maximal path of descendants of a structure S is a list of structure identifier, element pointer pairs ((S,E0), (D1,E1), ..., (Dn,0)). In this list E0 is the element pointer within the structure S of the element, EXECUTE STRUCTURE(D1), and so on until structure Dn, which contains no EXECUTE STRUCTURE elements. If the path order is TOPFIRST, then the returned paths start with the specified structure. A path order of BOTTOMFIRST reverses the order of the returned paths, so that the structure at the bottom of the hierarchy is at the top of the path.

The path depth parameter specifies the maximum number of hierarchy levels to return. A path depth of 0 is used to signify that all paths should be returned in their entirety. A positive integer truncates the returned paths to the specified depth. For example, to get a list of all immediate children of the structure *Room*, one would use the command:

INQUIRE PATHS TO DESCENDANTS(Room, TOPFIRST, 2, err, paths)

Using the structures as defined in Figure 10.1, one gets the paths:

Path 1	*Path 2*	*Path 3*	*Path 4*
Room,5	Room,5	Room,12	Room,21
Table,7	Table,8	Light,3	Desk,2

Using the path order BOTTOMFIRST and a positive path depth can cause the upper portion of the hierarchy to be discarded. For example,

INQUIRE PATHS TO DESCENDANTS(Room, BOTTOMFIRST, 2, err, paths)

with the structures in Figure 10.1 results in the following returned paths:

Path 1	*Path 2*	*Path 3*
Pen,0	Bulb,0	Bulb,0
Blotter,3	Table,8	Light,3

Notice that there are three paths to the structure *Bulb*, but only 2 are returned. This is because the paths have been truncated such that two paths would have been identical. The redundant path is not returned.

The procedure to get the paths to a structure's ancestors is similar. One needs to use the command:

INQUIRE PATHS TO ANCESTORS   (PHOP,*,*,*)
Arguments:

in	structure identifier	integer
in	path order	(TOPFIRST,BOTTOMFIRST)

in	path depth	(0,..,n)
out	error indicator	integer
out	list of structure paths	list of paths

This routine will search the CSS for all maximal paths to ancestors of the specified structure. A maximal path of ancestors of a structure S is a list of structure identifier, element pointer pairs ((A1,E1), (A2,E2), ..., (S,0)), where A1 is not referenced by any other structure in the CSS. The path order and path depth determine what portion of the path to return. A path depth of 0 specifies that entire paths are to be returned. A positive path depth will return paths with up to the specified number of levels. Once again, only unique paths are returned, since truncated paths caused by the path depth could be redundant.

The path order determines whether the returned path should begin with the highest structure in the hierarchy, TOPFIRST, or with the structure whose ancestors are being searched for, BOTTOMFIRST. Similarly to INQUIRE PATHS TO DESCENDANTS, a non-zero path depth and the path order TOPFIRST can cause the lower portion of the returned paths to be discarded. The path order BOTTOMFIRST could also cause the upper portion of the paths to be discarded. In our previous example, the commands:

INQUIRE PATHS TO ANCESTORS(Bulb, TOPFIRST, 2, err, paths)

yields

Path 1	*Path 2*	*Path 3*
Room,5	Room,12	Room,21
Table,8	Light,3	Desk,2

and

INQUIRE PATHS TO ANCESTORS(Bulb, BOTTOMFIRST, 2, err, paths)

yields

Path 1	*Path 2*
Bulb,0	Bulb,0
Table,8	Light,3

10.1.3 Searching for elements in the CSS

In addition to using inquiry functions to get information about structures in the CSS, there are several functions to search for structure elements which meet specified requirements. In order to find an element of a certain type in the CSS, one can use the function:

ELEMENT SEARCH   (PHOP,*,*,*)

178

Arguments:

in	structure identifier	integer
in	start element position	(0,..,n)
in	search direction	(BACKWARD,FORWARD)
in	element inclusion set	list of element types
in	element exclusion set	list of element types
out	error indicator	integer
out	status indicator	(FAILURE,SUCCESS)
out	found element position	(0,..,n)

This function is used to look for specific structure elements. A structure identifier must be specified since the operating state is (PHOP,*,*,*). The search will start at the specified element position and will search either forwards or backwards, depending on the search direction. The search looks for elements which are in the inclusion set but not in the exclusion set. Any element in both sets is excluded from the search. These sets consist of a list of structure element types which are found in Tables 10.1 and 10.2. In addition to the elements in the table, the element ALL is provided to indicate all possible structure elements.

A status of FAILURE is returned if either the beginning or the end of the structure is reached without finding an element meeting the search criteria. A status of SUCCESS is returned, as well as the found element's position, if the search is successful. It is important to note that only the specified structure is searched. Referenced structures are not searched.

10.2 Archiving structures

The CSS maintains the application's graphics data in structures. These structures can be interactively edited such that their contents can be drastically changed. Without a facility to save and restore contents of the CSS to a file, it is difficult to save the results of editing the CSS from one session to another. Archive files have been introduced to address this requirement as well as to facilitate transferring structure definitions between different graphics systems. Archive files are used to save structures and structure networks as illustrated in Figure 10.2.

The archive file is a file whose format has been standardized in order for it to be read by different PHIGS implementations. It has a clear text encoding so that it is human readable as well as editable. The format of the archive file is specified in the PHIGS standard and details of its grammar and syntax are beyond the scope of this book.

It is important to remember that only structures are archived. Often a structure will use an index to refer to attributes which are kept in the workstation state list, WSL. The values of these table entries will not be archived, because they are maintained by the workstation and are not in the CSS. A common example of an indexed entry is the view index, which points to a viewing transformation in the WSL. It is common that

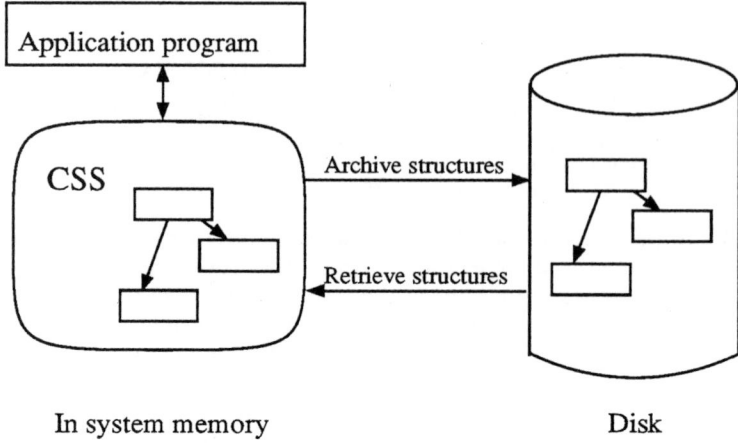

In system memory   Disk

Figure 10.2 Saving structures in an archive file.

the application will retrieve a structure from an archive file that assumes a certain viewing transformation is in the WSL. There are several methods of dealing with this problem. One method is to use inquiry functions to determine the contents of the workstation tables. A structure can then be created containing all relevant workstation table entries. This structure would contain an APPLICATION DATA (see Section 10.4) structure element with the necessary information. The application would need to encode and decode the data from this structure element in a consistent manner. If this technique is to be used to archive bundled table entries, then care must be taken to check that the workstation that uses the retrieved table entries has similar resources.

All routines which access archive files, need an archive identifier that specifies which file is meant. Before the file can be used, it must be opened:

OPEN ARCHIVE FILE   (PHOP,*,*,*)
Arguments:
           in   archive identifier   integer
           in   file   file name

This routine is called with an integer, the archive identifier, and the name of the archive file to be opened. The identifier is used to reference the open file. The specified file is opened and the archive state is set to AROP. If the file does not exist, a new file is created. More than one archive file can be simultaneously open, and each open file should have its own identifier. The maximum number of open archive files is implementation dependent, but it can be determined with the function INQUIRE PHIGS FACILITIES.

When finished using an archive file, it should be closed with the function:

CLOSE ARCHIVE FILE   (PHOP,*,*,AROP)
Arguments:
        in   archive identifier   integer

This routine closes the archive file associated with the archive identifier. The archive operating state is changed to ARCL if no further archive files are open.

10.2.1 Saving structures in an archive file

Once the archive file is open, there are several routines to save the contents of the CSS. The most obvious routine to have is:

ARCHIVE ALL STRUCTURES   (PHOP,*,*,AROP)
Arguments:
        in   archive identifier   integer

This routine saves all structures in the CSS in the file referenced by the archive identifier. This function should be called once all changes which need to be saved have been made to the CSS.

The next function is more specific. It will only archive the structure networks which it is told to:

ARCHIVE STRUCTURE NETWORKS   (PHOP,*,*,AROP)
Arguments:
        in   archive identifier   integer
        in   list of structure identifiers list of integers

This function will save all structures networks in the list. This means saving the structures in the list as well as all their descendants (child structures, children of children, ...). If a non-existent structure is referenced in the network, a warning is generated and the network which referenced the structure is not archived.

If only certain structures are to be saved, then the following routine should be used:

ARCHIVE STRUCTURES   (PHOP,*,*,AROP)
Arguments:
        in   archive identifier   integer
        in   list of structure identifiers list of integers

This will only save the listed structures in the archive file. All structures which are referenced by a structure in the list, but are not in the list themselves, are not archived.

10.2.2 Retrieving structures from an archive file

As would be expected, each of the previous routines has a corresponding routine to retrieve structures from the archive file. The following function retrieves all structures from an archive file:

RETRIEVE ALL STRUCTURES   (PHOP,*,*,AROP)
Arguments:

in	archive identifier	integer

If not all structures are to be retrieved, but only certain structure networks, then the following function should be used:

RETRIEVE STRUCTURE NETWORKS   (PHOP,*,*,AROP)
Arguments:

in	archive identifier	integer
in	list of structure identifiers	list of integers

This implies that all structures in the list, as well as any structures which are referenced with EXECUTE STRUCTURE, are retrieved. If a structure is referenced in a network to be retrieved, which is not in the archive file, a warning is generated and an empty structure is created with the offending structure's identifier.

If the application knows which structures are to be restored, and does not want to retrieve entire networks, then the following routine can be used:

RETRIEVE STRUCTURES   (PHOP,*,*,AROP)
Arguments:

in	archive identifier	integer
in	list of structure identifiers	list of integers

If a structure in the list does not exist in the archive file, a warning is generated and an empty structure is created in the CSS.

If one is not sure what is in an archive, it would be useful to get a list of structures which are archived in the file. This is similar to getting a directory listing and can be done with the function:

RETRIEVE STRUCTURE IDENTIFIERS   (PHOP,*,*,AROP)
Arguments:

in	archive	integer
out	list of structure identifiers	list of integers

Some readers might be thinking that this is too easy to be true. Unfortunately they are correct. What we have been ignoring so far, is how to deal with archiving a structure which is already in the archive file, or to retrieving a structure which is already in the CSS. Fortunately there is a mechanism to deal with these problems, namely conflict resolution.

10.2.3 Resolving conflicts in archiving

If an archive file is used several times from a given application, it will eventually contain a copy of some or all of the structures in the CSS.

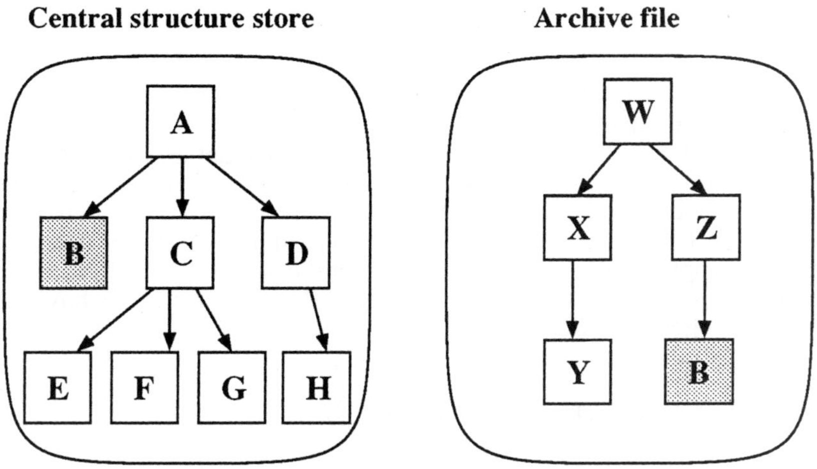

Central structure store   **Archive file**

Figure 10.3 Diagram of PHIGS archiving conflict.

Once this state has been reached, the question arises: how should one archive or restore structures which are in both the CSS and the archive file? Sometimes one will want to overwrite a structure which is in the archive, because it has been edited since the last time it was saved. On other occasions structures in the archive might be master copies which should not be overwritten.

Conflict resolution is the method with which structures in the CSS or the archive file can be write protected. The following function is used to specify how to deal with conflicts between the CSS and the archive file:

SET CONFLICT RESOLUTION   (PHOP,*,*,*)
Arguments:
      in   archival conflict   (MAINTAIN,ABANDON,UPDATE)
      in   retrieval conflict   (MAINTAIN,ABANDON,UPDATE)

This function specifies what to do with conflicts when archiving or retrieving structures. It is passed two flags: one to deal with archival conflicts and one for retrieval conflicts. Each of these flags can have one of three values. In the case of an archival conflict (see Figure 10.3), the structure B is in both the CSS and the archive file. If the CSS is to be archived, the value of the archival flag will cause the following actions:

MAINTAIN   The structure B in the archive is not overwritten by B from the CSS. All other structures from the CSS will be archived.

ABANDON   The conflict caused by structure B in both the CSS and the archive file generates an error and nothing is archived. Both the archive file and the CSS remain unchanged.

183

UPDATE   The structure in the archive file is overwritten by the structure from the CSS.

The retrieval conflict flag behaves analogously when retrieving structures from an archive file.

The conflict resolution flag can be used to maintain the integrity of the CSS or the archive file. Of course, the application needs to know which structures can be overwritten in order to use conflict resolution correctly. There are a number of archive inquiry functions which can help the application anticipate conflicts and determine how the structure networks in the archive file are organized. All these functions have been grouped together in Section 10.2.5.

10.2.4 Deleting archived structures

Structures can also be deleted in the archive file. The following three functions are used to delete structures in an archive file. The first function is:

DELETE ALL STRUCTURES FROM ARCHIVE   (PHOP,*,*,AROP)
Arguments:

in	archive identifier	integer

This routine deletes all structures in the specified archive file. After this operation, the file is as if it had been opened for the very first time.

If only certain structure networks should be deleted, then the following function should be used:

DELETE STRUCTURE NETWORKS FROM ARCHIVE   (PHOP,*,*,AROP)
Arguments:

in	archive identifier	integer
in	list of structure identifiers	list of integers

This routine will delete all structures in the list and their ancestors from the archive file. No check is made to see whether a deleted structure is referenced by another structure in the archive. In this case there will be structures in the file which execute structures which are not in the archive file. The inquiry functions described in Section 10.2.5 can be used to determine what structure networks are in an archive file in order to avoid unintentionally deleting structures which are referenced from two networks.

Finally one can delete individual structures in an archive file. This is done with:

DELETE STRUCTURES FROM ARCHIVE   (PHOP,*,*,AROP)
Arguments:

in	archive identifier	integer
in	list of structure identifiers	list of integers

In this case only the structures in the list of identifiers are deleted from the specified archive file. Once again, no check is made to see whether a deleted structure is executed by another structure in the archive. It is the application's responsibility to make sure that no structures are accidentally deleted.

10.2.5 Archive inquiry functions

This section covers the archive inquiry functions, which can help an application determine what is in the archive file. This can be especially useful when reading an archive file whose contents are not known. In this case one can determine what structure networks are in the archive file and conclude what should be retrieved and which structures are the root structures that should be posted.

Many of these inquiry functions return an error indicator. If the requested information is not available, a non-zero value is returned. Some reasons for a non-zero error indicator can be either PHIGS or the specified archive file are not open. The values that the error indicator can have are summarized in Appendix F. The first function in this list is certainly the most basic inquiry function:

INQUIRE ARCHIVE STATE VALUE   (*,*,*,*)
Arguments:
        out archive state value   (ARCL,AROP)

This function will return the archive operating state. This can be used if one is not sure if any archive files are open. Notice that this function can be called at any time, even before PHIGS has been opened. In order to find out which archive files are open and what their identifiers are, one can use:

INQUIRE ARCHIVE FILES   (PHOP,*,*,*)
Arguments:
        out error indicator   integer
        out list of archive identifiers   list of integers
        out list of archive file names list of filenames

This functions returns a list of all open archive files. This consists of a list of archive file identifiers and a list of the corresponding file names. If requested information is not available, the error indicator is set to a non-zero value. The next function will return the current state of the two conflict resolution flags:

INQUIRE CONFLICT RESOLUTION   (PHOP,*,*,*)
Arguments:
        out error indicator   integer
        out archival conflict flag   (MAINTAIN,ABANDON,UPDATE)
        out retrieval conflict flag   (MAINTAIN,ABANDON,UPDATE)

The next function will determine whether there are any conflicts between the CSS and an archive file:

INQUIRE ALL CONFLICTING STRUCTURES   (PHOP,*,*,AROP)
Arguments:

in	archive identifier	integer
out	error indicator	integer
out	list of structure identifiers	list of integers

This function returns a list of all structures in the specified archive file which conflict with structures in the CSS. If one only wants to find out whether there is a conflict in a specific network, then the next function should be used:

INQUIRE CONFLICTING STRUCTURES IN NETWORK   (PHOP,*,*,AROP)
Arguments:

in	archive identifier	integer
in	structure identifier	integer
in	structure network source	(CSS,ARCHIVE)
out	error indicator	integer
out	list of structure identifiers	list of integers

In this case a structure network is inspected to see whether it causes any conflicts. Depending on the network source flag either one of the following actions can occur:

CSS   The structure identifier and all its descendants in the CSS are compared with the structures in the archive file. All structure identifiers found in the archive that are also in the specified network are returned in a list.

ARCHIVE   The structure identifier and all its descendants in the archive are compared with the structures in the CSS. All structure identifiers found in the CSS that are also in the specified network are returned in a list.

If it is not clear how the networks in the archive file are organized, then the next two functions will be helpful in determining their structure. The first function is used to find the ancestors of a structure in the archive file:

RETRIEVE PATHS TO ANCESTORS   (PHOP,*,*,AROP)
Arguments:

in	archive file identifier	integer
in	structure identifier	integer
in	path order	(TOPFIRST,BOTTOMFIRST)
in	path depth	integer
out	paths	list of paths

This function returns a list of structure paths which reference the specified structure identifier in the specified archive file. The format of the returned list is determined by the path order and path depth parameters. The returned list of paths is exactly the same as in the function IN-

QUIRE PATHS TO ANCESTORS (see Section 10.1.2), so a description of the format in not repeated here.

RETRIEVE PATHS TO DESCENDANTS   (PHOP,*,*,AROP)
Arguments:

	in archive file identifier	integer
	in structure identifier	integer
	in path order	(TOPFIRST,BOTTOMFIRST)
	in path depth	integer
	out paths	list of paths

This function returns a list of structure paths in the specified archive file which are referenced by the specified structure. The format of the returned list is determined by the path order and path depth parameters. The returned list of paths is exactly the same as in the function INQUIRE PATHS TO DESCENDANTS (see Section 10.1.2), so a description of the format in not repeated here.

10.3 Generalized structure element

It is possible that a given PHIGS implementation might want to add functionality that is not defined by the PHIGS standard. Generalized drawing primitives have already been covered as a means for a PHIGS implementor to define additional output primitives. The generalized structure element, GSE is similar in that it provides a PHIGS-compatible interface to define non-standard functions. The GSE, however, may not be used to define output primitives and can only be used whan a structure is open.

GSEs are often used to define operations which should take place during structure traversal but do not directly generate graphical output. A GSE is created with the function:

GENERALIZED STRUCTURE ELEMENT   (PHOP,*,STOP,*)El
Arguments:

in	GSE identifier	GSE identifier
in	data record	data record

The data type of the GSE identifier and its data record are implementation specific. The identifier is usually declared as an integer type. Positive identifiers are reserved for registration by ISO. To illustrate how GSEs can be used, the following list shows some of the GSEs that have been implemented:

- pause structure traversal a specified number of seconds
- toggle display buffer and write buffer (used in double buffering)
- change image buffer's write mode, (INSERT,XOR,AND,OR, etc.)
- change boolean operation for Z buffering, (GT, LT, GE, LE, etc.).

Where additional data are required, such as the timeout in the first example, it is provided in the GSE data record. These functions are not registered by ISO. Many GSEs are specific to certain workstation types. For example, the last three functions require a physical workstation with certain hardware resources. The workstation should ignore any GSEs that it does not recognize.

Your PHIGS supplier should list what GSEs are available. One can additionally use the function INQUIRE GENERALIZED STRUCTURE ELEMENT FACILITIES to obtain a list of available GSE identifiers, as well as a list of indicators specifying whether each GSE uses workstation dependent resources. To see whether a given workstation type can use a GSE, one should use the function INQUIRE LIST OF AVAILABLE GENERALIZED STRUCTURE ELEMENTS. This function is passed a workstation type and returns a list of GSEs that are supported by the workstation. Before using GSEs, one must consider that the portability of the application will suffer through using non-standard functionality.

10.4 Application data

At times one will want to use the CSS as a database to keep information that is not directly involved with generating graphical output. This can be done with the structure element APPLICATION DATA. For example, a CAD application might want to store an object's material properties in the structure where the object is defined. When the object is picked, the structure is identified and this data could be easily retrieved.

Another possible use for APPLICATION DATA is to store information from the WSL in an archive file, as was mentioned in Section 10.2. For example, one might want to store the viewing transformations used by a structure network. In this case an application specific data record can be defined containing data from the WSL to be stored. This data record is passed to an APPLICATION DATA element belonging to a control structure that is archived. The control structure can be retrieved at a later time, interpreted and the WSL updated.

This structure element is created with the function:

```
APPLICATION DATA                                    (PHOP,*,STOP,*)El
Arguments:
          in    size of data record        integer
          in    data record                application data record
```

This element is not interpreted by PHIGS at all, so the programmer can put whatever information is necessary in the data record. The contents of the data record can be retrieved with the functions INQUIRE ELEMENT TYPE AND SIZE and INQUIRE ELEMENT CONTENT.

CHAPTER 11

Additional PHIGS Topics

This chapter addresses a number of PHIGS components that have little in common, other than they are not quite large enough to justify having a chapter dedicated to them. These components are error handling, escape functions and language binding issues.

11.1 PHIGS error handling

Throughout this text conditions have been referred to, that will result in an error being generated. This can be caused by factors varying from passing a function incorrect parameters, to trying to use resources that are not available in a particular PHIGS implementation. Some functions explicitly return an error indicator, whereas others will cause PHIGS directly to report the error condition. If the function returns an error indicator, it is the responsibility of the programmer to test it for an error condition.

Those functions which directly report error conditions, use an error handling mechanism which the applications programmer can access. This mechanism consists of two stages: error handling and error logging. Should an error be detected inside a PHIGS function, it will call:

ERROR HANDLING   (*,*,*,*)
Arguments:

in	error number	integer
in	PHIGS function identifier	function identifier
in	error file	file identifier

The application can supply its own error handling function, which will be called by PHIGS. How the error handling function is defined depends on the programming language. Section 11.3.1 covers defining an error handler from the C programming language. It will be passed the error number, an identifier of the PHIGS function which generated the error and a file identifier to report the error to. The possible error numbers are listed in Appendix F. The default error handler, supplied by PHIGS, will log errors to the error file. This is the file that was specified by the application when PHIGS was opened. The error is reported by directly calling the error logging function.

The only PHIGS functions that may be called from within an error handler are: inquiry functions, ERROR LOGGING and, if necessary, EMERGENCY CLOSE PHIGS. The error handler supplied by the application may call inquiry functions to identify what state PHIGS is in. It can then set global variables to be interpreted by the rest of the application. After the error handler is finished, it should return to the PHIGS. Generally the error handler supplied by the application will only deal with certain special cases. A structure that is found in many error handlers is:

```
ERROR HANDLING(error number, PHIGS function id, error file)
    Interpret error number and function identifier
    if( error = CATASTROPHIC )
        EMERGENCY CLOSE PHIGS()
    else if( error = special_treatment )
        Inquire PHIGS state
        Set state variables in application's global area
        Return to calling function in PHIGS
    else if( error = standard_treatment )
        Call ERROR LOGGING(error number, PHIGS function id, error file)
        Return to calling function in PHIGS
    endif
```

Logging an error consists of writing a message to an error file indicating what error was generated by which function. The following function gives the application's error handler access to PHIGS error logging utilities:

ERROR LOGGING   (*,*,*,*)
Arguments:
        in   error number   integer
        in   PHIGS function identifier function identifier
        in   error file   file identifier

This function should only be called by an error handler. The error logging function is called with the same parameters passed by PHIGS to the error handler.

The entire error handling mechanism can be disabled with the function:

SET ERROR HANDLING MODE   (PHOP,*,*,*)
Arguments:

    in   error handling mode   (OFF,ON)

When the error handling mode is set to OFF, the error handler will not be called, even when an error has occured. The default is, of course, ON.

Sometimes an error can occur that is so catastrophic that the application cannot continue. In order to save as much graphics data as possible, PHIGS provides a 'graceful' way to respond to the situation. This is done by calling the function:

EMERGENCY CLOSE PHIGS   (*,*,*,*)
Arguments:
        none

Exactly how this function behaves is implementation dependent, but it should try to perform the following steps:

1. Close the structure, if open.
2. Close any open archive files.
3. Update all open workstations.
4. Close all open workstations.
5. Close PHIGS.

This function may be called by the application if it detects an irrecoverable error, but it may also be called by PHIGS directly.

11.2 PHIGS escape functions

The escape function is a means for a implementor to add non-standard functionality to PHIGS. This is accessed through the function:

ESCAPE   (PHOP,*,*,*)
Arguments:
        in   escape function identifier   identifier
        in   escape input data record   data record
        out escape output data record   data record

One should note that escape functions can both accept and return data. Examples of escape functions that have been implemented are interfaces to a windowing system on a physical workstation, such as the MIT X11 system. For example, changing the title of the window on the screen, getting the window identifier of an open workstation, etc. Other implementations use escapes to read and write the contents of the drawing surface or Z buffer on a physical workstation. There are a number of restrictions on what escapes can do. They must not cause output to be drawn, create structure elements or change the PHIGS state list. If escape functions are provided, they will be documented by the PHIGS supplier.

11.3 Language bindings

The PHIGS functions have been discussed independently of any particular programming language. The application accesses PHIGS through calls to library functions. The interface to PHIGS, defined by a set of function calls, arguments, and parameter constants, is known as the *language binding*. Each language has certain features which must be addressed when defining the binding. Here only the C and FORTRAN bindings are considered.

11.3.1 The ISO C binding

The ISO C binding was standardized in late 1991. Prior to this, a large number of hardware and software companies have been releasing PHIGS libraries with a proprietary C binding. These bindings are in general not compatible with the ISO standard. Currently (early 1992) most PHIGS libraries are using the old C binding. The most obvious difference between the ISO binding and these proprietary interfaces is that the ISO call decomposes the PHIGS function name and data types into a set of keywords separated by underscores. So, for example, the function SET LOCAL TRANSFORMATION 3 is commonly implemented as:

```
psetlocaltran3( Pmatrix3 Mat, Pcomptype );
```

is as follows in the ISO binding:

```
pset_local_tran3( Pmatrix3 Mat, Pcompose_type );
```

It is expected that in the next several years the various proprietary bindings will eventually converge to the ISO standard. This will require a limited amount of porting effort for those applications using the old C binding. Other functions have slight differences in their arguments. For example, the function:

```
pawaitevent( Pfloat Timeout, Pevent *Event );
```

is under the ISO binding:

```
pawait_event( Pfloat Timeout, Pint *WsId,
              Pin_class *DevClass, Pint *DevNumber );
```

An important part of the ISO C binding are several additional functions to simplify using PHIGS. The first function belonging to the C binding is used to define an application specific error handler. How this function is used was covered in Section 11.1. This is done with the function:

SET ERROR HANDLER   (*,*,*,*)
Arguments:
            in   new error handler   function pointer

192

out   old error handler   function pointer

This has been realized in C as follows:

```
pset_err_hand( void( *new_func)(),void( **old_func)() );
```

The last two binding-specific utility functions are used in conjunction with a number of inquiry routines that return complex data structures. These utilities allocate and free memory needed by these inquiry functions. The C binding defines two functions: CREATE STORE and DELETE STORE. The store is memory that has been allocated by the implementation to contain data that is being returned by these inquiry functions. The application must create a store prior to using a function that needs it. The functions to create and delete stores are:

CREATE STORE   (PHOP,*,*,*)
Arguments:

out	error indicator	integer
out	store	store

DELETE STORE   (PHOP,*,*,*)
Arguments:

out	error indicator	integer
in/out	store	store

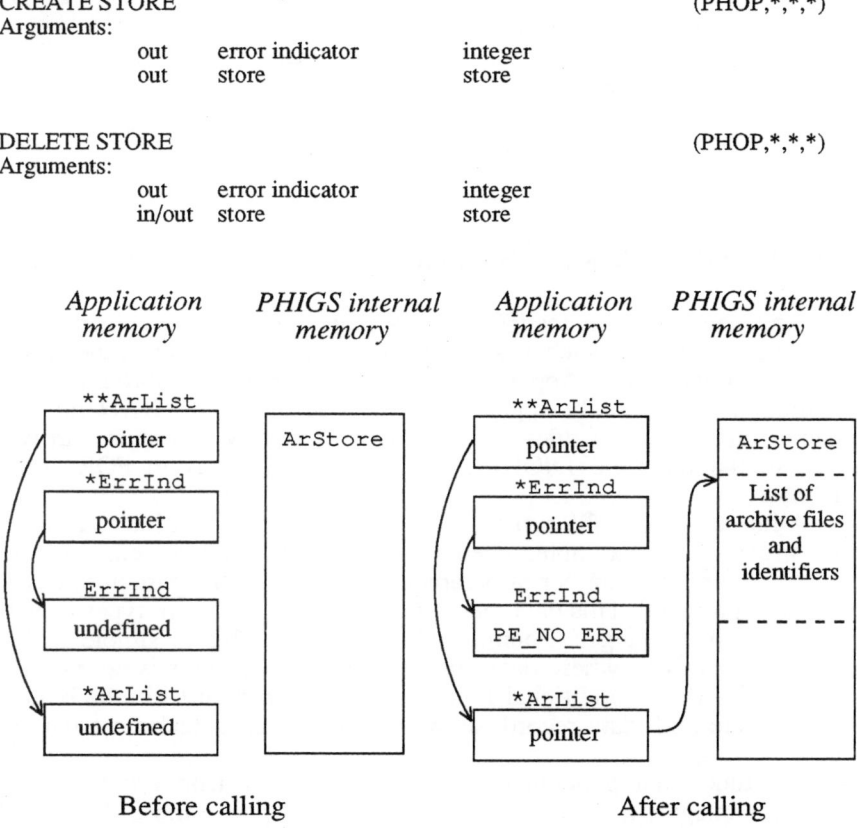

Figure 11.1 Using the store resource in the ISO C binding.

193

The internal structure of the store is transparent to the application. The data in the store will be accessed by de-referencing pointers that are returned by the inquiry functions. For example, the function INQUIRE ARCHIVE FILES returns a list of file names and their identifiers. These lists are kept in the store. Figure 11.1 shows how the store is being used by this inquiry function. Before reusing a store, one should copy all data out of it into application memory otherwise they will be overwritten. To use this inquiry function one would need code similar to the following:

```
Pint            ErrInd;
Pint            NumFiles;
Pstore          ArStore;
Par_file_list   *ArList;

pcreate_store( &ErrInd, &ArStore );
pinq_ar_files( ArStore, &ErrInd, &ArList );
NumFiles = ArList->num_ar_files;
/* etc.  . . . etc. */
pdelete_store( &err, ArStore );
```

11.3.2 The ISO FORTRAN binding

Several constraints in the FORTRAN language must be considered in defining its binding, such as six character function names and the lack of structured data types. Appendix C lists the FORTRAN subroutine calls. Although they initially appear to be cryptic, the FORTRAN function names follow a set of rules. For example, all inquiry functions start with PQ, so the function: INQUIRE ARCHIVE FILES is in FORTRAN: PQARF.

A number of PHIGS functions require arguments that have an intrinsic structure. For example, when an input device is initialized, a data record containing a number of parameters specific to that particular device must be provided. This data record might contain different types of variables, such as integer, floating point or string. This is simple in languages such as C, where data types can be defined. This is not possible in FORTRAN, so additional functions have been defined in the binding to generate both data records as well as to extract data from a data record.

The function to generate the data record is straightforward. It is called with an integer, a real and a string array and packs these data into a CHARACTER*80 array. This array is then passed to the function which required the data record, for example, INITIALIZE STRING. The exact syntax of the data packing routine is:

```
CALL PPREC(IL,IA, RL,RA, SL,LSTR,SA, MLDR,ERR,LDR,DATREC)
```

Input arguments:

INTEGER	IL	: length of integer array
INTEGER	IA(*)	: integer array
INTEGER	RL	: length of real array
REAL	RA(*)	: real array
INTEGER	SL	: length of string array
INTEGER	LSTR(*)	: array of string lengths
CHARACTER*(*)	SA	: string array
INTEGER	MLDR	: dimension of array DATREC

Output arguments:

INTEGER	ERR	: error indicator
INTEGER	LDR	: no. elements used in DATREC
CHARACTER*80	DATREC(MLDR)	: data record

One should point out that the argument MLDR is necessary for PPREC to determine if DATREC is large enough to contain the data to be packed. If it is not, then a non-zero error indicator will be returned. The actual contents of the integer, real and string arrays depends on the function requiring the data record and on how it is being used. For example, to initialize the input devices one must use different data for different prompt and echo types (see Chapter 8). Appendix A contains a FORTRAN example which uses PPREC to prepare data records for two different input devices. The documentation provided by the PHIGS supplier should list exactly what data is required for each function needing a packed data record.

Other PHIGS functions, such certain inquiry functions, return a record containing integer, real and string data. This record must be unpacked in order to interpret the data. This is done with the function:

```
CALL PUPREC( LDR,DATREC, MIL,MRL,MSL, ERR,
+                  IL,IA, RL,RA, SL,LSTR,SA )
```

Input arguments:

INTEGER	LDR	: no. elements used in DATREC
CHARACTER*80	DATREC(LDR)	: data record
INTEGER	MIL	: maximum integer array length
INTEGER	MRL	: maximum real array length
INTEGER	MSL	: maximum string array length

Output arguments:

INTEGER	ERR	: error indicator
INTEGER	IL	: number of unpacked integers
INTEGER	IA(*)	: integer array
INTEGER	RL	: number of unpacked reals
REAL	RA(*)	: real array

```
INTEGER      SL          : number of unpacked strings
INTEGER      LSTR(*)     : array of string lengths
CHARACTER*(*) SA         : string array
```

The arguments for this function are similar to those in PPREC, except now that the data record and its length are input parameters and the unpacked data are returned in the integer, real and string arrays. The data record and its length were returned by the inquiry function. Now we need to specify the maximum lengths of the integer, real and string arrays to avoid PUREC overrunning the declared sizes of these arrays. If an overrun occurs, a non-zero error indicator is returned, otherwise the unpacked data is returned in the arrays.

CHAPTER 12

PHIGS PLUS Output Primitives

In 1986 an *ad hoc* working group was formed in the USA, with partici-
pants from the academic and industrial communities, whose goal was to
define extensions to PHIGS. These extensions were to address emerging
technologies such as lighting and shading, as well as advanced primitives. The result of these efforts is currently a draft international standard, PHIGS PLUS. Since it has not yet been formally adopted as a standard, the PHIGS PLUS specification might change. This text is based on
the ISO draft standard dated 1991 [ISOe].

At the time the PHIGS PLUS working group was formed, lighting
and shading techniques were available through a number of proprietary
graphics libraries. In many cases these libraries were provided by manufacturers of 3D graphics hardware. It became apparent that the acceptance of PHIGS in the 3D graphics community would be severely affected if no means were provided to use these advanced rendering techniques. Now most available PHIGS implementations contain some
features which have been defined in the PHIGS PLUS specification.
PHIGS PLUS extends PHIGS by providing the following functionality:

- advanced rendering: lighting, shading, depth cueing, data mapping
- advanced primitives: curves, surfaces, triangular strip, quadrilateral
  mesh, etc.
- differentiation between front and back facing primitives
- direct colour specification.

Prior to introducing the PHIGS PLUS output primitives, direct colour
needs to be mentioned, since it is used by many primitives.

197

12.1 Direct colour

PHIGS PLUS addresses the needs of the 3D computer graphics market requiring a high degree of realism. The PHIGS colour model is limited, because colours are defined as entries in a table that are selected with an index. Physical workstations with 24 bitplanes of image memory, allowing one to use up to 16.7 million colours, are now common in the 3D graphics community. Realistic graphics require a more general way to specify colours. PHIGS PLUS meets this requirement with the *direct colour* specification. This gives the application writer the freedom to use more colours than could be defined in a colour table.

Direct colour uses a *general colour* which contains two fields, a colour type and a colour. The colour type can be one of the following:

0	INDIRECT
1	RGB
2	CIE LUV
3	HSV
4	HLS

In the case that the colour type is INDIRECT the colour is an integer which is used as an index in the PHIGS colour table. This is similar to the PHIGS attribute SET XXX COLOUR INDEX. When the colour type is greater than zero the colour is a tuple containing the components in the specified colour model (see Section 5.2). For the colour types listed above, the colour is defined as three real numbers. Examples of general colour are:

RED	{ 1, { 1.0, 0.0, 0.0 } }
BLUE	{ 1, { 0.0, 0.0, 1.0 } }
YELLOW	{ 1, { 1.0, 1.0, 0.0 } }

In these examples the colour type was 1, or RGB, and the colour was a triplet specifying the red, green and blue components.

Introducing direct colour requires a number of attribute specification functions which use the general colour. These functions are:

SET POLYLINE COLOUR   (PHOP,*,STOP,*)El
Arguments:
        in   polyline colour   general colour

SET POLYMARKER COLOUR   (PHOP,*,STOP,*)El
Arguments:
        in   polymarker colour   general colour

SET TEXT COLOUR   (PHOP,*,STOP,*)El
Arguments:
        in   text colour   general colour

SET INTERIOR COLOUR   (PHOP,*,STOP,*)El
Arguments:
      in   interior colour   general colour

SET EDGE COLOUR   (PHOP,*,STOP,*)El
Arguments:
      in   edge colour   general colour

12.2 PHIGS PLUS output primitives

To use advanced rendering effectively, one needs to specify more than just coordinate data defining the shape of the primitive. PHIGS PLUS has added a number of new output primitives, most of which allow additional data to be defined, These primitives will be referred to as *'with data primitives'*. Table 12.1 lists all primitives defined in PHIGS PLUS:

Table 12.1   PHIGS PLUS output primitives.

Direct colour primitive:
    CELL ARRAY 3 PLUS

Line drawing primitive:
    POLYLINE SET 3 WITH DATA

Primitives which define facets:
    FILL AREA SET 3 WITH DATA
    FILL AREA SET WITH DATA
    SET OF FILL AREA SET 3 WITH DATA
    SET OF FILL AREA SET WITH DATA
    TRIANGLE SET 3 WITH DATA
    TRIANGLE SET WITH DATA
    TRIANGLE STRIP 3 WITH DATA
    TRIANGLE STRIP WITH DATA
    QUADRILATERAL MESH 3 WITH DATA
    QUADRILATERAL MESH WITH DATA

Spline primitives:
    NON-UNIFORM B-SPLINE CURVE
    NON-UNIFORM B-SPLINE CURVE WITH COLOUR
    NON-UNIFORM B-SPLINE SURFACE
    NON-UNIFORM B-SPLINE SURFACE WITH DATA

Table 12.1 shows that all but three of the PHIGS PLUS output primitives define additional data. The 'with data primitives' can be grouped into three classes: lines, primitives which define facets, and spline primitives (see Table 12.1). Only one function belongs to the line drawing class, namely POLYLINE SET 3 WITH DATA. This function allows one to define a colour in addition to the coordinates at each vertex and will be discussed later. The majority of the PHIGS PLUS primitives define facets. A facet is simply a polygon. For example, a FILL AREA SET 3 WITH DATA containing one fill area consists of a single facet, whereas the QUADRILATERAL MESH 3 WITH DATA defines a grid of facets. The actual geometric structure of each primitive will be discussed later. These primitives occur in both a 2D and a 3D form. Only the 3D form of these primitives will be treated here. All the PHIGS PLUS faceted primitives use the same mechanism to define additional data. This mechanism will be treated here and will be referred to throughout the rest of the chapter. To achieve realism and flexibility, PHIGS PLUS has defined the following types of data which can be associated with an output primitive in addition to the coordinates:

- none
- colour
- normal vectors
- application specific data

These data may be defined for each facet as well as for each vertex of the facet. PHIGS PLUS uses two flags to identify what additional data is being defined: the *facet data flag* and the *vertex data flag*. Figure 12.1 illustrates the relationship between the primitive data and the facet. These flags can take one of the following values:

Table 12.2   PHIGS PLUS primitive data types.

Facet data	*Vertex data:* (COORDINATES &)
NONE	NONE
COLOUR	COLOUR
NORMAL	NORMAL
DATA	DATA
COLOUR & NORMAL	COLOUR & NORMAL
COLOUR & DATA	COLOUR & DATA
NORMAL & DATA	NORMAL & DATA
COLOUR & NORMAL & DATA	COLOUR & NORMAL & DATA

Defining colour data allows the application to bind a colour with either each facet of a multi-faceted primitive, or with each vertex. This colour is either an index or a colour-tuple, depending on the colour type. An area filling attribute, INTERIOR SHADING METHOD, determines how colours defined at the vertices are mapped onto the entire primitive. This will be covered in the subsequent chapter on PHIGS PLUS rendering. The colour data is defined with the primitive's geometry, allowing one to directly associate a colour field with the shape of a primitive. This simplifies defining a coloured, multi-faceted object.

Normal vectors are used to define the orientation of a primitive in MC. The orientation is required by the lighting model, and in determining which primitives are backfacing. If each facet were flat, then only a normal vector per facet would be needed. The lighting and shading

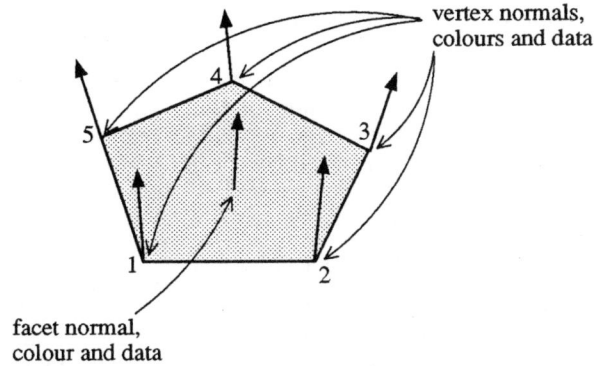

vertex normals, colours and data

facet normal, colour and data

Figure 12.1 Data with area filling primitives.

stages of the rendering pipeline can be used to approximate the appearance of a curved facet by specifying a different normal for each vertex. It is important to note that the shape of a primitive is still only determined by the coordinates. Lighting and shading will be covered in more detail in the subsequent chapter on rendering in PHIGS PLUS.

PHIGS PLUS provides a utility routine to calculate the facet normal. This routine takes the vector cross product of the first three non-colinear vertices. The sign of the normal vector depends, of course, on the order of the vertices (see Figure 12.1). The normal vector is calculated with the function:

COMPUTE FILL AREA SET GEOMETRIC NORMAL   (PHOP,*,*,*)
Arguments:

in	vertex coordinates	array of vertex arrays in MC
out	error indicator	integer
out	normal vector	normal vector

The application data is a recent addition to the PHIGS PLUS draft proposal. This enables one to bind additional data to either each facet or to each vertex. These data can be mapped to a primitive's *intrinsic colour*. A primitive's intrinsic colour is the colour it assumes independent of lighting or the rest of the rendering pipeline. Whether the application data is used to define the intrinsic colour, or how it is used depends on the *data mapping method*. This will be covered in detail in the subsequent chapter on rendering.

For now it suffices to say that the application data can consist of one or more real values that may be mapped to a colour. These data are bound to either the facets or the vertices. More data can be defined with the primitive than can be used in any given rendering. This can be useful to visualize a scalar field associated with the surface of an object. These fields could represent the temperature or the pressure at each vertex of the object. In order to map a given field, such as temperature, to the sur-

201

face's colour one needs only to select the appropriate data mapping method.

Finally, edge data can also be bound to an output primitive in PHIGS PLUS. Edge data consist of a flag for each edge of a facet. This flag determines whether the given edge is visible or not. Whether a primitive contains edge data is determined by the *edge data flag* that can assume one of the two values:

> NONE
> EDGE_VISIBILITY_FLAGS

When edge data is specified, an array of edge flags is defined with the primitive, one flag for each edge. For example, a triangular facet would have three edge flags, which could be either ON or OFF.

The first primitive we encounter that uses these data is FILL AREA SET 3 WITH DATA. The discussion of this function will clarify how to use primitive data. The remaining 'with data' functions will go into lesser depth on how to define the data, since it relies on the same mechanism. Before starting with the faceted primitives, the POLYLINE SET 3 WITH DATA should be covered.

12.2.1 Polyline set 3 with data

This function serves two purposes: it can be used to define more than one polyline in one primitive and it can be used to bind colour data to each vertex in a polyline. This primitive is created with the function:

POLYLINE SET 3 WITH DATA   (PHOP,*,STOP,*)El
Arguments:

in	vertex data flag	(COORDINATES, COORDINATES_COLOUR)
in	colour type	(INDEXED,RGB,CIELUV,HLS,HSV)
in	number of polylines	integer
in	vertices per polyline	array of integers
in	vertex data	array of 3D points in MC and vertex colours

The vertex data flag determines whether just coordinates or coordinates and colours are passed as vertex data. The colour type identifies how the colours have been defined, either from the workstation colour table or directly. Multiple polylines can be defined with this single primitive. In cases where only coordinate vertex data is defined, it is often more efficient to process one primitive containing many polylines than independent primitives. In many PHIGS implementations this primitive can render the same set of polylines faster than independent calls to POLYLINE 3.

When colour data is defined per vertex, an attribute is used to determine how to render the primitive, the *polyline shading method*. This attribute determines whether to draw the line segment between two adjacent vertices in a single colour, or to blend the colour linearly from one vertex to the next. The later form of shading is also referred to as linearly interpolating the colour. This attribute can be set directly with the function:

SET POLYLINE SHADING METHOD   (PHOP,*,STOP,*)El
Arguments:
      in   polyline shading method   (NONE,COLOUR)

12.2.2 Fill area set 3 with data

This primitive is similar to the PHIGS function FILL AREA SET 3. It differs in that one can define additional data as described in Section 12.2. The function to create this primitive is:

FILL AREA SET 3 WITH DATA   (PHOP,*,*STOP,*)El
Arguments:
in	facet data flag	see Table 12.2
in	edge data flag	(NONE,EDGE_VISIBILITY_FLAGS)
in	vertex data flag	see Table 12.2
in	colour type	(INDEXED,RGB,CIELUV,HLS,HSV)
in	facet data	array of facet data
in	edge flags	array of edge flags
in	vertex data	array of vertex data arrays, see text

The first three arguments are flags that determine what data is provided in the subsequent arguments. Depending on the facet data flag, the facet data will consist of either: an array of colours, an array of normal vectors, or an array of application data that can be mapped to a colour. These arrays will contain one entry per fill area in the set. Table 12.2 shows that any combination of these three arrays can be defined, or none at all. The edge data flag determines whether an edge data array is provided. If it is, an edge flags array should be defined with a flag per edge, determining whether to display the edge or not.

There is more structure to the vertex data than is shown in this function declaration. This is because the PHIGS PLUS. function is defined independent of a specific language binding. It should, however, not interfere with understanding how to use this function from any given language. The vertex data specifies how many fill areas are in the set, as well as how many vertices each fill area has. In addition to this, up to four arrays can be provided. An array of 3D coordinate data in MC is always specified. The vertex data flag determines which of the following additional arrays needs to be defined: colour, normal vectors or application data. The subsequent chapter on rendering will deal with the facet and vertex data in more detail.

12.2.3 Set of fill area set 3 with data

This function will generate a number of fill area sets with one primitive. The primary feature of this function is that the vertices are defined as a set of indices pointing into a single vertex array, which contains the co-ordinate and other vertex data. This gives a level of indirection so, should two fill areas share a common vertex, the actual vertex data does not have to be duplicated. This function has replaced a function found in earlier PHIGS PLUS drafts: POLYHEDRON 3 WITH DATA. The former name indicates that this function can be used to define tetrahedrons, cubes, etc.; but it was misleading since the function is much more general than that. This primitive is created with the function:

SET OF FILL AREA SET 3 WITH DATA   (PHOP,*,STOP,*)El
Arguments:

in	facet data flag	see Table 12.2
in	edge data flag	(NONE,EDGE_VISIBILITY_FLAGS)
in	vertex data flag	see Table 12.2
in	colour type	(INDEXED,RGB,CIELUV,HLS,HSV)
in	facet data	array of facet data
in	edge flags	array of edge flags
in	vertex data	array of vertex data, see text
in	vertex indices	list of arrays of integer arrays

Once again one has three flags indicating what type of data is provided. In addition to the arguments described here, one must specify the number of fill area sets, the number of fill areas per fill area set, and the number of vertices for each fill area. The vertex indices consist of a list of integers pointing into the vertex array for each fill area in the fill area

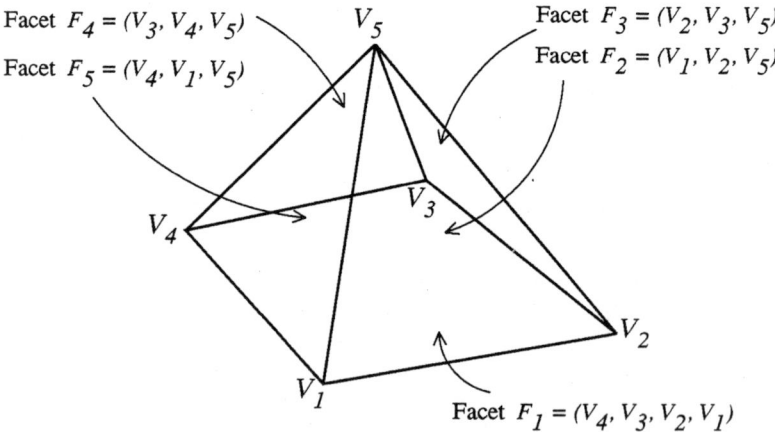

$\text{Facet } F_4 = (V_3, V_4, V_5)$

$\text{Facet } F_5 = (V_4, V_1, V_5)$

$\text{Facet } F_3 = (V_2, V_3, V_5)$

$\text{Facet } F_2 = (V_1, V_2, V_5)$

$\text{Facet } F_1 = (V_4, V_3, V_2, V_1)$

Figure 12.2 A pyramid as a set of fill area set 3 with data.

set. Each fill area set is defined by an array of index arrays, one array per fill area. Finally, the set of fill area set is specified by a list of fill area set arrays. The facet and vertex data is used as described in Section 12.2. The fill areas that are defined are the facets in this primitive. The application programmer should ensure that the vertices of the fill areas are coplanar.

As an example of how this function can be used, consider drawing a pyramid. It consists of a square and four triangles, a total of sixteen vertices. Each vertex is shared by several fill areas. Using the set of fill area set 3 with data, one need only define an array containing five vertices, and set the appropriate indices for each fill area, see Figure 12.2.

12.2.4 Triangle set 3 with data

This function is similar to SET OF FILL AREA SET 3 WITH DATA, except that it is more restrictive. A large number of applications, for example finite element analysis, use sets of triangles to define the shape of a surface. The triangle set meets this requirement. Each facet in this primitive is a triangle, defined by three indices into the vertex data array. To define this primitive one should call:

TRIANGLE SET 3 WITH DATA   (PHOP,*,STOP,*)El
Arguments:

in	facet data flag	see Table 12.2
in	edge data flag	(NONE,EDGE_VISIBILITY_FLAGS)
in	vertex data flag	see Table 12.2
in	colour type	(INDEXED,RGB,CIELUV,HLS,HSV)
in	facet data	array of facet data see Section 12.2
in	edge flags	array of edge flags
in	vertex data	array of vertex data see Section 12.2
in	vertex indices	array of integers

With this function one also needs to specify how many triangles are in the triangle set. Each group of three indices defines a separate facet. One should consult the PHIGS supplier's documentation for details on how to define this primitive.

12.2.5 Triangle strip 3 with data

This function is very similar to TRIANGLE SET 3 WITH DATA, but has been a part of the PHIGS PLUS specification much longer. This function defines a strip of connected triangles. Each triangle in the strip shares two vertices with the previous triangle (see Figure 12.3). After defining the first triangle, each subsequent triangle is created by defining an additional vertex. This allows one to define n triangles with just $n+2$ vertices. Because the vertices are directly specified, instead of being de-

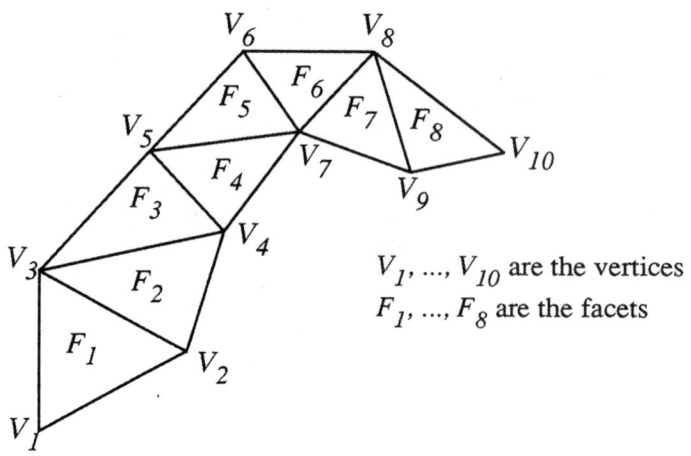

Figure 12.3 Triangle strip 3 with data primitive.

fined through indices, and because of its compact notation, triangle strips are drawn by many PHIGS implementations using special algorithms and hardware. Performance sensitive applications should consider using this primitive when possible. A triangle strip is created with the primitive:

TRIANGLE STRIP 3 WITH DATA   (PHOP,*,STOP,*)El
Arguments:

in	facet data flag	see Table 12.2
in	edge data flag	(NONE,EDGE_VISIBILITY_FLAGS)
in	vertex data flag	see Table 12.2
in	colour type	(INDEXED,RGB,CIELUV,HLS,HSV)
in	facet data	array of facet data see Section 12.2
in	edge flags	array of edge flags
in	vertex data	array of vertex data see Section 12.2

The vertex data is arranged such that vertices V_1, V_2, V_3 define the first triangle; vertices V_2, V_3, V_4 the second and so on. Each triangle is a facet, so if facet data is defined for a triangle strip with n vertices, the facet data array will have $n-2$ entries.

12.2.6 Quadrilateral mesh 3 with data

The quadrilateral mesh defines a grid of quadrilaterals, four-sided polygons. This is often useful when drawing surfaces that can be defined as a function of two variables, for example, a torus. Each vertex is defined once, and will be shared by adjacent facets. For example, an interior vertex will be shared by four quadrilaterals (see Figure 12.4). This primitive is created with the function:

QUADRILATERAL MESH 3 WITH DATA   (PHOP,*,STOP,*)El
Arguments:

in	facet data flag	see Table 12.2
in	edge data flag	(NONE,EDGE_VISIBILITY_FLAGS)
in	vertex data flag	see Table 12.2
in	colour type	(INDEXED,RGB,CIELUV,HLS,HSV)
in	facet data	array of facet data see Section 12.2
in	edge flags	array of edge flags
in	vertex data	array of vertex data see Section 12.2

The number of facets in each direction of the mesh will also have to be specified when defining the size of the vertex data array. A mesh consisting of m rows by n columns of four-sided facets requires $m+1$ by $n+1$ vertices. Since adjacent facets share the same edges, a quadmesh contains $m(n+1) + n(m+1)$ edges. This can be verified by counting the facets, edges and vertices in Figure 12.4. These numbers also indicate the size of the facet, edge and vertex arrays. One needs to consult the documentation provided by your PHIGS supplier for details on the parameters used when defining this primitive.

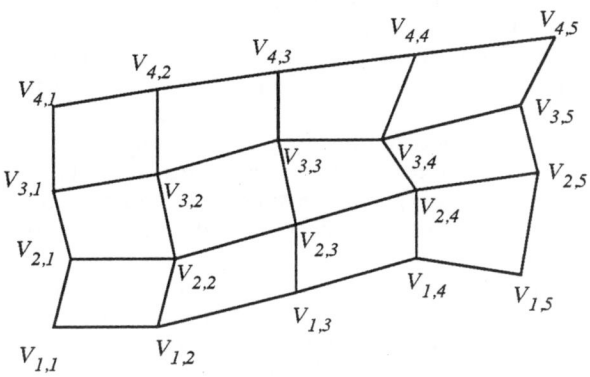

Figure 12.4 Quadrilateral mesh 3 with data primitive.

12.2.7 Cell array 3 plus

This function has been added to PHIGS PLUS to take advantage of direct colour. It is similar to the function CELL ARRAY 3, described in Chapter 4. The only difference is that CELL ARRAY 3 was defined with a grid of colour indices, whereas CELL ARRAY 3 PLUS uses general colour. The colour type determines what data is defined in the colour array. If the type is INDEXED, then the array is a grid of indices, otherwise it is a grid of floating point triplets in the specified colour model. This primitive is created with the function:

CELL ARRAY 3 PLUS   (PHOP,*,STOP,*)El
Arguments:

in	cell parallelogram	three 3D points in MC
in	rows	integer
in	columns	integer
in	colour type	(INDEXED,RGB,CIELUV,HLS,HSV)
in	array of colours	array of general colours

See Section 4.6 for details on cell array.

12.3 Spline functions

PHIGS PLUS has introduced four different spline functions, two for defining curves and two for surfaces. Splines differ from other PHIGS primitives in that one does not explicitly define vertices. The shape of a spline function is determined by a set of *control points*. Whereas previous output primitives connected vertices with either straight line segments, or 'flat' facets; splines are higher order functions. A spline curve maps an interval in a parameter space onto a curve in modelling coordinates (see Figure 12.5), while a spline surface maps a two-dimensional area in a parameter space onto a surface in MC. PHIGS PLUS uses *non-uniform rational B-splines*, NURB's, to define curves and surfaces.

It is beyond the scope of this text to cover spline functions in any depth, so the reader is referred to the excellent texts on the subject [Farin; Rogers and Adams]. For the sake of simplicity, this introduction to spline functions will focus on curves, a generalization to surfaces will follow.

Spline theory is based on piecewise continuous polynomials. This requires defining a *knot vector* that partitions the interval in parameter space. The knots are used to generate B-spline basis functions, which are weighted by the control points to define the curve:

$$C(t) = \sum_{i=1}^{n} B_{ik}(t)\, P_i$$

The knot vector is an array of real numbers $\{t_i\}_{i=1..n+k}$ partitioning the interval *[a,b]* such that:

$$a = t_1 \le t_2 \le \ldots \le t_{n+k} = b$$

$$t_i < t_{i+k} \quad \text{for} \quad i=1,\ldots,n$$

In this case the knots are defined for a kth order spline. The knot vec-

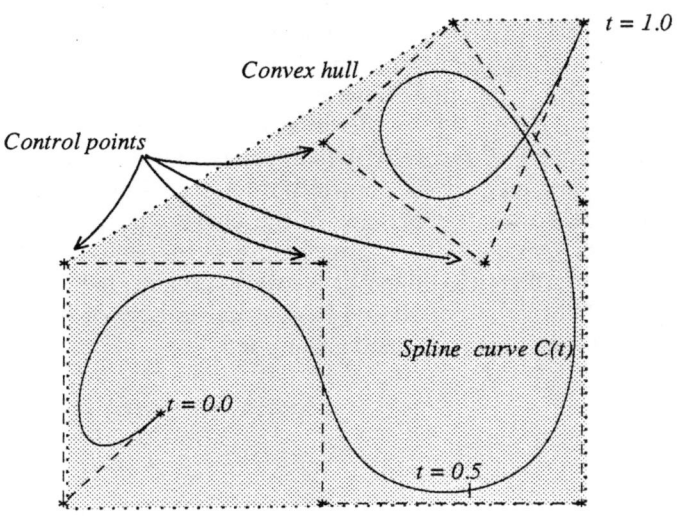

Figure 12.5 Cubic B-spline curve with 11 control points.

tor is an array of increasing real numbers, where up to k knots can assume the same value. The number of times a knot is repeated is known
as its *multiplicity*. A kth order spline can have a multiplicity of up to k.
The knots define the B-spline basis functions through the following recursion formula:

$$B_{i1}(t) = \begin{cases} 1, & \text{for} \quad t_i \leq t \leq t_{i+1} \\ 0, & \text{otherwise} \end{cases}$$

$$B_{ik}(t) = \begin{cases} \dfrac{(t - t_i)\, B_{i,k-1}(t)}{(t_{i+k-1} - t_i)} + \dfrac{(t_{i+k} - t)\, B_{i+1,k-1}(t)}{(t_{i+k} - t_{i+1})} & \text{for} \quad t_i \leq t \leq t_{i+k} \\ 0 & \text{otherwise} \end{cases}$$

If $(t_{i+1} - t_i)$ is the same for $i = k,...,n$, the resulting spline is called *uniform*. The smoothness or continuity of a spline is determined by the multiplicity of the knot vector. A kth order spline with a knot of multiplicity
k-1 results in a curve whose first derivative is not continuous, resulting
in a sharp corner (see Figure 12.6). The lower the multiplicity, the
smoother the curve, up to a multiplicity of one, which results in a
curve continuous up to the $(k$-$1)^{st}$ derivative.

In addition to a knot vector in parameter space, one needs to define control points in MC, to determine the shape of the curve. A kth order spline with n control points must have $n+k$ knots. The number of control points must be at least as large as the order k. An interesting property of splines is the *convex hull property*, which states that the spline will remain in the area spanned by its control points, (see Figure 12.5). This property helps one to relate the shape of the curve with the position of the control points. Another interesting feature is that moving a control point only locally affects the shape of a spline. Finally, the knots at the end points of a kth order spline should have a multiplicity of k which will force the spline to pass through the control point.

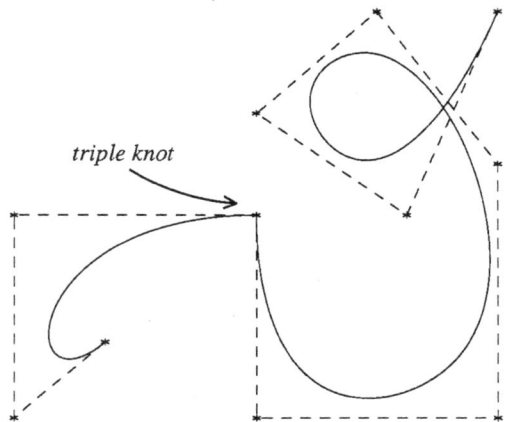

Figure 12.6 Fourth order spline curve with a triple knot.

To determine the shape of the curve, the PHIGS PLUS programmer needs to specify the order of the spline, k; the knot vector with $n+k$ knots; and n control points.

So far we have been discussing non-rational splines. PHIGS PLUS also allows one to define rational splines, which were introduced in a dissertation [Versprille]. Rational B-splines were introduced to a wider audience via an article [Tiller]. Rational splines combine spline theory with projective geometry. This results in having to define the control points in homogeneous coordinates (see Section 6.1):

$$P_i^h = (x_i w_i,\ y_i w_i,\ z_i w_i,\ w_i) = (P_i\ w_i,\ w_i)$$

$P_i = (x_i, y_i, z_i)$ is the position of the control point in MC, and the fourth component, w_i, is known as the weight coefficient. PHIGS PLUS requires the weights to be positive, although zero valued, or even negative weights, are theoretically possible and result in splines with interesting properties [Piegl a; Versprille]. Rational splines are calculated in homogeneous coordinates and are then projected onto MC. This results in the following formula for the rational spline curve:

$$C(t) = \frac{\sum_{i=1}^{n} B_{ik}(t)\, w_i\, P_i}{\sum_{i=1}^{n} B_{ik}(t)\, w_i}$$

Rational splines have a number of advantages over non-rational splines:

* closed under perspective transformations
* individual control points can be weighted
* exact representation for quadratic curves and surfaces.

The first point is especially important for 3D graphics, since it states that it does not matter whether one applies a perspective transformation to the control points and then calculates the NURB curve, or transforms the curve. The weight coefficient can be used to specify the influence of an individual control point without affecting the continuity of the spline. It can be shown [Piegl b] that one can calculate exactly how to change a weight coefficient to move the curve a fixed distance towards a given control point, (see Figure 12.7, Colour Plates 6 and 8). The influence of a control point is determined by the relative magnitude of its weight coefficient. Finally, one can exactly represent quadric curves and surfaces with NURBs; for example, a circle, sphere, torus, surface of revolution, etc. These objects can only be approximated by non-rational splines.

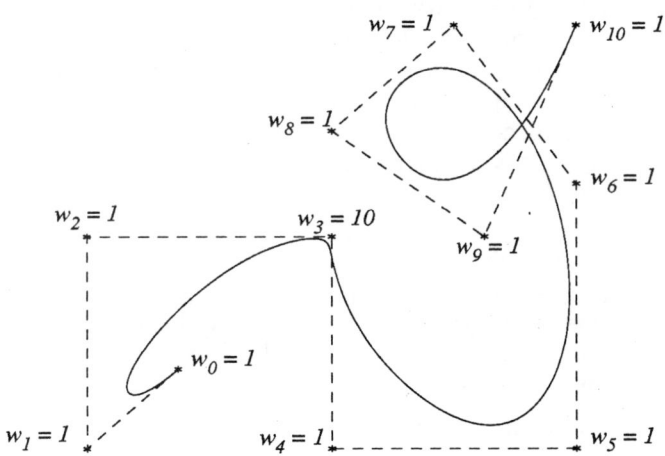

Figure 12.7 Effect of changing a rational spline's weight.

12.3.1 Spline curves

Now that the theory of splines has been briefly introduced, we can look at how PHIGS PLUS has implemented spline curves. There are two spline curves, the only difference being that one only defines the curve's shape and the other also allows one to determine how the colour is to change along the length of the curve. A spline curve primitive is defined with the function:

NON-UNIFORM B-SPLINE CURVE   (PHOP,*,STOP,*)El
Arguments:

in	spline order	integer
in	knots	array of real numbers
in	parameter limits	two real numbers
in	rationality	(RATIONAL,NON-RATIONAL)
in	control points	list of points in MC or homogeneous space

Here the order is an integer k, which should be greater than 1. For $k=2$, the spline is linear, so the control points will be connected by straight line segments. The knots are a sequence of real numbers $(t_1,...,t_{n+k})$ for a spline with n control points. The knots follow the restrictions that the sequence is non-decreasing and that no knot value is repeated more than k times. The parameter limits t_{min},t_{max} are two real numbers where:

$$t_{min} \geq t_k \quad \text{and} \quad t_{max} \leq t_{n+1}$$

This defines the parameter range used to draw the spline curve. The *rationality* is a flag to identify whether the spline curve is a non-rational curve with control points in MC, or a rational curve with control points in homogeneous space. For the case of a non-rational curve, one needs to specify a list of n controls points in MC. Remember at least k control points must be defined. A rational curve consists of a list of points in homogeneous space. It is simpler to understand the rational control point as a point in MC $P_i = (x_i, y_i, z_i)$ and a weight $w_i > 0$. Each point is then specified as $(x_i w_i, y_i w_i, z_i w_i, w_i)$. By increasing the weight w_i, the curve will pass closer to P_i.

The second curve defined in PHIGS PLUS adds, in addition to the coordinate spline, a colour spline. The colour spline determines how the colour of the curve varies along its length. This primitive is generated with the function:

NON-UNIFORM B-SPLINE CURVE WITH COLOUR   (PHOP,*,STOP,*)El
Arguments:

in	spline order	integer
in	knots	array of real numbers

in	parameter limits	two real numbers
in	rationality	(RATIONAL,NON-RATIONAL)
in	control points	list of points in MC or homogeneous space

COLOUR SPLINE consisting of:

in	spline order	integer
in	knots	array of real numbers
in	parameter limits	two real numbers
in	rationality	(RATIONAL,NON-RATIONAL)
in	colour type	(RGB,CIELUV,HLS,HSV,...)
in	control points	list of points in colour space or homogeneous colour space

The first five arguments refer to the geometry spline, so are the same as in NON-UNIFORM B-SPLINE CURVE. The colour spline is essentially the same as the coordinate spline, except that the control points are defined in colour space, for example, within the RGB colour cube. This spline has its own order, and knot vector. The *colour type* can be any type except INDEXED and determines which colour space the control points are defined in. The control points establish how the colour varies as a function of its parameter. The colour spline can either be non-rational, or rational in which case each colour coordinate is weighted by the fourth coefficient.

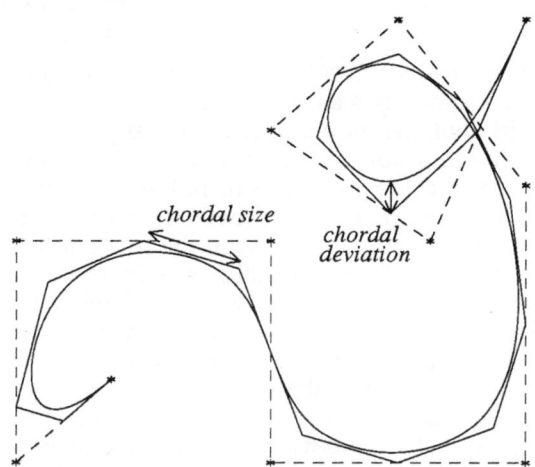

Figure 12.8 Spline curve approximation criteria.

12.3.2 Spline curve attributes

When a spline is drawn by PHIGS, it is reduced to a set of straight line segments that approximate the curve. It is possible to control how smoothly a curve should be drawn with the PHIGS PLUS attribute CURVE APPROXIMATION CRITERIA. This attribute is set with the function:

SET CURVE APPROXIMATION CRITERIA   (PHOP,*,STOP,*)El
Arguments:

in	approximation type	integer
in	approximation data record	data record

The approximation type determines the contents of the data record. One of the following approximation type can be specified:

Approximation type	*Data record*
1. Workstation dependent	none
2. Constant parametric subdivision	integer
3. Chordal size in WC	real
4. Chordal size in NPC	real
5. Chordal size in DC	real
6. Chordal deviation in WC	real
7. Chordal deviation in NPC	real
8. Chordal deviation in DC	real
9. Relative in WC	real between 0 and 1
10. Relative in NPC	real between 0 and 1
11. Relative in DC	real between 0 and 1

The *constant parametric subdivision* method divides each non-empty interval between knots into an equal number of straight line segments. The data record contains the number of line segments to use in the approximation. The *chordal size* method generates enough segments so that the length of the longest segment is less than value passed in the data record. The *chordal deviation* method generates enough segments so that the maximum deviation between the true curve and the approximation is less than a given threshold (see Figure 12.8). The *relative* method simply allows one to specify a real number between zero and one, which determines the relative quality of the rendering. Higher numbers result in a better quality rendering. Each of the methods: chordal size, chordal deviation and relative, specify a quality factor which is relative to a coordinate system. If, for example, one were to zoom in on a curve with a fixed chordal deviation in *WC*, the display of the curve in *DC* would deteriorate. As a result one can choose the coordinate system in which the approximation is to be evaluated, either *WC*, *NPC*, or *DC*.

All attributes that apply to polylines also apply to spline curves. Appendix E summarizes what attributes apply to each primitive.

12.3.3 Spline surfaces

PHIGS PLUS uses B-splines to define curved surfaces. The surface is a function of two parameters, with each parameter corresponding to an independent set of B-spline basis functions. The control points are now arranged as a grid of points in MC space. The surface is defined by the formula:

$$S(s,t) = \sum_{i=1}^{m} \sum_{j=1}^{n} B_{ik}(s) B_{jl}(t)\, P_{ij}$$

In order to define the B-spline basis functions, one needs to specify the spline's order and a knot vector for each parameter. To form the basis functions in the above example one needs the two knot vectors:

$$\sigma_1, \, ..., \, \sigma_{m+k} \qquad \text{for the } k^{th} \text{ order functions } B_{ik}(s)$$

$$\tau_1, \, ..., \, \tau_{m+k} \qquad \text{for the } l^{th} \text{ order functions } B_{jl}(t)$$

The control points are defined in the $m \times n$ array P_{ij}. Of course, the same rules regarding the knots apply to each knot vector of the surface. In summary they are for a kth order B-spline:

- the knots are non-decreasing,   i.e. $t_i \le t_{i+1}$ for $i=1,...,n+k-1$
- interior knot multiplicity up to $k-1$, i.e. $t_{i+1} < t_{i+k}$ for $i=k, \, ..., \, n-1$
- end knots have a multiplicity of k,   i.e. $t_1 = ... = t_k$ and
  $$t_{n+1} = ... = t_{n+k}$$

The same relationship between the continuity of the spline and the multiplicity of a knot applies to surfaces. The only difference is now a knot with a multiplicity of $k-1$, results in a sharp edge running across the entire surface. Colour Plate 7 shows the effect of knots with a multiplicity of three on a fourth order spline surface. In this case both knot vectors have knots with a multiplicity of three.

The control points for a B-spline surface are either a grid in MC, for a non-rational surface, or a grid of homogeneous points for a rational surface. The number of control points along each parameter's dimension can not be less than the order of the corresponding spline's basis function. So for the surface $S(s,t)$ m is greater than or equal to k and n is greater than or equal to l. Similar to curves, a rational surface can be defined by taking the grid of control points in MC and then applying an array of weights. This results in a grid of homogeneous coordinates:

$$P_{ij}^{h} = (\, x_{ij} w_{ij},\ y_{ij} w_{ij},\ z_{ij} w_{ij},\ w_{ij}\,)$$

An advantage of using the weight vector can be seen in Colour Plate 8. In this case the control point P_{33} has been given the weight 10.0.,

215

whereas all other points are weighted with 1.0. The point P_{33} is weighted without forming a ridge, as in Colour Plate 7 with multiple knots.

PHIGS PLUS has two primitives for B-spline surfaces. The first primitive is used if only the shape of the surface is to be defined, the second is used if additional data to be mapped onto colour is also present. If only the shape is to be defined, then one should use the function:

NON-UNIFORM B-SPLINE SURFACE   (PHOP,*,STOP,*)El
Arguments:

in	s spline order integer	
in	t spline order integer	
in	s knot vector	array of reals
in	t knot vector	array of reals
in	rationality	(RATIONAL,NON-RATIONAL)
in	control points	array of points in MC, or in homogeneous coordinates

Trimming curve definitions:

in	approximation type	integer
in	approximation data record	real
in	curve visibility flag	(OFF,ON)
in	curve order	integer
in	curve knot vector	array of real numbers
in	parameter limits	two real numbers
in	rationality	(RATIONAL,NON-RATIONAL)
in	control points	array of points in parameter space or homogeneous points

What might not have been expected in the definition of the B-spline surface are the trimming curves. They identify a region in the two dimensional parameter space to use to map onto the surface. Without trimming curves, all surfaces would appear as warped rectangular sheets. Trimming curves have their control points in the *(s,t)* parameter space, or its homogeneous equivalent for rational curves. They should form closed loops and not intersect themselves or each other. More than one trimming curve can be defined, allowing one to have holes in the surface. The region in parameter space that is used is identified by the *curve orientation rule,* which states the region inside a counterclockwise oriented loop is mapped onto the surface. A loop's orientation is determined by the path traced by increasing its parameter, (see Colour Plates 12 and 15).

One can also define spline surfaces with additional data. This is done with the primitive:

NON-UNIFORM B-SPLINE SURFACE WITH DATA   (PHOP,*,STOP,*)El
Arguments:

in	s spline order	integer
in	t spline order	integer
in	s knot vector	array of reals
in	t knot vector	array of reals
in	rationality	(RATIONAL,NON-RATIONAL)

in	control points	array of points in MC, or in homogeneous coordinates
in	trimming curves	list of trimming curves
in	colour spline	spline surface with control points in colour space
in	data spline	spline surface with application data for control points

This is the last and most complex output primitive defined in PHIGS PLUS. It consists of one spline surface for the coordinates, with its trimming curves, and two optional splines to define colour and data to be mapped onto the surface. Both of these splines are a function of two parameters, with their own orders and knot vectors. The colour of the spline surface at any given point is determined by evaluating the colour spline at that parameter value. The data values are determined analogously. The intrinsic colour the spline surface assumes depends on the data mapping method. This will be covered in the subsequent chapter.

12.3.4 Spline surface attributes

Spline surfaces share the same attributes as FILL AREA SET WITH DATA 3 with two additional aspects articular to surfaces: SURFACE APPROXIMATION CRITERIA and PARAMETRIC SURFACE CHARACTERISTICS. Surfaces are approximated by a set of flat facets internal to the PHIGS PLUS implementation. The degree to which the surface is approximated is determined by the SURFACE APPROXIMATION CRITERIA. This aspect is analogous to its counterpart for spline curves. It is set with the function:

SET SURFACE APPROXIMATION CRITERIA   (PHOP,*,STOP,*)El
Arguments:

in	approximation type	integer
in	approximation data record	data record

The following approximation types are supported:

Approximation type	*Data record*
1. Workstation dependent	none
2. Constant parametric subdivision	two integers
3. Chordal size in WC	two reals
4. Chordal size in NPC	two reals
5. Chordal size in DC	two reals
6. Planar deviation in WC	real
7. Planar deviation in NPC	real
8. Planar deviation in DC	real
9. Relative in WC	real between 0 and 1
10. Relative in NPC	real between 0 and 1
11. Relative in DC	real between 0 and 1

The aspect PARAMETRIC SURFACE CHARACTERISTICS controls the appearance of a spline surface by drawing a set of curves. These curves are drawn on the surface using the current polyline attributes. The following function is used to set this aspect:

SET PARAMETRIC SURFACE CHARACTERISTICS   (PHOP,*,STOP,*)El
Arguments:

in	type	integer
in	data record	data record

The following parametric surface characteristics are registered:

1. none
2. workstation dependent
3. isoparametric curves
4. level curves in MC
5. level curves in WC.

The contents of the data record depends on the characteristic type. It determines how to display the isoparametric and level curves. Isoparametric curves are drawn at constant parameter values in both the *s* and *t* directions on the surface. The data record for isoparametric curves will specify how many curves to draw in each direction.

Level curves are drawn at the intersection between the surface and a set of planes perpendicular to a direction vector. The direction vector, and the position of the planes along the vector are specified in the data record. These level planes can either be defined in MC or *WC*.

The two aspects SURFACE APPROXIMATION CRITERIA and PARAMETRIC SURFACE CHARACTERISTICS can be bundled together in a workstation table with the function SET PARAMETRIC SURFACE REPRESENTATION. This table entry is selected with the structure element SET PARAMETRIC SURFACE INDEX. As is the case with all aspects, whether the parametric surface aspects are selected with an index or not depends on the aspect source flag. See Section 5.1 for details on the ASF.

This concludes the chapter on PHIGS PLUS output primitives. A large number of primitives covering a broad range of complexity have been introduced. Not every PHIGS PLUS implementation will necessarily support all the output primitives treated here. These primitives have defined data that are to be used by the rendering pipeline. The next chapter will show how these data are used.

CHAPTER 13

Rendering with PHIGS PLUS

The goal of a three dimensional computer graphics system is to compute a 2D image of a 3D scene as it would be formed in a real imaging system, such as a camera or the eye. This involves simulating the optics involved with viewing and illuminating a scene. The previous chapter on PHIGS PLUS output primitives introduced a mechanism to define additional data, such as normal vectors, colour or application data at the primitive's vertices or facets. Now we want to look into the rendering algorithms that use these data to calculate the colour and brightness of the objects drawn.

A major contribution of the PHIGS PLUS extension to PHIGS is the rendering pipeline. This consists of the data mapping, lighting, shading, depth cueing and colour mapping stages. PHIGS PLUS uses a relatively simple physical model of the optics used to light a scene. The goal of rendering in PHIGS PLUS is not to generate photorealistic images, but it is, however, accurate enough to give the visual cues needed to discern the shape of a three dimensional object. The shading stage of the rendering pipeline determines how to colour the interior of a primitive, such as a polygon, from information which is specified at the vertices. Depth cueing attenuates the colour of a primitive by it depth coordinate. This adds an additional visual cue of the three dimensional nature of an object. Colour mapping is used to map the colour that has been calculated for the primitive onto a colour that is available on the workstation.

Before area filling primitives enter the rendering pipeline during traversal, they pass through a backface processing stage. This separates the primitives into those that face the viewer and those which do not. One can specify different aspects for backfacing primitives or chose not to draw either front- or backfacing facets. Figure 13.1 illustrates all the stages used to process output primitives provided by PHIGS PLUS.

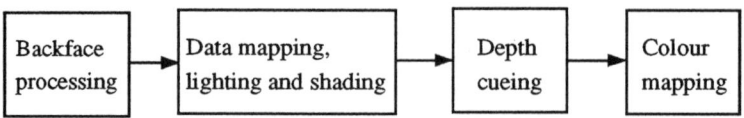

Figure 13.1   PHIGS PLUS output primitive processing.

13.1 Backface processing

PHIGS PLUS lets an application determine whether to distinguish between front- and backfacing primitives or not. Backfacing primitives are area filling primitives which are facing away from the viewer after they have been transformed to *NPC*. If it does distinguish between the frontfacing and backfacing primitives, it can either cull or use different aspects for each set of primitives.

A culled primitive is not drawn, so it requires no further processing. For example, a closed object such as a sphere, does not need to have its backfacing primitives drawn since they are being occluded by the front. Culling can lead to an increase in performance on some workstations, because most of the rendering pipeline can be skipped for the culled primitives. One can also render backfacing primitives differently than those which are frontfacing. This allows the PHIGS PLUS programmer to easily create surfaces which have a different colour and appearance on each side.

Whether PHIGS PLUS distinguishes between front and backfacing primitives is determined by a flag that is set with the structure element:

SET FACET DISTINGUISH MODE   (PHOP,*,STOP,*)El
Arguments:
        in   face distinguish mode   (OFF,ON)

The default face distinguish mode is OFF. A primitive is backfacing if the z component of its normal vector in *NPC* space is negative. The normal vector used for backface processing is known as the *geometric normal*. Each facet in an area filling primitive has a geometric normal. The geometric normal is either provided by the application as a facet normal, or will be automatically computed. This makes it possible to have backface processing apply even to primitives defined in PHIGS.

It is important to note that the order of the vertices determines which

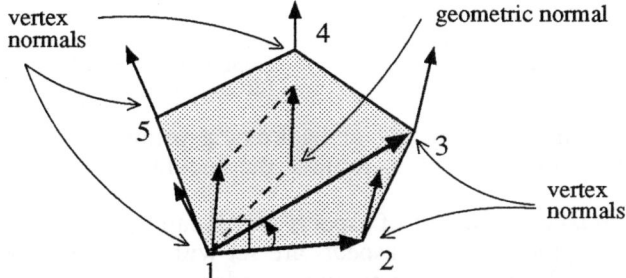

Figure 13.2 The geometric normal for a facet.

direction the facet is facing. If no facet normal is present, PHIGS PLUS take the first three non-colinear vertices and computes the geometric normal with a vector cross product (see Figure 13.2).

Multi-faceted primitives and surfaces need more involved methods for computing the geometric normal. Generally the sign of the geometric

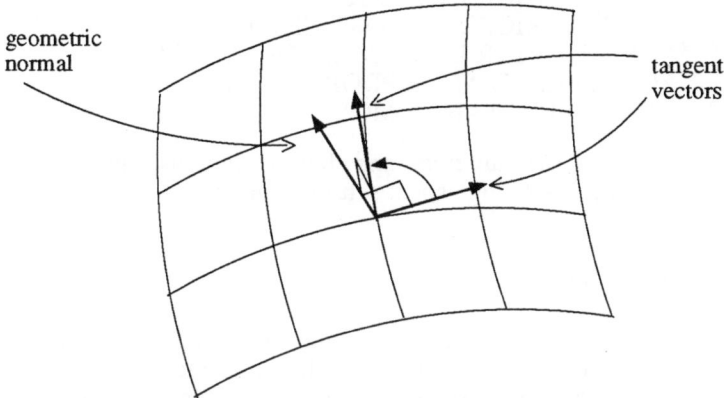

Figure 13.3 The geometric normal for a surface primitive.

normal is determined by the right-hand rule. In the case of the triangular strip it is not as simple. The order of the points would cause the sign of a flat strip to alternate. This is taken into account by PHIGS PLUS. Geometric normals for a B-spline surface can be determined from its tangent vectors at each point (see Figure 13.3). The applications programmer only needs to consider the order of the control points in the grid to establish which direction the geometric normal is facing. Similar arguments apply to QUADRILATERAL MESH 3 WITH DATA.

Once the face distinguish mode has been set to ON, facets or portions of surfaces can be culled through using the following structure element:

SET FACET CULLING MODE   (PHOP,*,STOP,*)El
Arguments:
      in   face culling mode   (NONE,BACKFACING,
                                        FRONTFACING)

Although either frontfacing or backfacing primitives can be culled, most applications will want to remove the backfacing primitives, if any at all.

There are a large number of aspects which can be separately specified for backfacing facets. These aspects are set with an independent routine and will be used if the face distinguish mode is set to ON. The functions to set the backfacing aspects are identified by the keyword BACK preceding the aspect name. These functions are summarized in the following list:

- SET BACK INTERIOR INDEX
- SET BACK DATA MAPPING INDEX
- SET BACK REFLECTANCE INDEX
- SET BACK INTERIOR STYLE
- SET BACK INTERIOR STYLE INDEX
- SET BACK INTERIOR COLOUR
- SET BACK INTERIOR SHADING METHOD
- SET BACK INTERIOR DATA MAPPING METHOD
- SET BACK REFLECTANCE PROPERTIES
- SET BACK REFLECTANCE MODEL.

A description of the functions and their arguments can be found by looking at the corresponding aspect setting routines.

13.2 Data mapping

A number of PHIGS PLUS primitives, the 'with data' primitives, allow one to specify additional data at the vertices and facets. These data are used by the rendering pipeline to determine the colour of the primitive. For the purposes of the data mapping stage, only the colour and the application data are considered. The normal vectors are used by the backface processing and lighting stages.

Both the colour and the application data defined with the primitive can be visualized as a colour field on the surface. Colour can be directly specified for each facet or vertex, or it can be indirectly defined as one or more fields of application data which are then mapped onto a colour. For example, these data can represent a temperature or a stress field defined at each vertex on the object's surface. The data mapping stage determines how to transform these data to a colour.

The data mapping method can be bundled in the workstation table and selected with an index, or set directly with the function SET DATA MAPPING METHOD. The DATA MAPPING ASF determines whether to use the directly specified method or not. The following function is used to directly set the data mapping method:

SET DATA MAPPING METHOD   (PHOP,*,STOP,*)El
Arguments:

| | in | data mapping method | integer |
| | in | data mapping record | data record |

So far five data mapping methods have been registered:

1. COLOUR
2. SINGLE VALUE, UNIFORM
3. SINGLE VALUE, NON-UNIFORM
4. BI-VALUE, UNIFORM
5. BI-VALUE, NON-UNIFORM

The method determines the contents of the data mapping record. The record consists of a list of source selectors and method dependent values. The list of source selectors determines the precedence of possible sources for the intrinsic colour. Remember, the intrinsic colour is the colour assigned to a primitive prior to the lighting calculations. The source selectors can be one of the following: COLOUR_ASPECT, FACET_COLOUR, FACET_DATA, VERTEX_COLOUR and VERTEX_DATA. If the data required by the highest precedence source selector is not available, then the next entry in the selector list is used, until the list is exhausted, in which case the colour aspect, e.g., the interior colour, is used. Not all source selectors can be used with every method.

The first data mapping method is *COLOUR*. It should be selected when one wants to use the colour provided with the primitive as the source for the intrinsic colour. The data mapping record is a list of the following source selectors: COLOUR_ASPECT, FACET_COLOUR, or VERTEX_COLOUR.

The simplest method using application data is *SINGLE VALUE, UNIFORM*. In this case only the source selectors FACET_DATA and VERTEX_DATA are meaningful. In addition to the list of source selectors, the data mapping record contains an index identifying the data value to use to map onto a colour. Remember, it is possible to define more than one data value per vertex or facet. The record also contains a colour type and a list of n colours $C_1,...,C_n$. Finally, the record contains two real numbers identifying the upper and lower limit of a range of data values, d_{low} and d_{high}. This range is divided into $n-2$ equally spaced partitions. The data are mapped as follows: primitive data less than the lower limit are mapped onto C_1, data above the upper limit are mapped onto C_n, otherwise they are mapped onto the colour corresponding to the partition containing its data value (see Figure 13.4).

The method *SINGLE VALUE, NON-UNIFORM* is a generalization of the previous method. In this case the only difference is that a list of $n-1$

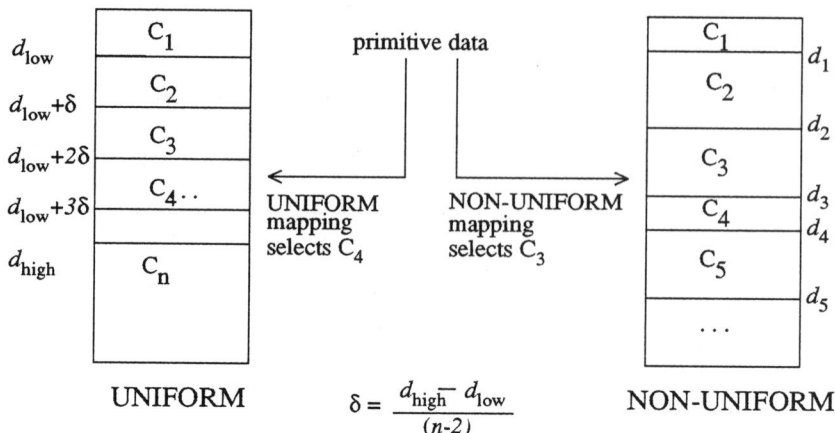

$$\delta = \frac{d_{high} - d_{low}}{(n-2)}$$

Figure 13.4 Single valued data mapping.

data values $(d_1,...,d_{n-1})$ is provided instead of an upper and lower limit. By providing this list one is not restricted to equally spaced partitions. These data values identify the borders between each partition (see Figure 13.4). Primitive data below d_1 are mapped to C_1, data above d_{n-1} are mapped to C_n, otherwise they are mapped to the colour corresponding to their data partition.

The last two methods map two data values onto a colour. This can be thought of as selecting a colour as a function of two variables. The method *BI-VALUE, UNIFORM* is the simpler of the two. Its data mapping record contains a list of source selectors, either FACET_DATA, or VERTEX_DATA or both. Additionally, it contains two indices identifying which data fields should be used for the mapping. Analogous to the single valued uniform method, two maximum and minimum pairs are provided to define two ranges which will be uniformly partitioned. Finally, a list of *m* colour arrays, each array containing *n* colours, is passed in the data record. The data value corresponding to the first index selects the colour list, whereas the second data value selects a colour out of the list.

The method *BI-VALUE, NON-UNIFORM* on the other hand lets the application explicitly identify partition boundaries. Similar to the uniform method, the data mapping record contains the source selector list, the two indices identifying the data fields, and the list of colour arrays. Now the record additionally contains a list of values identifying the partition boundaries for the first data value. It also contains a list of arrays containing partition boundaries for the second data value. The partition that the first data value lies in, identifies both an array of partition boundaries for the second data value as well as a colour array. The partition the second data value lies in selects a colour that the data pair is to be mapped onto out of the colour array.

If bundled data mapping methods are required, an entry containing the data mapping method and its data record should be placed in the workstation state list with the function SET DATA MAPPING REPRE-SENTATION. A given representation can be chosen with the function SET DATA MAPPING INDEX. Remember, the default aspect source flag is INDIVIDUAL, so the ASF must be set to BUNDLED prior to using bundled data mapping.

13.3 Lighting and shading with PHIGS PLUS

When we look at an object, we see the light which has reflected off of its surface. When light interacts with a surface it can be absorbed, transmitted or reflected. The lighting model in PHIGS PLUS only deals with reflected light. A coloured object will reflect only certain components of a white light, namely those which make up its colour. If the light which illuminates an object of a given colour does not contain any of the frequency components in the object's colour spectrum, it will appear black. For example, a green object looks black under a red light.

PHIGS PLUS uses a *reflectance equation* to model the interaction of light with a surface. Light is represented by four lights sources: ambient, point, directional and spot. A more accurate lighting model should also take into account illumination coming from surfaces, such as light sources which distend space or even light reflecting off of other surfaces in a scene. The optics of illumination is more accurately modelled by techniques such as ray tracing, or radiosity. PHIGS PLUS does not provide a mechanism to use these more sophisticated lighting techniques.

We will need the normal vector and the intrinsic colour of the object at every point where the lighting calculation is to be performed. At the very best this information can be defined at the vertices of the facet. As a result shading is closely coupled with lighting calculations; with the shading method being used to calculate terms needed by the lighting equation at points inside a facet. Lighting under PHIGS PLUS will first be introduced, followed by shading and how it interacts with lighting.

13.3.1 The reflectance equation

The reflectance equation calculates the colour of light reflected off of a surface from its intrinsic colour, its orientation and its reflectance properties as well as from parameters characterizing the light sources. This equation is composed of three terms: ambient, diffuse and specular equations. The ambient equation is used so that one can see surfaces even if they are not being explicitly lit. In the diffuse equation an incoming light ray is scattered evenly in all directions. The specular equation, on the other hand, is used to model shiny surfaces, where most of the light is reflected from the surface in a direction which depends on the angle between the incident ray and the surface's normal vector.

Most physical surfaces behave in a manner which can be modelled by a combination of these three components. A surface's appearance is determined by how much each term contributes. The application can control this by setting some of the surface's reflectance properties: the ambient coefficient K_a the diffuse coefficient K_d and the specular coefficient K_s. These coefficients are real numbers between 0.0 and 1.0 that scale each term of the reflectance equation.

In general the PHIGS PLUS reflectance formula can be represented by the equation:

$$\sum_{i=0}^{n} \; (C_{ai} + C_{bi} + C_{si}) \tag{13.1}$$

This equation sums over n separate light sources and C_{ai}, C_{di}, C_{si} are the ambient, diffuse, and specular terms from the ith light source. It is important to note here that C_{ai}, C_{di} and C_{si} are colours; so they are represented by a triplet. For example, using the RGB colour model C_{ai} contains a red, a green and a blue component each of which is separately computed.

One can specify which terms of the reflectance equation to use by setting the reflectance model aspect with:

SET REFLECTANCE MODEL   (PHOP,*,STOP,*)El
Arguments:
          in   reflectance model   integer

This function is passed an integer selecting one of the following possibilities:

1. No reflectance calculation.
2. Ambient reflectance term only.
3. Ambient and diffuse reflectance terms only.
4. Ambient, diffuse, and specular reflectance terms.

The default reflectance model is 1 (i.e. no lighting). The higher the reflectance model number, the more realistic the rendering can appear. On the other hand, if fewer terms of the reflectance equation are needed, less calculation is required, so the object can be rendered faster.

The contents of each term in the reflectance equation depends on which light source is being used. Before going into details on individual light sources, general properties of these terms should be briefly mentioned.

The simplest part of the PHIGS PLUS reflectance equation is the *ambient reflectance term,* which models the random scattering of light from the atmosphere and all other objects present. This term is due to ambient light. Ambient light is only specified by a colour; it comes from no particular location or direction. Without an ambient light only the surfaces directly illuminated are visible and the scene looks harshly lit. For example, the moon appears as a crescent when it is not full, because there is no ambient light in space. Only ambient lights contribute to the ambient term. This term is scaled by K_a, the *ambient reflectance coefficient,* which is defined in the reflectance properties.

The *diffuse reflectance term* in the lighting equation models the light which is uniformly scattered by a surface. The brightness of the reflected light varies with respect to the orientation of the surface relative to the light sources. Because the brightness of the object is the same no matter from what angle it is viewed, it has a matt look. The diffuse term is often the dominant component of the lighting equation, because it delivers the visual cues that make an object look three dimensional over an extended area of the surface. In contrast, ambient light does af-

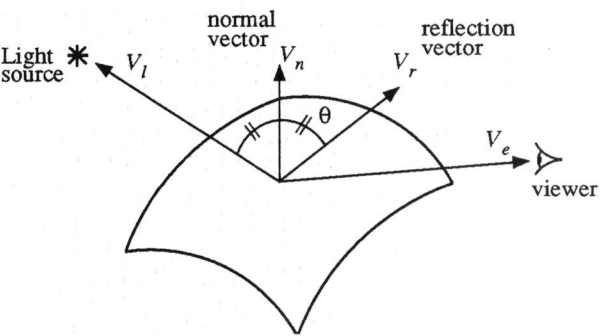

Figure 13.5 Illuminating a surface with a light source.

fect an extended area, but does not deliver the visual cues needed; and specular light, while delivering visual cues, as shall be seen shortly, only affects a limited portion of the surface. This term is weighted by the *diffuse reflection coefficient K_d,* a reflectance property.

The mathematics of the diffuse lighting equation is based on Lambert's cosine law, which states that the intensity of the light reflected from a surface is proportional to the cosine of the angle between the incident light ray and the surface normal θ (see Figure 13.5). Fortunately, the cosine of the angle between these two vectors is equal to their dot product, which is much simpler to calculate than a cosine. The value of the dot product is a maximum when the surface normal is parallel to the vector to the light source and zero when they are perpendicular. When the angle between these vectors is greater than 90 degrees, the value of the dot product is forced to zero, so that light sources which are behind the surface do not contribute to the lighting equation.

The final component of the lighting equation is the *specular reflectance term*. This is used to model shiny surfaces and is computationally the most demanding component of the lighting equation. This term is often computed using equations based on work done by Bui Tuong Phong. Thus the lighting model used in PHIGS PLUS is referred to as Phong lighting, not to be confused with Phong shading which will be dealt with later. Light is reflected from a specular surface in a direction which makes the same angle with the surface normal, V_n, as the incident ray, V_l, and lies in the same plane as both V_l and V_n. This reflected vector is known as the reflection vector V_r, (see Figure 13.5), and can be calculated from the surface normal and the light vector as follows:

$$V_r = 2 * (V_n \cdot V_l) * V_n - V_l \qquad (13.2)$$

An ideal specular surface is a mirror. Of course, mirrors cannot be modelled with the PHIGS PLUS, because the only light which can be specularly reflected comes from the light sources and not other objects. The contributions from the specular term are called specular highlights. Obviously, the position of the specular highlights on an object depends on where the viewer is. This is because a specular surface reflects all incident light in the direction of the reflection vector.

In reality most surfaces are not perfect specular reflectors and PHIGS PLUS tries to model their behaviour. In the Phong lighting model a reflected ray generates a cone of light with V_r as its axis. The intensity of the specularly reflected light is brightest when the angle between V_r and the vector to the viewer, V_e, is zero and decreases as the angle increases (see Figure 13.6). How quickly the intensity drops is parameterized by the *specular exponent*, e_s. The formula determining the intensity of reflected light is:

$$I_s = (V_r \cdot V_e)^{e_s} \qquad (13.3)$$

This equation suggests that the intensity drops faster, the larger the exponent is. For a very large exponent, $I_s = 1$ when V_r and V_e are parallel, and zero otherwise. This is the behaviour of an ideal specular reflector. Large exponents generate bright, sharply defined specular highlights which cover a relatively small area and are used to model shiny surfaces.

The specular exponent belongs to the reflectance properties of the ob-

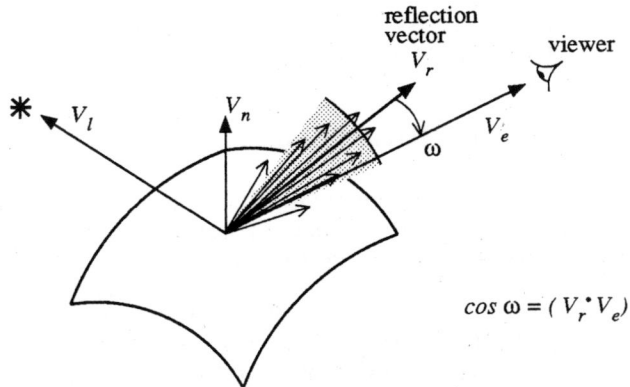

Figure 13.6 Specularly reflected light.

ject. In addition to the exponent, a *specular colour, O_s,* is defined for the surface as well. The colour that is specularly reflected is not necessarily the same as the intrinsic colour. An example is a coloured plastic object. Its specular colour is white, whereas copper has reddish specular highlights. Finally, the specular term is weighted by the *specular reflectance coefficient, K_s,* a number between 0 and 1.0.

In this discussion of the reflectance equation a number of parameters belonging to the surface have been mentioned. These are the reflectance properties of the object being rendered. They can be directly specified with the PHIGS PLUS function:

SET REFLECTANCE PROPERTIES   (PHOP,*,STOP,*)El
Arguments:

in	properties type	integer
in	data record	data record

The properties type field is present in order to allow for reflectance equations based on different models. Currently only simple reflectance is registered. It is selected by setting the property type to 1 and is accompanied by a data record containing:

- ambient reflectance coefficient   real number between 0 and 1
- diffuse reflectance coefficient   real number between 0 and 1
- specular reflectance coefficient   real number between 0 and 1
- specular colour   general colour
- specular exponent   positive real number

An alternative method is to use bundled aspects and define an entry in the WSL with the function SET REFLECTANCE REPRESENTATION. This bundles both the reflectance properties and the reflectance model in one table entry. A bundled entry is selected with the structure element SET REFLECTANCE INDEX. Of course to use the bundled aspects, one needs to set the appropriate ASF to BUNDLED.

13.3.2 Light sources in PHIGS PLUS

Each type of light source has its own reflectance equation. The principles of the reflectance equation remain the same, but each light is parameterized to model the nature of the source. These parameters determine the light's colour, its brightness and where it is coming from. Each light is defined as an entry in the workstation state list. Once defined it is referred to by an index. More lights can be defined than are needed in any given rendering. The maximum number of lights that can be simultaneously defined can be determind by calling the function INQUIRE WORKSTATION STATE TABLE LENGTHS PLUS.

A light is defined with the function:

SET LIGHT SOURCE REPRESENTATION   (PHOP,WSOP,*,*)
Arguments:

in	workstation identifier	integer
in	light source index	integer
in	light source type	integer
in	light source data record	data record

This light will be referred to by the light source index. The light source type identifies which of the four types of lights is being defined. It can be one of:

1. AMBIENT.
2. DIRECTIONAL.
3. POSITIONAL.
4. SPOT.

The contents of the data record obviously depend on the type of light. The simplest type of light is AMBIENT. Only *ambient light* sources contribute to the ambient term in the reflectance equation (see Section 13.3.1). Remember, the ambient light source is only characterized by a colour, which is multiplied by the colour of the surface, term by term. The colour of the light L_c is specified by a general colour that is passed in the data record. Table 13.1 shows the reflectance equation for an ambient light.

A *directional light* has both a colour L_c and a vector V_l associated with it. The vector is used to specify the direction the light is coming from. All rays from a directional light source are parallel to each other. They are sometimes called infinite light sources, because a light infinitely far away would also have parallel rays. Table 13.1 contains a commonly used reflectance equation for directional lights. Table 13.2 lists the values that must be specified in the light source data record.

A *point light* source, also known as a positional source, is used to model a light which has a specific location and colour. Light from a point source has a spherical wavefront centred at the location of the source. In other words, the light rays start at the source's position and are radiated in all directions. The optics of a point source would demand that the intensity of the light should be proportional to the reciprocal of the distance from the source squared. The physical model attenuates the brightness too quickly for computer graphics. In PHIGS PLUS the brightness is attenuated by a term which is proportional to the reciprocal of the distance from the source. This term is used in the diffuse and specular reflectance equations, and requires two coefficients. It is given by the equation:

$$L_a = \frac{1}{(A_1 + A_2\, r)}$$

$$r = \lVert P_l - P_o \rVert$$

(13.4)

In Equation 13.4 r is the distance between the posistion of the light source P_l and the object P_o. The two attenuation coefficients allow the PHIGS PLUS programmer to specify how rapidly the point light's intensity should fall as a function of the distance to the light. The light vector needed in the reflectance equation is derived from the position of the light relative to the object. Table 13.1 lists the reflectance equations for the point light and Table 13.2 lists the parameters needed for the light source data record.

The final light source type used in PHIGS is a *spot light*. It can be used to create special effects which cannot be generated with the other light types. As its name implies, a spot light source models a light which radiates from a given position, but it can also be aimed in a specific direction. It has a cone of influence with an aperture given by a spread angle and an axis passing through the light source's position and parallel to the direction of the light (see Figure 13.7). If the angle between the

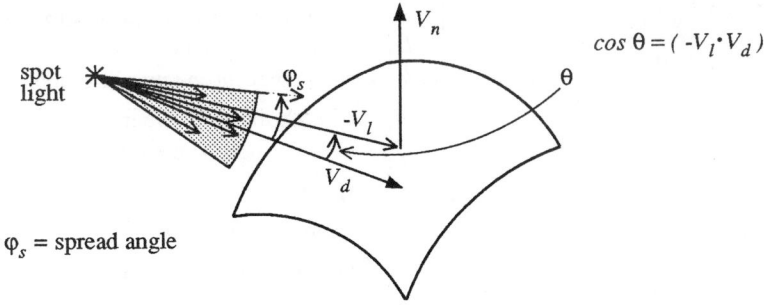

φ_s = spread angle

Figure 13.7 The spot light source.

light's directional vector and the vector from the object to the light's position is greater than the spread angle of the light φ_s, then the brightness of the spot is set to zero. There is also a concentration exponent which determines how rapidly the brightness of the light falls of as a function of the angle between the light ray and the central axis of the spot. This concentration function is given by the cosine of the angle between the central axis and the light ray raised to the exponent. This is the same function as was used in calculating the specular term of the reflectance equation. The dot product of the two vectors is the cosine of the angle, so the concentration factor can be written as:

$$L_s = (-V_l \cdot V_d)^{e_c} \tag{13.5}$$

Here e_c is the concentration exponent and V_d is the unit vector specifying the central axis of the spot's cone of influence. The unit vector from the light's position to object is $-V_l$.

As with the point light source, the spot light's brightness also depends on the distance between the light and the object. This is determined by the attenuation factor L_a from Equation 13.4. Table 13.1 shows the reflectance equation for an object being lit by spot light where the angle between V_d and $-V_l$ less than the spread angle.

Table 13.1 Reflectance equations for each light source type.

Ambient light: $C_a = K_a L_c O_c$ $C_d = 0$ $C_s = 0$	A_1 = scalar attenuation coefficient A_2 = linear attenuation coefficient e_c = spot light's concentration exponent e_s = specular exponent I_s = specular intensity (Equation 13.3)
Directional light: $C_a = 0$ $C_d = K_d L_c O_c (V_n \cdot V_l)$ $C_s = K_s L_c O_s I_s$	K_a = ambient reflectance coefficient K_d = diffuse reflectance coefficient K_s = specular reflectance coefficient L_a = attenuation factor (Equation 13.4) L_c = light source colour
Point light: $C_a = 0$ $C_d = K_d L_c O_c (V_n \cdot V_l) L_a$ $C_s = K_s L_c O_s I_s L_a$	L_s = spot light concentration (Equation 13.5) O_c = object's intrinsic colour O_s = object's specular colour V_d = spot light's central axis vector
Spot light: $C_a = 0$ $C_d = K_d L_c O_c (V_n \cdot V_l) L_s L_a$ $C_s = K_s L_c O_s I_s L_s L_a$	V_e = vector from object to viewer V_l = vector from object to light source V_n = normal vector of object V_r = reflection vector (Equation 13.2)

Table 13.2   Data record contents for light sources.

Ambient:		Directional:	
light's colour	direct colour	light's colour	direct colour
		light's direction	3D vector in WC
Point:		**Spot:**	
light's colour	direct colour	light's colour	direct colour
light's position	3D point in WC	light's direction	3D vector in WC
attenuation coeff.	two real numbers	light's position	3D point in WC
		attenuation coeff.	two real numbers
		concentr. exponent	real number > 0
		spread angle	real from 0 to π

So far we have covered how to define these lights. Each light can be referred to by the index passed to the function SET LIGHT SOURCE REPRESENTATION when it was defined. In order to use the lights in the WSL, one needs the structure element:

```
SET LIGHT SOURCE STATE                              (PHOP,*,STOP,*)El
Arguments:
          in   on list                list of light source indices
          in   off list               list of light source indices
```

The lights selected by the on list are added to the list of active lights in the traversal state list. In other words, they are 'turned on'. Lights selected by the off list are removed from the list of active lights, or 'turned off'. The list of active lights in the TSL is empty by default; so this function must be called if lights are to be used. A common source of error is to render a scene without turning on the lights.

13.3.3 Shading

Shading is used by two types of primitives: line drawing primitives and three dimensional area filling primitives. Shading area filling primitives is closely coupled with lighting, because components used by the reflectance equation can be derived from the shading stage. Shading takes geometric and colour data specified at the vertices and interpolates them across the primitive to generate colour data in the interior of the primitive.

The line drawing primitives are the simplest to shade. They consist of the two primitives: POLYLINE SET 3 WITH DATA and NON-UNIFORM B-SPLINE CURVE WITH COLOUR. In defining POLY-LINE SET 3 WITH DATA, a colour could optionally be specified at each vertex. The curve approximation criteria aspect reduces the NON-UNIFORM B-SPLINE CURVE WITH COLOUR to a set of line segments. The colour spline associated with this primitive determines the colour at each vertex of this tesselated curve. Each segment of this approximated curve is shaded with the polyline shading method aspect.

In PHIGS PLUS there are two ways to shade a polyline: do not shade and linearly interpolate the colour. If colour data is given at the vertices and shading has been disabled, then each segment between two vertices is drawn with a solid colour. This can either be one of the two colours defined at the bordering vertices, or an average of the two. Which colour is chosen, depends on the particular PHIGS PLUS implementation. If shading has been enabled and colour data is given at the vertices, then the colour at a point on the polyline is determined by linearly interpolating the vertex colours. Linear interpolation is a method to create a weighted average of the two vertex colours. One of these two shading options can be chosen directly with the structure element:

SET POLYLINE SHADING METHOD   (PHOP,*,STOP,*)El
Arguments:
        in   polyline shading method   (NONE,COLOUR)

Shading area filling primitives is slightly more involved than polylines. Once again, the objective of shading is to specify the colour in the interior of the primitive from data specified at the vertices. The previous section dealt with how light interacts with a surface to produce a given colour. The surface was characterized by a position in space, a normal vector and a set of surface properties. In order to illuminate the primitive, this information is required at all points on the surface. The area filling primitives in PHIGS PLUS, with the exception of NURB surfaces, are defined in terms of data specified for each facet and data specified at the vertices. How to derive these data at interior points is determined by the shading method which is set with the function:

SET INTERIOR SHADING METHOD   (PHOP,*,STOP,*)El
Arguments:
        in   shading method   (NONE,COLOUR,DATA,
                                     DOT, NORMAL)

The shading method is used to specify what data are to be interpolated across the interior of the primitive. The first conclusion from this statement is that if one is to use shading at all, then data must be specified at the vertices. PHIGS PLUS has defined five different shading methods: NONE, COLOUR, DOT, DATA and NORMAL. This order reflects the amount of calculation involved, with NONE requiring the least and NORMAL using the most computation.

The shading method *NONE* disables shading and fills the interior of each facet with a solid colour. This method is also known as flat shading.

The shading method *COLOUR,* commonly known as Gouraud shading, determines the intrinsic colours at each vertex with the data mapping method, applies the lighting calculation to calculate the reflected colour at each vertex. These reflected colours are bilinearly interpolated across the interior of the primitive.

The method *DATA* interpolates the data or colour, defined at the vertices, across the primitive and maps it to the intrinsic colour at interior points. This intrinsic colour is used by the reflectance equation, which is applied at all interior points

The method *DOT* also interpolates the data or colour at the vertices and generates the intrinsic colour at interior points. It also calculates the dot products used in the reflectance formula (see Table 13.1) at the vertices and interpolates these dot products across the primitive. The interpolated dot products are combined with the intrinsic colour to determine the reflected colour at interior points. This method is also known as 'cheap Phong' shading.

The last method *NORMAL* is also known as Phong shading. Here the colour and data are interpolated as well as the normal vectors. A full reflectance equation is performed at all interior points. By interpolating the normal vectors specular highlights can be rendered more realistically. Specular highlights are especially sensitive to the normal vector's orientation. If the specular reflectance equation is only performed at the vertices, as is the case with Gouraud shading, facets covering a large area can have anomalous specular highlights.

The shading method can also be specified as a bundled aspect. This is done by defining a bundle table entry with the function SET INTERIOR REPRESENTATION PLUS. This is similar to the function SET INTERIOR REPRESENTATION, but allows one to additionally define the interior colour and the interior shading method. Remember, the interior colour is a PHIGS PLUS aspect. This table entry is selected with the PHIGS function SET INTERIOR INDEX. The shading method's ASF will determine whether to use the individual or bundled aspect.

13.4 Depth cueing

After lighting has been performed, one can choose to use *depth cueing*. This scales a primitive's colour by its depth. Both PHIGS and PHIGS PLUS primitives are subject to depth cueing. The primitive's z coordinate in *NPC* is used to attenuate its colour. Since the intent of depth cueing is to have the colour of distant objects blend into the background colour, a *depth cue colour* needs to be specified, that the primitive's colour should be blended to as a function of depth. The depth cue colour is generally set to the background colour. To use depth cueing one must define two planes in *NPC* parallel to the *x-y* plane, the front and the back depth plane. One also defines two scale values, one for each of the depth planes. Figure 13.8 illustrates the relationship between the planes and the scale factors. The colour of the rendered primitive is a weighted combination of the depth cue colour and the primitive colour. The weight factors are determined by a combination of the scale factors and the objects depth coordinate. A suggested depth cue formula is given by Equation 13.6

$$C'_o = S_f C_o + (1 - S_f) C_d \qquad z > Z_f$$

$$C'_o = S_b C_o + (1 - S_b) C_d \qquad z < Z_b$$

$$C'_o = s C_o + (1 - s) C_d \qquad Z_b \leq z \leq Z_f \qquad (13.6)$$

$$s = S_b + (z - Z_b) \frac{(S_f - S_b)}{(Z_f - Z_b)}$$

This results in a linear scaling of the colour between the front and back planes. The colour set to a weighted sum of the depth cue colour C_d and the primitive's colour C_o. The weight factor is determined by the slope of the depth cueing scaling function (see Figure 13.8). If the depth

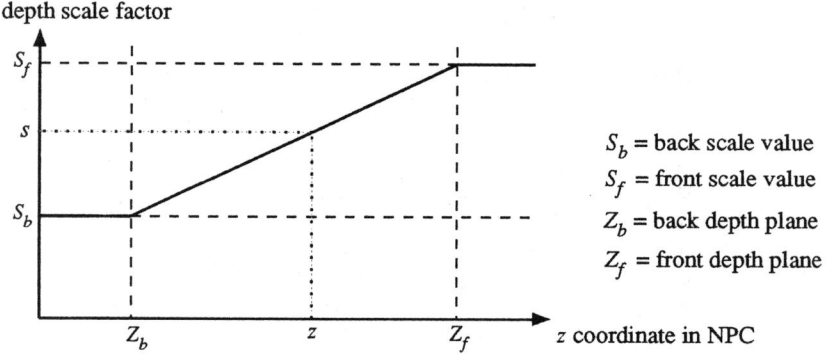

Figure 13.8 Depth cueing scaling function.

coordinate does not lie between the two planes, the colour is set to a fixed weighted sum of the C_d and C_o.

In order to use depth cueing, one needs to set a depth cue representation in the WSL defining the needed data, as well as an index to indicate which representation to use. The depth cue representation is defined with the function:

SET DEPTH CUE REPRESENTATION   (PHOP,WSOP,*,*)
Arguments:

in	workstation identifier	integer
in	depth cue index	integer
in	depth cue mode	(SUPPRESSED,ALLOWED)
in	depth reference planes	2 real z values in NPC
in	depth cue scale factors	2 real scale factors
in	depth cue colour	general colour

The depth cue mode indicates whether to use depth cueing or not. The reference planes must be defined such that the back plane is less than the front plane and the scale factors must lie between zero and one.

Once the depth cue representation is defined it needs to be selected with the structure element:

SET DEPTH CUE INDEX   (PHOP,*,STOP,*)El
Arguments:

in	depth cue index	integer

13.5 Colour mapping

The final stage of the rendering pipeline is colour mapping, which takes the colour derived from lighting, shading and depth cueing and maps it onto a colour that is available on a physical workstation. Physical workstations come with various different colour capabilities, ranging from black and white to true colour. The colour mapping stage can be used to optimise the use of the available colours. This is especially important in PHIGS PLUS, because lighting and shading generally require a large amount of colours. For example, lighting a scene can generate many different shades of the intrinsic colours. An example of how to use colour mapping on an eight-plane workstation, with 256 colours, is provided at the end of this chapter. Older versions of the PHIGS PLUS specification refer to colour approximation instead of mapping. Both terms imply the same mechanism.

Colour mapping takes the depth cued colour and maps it onto a colour maintained in a colour mapping table. PHIGS PLUS has defined three colour mapping methods, which determine how the colour is to be mapped. Finally, the mapped colour is rendered as accurately as possible on the physical workstation. To use colour approximation one must define a colour mapping representation in the WSL and use a colour mapping index to select the entry. The table entry contains the mapping method as well as method specific data. It is set with the function:

SET COLOUR MAPPING REPRESENTATION   (PHOP,WSOP,*,*)
Arguments:

in	workstation identifier	integer
in	colour mapping index	integer
in	colour mapping method	integer

in   data record   method dependent data record

The index refers to the table entry. The three mapping methods which have been registered are:

1. TRUE colour.
2. PSEUDO colour.
3. PSEUDO-N colour.

Obviously not all workstations will support all methods. One can find out what methods are available with the function INQUIRE COLOUR MAPPING FACILITIES. A workstation must support at least the colour mapping method TRUE. This method does nothing but passes the colours to be rendered as accurately as possible on the device in a workstation dependent manner.

Colour mapping becomes interesting with the method PSEUDO. Basically it converts the input colour to an integer index which selects a mapped colour out of a list. This method requires the data record to contain the following information:

colour model   (RGB,CIELUV,HSV,HLS)
weight vector   three reals colours
colour list   list of colours

The input colour is first converted to the specified model and then normalized. The weight vector is also normalized and is used to scale each component of the input colour. It actually has as many terms as components in the colour model. This is three for all registered models. The colour and the weight vector are multiplied term by term and then summed. Now we have a number between 0 and 1. This is multi-

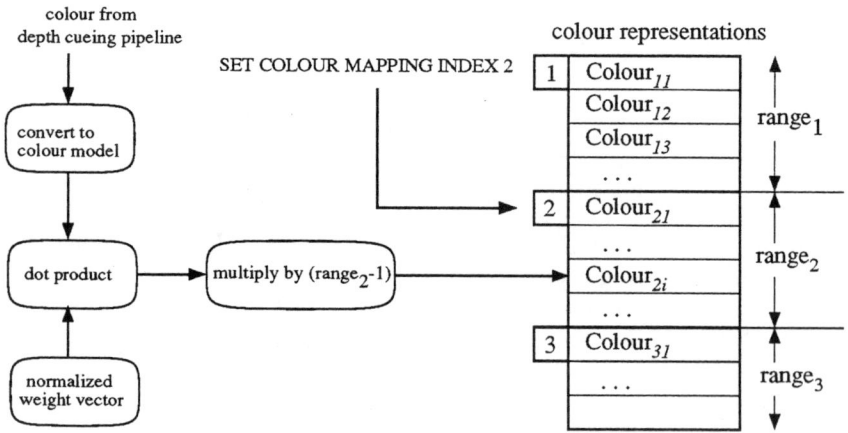

Figure 13.9 PSEUDO colour mapping flowchart.

plied by the length of the colour list minus 1 to get an index into the list. Figure 13.9 illustrates this procedure.

Obviously the list of colours cannot be arbitrarily long. The maximum number of pseudo colour entries available on a workstation can be determined using the function INQUIRE COLOUR MAPPING METHOD FACILITIES. For example, a workstation with 256 available colours would return a number not exceeding 256. The example at the end of this chapter illustrates how to use this colour mapping method.

The final method is PSEUDO-N. This is similar to pseudo, except that the colour components are mapped separately. This requires a colour list for each component in the model; we shall use three lists. This method's data record requires:

colour model	(RGB,CIELUV,HSV,HLS)
colour lists	three lists of colour terms

As in the method PSEUDO the input colour is first converted to the specified model and normalized. Each colour component is then multiplied by the length of its corresponding list minus 1 to get an index into the list. The three separately derived components are combined to yield the mapped colour.

So far the mechanism of colour mapping has been described. It is now time to see how to use colour mapping. This is done by selecting a representation with the function:

SET COLOUR MAPPING INDEX   (PHOP,*,STOP,*)El
Arguments:
         in   colour mapping index   integer

Using colour mapping can be illustrated by considering the method PSEUDO on an eight-plane physical workstation. In this example, let us assume that the colour mapping tables can contain up to 255 entries, with the 256th colour reserved for the background. In this example a scene is to be lit containing various objects in a number of different colours. In order to use lighting and shading one would need several gradations of each colour. This can be achieved by using colour mapping.

In order to use the available colours optimally, a colour mapping representation using the method PSEUDO can be defined for each colour in the scene. The list in each representation would consist of a colour ramp, from the background colour to the colour of the object. Here one can use the model RGB and a weight vector of *(1,1,1)*. This will weight each of the RGB components equally. When defining the structure, the intrinsic colour should be set to white, and the function SET COLOUR MAPPING INDEX is used instead to select the colour. The lighting stage will produce various shades of grey, which are used to index into the appropriate colour mapping representation. It is important to realize that this can only simulate achromatic lights.

The following is a sample subroutine used to set the colour mapping representation.

```
#include <phigs.h>

#define MAXCOLOURS 255
Pcolr_rep bg;                    /* background colour of window*/

/**********************************************************
 This routine will define pseudo colour mapping
 representations in order to shade a number of
 colours. It is passed:
     wsid   : workstation identifier to use
     ncol   : how many colour ramps to define
     lsize  : size of each colour list
     colour : ncol lists of colour, in RGB

   It assumes the colour are in the RGB model. It also
   assumes that up to 255 colour mapping entries can be
   entered. It is the responsibility of the caller to
   assure that ncol * lsize < 255. If it detects an error
   in the arguments -1 is returned, otherwise 0.
 **********************************************************/
int define_colours( Pint wsid, int ncols,
                    int lsize, Pcolr_rep *colour )
{
int             i,j;
float           f;
static Pfloat   wght[3] = { 0.33333, 0.33333, 0.33333 };
static Pfloat_list wght_list;
Pcolr_rep          col[MAXCOLOURS];
Pcolr_rep_list colr_list;
Pcolr_map_data cdata;

if( ncols < 0 || lsize < 0 ) return( -1 );
if( ncols*lsize > MAXCOLOURS ) return( -1 );

wght_list.num_floats = 3;
wght_list.floats     = wght;

for( i=0; i<ncols; i++ ){
 for( j=0; j<lsize; j++ ){
  /* calculate the colour ramp */
  f           = (float)j/(float)lsize;
  col[j].rgb.red = f*colour->rgb.red  +(1-f)*bg.rgb.red;
  col[j].rgb.green=f*colour->rgb.green+(1-f)*bg.rgb.green;
```

```
  col[j].rgb.blue = f*colour->rgb.blue+(1-f)*bg.rgb.blue;
} /* colour ramp loop */

/* set colour approximation representations */
colr_list.num_colr_reps  = lsize;
colr_list.colr_reps      = col;
cdata.meth_r2.colr_model = PMODEL_RGB;
cdata.meth_r2.colrs      = colr_list;
cdata.meth_r2.weights    = wght_list;
pset_colr_map_rep (wsid, i, PCOLR_MAP_PSEUDO, &cdata);
colour++;
} /* loop over colours */

return(0);
}
```

Bibliography

[**Abi-Ezzi**] Abi-Ezzi S., Bunshaft A.J., An Implementer's View of PHIGS, IEEE Computer Graphics and Applications 2, 1986.

[**ANSI**] American National Standards Institute, Computer Graphics Programmer's Hierarchical Interactive Graphics System (PHIGS), ANSI X3.144,1988.

[**Arnold and Duce**] Arnold D.B., Duce D.A., ISO Standards for Computer Graphics: The First Generation, Computer Graphics Standards Series, Butterworths, 1990.

[**Blinn**] Blinn J. F., Me and my fake shadow, IEEE Computer Graphics and Applications, January 1988.

[**Brown and Heck**] Brown M.D., Heck M., Understanding PHIGS, Template Software Division of Megatek Corp., 1985.

[**Cahn et al.**] Cahn D., Abi-Ezzi S., McGinnis E., Shuey D., SIGGRAPH '87 Course #12: Using the PHIGS Standard, 1987.

[**Farin**] Farin G., Curves and Surfaces for Computer Aided Geometric Design: A Practical Guide, Academic Press, 1990.

[**Foley et al.**] Foley J.D., van Dam A., Feiner S.K., Hughes J.F., Computer Graphics Principles and Practice, Second Edition, Addison-Wesley, 1990.

[**Gaskins**] Gaskins T., PHIGS Programming Manual: 3D Programming in X, O'Reilly & Associates, 1992.

[**Henderson and Mumford**] Henderson L.R., Mumford A.M., The Computer Graphics Metafile, Butterworths, 1990.

[**Hopgood et al.**] Hopgood F.R.A., Duce D.A., Gallop J.R., Sutcliffe D.C., Introduction to the Graphical Kernel System GKS, Academic Press, 1986.

[Hopgood and Duce] Hopgood F.R.A., Duce D.A., A Primer for PHIGS, John Wiley & Sons, 1991.

[Howard] Howard T.L.J., TopDraw: A Structure Network Visualiser for PHIGS, Computer Graphics Forum **9**, 139-147, 1990.

[Howard et al.] Howard T.L.J., Hewitt W.T., Hubbold R.J., Wyrwas K.M., A Practical Introduction to PHIGS and PHIGS PLUS, Addison-Wesley, 1991.

[ISOa] International Organisation for Standardization, Information processing systems – Computer graphics, Graphical Kernel System GKS, ISO 7942, 1985.

[ISOb] International Organisation for Standardization, Information processing systems – Computer graphics, Computer Graphics Metafile, ISO/IEC 8632, 1987.

[ISOc] International Organisation for Standardization, Information processing systems – Computer graphics, Graphical Kernel System for three dimensions (GKS-3D) functional description, ISO 8805, 1987.

[ISOd] International Organisation for Standardization, Information processing systems – Computer graphics, Programmer's Hierarchical Interactive Graphics System (PHIGS), ISO/IEC IS 9592, 1989.

[ISOe] International Organisation for Standardization, Information processing systems – Computer graphics, Programmer's Hierarchical Interactive Graphics System (PHIGS PLUS), ISO/IEC DIS 9592-4, 1991.

[ISOf] International Organisation for Standardization, Information processing systems – Computer graphics, Programmer's Hierarchical Interactive Graphics System (PHIGS) FORTRAN-Binding, ISO/IEC IS 9593-1, 1990.

[ISOg] International Organisation for Standardization, Information processing systems – Computer graphics, Programmer's Hierarchical Interactive Graphics System (PHIGS) Ada-Binding, ISO/IEC 9593-3, 1990.

[ISOh] International Organisation for Standardization, Information processing systems – Computer graphics, Programmer's Hierarchical Interactive Graphics System (PHIGS) C-Binding, ISO/IEC IS 9593-4, 1991.

[ISOi] International Organisation for Standardization, Information processing systems – Computer graphics, Programmer's Hierarchical Interactive Graphics System (PHIGS) PHIGS PLUS FORTRAN-Binding, Draft amendment to ISO/IEC 9593-1, July 3, 1992.

[ISOj] International Organisation for Standardization, Information processing systems – Computer graphics, Programmer's Hierarchical Interactive Graphics System (PHIGS) PHIGS PLUS C-Binding, Draft amendment to ISO/IEC IS 9593-4, March 25, 1992.

[**Penna and Patterson**] Penna M. A., Patterson R. R., Projective Geometry and its Application to Computer Graphics, Prentice Hall, 1986.

[**PEX**] PEXlib C Language Binding Specification, Digital Equipment Corp., 1992.

[**Piegl a**] Piegl L., A Geometric Investigation of the Rational Bezier Scheme of Computer Aided Design, Computers in Industry, **7**, pp 401-410, 1986.

[**Piegl b**] Piegl L., On the use of infinite control points in CAGD, Computer Aided Geometric Design, **4**, pp. 155-166, 1987.

[**Plaehn**] Plaehn M., PHIGS: Programmer's Hierarchical Interactive Graphics Standard, BYTE, 1987.

[**Poller et al.**] Poller J., Noll S., Rix J., Migration of GKS/GKS-3D and PHIGS: Discussed under the View of the Computer Graphics Reference Model, Computer Graphics Forum **8**, pp. 239-248, 1989.

[**Rogers**] Rogers D.F., Procedural Elements for Computer Graphics, McGraw Hill Book Company, 1985.

[**Rogers and Adams**] Rogers D.F., Adams J.A., Mathematical Elements for Computer Graphics, Second Edition, McGraw-Hill Book Company, 1990.

[**Tiller**] Tiller W., Rational B-Splines for Curve and Surface Representation, IEEE Computer Graphics & Applications, **3**, pp. 61-69, 1985.

[**Versprille**] Versprille K., Computer-aided design applications of the rational B-spline approximation form. Dissertation, Syracuse University, USA, 1975.

Appendix A

A FORTRAN Example

```
c==============================================================
c This program demonstrates the use of PHIGS to define and
c draw a very simple object. It demonstrates:
c
c 1. Use of CSS to define structures
c 2. Defining viewing transformations
c 3. Using the locator input device in sample mode
c 4. Using the choice device in event mode
c 6. Updating modelling transformations
c 7. Rotating about an arbitrary centre of rotation
c 8. Updating workstations
c
c==============================================================
        include '/usr/include/PHIGS/phigs_for_bnd_consts.f'

        real matrix(4,4), matrix1(4,4),
        real matrix2(4,4), idmtrx(4,4)
        real pi
        real oldx, oldy, lpx, lpy, xrot, yrot
        integer icl, viewi, errind
        integer conid,wtype

C Define variables needed for input devices
        integer il,rl,sl, lstr(4),mldr,ldr
```

```
      integer ia(1)
      integer ra(1)
      integer ch_1, done
      integer chstat, chonr, wsch
      integer devnum, locdev
      integer rasterx, rastery, dcunit
      real dcx,dcy
      real chxmin,chxmax, chymin,chymax
      character*8 str(4), chorec(10)
      character*5 title
      data title /'Title'/

C Define structure names and labels
      integer ROOT,BOX, TRANSFORM
      parameter( ROOT=0, BOX=1 )
      parameter( TRANSFORM=1 )
      parameter (locdev=1 )

C Define our workstation id
      integer wkid
      parameter ( wkid=1 )

c Define the base colours used for the pseudocolour LUT.
      real backg(3), col( 3,6 )

      data backg / 0.4, 0.4, 0.4 /
      data col / 1.0, 0.3, 0.2,
     *           1.0, 0.2, 0.7,
     *           0.9, 0.9, 0.4,
     *           0.2, 0.9, 0.2,
     *           0.2, 0.7, 0.9,
     *           0.2, 0.2, 1.0 /

c Define identity matrix
      data idmtrx / 1, 0, 0, 0,
     *              0, 1, 0, 0,
     *              0, 0, 1, 0,
     *              0, 0, 0, 1 /

c*******************************************************************
c    START OF EXECUTABLE
c*******************************************************************
      pi = 4 * atan(1.0)
c
c Before we can do anything we have to open PHIGS
c
```

```
        open( unit= 1, file='box.err',status='unknown' )
        call popph(1,0)
```

```
c Create the main structure. The second SET LOCAL TRANS
c FORM element will be edited and given different trans-
c formations once this demo gets started. The label is
c used to identify where the element that is to be edited
c is. The two additional set local transformations, one
c before and one after the rotation placeholder are there
c in order to specify a different centre of rotation. One
c must simply tranform the COR to the origin, rotate about
c the origin, and then transform back to its original
c position. One must make sure that all calls to SET LOCAL
c TRANSFORMATION are postconcatenated, otherwise the xform
c order is incorrect. The structure contains the following
c elements:
c
c EP  Element                    Comment
c --  ------                     ---------
c 1 set view index              identifies viewing transform
c 2 set hlhsr id to 1           enable hidden surface removal
c 3 set interior style solid    enable filling polygons
c 4 translate                   move COR to origin
c 5 label                       label to mark where xform is
c 6 set local transform         3D rotation placeholder
c 7 translate                   move object back to its COR
c 8 execute structure box       contains object to be drawn
```

```
        call popst (ROOT)
           call psvwi (1)
           call pshrid (PHRIZB)
           call psis ( PSOLID )
           call ptr3 ( -0.5, -0.5, -0.5, errind, matrix1 )
           call pslmt3 ( matrix1, PCPOST )
           call plb ( TRANSFORM )
           call pslmt3 ( idmtrx, PCPOST )
           call ptr3 ( 0.5, 0.5, 0.5, errind, matrix1 )
           call pslmt3 ( matrix1, PCPOST )
           call pexst ( BOX )
        call pclst
```

```
c Now define a cube and put it in the structure: BOX
        call ldbox (BOX)
```

```
c Open an OUTIN workstation with, define a viewing
c transformation and enable the Z-Buffer.
```

```
      call popwk(wkid,0,0)
      call ldview(wkid,1)
      call pshrm( wkid,PHRMZB )

c Initialize the input devices: locator and choice
c First initialize the locator and put it in sample mode.
c This will be used to update the local transformation.
      il    = 0
      ia(1) = 0
      rl    = 0
      ra(1) = 0
      sl    = 0
      lstr(1) = 0
      mldr    = 10
      call pprec( il,ia, rl,ra, sl,lstr,str, mldr,
     +            errind,ldr,chorec )
      call pinlc(wkid, locdev, 1, 0.5,0.5, 1,
     +            0,dcx,0,dcy, ldr, chorec)
      call pslcm(wkid,locdev,PSAMPL,PECHO)
      call psvtip( wkid, 1, 0, PHIGHR )

C Now initialze a choice button to use to tell the program
C we are done. FORTRAN has no data structures, so we must
C use the phigs call PACK DATA RECORD to shuffle data into
C the string: chorec, which is passed to the call
C INITIALIZE CHOICE. We are using PET -1 which is a
C button. This choice device is in event mode so that we
C can take the choice out of the input queue.
      il    = 2
      ia(1) = %loc(title)
      ia(2) = len( title )
      rl    = 0
      ra(1) = 0
      sl    = 1
      lstr(1) = 4
      str(1)  = 'Done'
      mldr    = 10
      call pprec( il,ia, rl,ra, sl,lstr,str, mldr,
     +            errind, ldr,chorec )
      if( errind .ne. 0 )
         write(*,*)'Error making choice datarec',errind

      ch_1  = 1
      done  = 0
      chxmin = 0.9*dcx
      chxmax = dcx
```

```
          chymin = 0.9*dcy
          chymax = dcy
          call pinch( wkid, ch_1,POK,done,3, chxmin,chxmax,
     +                chymin,chymax, ldr,chorec )
          call pschm( wkid, ch_1,PEVENT, PECHO )

c First define the colour representations. Colour rep
c 0 is always the background colour. Each colour
c representations will be used by a face of the box.
c The colours will be selected by setting the INTERIOR
c COLOUR INDEX to point to one of the colours defined
c here.
          call pscr(wkid, 0, backg(1), backg(2), backg(3) )
          call pscr(wkid, 1, col(1,1), col(2,1),col(3,1) )
          call pscr(wkid, 2, col(1,2), col(2,2),col(3,2) )
          call pscr(wkid, 3, col(1,3), col(2,3),col(3,3) )
          call pscr(wkid, 4, col(1,4), col(2,4),col(3,4) )
          call pscr(wkid, 5, col(1,5), col(2,5), col(3,5) )
          call pscr(wkid, 6, col(1,6), col(2,6), col(3,6) )

c Post the root structure. This will associate ROOT with
c the workstation, wkid. Nothing is drawn yet. This is
c because the default deferral mode is PWAIT. One must
c either call REDRAW ALL STRUCTURES or UPDATE WORKSTATION
c to get something drawn in the mode PWAIT.

          call ppost(wkid, ROOT, 0.0)

c Now open the ROOT structure to edit, set edit mode to
c replace, and point to the element after the label
c TRANSFORM. This is the transformation which will be
c overwritten with a new local transformation each time
c through the loop.

          call popst(ROOT)
          call psedm(PREPLC)
          call psep(0)
          call pseplb(TRANSFORM)
          call posep(1)
          call prst(wkid,PALWAY)

C*************************************************************
C   Main loop which is exited when we push the done choice
C   button. If we get an event, read it from the input
C   queue, and if the done button was picked then update
C   the variable, done.
```

Appendix A

```
C*****************************************************
      oldx = -10.0
      oldy = -10.0
100   continue
        call pwait( 0.0, wsch,icl,devnum )
         if( (icl.eq.PCHOIC).and.(devnum.eq.ch_1) ) then
           call pgtch( chstat, chonr )
            if( (chstat.eq.POK).and.(chonr.eq.1)) done = 1
         endif

        call psmlc( wkid, locdev, viewi, lpx, lpy )
        xrot = 4*pi*lpy
        yrot = 4*pi*lpx
        call prox(xrot, errind, matrix1)
        call proy(yrot, errind, matrix2)
        call pcom3(matrix1, matrix2, errind, matrix)
        if( lpx.ne.0.0 .or. lpy.ne.0.0 )
            call pslmt3(matrix,PCPOST)

        if((oldx.ne.lpx) .or. (oldy.ne.lpy))
            call prst(wkid,PALWAY)

        oldx = lpx
        oldy = lpy
      if( done.eq.0 ) goto 100

c Tidy up before exiting. (ie. close the open root
c structure, the workstation and PHIGS).
      call pclst
      call pclwk(wkid)
      call pclph
      end

      subroutine ldbox(sid)
C*****************************************************
c This function defines a cube in the CSS. Here the
c object defined with FILL AREA 3. Each face has a
c different colour
C*****************************************************
      integer sid
      real xf_1(4), yf_1(4), zf_1(4)
      real xf_2(4), yf_2(4), zf_2(4)
      real xf_3(4), yf_3(4), zf_3(4)
      real xf_4(4), yf_4(4), zf_4(4)
      real xf_5(4), yf_5(4), zf_5(4)
      real xf_6(4), yf_6(4), zf_6(4)
```

```
      data xf_1 / 0.25, 0.25, 0.75, 0.75 /
      data yf_1 / 0.25, 0.25, 0.25, 0.25 /
      data zf_1 / 0.75, 0.25, 0.25, 0.75 /

      data xf_2 / 0.25, 0.25, 0.75, 0.75 /
      data yf_2 / 0.75, 0.75, 0.75, 0.75 /
      data zf_2 / 0.75, 0.25, 0.25, 0.75 /

      data xf_3 / 0.25, 0.25, 0.25, 0.25 /
      data yf_3 / 0.25, 0.75, 0.75, 0.25 /
      data zf_3 / 0.75, 0.75, 0.25, 0.25 /

      data xf_4 / 0.75, 0.75, 0.75, 0.75 /
      data yf_4 / 0.25, 0.75, 0.75, 0.25 /
      data zf_4 / 0.75, 0.75, 0.25, 0.25 /

      data xf_5 / 0.25, 0.25, 0.75, 0.75 /
      data yf_5 / 0.25, 0.75, 0.75, 0.25 /
      data zf_5 / 0.75, 0.75, 0.75, 0.75 /

      data xf_6 / 0.25, 0.25, 0.75, 0.75 /
      data yf_6 / 0.25, 0.75, 0.75, 0.25 /
      data zf_6 / 0.25, 0.25, 0.25, 0.25 /

C*************************************************************
c Create a structure with the name sid. Put the geometry
c and colour information into the structure.
C*************************************************************
      call popst(sid)
        call psici( 1 )
        call pfa3( 4, xf_1, yf_1, zf_1 )
        call psici( 2 )
        call pfa3( 4, xf_2, yf_2, zf_2 )
        call psici( 3 )
        call pfa3( 4, xf_3, yf_3, zf_3 )
        call psici( 4 )
        call pfa3( 4, xf_4, yf_4, zf_4 )
        call psici( 5 )
        call pfa3( 4, xf_5, yf_5, zf_5 )
        call psici( 6 )
        call pfa3( 4, xf_6, yf_6, zf_6 )
      call pclst
c
      return
      end
```

Appendix A

```
      subroutine ldview(ws, ind)
c

      integer ws, ind   integer errind
      real vwormt(4,4), vwmpmt(4,4)
      real vwwnlm(4), pjvplm(6), vwcplm(6)
c

      data vwwnlm / -1.0, 1.5, -1.0, 1.5 /
      data pjvplm / 0.0, 1.0, 0.0, 1.0, 0.0, 1.0 /
      data vwcplm / 0.0, 1.0, 0.0, 1.0, 0.0, 1.0 /

      include '/usr/include/PHIGS/phigs_for_bnd_consts.f'
C**********************************************************
C             Start of executable                       *
C**********************************************************
c
c Define the view orientation matrix. This determines what
c in WC space is being looked at and how the WC is
c oriented relative to the screen.  The routine EVALUATE
c VIEW ORIENTATION MATRIX3 generates a matrix which
c will map the WC space to the VRC space. The point, VRP,
c is in WC coordinates and defines the origin of the VRC
c (View Reference Coordinates).  The VRC has the right
c handed axes (U,V,N). The vectors VPN and VUP are the
c N and V axes of the VRC respectively. The U axis is
c determined by the cross product. Therefore this
c mapping needs the following information:
c
c View Reference Point (VRC origin)        = (0,0,0)
c View Plane Normal (the N axis of the VRC) = (0,0,1)
c View Up vector ( the V axis of the VRC)   = (0,1,0)
c
      call pevom3(0.0, 0.0, 0.0,
     *      0.0, 0.0, 1.0,
     *      0.0, 1.0, 0.0,
     *      errind, vwormt)

      if( errind.ne.0 ) write( 6,10 ) errind
10    format( 'view orientation error #',i10 )
c
c Define the view mapping matrix. This matrix transforms
c the VRC onto the NPC, Normalized Projection
c Coordinates. This is the projection transformation. We
c need to determine a window in the VRC which is
c projected onto a viewport in NPC. The VRC window is in
c (U and V) the volume in VRC is then determined by the
c front, view and back planes. The position of these
```

```
c planes is given by an N coordinate, and they are
c orthogonal to the N axis. This is where it is
c determined whether perspective is used or not, and
c where is the perspective reference point. All
c coordinates are VRC coordinates, EXCEPT the NPC viewport
c which is in NPC coordinates. NPC coordinates are by
c definition normalized.  That means all NPC coordinates
c must be between 0 and 1. So, we must specify the:
c
c     VRC window (umin,umax, vmin,vmax):  (-1,1.5, -1,1.5)
c     NPC viewport:                       (0,1, 0,1, 0,1)
c     Projection type:                    Perspective
c     VRC Projection Reference Point: ( 0.5, 0.5, 3.0 )
c     VRC view plane:   0.0
c     VRC front plane: 1.0
c     VRC back plane: -1.0
c
      call pevmm3(vwwnlm, pjvplm, PPERS, 0.5, 0.5, 3.0,
     *           0.0, -1.0, 1.0, errind, vwmpmt)
c
      if(errind.ne.0)
      write(6,20)errind
20    format(' view mapping error #',i10)

c Now we have our transformations. Let's pass this over to
c the workstation, ws, and give this viewing
c transformation the index ind. Whenever we need this
c viewing transformation, we need to call SET VIEW INDEX
c with the value ind. One other thing that we must
c specify is whether we want to clip or not, and if so
c what is the clipping volume. The clipping volume is
c given in NPC coordinates.
c
c     NPC clipping limits: ( 0,1, 0,1, 0,1)
c     X-Y clipping: YES
c     Front plane clipping: YES
c     Back plane clipping: YES
c
      call psvwr3(ws, ind, vwormt, vwmpmt, vwcplm,
     +           PCLIP,PCLIP,PCLIP)
c
      return
      end
```

Appendix B

A PHIGS PLUS Example

The following example program demonstrates a number of PHIGS PLUS features as well as the structure of a typical PHIGS program. The following components of PHIGS PLUS are demonstrated: backface processing, lighting and depth cueing. The original example was written with DEC-PHIGS Version 2.3, but was ported to SUN-PHIGS in order to take advantage of the ISO C binding. It took four hours to port this example program.

The example uses a simple geometric object, a torus, which is defined with the primitive QUADRILATERAL MESH 3 WITH DATA. Both the vertices and the normal vectors are defined. The normal vectors are used in the lighting calculation. The tesselation of the torus can be controlled with a valuator, ranging from 3 to 150, enabling one to define an object whose complexity can range from nine to 22,500 polygons.

The torus can be rotated by moving the mouse while holding down the left mouse button. The mouse position is used to determine the latitude and longitude of the viewer in spherical coordinates. The torus can be zoomed with an additional slider bar. There are also three sliders which can be used to translate the object. The viewing transformations are generated using a simplistic camera-based viewing model, which was introduced in Section 7.5.

The user is presented with one menu containing five choices. The first choice is self-evident, 'Exit'. The next choice 'Tumble' causes the torus to rotate on the screen. When 'Tumble' is selected a second time, performance data consisting of frame rate and polygons/second is printed to the screen and the tumbling stops. The third choice 'Toggle wireframe' toggles between three different interior styles:

Toggle state	Front facing facets	Back facing facets
1	SOLID	SOLID
2	HOLLOW	SOLID
3	HOLLOW	HOLLOW

The torus appears as a lit and shaded surface under toggle state 1. Toggle state 2 causes the front facets to appear as a wireframe and the back facing facets to appear solid. This allows one to look inside the torus. The last toggle state causes both front- and backfacing facets to appear as a wireframe. The wireframe is drawn with the same aspects as the solid surface, so it appears as if it was lit (see Colour Plate 14).

The fourth menu choice toggles polygon edge display on and off. When on, the edges of each quadrilateral are rendered with the edge aspects. This allows one to see the edges even when the interior style is SOLID. The fifth menu choice is used to toggle depth cueing on and off. A fixed depth cueing representation is hard-coded in the example.

```
#include <stdio.h>
#include <math.h>
#include <sys/types.h>
#include <sys/time.h>
#include <phigs.h>

#define TRUE (1==1)
#define FALSE (1==0)
#define PI 3.141592654
#define DEGRAD (PI/180.0)

#define RootStruct   1
#define ViewInd      1
#define WSID         1
#define AttrLab      2
#define ObjLab       3

#define BackColInd   0
#define SurfColInd   1

/*   LIGHT SOURCES */
#define AMBI 1
#define INF1 2
#define INF2 3
```

```
#define DQ_OFF 1
#define DQ_ON  2
/*****************************************/
/******** Input device parameters ******/
/*****************************************/
/* Menu choice device number */
#define CH_MAIN  1
/* valuator device numbers */
#define S_XPOS   1
#define S_YPOS   2
#define S_ZPOS   3
#define S_ZOOM   4
#define S_TESS   5
/* Locator device number */
#define MOUSE    5


Prefl_props refl_prop;

/**************************/
/*** Function prototypes ***/
/**************************/
void define_dqrep( Pint, Pcolr_rep );
void define_lights( Pint, Pint_list *, Pint_list * );
void InitInput( Pint );
void printperf( int, float );
void ProcessInput( Pint );
Pint set_camera_view( Pint, Pint, Ppoint3, Ppoint3,
                      Pvec3 *, float, float);
double stopwatch( int );
void torus( int, int, float, float );
void ToggleWire( int * );
void ToggleEdge(void);
void ToggleDQ(void);

/********************************/
/*** Global variables and flags ***/
/********************************/
Pfloat xmaxDC, ymaxDC;
static Ppoint3 viewer = { 0.0, 0.5, 5.0 };
static Ppoint3 viewee = { 0.0, 0.0, 0.0 };
static Pvec3   vup    = { 0.0, 1.0, 0.0 };
static float   aper = 60.0;
static float   depth = 0.5;
Pfloat xmaxDC, ymaxDC;
static Ppoint3 viewer = { 0.0, 0.5, 5.0 };
static Ppoint3 viewee = { 0.0, 0.0, 0.0 };
```

```
static Pvec3    vup    = { 0.0, 1.0, 0.0 };
static float    aper   = 60.0;
static float    depth = 0.5;
int        i,s,t;
int        Done,update;
static int tess = 10;
static int Tumble = FALSE;
static int EdgeF  = FALSE;
static int DcueF  = FALSE;

void
main( int argc, char *argv[] )
{
/****************************************************/
/* Main program. First define a number of variables */
/* needed in the main program and their values.     */
/****************************************************/
Pint err;
Pint wstype;
Pdisp_space_size dsize;

/* Transformation variables */
/* ----------------------- */
Pmatrix3 mat;
static Pvec3 zero  = { 0, 0, 0 };
static Ppoint3 cor = { 0.5,0.5,0.5 };
static Pfloat xang = 5.0*DEGRAD;
static Pfloat yang = -5.0*DEGRAD;
static Pfloat zang = 0.0;
static Pvec3 scale = { 1.0, 1.0, 1.0 };

Pcolr_rep BackCol;
Pcolr_rep SurfCol;
Pint_list on, off;

/****************************************************/
/* ================================== */
/* Before using PHIGS, it must be opened */
/* ================================== */
   popen_phigs( PDEF_ERR_FILE, PDEF_MEM_SIZE );

/* ========================================= */
/* Open a workstation to display structure on    */
/* On SUN-PHIGS one must use a proprietary function */
/* to generate the workstation type.             */
/* ========================================= */
```

```
  wstype = phigs_ws_type_create( phigs_ws_type_x_tool,
      PHIGS_TOOL_LABEL, "SunPHIGS X Tool Workstation",
      PHIGS_WS_CATEGORY, PCAT_OUTIN,
      PHIGS_X_BUF_MODE, PHIGS_BUF_DOUBLE,
      0);
  if ( !wstype ) {
      pclose_phigs();
      exit(1);
  }

  pinq_disp_space_size( wstype, &err, &dsize );
  xmaxDC = dsize.size_dc.size_x;
  ymaxDC = dsize.size_dc.size_y;
  popen_ws( WSID, (void *)NULL, wstype );

/* ------------------------------------- */
/* Define some colours on the workstation */
/* ------------------------------------- */
  BackCol.rgb.red   = 0.1;
  BackCol.rgb.green = 0.2;
  BackCol.rgb.blue  = 0.3;
  SurfCol.rgb.red   = 0.9;
  SurfCol.rgb.green = 0.9;
  SurfCol.rgb.blue  = 0.9;
  pset_colr_rep( WSID, BackColInd, &BackCol );
  pset_colr_rep( WSID, SurfColInd, &SurfCol );

/* ------------------------------------------- */
/* Initialize viewing transformation, lights, */
/* depth cueing, HLHSR and input devices.      */
/* ------------------------------------------- */
  set_camera_view( WSID, ViewInd, viewer, viewee,
                     &vup, aper, depth );
  define_lights(WSID, &on, &off );
  define_dqrep( WSID, BackCol );
  pset_hlhsr_mode (WSID, PHIGS_HLHSR_MODE_ZBUFF );
  InitInput( WSID );

/* Define a transformation to tilt the torus a bit */
/* ------------------------------------------------- */
  pbuild_tran_matrix3( &cor, &zero, xang,yang,zang,
                         &scale, &err, mat );

/* ===================================== */
/* Now define the objects in a structure */
/* ===================================== */
```

```
  popen_struct( RootStruct );
    pset_view_ind( ViewInd );
    pset_hlhsr_id (PHIGS_HLHSR_ID_ON );
  plabel( AttrLab );
    pset_line_colr_ind( SurfColInd );
    pset_int_colr_ind( SurfColInd );
    pset_edge_flag( PEDGE_OFF );
    pset_int_style (PSTYLE_SOLID);
    pset_back_int_style( PSTYLE_SOLID);
    pset_dcue_ind( DQ_OFF );
    pset_refl_eqn (PREFL_AMB_DIFF_SPEC);
    pset_int_shad_meth (PSD_COLOUR);
    pset_light_src_state( &on, &off );
    pset_refl_props(&refl_prop);
    pset_face_disting_mode( PDISTING_YES );
    pset_back_refl_props(&refl_prop);
    pset_back_refl_eqn (PREFL_AMB_DIFF_SPEC);
    pset_back_int_shad_meth (PSD_COLOUR);
    pset_global_tran3( mat );
  plabel( ObjLab );
    torus( tess, tess, 0.5, 0.3 );
  pclose_struct();

/* ================================================== */
/* Now post structure to the workstation and update */
/* ================================================== */
  ppost_struct( WSID, RootStruct, 1.0 );
  pupd_ws( WSID, PFLAG_PERFORM );

/* -------------------------------------------------- */
/* Now enter the input loop, processing input devices */
/* until the user selects 'Exit'.                     */
/* -------------------------------------------------- */
  Done = FALSE;
  update = TRUE;
  while( !Done ){
    ProcessInput(WSID);
    if( update ) {
      pupd_ws( WSID, PFLAG_PERFORM );
      update = FALSE;
      }
    }

/* We're done, so close everything and exit */
/* ======================================== */
  pclose_ws( WSID );
```

```
    pclose_phigs();
}


void
define_dqrep( Pint wsid, Pcolr_rep Backg )
/*----------------------------------------------------------*/
/* Define 2 depth cue representations. One disabling    */
/* depth cueing, the other enabling it.                 */
/*----------------------------------------------------------*/
{
   Pdcue_bundle dq;

   dq.mode = PSUPPRESSED;
   pset_dcue_rep( wsid, DQ_OFF, &dq );

   dq.mode          = PALLOWED;
   dq.ref_planes[0] = -0.5;
   dq.ref_planes[1] = 0.5;
   dq.scaling[0]    = 0.0;
   dq.scaling[1]    = 1.0;
   dq.colr.type     = PMODEL_RGB;
   dq.colr.val.general.x = Backg.rgb.red;
   dq.colr.val.general.y = Backg.rgb.green;
   dq.colr.val.general.z = Backg.rgb.blue;
   pset_dcue_rep( wsid, DQ_ON, &dq );
}


void
define_lights(Pint wsid, Pint_list *on, Pint_list *off)
/*----------------------------------------------------------*/
/* Define 3 light sources (1 ambient and 2 directional) */
/* and return the light source indices in the on list   */
/*----------------------------------------------------------*/
{
static Pint onlist[8], offlist[8];
Plight_src_bundle lights;
Plight_src_rec    lrec;

   refl_prop.ambient_coef  = 0.1;
   refl_prop.diffuse_coef  = 0.8;
   refl_prop.specular_coef = 0.3;
   refl_prop.specular_colr.type = PMODEL_RGB;
   refl_prop.specular_colr.val.general.x = 1.0;
   refl_prop.specular_colr.val.general.y = 1.0;
   refl_prop.specular_colr.val.general.z = 1.0;
   refl_prop.specular_exp = 3;
```

```
    lights.type  = PLIGHT_AMBIENT;
    lights.rec.ambient.colr.type = PMODEL_RGB;
    lights.rec.ambient.colr.val.general.x = 0.2;
    lights.rec.ambient.colr.val.general.y = 0.2;
    lights.rec.ambient.colr.val.general.z = 0.2;
    pset_light_src_rep( wsid, AMBI, &lights );

    lights.type  = PLIGHT_DIRECTIONAL;
    lights.rec.directional.colr.type = PMODEL_RGB;
    lights.rec.directional.colr.val.general.x = 1.0;
    lights.rec.directional.colr.val.general.y = 0.5;
    lights.rec.directional.colr.val.general.z = 0.2;
    lights.rec.directional.dir.delta_x = -0.4;
    lights.rec.directional.dir.delta_y = -0.2;
    lights.rec.directional.dir.delta_z = -1.0;
    pset_light_src_rep( wsid, INF1,  &lights );

    lights.type  = PLIGHT_DIRECTIONAL;
    lights.rec.directional.colr.type = PMODEL_RGB;
    lights.rec.directional.colr.val.general.x = 0.2;
    lights.rec.directional.colr.val.general.y = 0.6;
    lights.rec.directional.colr.val.general.z = 0.6;
    lights.rec.directional.dir.delta_x = 0.4;
    lights.rec.directional.dir.delta_y = -0.2;
    lights.rec.directional.dir.delta_z = -1.0;
    pset_light_src_rep( wsid, INF2, &lights );
    onlist[0] = AMBI;
    onlist[1] = INF1;
    onlist[2] = INF2;
    on->num_ints  = 3;
    on->ints      = onlist;
    off->num_ints = 3;
    off->ints     = offlist;

}


void
InitInput( Pint wsid)
{
static Pint ChPET = 3;
static char  *mmenstr[5] = { "Exit",
                             "Tumble",
                             "Toggle wireframe",
                             "Toggle edges",
                             "Depth cue" };
```

```
static Plimit ChSize      = { 0.0,0.75, 0.0,0.25 };
Pchoice_data chrec;

Plimit valsize;

Pint i, err;
Pval_data dial_rec;
Plimit dial_area;
char   low_lab[10];
char   high_lab[10];

static Ppoint    inipos = { 0.5, 0.5 };
Ploc_data locrec;
static  Plimit mouse_area = { 0.0, 0.1, 0.0, 0.1 };

/*---------------------------------------------------------*/
/* Initialize choice device with a menu containing the */
/* options:                                            */
/*  "Exit",              leave the program             */
/*  "Tumble",            tumble torus measuring speed   */
/*  "Toggle wireframe", Toggle between SOLID, HOLLOW    */
/*                       front and HOLLOW front&back    */
/*                       interior styles               */
/*  "Toggle edges",      toggle edge visibility         */
/*  "Depth cue",         toggle depth cueing on/off     */
/*---------------------------------------------------------*/
ChSize.x_min *= xmaxDC; ChSize.x_max *= xmaxDC;
ChSize.y_min *= ymaxDC; ChSize.y_max *= ymaxDC;
chrec.pets.pet_r3.num_strings = 5;
chrec.pets.pet_r3.strings      = mmenstr;
pinit_choice( wsid, CH_MAIN, PIN_STATUS_OK, 1, ChPET,
              &ChSize,&chrec );
pset_choice_mode(wsid, CH_MAIN, POP_EVENT, PSWITCH_ECHO);

/*---------------------------------------------------------*/
/* Initialize three valuators, as sliders for inputing */
/* the position of the view reference point            */
/*---------------------------------------------------------*/
/* VRP's x position */
/*-----------------*/
dial_rec.low = -2;
dial_rec.high = 2;
dial_rec.pets.pet_u1.label  = "X-Position  ";
dial_rec.pets.pet_u1.format = "%6.2f";
sprintf( low_lab, "%6.2f", dial_rec.low );
sprintf( high_lab, "%6.2f", dial_rec.high );
```

```
dial_rec.pets.pet_u1.low_label  = low_lab;
dial_rec.pets.pet_u1.high_label = high_lab;
dial_area.x_min=0.75*xmaxDC; dial_area.x_max=xmaxDC;
dial_area.y_min=0.45*ymaxDC; dial_area.y_max=0.6*ymaxDC;
pset_val_mode( wsid, S_XPOS, POP_REQ, PSWITCH_NO_ECHO );
pinit_val( wsid, S_XPOS, viewee.x, -1,
            &dial_area, &dial_rec);
pset_val_mode( wsid, S_XPOS, POP_SAMPLE, PSWITCH_ECHO );

/* VRP's y position */
/*------------------*/
dial_rec.low = -2;
dial_rec.high = 2;
dial_rec.pets.pet_u1.label  = "Y-Position";
dial_rec.pets.pet_u1.format = "%6.2f";
sprintf( low_lab, "%6.2f", dial_rec.low );
sprintf( high_lab, "%6.2f", dial_rec.high );
dial_rec.pets.pet_u1.low_label  = low_lab;
dial_rec.pets.pet_u1.high_label = high_lab;
dial_area.x_min=0.75*xmaxDC; dial_area.x_max=xmaxDC;
dial_area.y_min=0.3*ymaxDC; dial_area.y_max=0.45*ymaxDC;
pset_val_mode( wsid, S_YPOS, POP_REQ, PSWITCH_NO_ECHO );
pinit_val( wsid, S_YPOS, viewee.y, -1,
            &dial_area, &dial_rec);
pset_val_mode( wsid, S_YPOS, POP_SAMPLE, PSWITCH_ECHO );

/* VRP's z position */
/*------------------*/
dial_rec.low = -2;
dial_rec.high = 2;
dial_rec.pets.pet_u1.label  = "Z-Position";
dial_rec.pets.pet_u1.format = "%6.2f";
sprintf( low_lab, "%6.2f", dial_rec.low );
sprintf( high_lab, "%6.2f", dial_rec.high );
dial_rec.pets.pet_u1.low_label  = low_lab;
dial_rec.pets.pet_u1.high_label = high_lab;
dial_area.x_min=0.75*xmaxDC; dial_area.x_max=xmaxDC;
dial_area.y_min=0.15*ymaxDC; dial_area.y_max=0.3*ymaxDC;
pset_val_mode( wsid, S_ZPOS, POP_REQ, PSWITCH_NO_ECHO );
pinit_val( wsid, S_ZPOS, viewee.z, -1,
              &dial_area, &dial_rec);
pset_val_mode( wsid, S_ZPOS, POP_SAMPLE, PSWITCH_ECHO );

/*-----------------------------------------------------*/
/* Initialize a valuator, to input a zoom factor       */
/*-----------------------------------------------------*/
```

```
dial_rec.low = 0;
dial_rec.high = 15;
dial_rec.pets.pet_u1.label  = "Zoom";
dial_rec.pets.pet_u1.format = "%6.2f";
sprintf( low_lab,  "%6.2f", dial_rec.low );
sprintf( high_lab, "%6.2f", dial_rec.high );
dial_rec.pets.pet_u1.low_label  = low_lab;
dial_rec.pets.pet_u1.high_label = high_lab;
dial_area.x_min=0.75*xmaxDC; dial_area.x_max=xmaxDC;
dial_area.y_min=0.0*ymaxDC;  dial_area.y_max=0.15*ymaxDC;
pset_val_mode( wsid, S_ZOOM, POP_REQ, PSWITCH_NO_ECHO );
pinit_val( wsid, S_ZOOM, 4.0, -1,
           &dial_area, &dial_rec);
pset_val_mode( wsid, S_ZOOM, POP_SAMPLE, PSWITCH_ECHO );

/*-------------------------------------------------------*/
/* Initialize a valuator, to input a tesselation factor*/
/* This factor is used to determine how many polygons  */
/* to generate per torus.                              */
/*-------------------------------------------------------*/
dial_rec.low = 3;
dial_rec.high = 150;
dial_rec.pets.pet_u1.label  = "Tesselation";
dial_rec.pets.pet_u1.format = "%6.2f";
sprintf( low_lab,  "%6.2f", dial_rec.low );
sprintf( high_lab, "%6.2f", dial_rec.high );
dial_rec.pets.pet_u1.low_label  = low_lab;
dial_rec.pets.pet_u1.high_label = high_lab;
dial_area.x_min=0.75*xmaxDC; dial_area.x_max=xmaxDC;
dial_area.y_min=0.0*ymaxDC;  dial_area.y_max=0.15*ymaxDC;
pset_val_mode( wsid, S_TESS, POP_REQ, PSWITCH_NO_ECHO );
pinit_val( wsid, S_TESS, tess, -1,
           &dial_area, &dial_rec);
pset_val_mode( wsid, S_TESS, POP_SAMPLE, PSWITCH_ECHO );

/*------------------------------------------*/
/* Initialize the mouse as a locator */
/*------------------------------------------*/
pset_loc_mode(wsid, MOUSE, POP_REQ, PSWITCH_NO_ECHO);
pinit_loc(wsid,MOUSE, 1,&inipos, 1, &mouse_area,&locrec);
pset_loc_mode(wsid, MOUSE, POP_SAMPLE, PSWITCH_NO_ECHO);
}

void printperf( int iter, float interval )
{
  if( iter != 0 && interval != 0.0 ){
```

```
    printf("-------------------------------------------\n");
    printf("Torus is one quad mesh with %d quads\n",
            tess*tess);
    printf("   Tumble drew torus %d times in %f secs\n",
            iter,interval);
    printf("   Drew %8.2f quads/sec, refresh is %3.1fHz\n",
            tess*tess*iter/interval, iter/interval );
  }
}


void ProcessInput( Pint wsid )
{
Pint wsid_in, DevNum;
Pin_status status;
Pin_class DevClass;
Pint err;
Pint    choice;
Ppoint  mpos;
Pint     vind;
Pfloat knob_val;
static Ppoint3 oldv;
static Pfloat oldlat, oldlong,oldzoom;

static Pfloat lati = 0;
static Pfloat longi = 0;
static Pfloat zoom = 10;
        Pfloat NewTessel;

static int iter;
static double interval;
static int Wiref = 0;

/* Process all event driven devices */
/* ================================= */
pawait_event( 0.01, &wsid_in, &DevClass, &DevNum );
  if( wsid_in == wsid && DevClass == PIN_CHOICE ){
    pget_choice( &status, &choice );
    if( status == PIN_STATUS_OK && DevNum == CH_MAIN ){
      switch( choice ){
        case 1:{           /* Exit" chosen */
          Done = TRUE;
          break;
        }
        case 2:{           /* "Tumble" chosen */
            if(Tumble ){
            interval = stopwatch( 1 );
```

265

```
                printperf( iter,interval );
            }
            else{
                iter = 0;
                stopwatch( 0 );
            }
            Tumble = ~Tumble;
            break;
        }
        case 3:{          /* "Toggle wireframe" chosen */
            ToggleWire( &Wiref );
            update = TRUE;
            break;
        }
        case 4:{          /* "Toggle edge" chosen */
            ToggleEdge();
            update = TRUE;
            break;
        }
        case 5:{          /* Depth cue" chosen */
            ToggleDQ();
            break;
        }
        default:
            break;
    }
  }
}


/* --------------------------------------------- */
/* Now sample all six valuators                  */
/* --------------------------------------------- */
psample_val(wsid,S_XPOS,&(viewee.x));
psample_val(wsid,S_YPOS,&(viewee.y));
psample_val(wsid,S_ZPOS,&(viewee.z));
psample_val(wsid,S_ZOOM,&zoom);
psample_val(wsid,S_TESS,&NewTessel);
psample_loc(wsid, MOUSE, &vind, &mpos );

/*-----------------------------------------------------*/
/* Update viewer's position, either through tumbling */
/* or with the mouse                                 */
/*-----------------------------------------------------*/
if( Tumble ){
  lati++;
  longi++;
```

```
      iter++;
   }
   else{
      lati  = 180*mpos.x;
      longi = 360*mpos.y;
   }
   viewer.x = (15-zoom)*sin(DEGRAD*lati)*cos(DEGRAD*longi);
   viewer.y = (15-zoom)*                 sin(DEGRAD*longi);
   viewer.z = (15-zoom)*cos(DEGRAD*lati)*cos(DEGRAD*longi);
   vup.delta_x  = -sin(DEGRAD*lati)*sin(DEGRAD*longi);
   vup.delta_y  =                   cos(DEGRAD*longi);
   vup.delta_z  = -cos(DEGRAD*lati)*sin(DEGRAD*longi);
   set_camera_view( wsid, ViewInd, viewer,viewee, &vup,
                    aper, depth );

   /* ---------------------------------------------------*/
   /* If a new tesselation factor was input, regenerate */
   /* the torus.                                         */
   /* ---------------------------------------------------*/
   if( (int)NewTessel != tess ){
      pset_edit_mode( PEDIT_REPLACE );
      popen_struct( RootStruct );
        pset_elem_ptr( 0 );
        pset_elem_ptr_label( ObjLab );
        poffset_elem_ptr(1);
        tess = (int)NewTessel;
        torus( tess, tess, 0.5, 0.3 );
      pclose_struct();
      update = TRUE;
   }

   /*--------------------------------------------------*/
   /* If anything else has changed, update             */
   /*--------------------------------------------------*/
   if( oldv.x != viewee.x || oldv.x != viewee.y ||
       oldv.x != viewee.z || oldlat != lati ||
       oldlong != longi || oldzoom != zoom ) update = TRUE;

   oldv.x = viewee.x; oldv.y = viewee.y; oldv.z = viewee.y;
   oldlat = lati; oldlong = longi; oldzoom = zoom;
}


Pint
set_camera_view( Pint wsid, Pint index,
          Ppoint3 viewer,
          Ppoint3 viewee,
```

```
            Pvec3 *vup,
            float aperture, float depthrat )
{

  Pint err;

  float width, viewdist;
  Ppoint3 vrp;
  Pvec3 vpn;
  Pview_map3 vmap;
  Pview_rep3 vrep;
  static Plimit3 allnpc = { 0.0, 1.0, 0.0,1.0, 0.0,1.0 };

  /* Initialize and check arguments*/
  /*================================*/
  err = 0;
  if( depthrat <= 0.0 || depthrat >= 1.0 ) return( -1 );
  if( aperture <= 0.0 || aperture >= 90.0 ) return(-2);
  vrp = viewee;

  /* Calculate distance between viewer and viewee */
  /*==============================================*/
  viewdist = sqrt( (viewer.x-vrp.x)*(viewer.x-vrp.x)
             + (viewer.y-vrp.y)*(viewer.y-vrp.y)
             + (viewer.z-vrp.z)*(viewer.z-vrp.z) );

  /*************************************/
  /* Create the view orientation matrix */
  /*************************************/

  /* Now get the VPN as vector from viewee to viewer */
  /*=================================================*/
  vpn.delta_x = (viewer.x-vrp.x) / viewdist;
  vpn.delta_y = (viewer.y-vrp.y) / viewdist;
  vpn.delta_z = (viewer.z-vrp.z) / viewdist;

  peval_view_ori_matrix3( &vrp, &vpn, vup, &err,
                          vrep.ori_matrix);
  if( err != 0 ) return( err );

  /*************************************/
  /* Create the view mapping matrix */
  /*************************************/

  /* First derive the window from the aperture angle */
  /*=================================================*/
```

```
    width = viewdist*sin( DEGRAD*aperture );
    vmap.win.x_min = -width/2.0;
    vmap.win.x_max = width/2.0;
    vmap.win.y_min = -width/2.0;
    vmap.win.y_max = width/2.0;

    /* Define the prp and use the whole NPC viewport */
    /*===================================================*/
    vmap.proj_ref_point.x = 0.0;
    vmap.proj_ref_point.y = 0.0;
    vmap.proj_ref_point.z = viewdist;
    vmap.proj_vp          = allnpc;
    vmap.proj_type        = PTYPE_PERSPECT;

    /* Now the viewing reference planes */
    /*===================================*/
    vmap.view_plane = 0.0;
    vmap.front_plane = depthrat*viewdist;
    vmap.back_plane = -vmap.front_plane;

    peval_view_map_matrix3( &vmap, &err,
                            vrep.map_matrix);
    if( err != 0 ) return( err );

    /* We have our matrices, now use them */
    /*=====================================*/
    vrep.xy_clip    = PIND_CLIP;
    vrep.back_clip  = PIND_CLIP;
    vrep.front_clip = PIND_CLIP;
    vrep.clip_limit = allnpc;
    pset_view_rep3( wsid, index, &vrep);

    return( 0 );
}


double stopwatch( int flag )
/*----------------------------------------------------------*/
/* Reset stopwatch if passed 0, otherwise return time   */
/* in seconds since last called.                        */
/*----------------------------------------------------------*/
{
    double elapse;
    double sec,usec;
    static double start,now;
    struct timeval tp;
    struct timezone tpz;
```

```
    gettimeofday( &tp, &tpz );
    sec = (double)tp.tv_sec; usec = (double)tp.tv_usec;
    now =  sec + usec/1000000.0;
    if( flag == 0 ){
      start = now;
      return( 0.0 );
    }
    else{
      elapse = now-start;
      return( elapse );
    }
}


void ToggleDQ( void )
/*--------------------------------------------------------*/
/* Toggle depth cueing. Assumes a fixed structure layout*/
/*--------------------------------------------------------*/
{
  DcueF = ~DcueF;
  pset_edit_mode( PEDIT_REPLACE );
  popen_struct( RootStruct );
  pset_elem_ptr( 0 );
  pset_elem_ptr_label( AttrLab );
  poffset_elem_ptr(6);
  if( DcueF )
    pset_dcue_ind( DQ_ON );
  else
    pset_dcue_ind( DQ_OFF );
  pclose_struct();
}


void ToggleEdge( void )
/*--------------------------------------------------------*/
/* Toggle edge visibility. Assumes a fixed structure    */
/* layout                                               */
/*--------------------------------------------------------*/
{
  EdgeF = ~EdgeF;
  pset_edit_mode( PEDIT_REPLACE );
  popen_struct( RootStruct );
  pset_elem_ptr( 0 );
  pset_elem_ptr_label( AttrLab );
  poffset_elem_ptr(3);
  if( EdgeF )
    pset_edge_flag( PEDGE_ON );
```

```
    else
      pset_edge_flag( PEDGE_OFF );
    pclose_struct();
}

void ToggleWire( int *wiref )
/*----------------------------------------------------------*/
/* Toggle interior style between: 1) Front and back      */
/* facing facets as solid, 2) Front Hollow & Back Solid,*/
/* 3) Front and back facing facets as Hollow. Assumes a */
/* fixed structure layout                                */
/*----------------------------------------------------------*/
{
 (*wiref)++;
 if( *wiref > 2 ) *wiref = 0;
 pset_edit_mode( PEDIT_REPLACE );
 popen_struct( RootStruct );
 pset_elem_ptr( 0 );
 pset_elem_ptr_label( AttrLab );
 poffset_elem_ptr(4);
 switch( *wiref ){
    case 0:{
        pset_int_style (PSTYLE_SOLID);
        poffset_elem_ptr(1);
        pset_back_int_style( PSTYLE_SOLID);
        break;
    }
    case 1:{
        pset_int_style (PSTYLE_HOLLOW);
        poffset_elem_ptr(1);
        pset_back_int_style( PSTYLE_SOLID);
        break;
    }
    case 2 :{
        pset_int_style (PSTYLE_HOLLOW);
        poffset_elem_ptr(1);
        pset_back_int_style( PSTYLE_HOLLOW);
        break;
    }
 }
 pclose_struct();
}

void
torus( int m, int n, float R1, float R2 )
{
```

```
float R;
float r;
Pint_size          dim;
Pfacet_data_arr3   fdata;
Pfacet_vdata_arr3  vdata;
Pcoval             fcolr;
Pvec3              fnorm;
Pconorm3           fconorm;
Pptnorm3          *ptnorm;

/* Allocate memory to contain torus' geometry */
ptnorm = (Pptnorm3 *)malloc((m+1)*(n+1)*
                              sizeof(Pptnorm3) );

/****************************************************/
/* Compute the vertices and normals of the torus */
/****************************************************/
R = R1;
r = R2;
i = 0;
for (s = 0; s <= n; s++) /* major radius */
{
   for (t = 0; t <= m; t++) /* minor radius */
   {
       (ptnorm+i)->point.x = cos(2*PI * s / n) *
                             (R + r * cos(2*PI * t / m));
       (ptnorm+i)->point.y = r * sin(2*PI * t / m);
       (ptnorm+i)->point.z = sin(2*PI * s / n) *
                             (R + r * cos(2*PI * t / m));

       (ptnorm+i)->norm.delta_x = -r*cos(2*PI * s / n)*
                                  cos(2*PI * t / m);
       (ptnorm+i)->norm.delta_y = -r * sin(2*PI * t / m);
       (ptnorm+i)->norm.delta_z = -r * sin(2*PI * s / n) *
                                  cos(2*PI * t / m);
       i++;
   }
}


/****************************************************/
/* Now pass geometry to quadrilateral mesh primitive */
/****************************************************/
dim.size_x = n+1;
dim.size_y = m+1;
fdata.colrs = &fcolr;
fdata.norms = &fnorm;
```

```
    fdata.conorms = &fconorm;
    vdata.ptnorms = ptnorm;
    pquad_mesh3_data( PFACET_NONE, PVERT_COORD_NORMAL,
                      PINDIRECT,
                      &dim, &fdata, &vdata );
    free( ptnorm );
}
```

Appendix C

The PHIGS C and FORTRAN Bindings

This Appendix lists all PHIGS and PHIGS PLUS functions alphabetically along with the corresponding C and FORTRAN function names. These function names have been standardized in the ISO bindings [ISOh; ISOf]. At this time the PHIGS PLUS bindings have not been standardized, so they may be subject to change. The PHIGS PLUS function names have been taken from the drafts [ISOi; ISOj].

All PHIGS functions begin with a 'p'. The function names in the C binding are built from a set of abbreviations of keywords, while the FORTRAN binding generally has abbreviated the keywords to a single letter. So, for example, all inquiry functions start with:

C binding	FORTRAN binding
C binding	*FORTRAN binding*
pinq_	PQ

The abbreviated keywords in the C binding are separated by an underscore, making the function name readable. The FORTRAN names are unfortunately rather cryptic, due to the restriction that they must be six characters long. These function names generally follow fixed rules, so that one can quickly identify the PHIGS function by looking at its FORTRAN call.

The following table lists the PHIGS function keywords and the corresponding C and FORTRAN abbreviations. A NULL signifies that there is no abbreviation associated with a keyword. This simplifies identifying the function name from either its C or FORTRAN call.

Keyword	*C abbreviation*	*FORTRAN abbreviation*
ANNOTATION TEXT	anno	AT
APPLICATION	appl	AP
ARCHIVE	ar	AR
CHARACTER	char	CH
CHOICE	choice	CH
CLOSE	close	CL
COLOUR	colr	C
CONFLICT	conf	CN
COMPOSE	compose	CO
DEFAULT	def	NULL
DELETE	del	D
DISPLAY	disp	D
EDGE	edge	ED
ELEMENT	elem	E
ERROR	err	ER
EVALUATE	eval	EV
EXECUTE	exec	EX
EXPANSION	expan	XP
FACILITIES	facs	F
FILTER	filter	FT
GET	get	GT
HEIGHT	ht	H
HIGHLIGHTING	highl	HL
IDENTIFIER	id	ID
INDEX	ind	I
INITIALIZE	init	IN
INQUIRE	inq	Q
INTERIOR	int	I
LOCATOR	loc	LC
MAPPING	map	M
MATRIX	matrix	M
MODE	mode	M
NETWORKS	nets	N
OPEN	open	OP
PICK	pick	PK
PHIGS	phigs	PH
POINTER	ptr	P
PREDEFINED	pred	P
REPRESENTATION	rep	R
REQUEST	req	RG
RETRIEVE	ret	R
SAMPLE	sample	SM
SET	set	S
STATE	st	S
STRING	string	ST
STROKE	stroke	SK
STRUCTURE	struct	ST
TEXT	text	TX
TRANSFORMATION	tran	T
VALUATOR	val	VL
VIEW	view	VW
VIEWPORT	vp	V
WINDOW	win	W
WORKSTATION	ws	WK

275

PHIGS function name	ISO bindings C	FORTRAN
ADD NAMES TO SET	padd_names_set	PADS
ANNOTATION TEXT RELATIVE	panno_text_rel	PATR
ANNOTATION TEXT RELATIVE 3	panno_text_rel3	PATR3
APPLICATION DATA	pappl_data	PAP
ARCHIVE ALL STRUCTURES	par_all_structs	PARAST
ARCHIVE STRUCTURES	par_structs	PARST
ARCHIVE STRUCTURE NETWORKS	par_struct_nets	PARSN
AWAIT EVENT	pawait_event	PWAIT
BUILD TRANSFORMATION MATRIX	pbuild_tran_matrix	PBLTM
BUILD TRANSFORMATION MATRIX 3	pbuild_tran_matrix3	PBLTM3
CELL ARRAY	pcell_array	PCA
CELL ARRAY 3	pcell_array3	PCA3
CELL ARRAY 3 PLUS	pcell_array3_plus	PCA3P
CHANGE STRUCTURE IDENTIFIER	pchange_struct_id	PCSTID
CHANGE STRUCTURE IDENTIFIER AND REFER-ENCES	pchange_struct_id_refs	PCSTIR
CHANGE STRUCTURE REFERENCES	pchange_struct_refs	PCSTRF
CLOSE ARCHIVE FILE	pclose_ar_file	PCLARF
CLOSE PHIGS	pclose_phigs	PCLPH
CLOSE STRUCTURE	pclose_struct	PCLST
CLOSE WORKSTATION	pclose_ws	PCLWK
COMPOSE MATRIX	pcompose_matrix	PCOM
COMPOSE MATRIX 3	pcompose_matrix3	PCOM3
COMPOSE TRANSFORMATION MATRIX	pcompose_tran_matrix	PCOTM
COMPOSE TRANSFORMATION MATRIX 3	pcompose_tran_matrix3	PCOTM3
COPY ALL ELEMENTS FROM STRUCTURE	pcopy_all_elems_struct	PCELST
DELETE ALL STRUCTURES	pdel_all_structs	PDAS
DELETE ALL STRUCTURES FROM ARCHIVE	pdel_all_structs_ar	PDASAR
DELETE ELEMENT	pdel_elem	PDEL
DELETE ELEMENTS BETWEEN LABELS	pdel_elem_labels	PDELLB
DELETE ELEMENT RANGE	pdel_elem_range	PDELRA
DELETE STRUCTURE	pdel_struct	PDST
DELETE STRUCTURES FROM ARCHIVE	pdel_structs_ar	PDSTAR
DELETE STRUCTURE NETWORK	pdel_struct_net	PDSN
DELETE STRUCTURE NETWORKS FROM ARCHIVE	pdel_struct_nets_ar	PDSNAR
ELEMENT SEARCH	pelem_search	PELS
EMERGENCY CLOSE PHIGS	pemergency_close_phigs	PECLPH
EMPTY STRUCTURE	pempty_struct	PEMST
ERROR HANDLING	perr_hand	PERHND
ERROR LOGGING	perr_log	PERLOG
ESCAPE	pescape	PESC
EVALUATE VIEW MAPPING MATRIX	peval_view_map_matrix	PEVMM
EVALUATE VIEW MAPPING MATRIX 3	peval_view_map_matrix3	PEVMM3
EVALUATE VIEW ORIENTATION MATRIX	peval_view_ori_matrix	PEVOM
EVALUATE VIEW ORIENTATION MATRIX 3	peval_view_ori_matrix3	PEVOM3
EXECUTE STRUCTURE	pexec_struct	PEXST
FILL AREA	pfill_area	PFA
FILL AREA 3	pfill_area3	PFA3
FILL AREA SET	pfill_area_set	PFAS
FILL AREA SET 3	pfill_area_set3	PFAS3
FILL AREA SET WITH DATA	pfill_area_set_data	PFASD
FILL AREA SET 3 WITH DATA	pfill_area_set3_data	PFAS3D
FLUSH DEVICE EVENTS	pflush_events	PFLUSH
GENERALIZED DRAWING PRIMITIVE	pgdp	PGDP
GENERALIZED DRAWING PRIMITIVE 3	pgdp3	PGDP3
GENERALIZED STRUCTURE ELEMENT	pgse	PGSE
GET CHOICE	pget_choice	PGTCH
GET ITEM TYPE FROM METAFILE	pget_item_type	PGTITM
GET LOCATOR	pget_loc	PGTLC

PHIGS function name	ISO bindings C	FORTRAN
GET LOCATOR 3	pget_loc3	PGTLC3
GET PICK	pget_pick	PGTPK
GET STRING	pget_string	PGTST
GET STROKE	pget_stroke	PGTSK
GET STROKE 3	pget_stroke3	PGTSK3
GET VALUATOR	pget_val	PGTVL
INCREMENTAL SPATIAL SEARCH	pincr_spa_search	PISS
INCREMENTAL SPATIAL SEARCH 3	pincr_spa_search3	PISS3
INITIALIZE CHOICE	pinit_choice	PINCH
INITIALIZE CHOICE 3	pinit_choice3	PINCH3
INITIALIZE LOCATOR	pinit_loc	PINLC
INITIALIZE LOCATOR 3	pinit_loc3	PINLC3
INITIALIZE PICK	pinit_pick	PINPK
INITIALIZE PICK 3	pinit_pick3	PINPK3
INITIALIZE STRING	pinit_string	PINST
INITIALIZE STRING 3	pinit_string3	PINST3
INITIALIZE STROKE	pinit_stroke	PINSK
INITIALIZE STROKE 3	pinit_stroke3	PINSK3
INITIALIZE VALUATOR	pinit_val	PINVL
INITIALIZE VALUATOR 3	pinit_val3	PINVL3
INQUIRE ALL CONFLICTING STRUCTURES	pinq_all_conf_structs	PQCST
INQUIRE ANNOTATION FACILITIES	pinq_anno_facs	PQANF
INQUIRE ARCHIVE FILES	pinq_ar_files	PQARF
INQUIRE ARCHIVE STATE VALUE	pinq_ar_st	PQARS
INQUIRE B-SPLINE SURFACE FACILITIES	pinq_b_spline_surf_facs	PQBSSF
INQUIRE CHOICE DEVICE STATE	pinq_choice_st	PQCHS
INQUIRE CHOICE DEVICE STATE 3	pinq_choice_st3	PQCHS3
INQUIRE COLOUR FACILITIES	pinq_colr_facs	PQCF
INQUIRE COLOUR MAPPING FACILITIES	pinq_colr_map_facs	PQCMF
INQUIRE COLOUR MAPPING METHOD FACILITIES	pinq_colr_map_method_facs	PQCMMF
INQUIRE COLOUR MAPPING REPRESENTATION	pinq_colr_map_rep	PQCMR
INQUIRE COLOUR MAPPING STATE	pinq_colr_map_st	PQCMS
INQUIRE COLOUR MODEL	pinq_colr_model	PQCMD
INQUIRE COLOUR MODEL FACILITIES	pinq_colr_model_facs	PQCMDF
INQUIRE COLOUR REPRESENTATION	pinq_colr_rep	PQCR
INQUIRE CONFLICT RESOLUTION	pinq_conf_res	PQCNRS
INQUIRE CONFLICTING STRUCTURES IN NETWORK	pinq_conf_structs_net	PQCSTN
INQUIRE CURRENT ELEMENT CONTENT	pinq_cur_elem_content	PQCECO
INQUIRE CURRENT ELEMENT TYPE AND SIZE	pinq_cur_elem_type_size	PQETS
INQUIRE CURVE FACILITIES	pinq_curve_facs	PQCVF
INQUIRE DATA MAPPING FACILITIES	pinq_data_map_facs	PQDMF
INQUIRE DATA MAPPING REPRESENTATION	pinq_data_map_rep	PQDMR
INQUIRE DEFAULT CHOICE DEVICE DATA	pinq_def_choice_data	PQDCH
INQUIRE DEFAULT CHOICE DEVICE DATA 3	pinq_def_choice_data3	PQDCH3
INQUIRE DEFAULT LOCATOR DEVICE DATA	pinq_def_loc_data	PQLC
INQUIRE DEFAULT LOCATOR DEVICE DATA 3	pinq_def_loc_data3	PQLC3
INQUIRE DEFAULT PICK DEVICE DATA	pinq_def_pick_data	PQPK
INQUIRE DEFAULT PICK DEVICE DATA 3	pinq_def_pick_data3	PQPK3
INQUIRE DEFAULT STRING DEVICE DATA	pinq_def_string_data	PQST
INQUIRE DEFAULT STRING DEVICE DATA 3	pinq_def_string_data3	PQST3
INQUIRE DEFAULT STROKE DEVICE DATA	pinq_def_stroke_data	PQSK
INQUIRE DEFAULT STROKE DEVICE DATA 3	pinq_def_stroke_data3	PQSK3
INQUIRE DEFAULT VALUATOR DEVICE DATA	pinq_def_val_data	PQVL
INQUIRE DEFAULT VALUATOR DEVICE DATA 3	pinq_def_val_data3	PQVL3
INQUIRE DEPTH CUE FACILITIES	pinq_depth_cue_facs	PQDCF
INQUIRE DEPTH CUE REPRESENTATION	pinq_depth_cue_rep	PQDCR
INQUIRE DIRECT COLOUR MODEL FACILITIES	pinq_direct_colr_model_facs	PQDCMF
INQUIRE DISPLAY SPACE SIZE	pinq_disp_space_size	PQDSP

PHIGS function name	ISO bindings C	FORTRAN
INQUIRE DISPLAY SPACE SIZE 3	pinq_disp_space_size3	PQDSP3
INQUIRE DISPLAY UPDATE STATE	pinq_disp_upd_st	PQDUS
INQUIRE DYNAMICS OF STRUCTURES	pinq_dyns_structs	PQDSTR
INQUIRE DYNAMICS OF WORKSTATION ATTRIBUTES	pinq_dyns_ws_attrs	PQDSWA
INQUIRE DYNAMICS OF WORKSTATION PLUS	pinq_dyns_ws_plus	PQDCWP
INQUIRE EDGE FACILITIES	pinq_edge_facs	PQEDF
INQUIRE EDGE REPRESENTATION	pinq_edge_rep	PQEDR
INQUIRE EDGE REPRESENTATION PLUS	pinq_edge_rep_plus	PQEDP
INQUIRE EDIT MODE	pinq_edit_mode	PQEDM
INQUIRE ELEMENT CONTENT	pinq_elem_content	PQECO
INQUIRE ELEMENT POINTER	pinq_elem_ptr	PQEP
INQUIRE ELEMENT TYPE AND SIZE	pinq_elem_type_size	PQETS
INQUIRE ERROR HANDLING MODE	pinq_err_hand_mode	PQERHM
INQUIRE GENERALIZED DRAWING PRIMITIVE	pinq_gdp	PQGDP
INQUIRE GENERALIZED DRAWING PRIMITIVE 3	pinq_gdp3	PQGDP3
INQUIRE GENERALIZED STRUCTURE ELEMENT FACILITIES	pinq_gse_facs	PQGSEF
INQUIRE HIGHLIGHTING FILTER	pinq_highl_filter	PQHLFT
INQUIRE HLHSR IDENTIFIER FACILITIES	pinq_hlhsr_id_facs	PQHRIF
INQUIRE HLHSR MODE	pinq_hlhsr_mode	PQHRM
INQUIRE HLHSR MODE FACILITIES	pinq_hlhsr_mode_facs	PQHRMF
INQUIRE INPUT QUEUE OVERFLOW	pinq_in_overf	PQIQOV
INQUIRE INTERIOR FACILITIES	pinq_int_facs	PQIF
INQUIRE INTERIOR FACILITIES PLUS	pinq_int_facs_plus	PQIFP
INQUIRE INTERIOR REPRESENTATION	pinq_int_rep	PQIR
INQUIRE INTERIOR REPRESENTATION PLUS	pinq_int_rep_plus	PQIP
INQUIRE INVISIBILITY FILTER	pinq_invis_filter	PQIVFT
INQUIRE LIGHT SOURCE FACILITIES	pinq_light_source_facs	PQLSF
INQUIRE LIGHT SOURCE REPRESENTATION	pinq_light_source_rep	PQLSR
INQUIRE LIST OF AVAILABLE GDP's	pinq_list_avail_gdp	PQEGDP
INQUIRE LIST OF AVAILABLE GDP's 3	pinq_list_avail_gdp3	PQEGD3
INQUIRE LIST OF AVAILABLE GSE's	pinq_list_avail_gse	PQEGSE
INQUIRE LIST OF AVAILABLE WORKSTATION TYPES	pinq_list_avail_ws_types	PQEWK
INQUIRE LIST OF COLOUR INDICES	pinq_list_colr_inds	PQECI
INQUIRE LIST OF COLOUR MAPPING INDICES	pinq_list_colr_map_inds	PQECMI
INQUIRE LIST OF DATA MAPPING INDICES	pinq_list_data_map_inds	PQEDMI
INQUIRE LIST OF DEPTH CUE INDICES	pinq_list_depth_cue_inds	PQEDCI
INQUIRE LIST OF EDGE INDICES	pinq_list_edge_inds	PQEEDI
INQUIRE LIST OF INTERIOR INDICES	pinq_list_int_inds	PQEII
INQUIRE LIST OF LIGHT SOURCE INDICES	pinq_list_light_source_inds	PQELSI
INQUIRE LIST OF PARAMETRIC SURFACE INDICES	pinq_list_param_surf_inds	PQEPSI
INQUIRE LIST OF PATTERN INDICES	pinq_list_pat_inds	PQEPAI
INQUIRE LIST OF POLYLINE INDICES	pinq_list_line_inds	PQEPLI
INQUIRE LIST OF POLYMARKER INDICES	pinq_list_marker_inds	PQEPMI
INQUIRE LIST OF REFLECTANCE INDICES	pinq_list_refl_inds	PQERFI
INQUIRE LIST OF TEXT INDICES	pinq_list_text_inds	PQETXI
INQUIRE LIST OF VIEW INDICES	pinq_list_view_inds	PQEVWI
INQUIRE LOCATOR DEVICE STATE	pinq_loc_st	PQLCS
INQUIRE LOCATOR DEVICE STATE 3	pinq_loc_st3	PQLCS3
INQUIRE MODELLING CLIPPING FACILITIES	pinq_model_clip_facs	PQMCLF
INQUIRE MORE SIMULTANEOUS EVENTS	pinq_more_simult_events	PQSIM
INQUIRE NUMBER OF AVAILABLE LOGICAL INPUT DEVICES	pinq_num_avail_in	PQLI
INQUIRE NUMBER OF DISPLAY PRIORITIES SUPPORTED	pinq_num_disp_pris	PQDP
INQUIRE OPEN STRUCTURE	pinq_open_struct	PQOPST
INQUIRE PARAMETRIC SURFACE FACILITIES	pinq_param_surf_facs	PQPSF

	ISO bindings	
PHIGS function name	C	FORTRAN

INQUIRE PARAMETRIC SURFACE REPRESENTATION	pinq_param_surf_rep	PQPSR
INQUIRE PATHS TO ANCESTORS	pinq_paths_ances	PQPAN
INQUIRE PATHS TO DESCENDANTS	pinq_paths_descs	PQPDE
INQUIRE PATTERN FACILITIES	pinq_pat_facs	PQPAF
INQUIRE PATTERN REPRESENTATION	pinq_pat_rep	PQPAR
INQUIRE PATTERN REPRESENTATION PLUS	pinq_pat_rep_plus	PQPAP
INQUIRE PHIGS FACILITIES	pinq_phigs_facs	PQPHF
INQUIRE PICK DEVICE STATE	pinq_pick_st	PQPKS
INQUIRE PICK DEVICE STATE 3	pinq_pick_st3	PQPKS3
INQUIRE POLYLINE FACILITIES	pinq_line_facs	PQPLF
INQUIRE POLYLINE FACILITIES PLUS	pinq_line_facs_plus	PQPLFP
INQUIRE POLYLINE REPRESENTATION	pinq_line_rep	PQPLR
INQUIRE POLYLINE REPRESENTATION PLUS	pinq_line_rep_plus	PQPLP
INQUIRE POLYMARKER FACILITIES	pinq_marker_facs	PQPMF
INQUIRE POLYMARKER REPRESENTATION	pinq_marker_rep	PQPMR
INQUIRE POLYMARKER REPRESENTATION PLUS	pinq_marker_rep_plus	PQPMP
INQUIRE POSTED STRUCTURES	pinq_posted_structs	PQPOST
INQUIRE PREDEFINED COLOUR REPRESENTATION	pinq_pred_colr_rep	PQPCR
INQUIRE PREDEFINED COLOUR MAPPING REPRESENTATION	pinq_pred_colr_map_rep	PQPCMR
INQUIRE PREDEFINED DATA MAPPING REPRESENTATION	pinq_pred_data_map_rep	PQPDMR
INQUIRE PREDEFINED DEPTH CUE REPRESENTATION	pinq_pred_depth_cue_rep	PQPDCR
INQUIRE PREDEFINED EDGE REPRESENTATION	pinq_pred_edge_rep	PQPEDR
INQUIRE PREDEFINED EDGE REPRESENTATION PLUS	pinq_pred_edge_rep_plus	PQPEDP
INQUIRE PREDEFINED INTERIOR REPRESENTATION	pinq_pred_int_rep	PQPIR
INQUIRE PREDEFINED INTERIOR REPRESENTATION PLUS	pinq_pred_int_rep_plus	PQPIP
INQUIRE PREDEFINED LIGHT SOURCE REPRESENTATION	pinq_pred_light_source_rep	PQPLSR
INQUIRE PREDEFINED PARAMETRIC SURFACE REPRESENTATION	pinq_pred_param_surf_rep	PQPPSR
INQUIRE PREDEFINED PATTERN REPRESENTATION	pinq_pred_pat_rep	PQPPAR
INQUIRE PREDEFINED PATTERN REPRESENTATION PLUS	pinq_pred_pat_rep_plus	PQPPAP
INQUIRE PREDEFINED POLYLINE REPRESENTATION	pinq_pred_line_rep	PQPPLR
INQUIRE PREDEFINED POLYLINE REPRESENTATION PLUS	pinq_pred_line_rep_plus	PQPPLP
INQUIRE PREDEFINED POLYMARKER REPRESENTATION	pinq_pred_marker_rep	PQPPMR
INQUIRE PREDEFINED POLYMARKER REPRESENTATION PLUS	pinq_pred_marker_rep_plus	PQPPMP
INQUIRE PREDEFINED REFLECTANCE REPRESENTATION	pinq_pred_refl_rep	PQPRFR
INQUIRE PREDEFINED TEXT REPRESENTATION	pinq_pred_text_rep	PQPTXR
INQUIRE PREDEFINED TEXT REPRESENTATION PLUS	pinq_pred_text_rep_plus	PQPTXP
INQUIRE PREDEFINED VIEW REPRESENTATION	pinq_pred_view_rep	PQPVWR
INQUIRE REFLECTANCE FACILITIES	pinq_refl_facs	PQRFF
INQUIRE REFLECTANCE REPRESENTATION	pinq_refl_rep	PQRFR
INQUIRE RENDERING COLOUR MODEL FACILITIES	pinq_rend_colr_model_facs	PQRCMF
INQUIRE SET OF OPEN WORKSTATIONS	pinq_open_wss	PQOPWK
INQUIRE SET OF WORKSTATIONS TO WHICH	pinq_wss_posted	PQWKPO

PHIGS function name	ISO bindings	
	C	FORTRAN

POSTED		
INQUIRE STRING DEVICE STATE	pinq_string_st	PQSTS
INQUIRE STRING DEVICE STATE 3	pinq_string_st3	PQSTS3
INQUIRE STROKE DEVICE STATE	pinq_stroke_st	PQSKS
INQUIRE STROKE DEVICE STATE 3	pinq_stroke_st3	PQSKS3
INQUIRE STRUCTURE IDENTIFIERS	pinq_struct_ids	PQSID
INQUIRE STRUCTURE STATE VALUE	pinq_struct_st	PQSTRS
INQUIRE STRUCTURE STATUS	pinq_struct_status	PQSTST
INQUIRE SYSTEM STATE VALUE	pinq_sys_st	PQSYS
INQUIRE TEXT EXTENT	pinq_text_extent	PQTXX
INQUIRE TEXT FACILITIES	pinq_text_facs	PQTXF
INQUIRE TEXT REPRESENTATION	pinq_text_rep	PQTXR
INQUIRE TEXT REPRESENTATION PLUS	pinq_text_rep_plus	PQTXP
INQUIRE TRIMMING CURVE FACILITIES	pinq_trim_curve_facs	PQTCF
INQUIRE VALUATOR DEVICE STATE	pinq_val_st	PQVLS
INQUIRE VALUATOR DEVICE STATE 3	pinq_val_st3	PQVLS3
INQUIRE VIEW FACILITIES	pinq_view_facs	PQVWF
INQUIRE VIEW REPRESENTATION	pinq_view_rep	PQVWR
INQUIRE WORKSTATION CATEGORY	pinq_ws_cat	PQWKCA
INQUIRE WORKSTATION CLASSIFICATION	pinq_ws_class	PQWKCL
INQUIRE WORKSTATION CONNECTION AND TYPE	pinq_ws_conn_type	PQWKC
INQUIRE WORKSTATION STATE TABLE LENGTHS	pinq_ws_st_table	PQWKSL
INQUIRE WORKSTATION STATE TABLE LENGTHS PLUS	pinq_ws_st_table_length_plus	PQWSLP
INQUIRE WORKSTATION STATE VALUE	pinq_ws_st	PQWKST
INQUIRE WORKSTATION TRANSFORMATION	pinq_ws_tran	PQWKT
INQUIRE WORKSTATION TRANSFORMATION 3	pinq_ws_tran3	PQWKT3
INTERPRET ITEM	pinterpret_item	PIITM
LABEL	plabel	PLB
MESSAGE	pmessage	PMSG
NON-UNIFORM B-SPLINE CURVE	pnon_uniform_b_spline_curve3	PBSC
NON-UNIFORM B-SPLINE CURVE WITH COLOUR	pnon_uniform_b_spline_curve3_colr	PBSCC
NON-UNIFORM B-SPLINE SURFACE	pnon_uniform_b_spline_surf3	PBSS
NON-UNIFORM B-SPLINE SURFACE WITH DATA	pnon_uniform_b_spline_surf3_data	PBSSD
OFFSET ELEMENT POINTER	poffset_elem_ptr	POSEP
OPEN ARCHIVE FILE	popen_ar_file	POPARF
OPEN PHIGS	popen_phigs	POPPH
OPEN STRUCTURE	popen_struct	POPST
OPEN WORKSTATION	popen_ws	POPWK
PACK COLOUR SPLINE CURVE	FORTRAN only	PPCSC
PACK COLOUR SPLINE SURFACE	FORTRAN only	PPCSS
PACK DATA SPLINE SURFACE	FORTRAN only	PPDSS
PACK TRIMMING CURVE	FORTRAN only	PPTC
POLYLINE	ppolyline	PPL
POLYLINE 3	ppolyline3	PPL3
POLYLINE SET 3 WITH COLOUR	ppolyline_set3_colr	PPLS3C
POLYMARKER	polymarker	PPM
POLYMARKER 3	polymarker3	PPM3
POST STRUCTURE	ppost_struct	PPOST
QUADRILATERAL MESH WITH DATA	pquad_mesh_data	PQMD
QUADRILATERAL MESH 3 WITH DATA	pquad_mesh3_data	PQM3D
READ ITEM FROM METAFILE	pread_item	PRDITM
REDRAW ALL STRUCTURES	predraw_all_struct	PRST
REMOVE NAMES FROM SET	premove_names_set	PRES
REQUEST CHOICE	preq_choice	PRQCH
REQUEST LOCATOR	preq_loc	PRQLC
REQUEST LOCATOR 3	preq_loc3	PRQLC3

PHIGS function name	ISO bindings	
	C	FORTRAN
REQUEST PICK	preq_pick	PRQPK
REQUEST STRING	preq_string	PRQST
REQUEST STROKE	preq_stroke	PRQSK
REQUEST STROKE 3	preq_stroke3	PRQSK3
REQUEST VALUATOR	preq_val	PRQVL
RESTORE MODELLING CLIPPING VOLUME	prestore_model_clip_vol	PRMCLV
RETRIEVE ALL STRUCTURES	pret_all_structs	PRAST
RETRIEVE PATHS TO ANCESTORS	pret_paths_ances	PREPAN
RETRIEVE PATHS TO DESCENDANTS	pret_paths_descs	PREPDE
RETRIEVE STRUCTURE IDENTIFIERS	pret_struct_ids	PRSID
RETRIEVE STRUCTURE NETWORKS	pret_struct_nets	PRESN
RETRIEVE STRUCTURES	pret_structs	PREST
ROTATE	protate	PRO
ROTATE X	protate_x	PROX
ROTATE Y	protate_y	PROY
ROTATE Z	protate_z	PROZ
SAMPLE CHOICE	psample_choice	PSMCH
SAMPLE LOCATOR	psample_loc	PSMLC
SAMPLE LOCATOR 3	psample_loc3	PSMLC3
SAMPLE PICK	psample_pick	PSMPK
SAMPLE STRING	psample_string	PSMST
SAMPLE STROKE	psample_stroke	PSMSK
SAMPLE STROKE 3	psample_stroke3	PSMSK3
SAMPLE VALUATOR	psample_val	PSMVL
SCALE	pscale	PSC
SCALE 3	pscale3	PSC3
SET ANNOTATION STYLE	pset_anno_style	PSANS
SET ANNOTATION TEXT ALIGNMENT	pset_anno_align	PSATAL
SET ANNOTATION TEXT CHARACTER HEIGHT	pset_anno_char_ht	PSATCH
SET ANNOTATION TEXT CHARACTER UP VECTOR	pset_anno_char_up_vec	PSATCU
SET ANNOTATION TEXT PATH	pset_anno_path	PSATP
SET BACK DATA MAPPING INDEX	pset_back_data_map_ind	PSBDMI
SET BACK DATA MAPPING METHOD	pset_back_data_map_method	PSBDMM
SET BACK INTERIOR COLOUR	pset_back_int_colr	PSBIC
SET BACK INTERIOR INDEX	pset_back_int_ind	PSBII
SET BACK INTERIOR SHADING METHOD	pset_back_int_shad_method	PSBISM
SET BACK INTERIOR STYLE	pset_back_int_style	PSBIS
SET BACK INTERIOR STYLE INDEX	pset_back_int_style_ind	PSBISI
SET BACK REFLECTANCE INDEX	pset_back_refl_ind	PSBRFI
SET BACK REFLECTANCE MODEL	pset_back_refl_model	PSBRFM
SET BACK REFLECTANCE PROPERTIES	pset_back_refl_props	PSBRFP
SET CHARACTER EXPANSION FACTOR	pset_char_expan	PSCHXP
SET CHARACTER HEIGHT	pset_char_ht	PSCHH
SET CHARACTER SPACING	pset_char_space	PSCHSP
SET CHARACTER UP VECTOR	pset_char_up_vec	PSCHUP
SET CHOICE MODE	pset_choice_mode	PSCHM
SET COLOUR MAPPING INDEX	pset_colr_map_ind	PSCMI
SET COLOUR MAPPING REPRESENTATION	pset_colr_map_rep	PSCMR
SET COLOUR MODEL	pset_colr_model	PSCMD
SET COLOUR REPRESENTATION	pset_colr_rep	PSCR
SET CONFLICT RESOLUTION	pset_conf_res	PSCNRS
SET CURVE APPROXIMATION CRITERIA	pset_curve_approx_crit	PSCAC
SET DATA MAPPING INDEX	pset_data_map_ind	PSDMI
SET DATA MAPPING METHOD	pset_data_map_method	PSDMM
SET DATA MAPPING REPRESENTATION	pset_data_map_rep	PSDMR
SET DEPTH CUE INDEX	pset_depth_cue_ind	PSDCI
SET DEPTH CUE REPRESENTATION	pset_depth_cue_rep	PSDCR
SET DISPLAY UPDATE STATE	pset_disp_upd_st	PSDUS
SET EDGE COLOUR	pset_edge_colr	PSEDC

PHIGS function name	ISO bindings C	FORTRAN
SET EDGE COLOUR INDEX	pset_edge_colr_ind	PSEDCI
SET EDGE FLAG	pset_edge_flag	PSEDFG
SET EDGE INDEX	pset_edge_ind	PSEDI
SET EDGE REPRESENTATION	pset_edge_rep	PSEDR
SET EDGE REPRESENTATION PLUS	pset_edge_rep_plus	PSEDP
SET EDGE TYPE	pset_edgetype	PSEDT
SET EDGEWIDTH SCALE FACTOR	pset_edgewidth	PSEWSC
SET EDIT MODE	pset_edit_mode	PSEDM
SET ELEMENT POINTER	pset_elem_ptr	PSEP
SET ELEMENT POINTER AT LABEL	pset_elem_ptr_label	PSEPLB
SET ERROR HANDLING	pset_err_hand	PSERH
SET ERROR HANDLING MODE	pset_err_hand_mode	PSERHM
SET FACET CULLING MODE	pset_facet_cull_mode	PSFCM
SET FACET DISTINGUISHING MODE	pset_facet_disting_mode	PSFDM
SET GLOBAL TRANSFORMATION	pset_global_tran	PSGMT
SET GLOBAL TRANSFORMATION 3	pset_global_tran3	PSGMT3
SET HIGHLIGHT FILTER	pset_highl_filter	PSHLFT
SET HLHSR IDENTIFIER	pset_hlhsr_id	PSHRID
SET HLHSR MODE	pset_hlhsr_mode	PSHRM
SET INDIVIDUAL ASF	pset_indiv_asf	PSIASF
SET INTERIOR COLOUR	pset_int_colr	PSIC
SET INTERIOR COLOUR INDEX	pset_int_colr_ind	PSICI
SET INTERIOR INDEX	pset_int_ind	PSII
SET INTERIOR REPRESENTATION	pset_int_rep	PSIR
SET INTERIOR REPRESENTATION PLUS	pset_int_rep_plus	PSIP
SET INTERIOR SHADING METHOD	pset_int_shad_method	PSISM
SET INTERIOR STYLE	pset_int_style	PSIS
SET INTERIOR STYLE INDEX	pset_int_style_ind	PSISI
SET INVISIBILITY FILTER	pset_invis_filter	PSIVFT
SET LIGHT SOURCE REPRESENTATION	pset_light_source_rep	PSLSR
SET LIGHT SOURCE STATE	pset_light_source_st	PSLSS
SET LINETYPE	pset_linetype	PSLN
SET LINEWIDTH SCALE FACTOR	pset_linewidth	PSLWSC
SET LOCAL TRANSFORMATION	pset_local_tran	PSLMT
SET LOCAL TRANSFORMATION 3	pset_local_tran3	PSLMT3
SET LOCATOR MODE	pset_loc_mode	PSLCM
SET MARKER SIZE SCALE FACTOR	pset_marker_size	PSMKSC
SET MARKER TYPE	pset_marker_type	PSMK
SET MODELLING CLIPPING INDICATOR	pset_model_clip_ind	PSMCLI
SET MODELLING CLIPPING VOLUME	pset_model_clip_vol	PSMCV
SET MODELLING CLIPPING VOLUME 3	pset_model_clip_vol3	PSMCV3
SET OF FILL AREA SET WITH DATA	pset_of_fill_area_sets_data	PSFASD
SET OF FILL AREA SET 3 WITH DATA	pset_of_fill_area_sets3_data	PSFAS3
SET PARAMETRIC SURFACE CHARACTERISTICS	pset_param_surf_chars	PSPSC
SET PARAMETRIC SURFACE INDEX	pset_param_surf_ind	PSPSI
SET PARAMETRIC SURFACE REPRESENTATION	pset_param_surf_rep	PSPSR
SET PATTERN REFERENCE POINT	pset_pat_ref_point	PSPARF
SET PATTERN REFERENCE POINT AND VECTORS	pset_pat_ref_point_vecs	PSPRPV
SET PATTERN REPRESENTATION	pset_pat_rep	PSPAR
SET PATTERN REPRESENTATION PLUS	pset_pat_rep_plus	PSPAP
SET PATTERN SIZE	pset_pat_size	PSPA
SET PICK FILTER	pset_pick_filter	PSPKFT
SET PICK IDENTIFIER	pset_pick_id	PSPKID
SET PICK MODE	pset_pick_mode	PSPKM
SET POLYLINE COLOUR	pset_line_colr	PSPLC
SET POLYLINE COLOUR INDEX	pset_line_colr_ind	PSPLCI
SET POLYLINE INDEX	pset_line_ind	PSLI
SET POLYLINE REPRESENTATION	pset_line_rep	PSLR
SET POLYLINE REPRESENTATION PLUS	pset_line_rep_plus	PSPLP

PHIGS function name	ISO bindings C	FORTRAN
SET POLYLINE SHADING METHOD	pset_line_shad_method	PSPLSM
SET POLYMARKER COLOUR	pset_marker_colr	PSPMC
SET POLYMARKER COLOUR INDEX	pset_marker_colr_ind	PSPMCI
SET POLYMARKER INDEX	pset_marker_ind	PSPMI
SET POLYMARKER REPRESENTATION	pset_marker_rep	PSPMR
SET POLYMARKER REPRESENTATION PLUS	pset_marker_rep_plus	PSPMP
SET REFLECTANCE INDEX	pset_refl_ind	PSRFI
SET REFLECTANCE MODEL	pset_refl_model	PSRFM
SET REFLECTANCE PROPERTIES	pset_refl_props	PSRFP
SET REFLECTANCE REPRESENTATION	pset_refl_rep	PSRFR
SET RENDERING COLOUR MODEL	pset_rend_colr_model	PSRCM
SET STRING MODE	pset_string_mode	PSSTM
SET STROKE MODE	pset_stroke_mode	PSSKM
SET SURFACE APPROXIMATION CRITERIA	pset_surf_approx_crit	PSSAC
SET TEXT ALIGNMENT	pset_text_align	PSTXAL
SET TEXT COLOUR	pset_text_colr	PSTXC
SET TEXT COLOUR INDEX	pset_text_colr_ind	PSTXCI
SET TEXT FONT	pset_text_font	PSTXFN
SET TEXT INDEX	pset_text_ind	PSTXI
SET TEXT PATH	pset_text_path	PSTXP
SET TEXT PRECISION	pset_text_prec	PSTXPR
SET TEXT REPRESENTATION	pset_text_rep	PSTXR
SET TEXT REPRESENTATION PLUS	pset_text_rep_plus	PSTXP
SET VALUATOR MODE	pset_val_mode	PSVLM
SET VIEW INDEX	pset_view_ind	PSVWI
SET VIEW REPRESENTATION	pset_view_rep	PSVWR
SET VIEW REPRESENTATION 3	pset_view_rep3	PSVWR3
SET VIEW TRANSFORMATION INPUT PRIORITY	pset_view_tran_in_pri	PSVTIP
SET WORKSTATION VIEWPORT	pset_ws_vp	PSWKV
SET WORKSTATION VIEWPORT 3	pset_ws_vp3	PSWKV3
SET WORKSTATION WINDOW	pset_ws_win	PSWKW
SET WORKSTATION WINDOW 3	pset_ws_win3	PSWKW3
TEXT	ptext	PTX
TEXT 3	ptext3	PTX3
TRANSFORM POINT	ptran_point	PTP
TRANSFORM POINT 3	ptran_point3	PTP3
TRANSLATE	ptranslate	PTR
TRANSLATE 3	ptranslate3	PTR3
TRIANGLE SET WITH DATA	ptri_set_data	PTSD
TRIANGLE SET 3 WITH DATA	ptri_set_data	PTS3D
TRIANGLE STRIP WITH DATA	ptri_strip_data	PTSTD
TRIANGLE STRIP 3 WITH DATA	ptri_strip3_data	PTST3D
UNPACK COLOUR SPLINE CURVE	FORTRAN only	PUCSC
UNPACK COLOUR SPLINE SURFACE	FORTRAN only	PUCSS
UNPACK DATA SPLINE SURFACE	FORTRAN only	PUDSS
UNPACK TRIMMING CURVE	FORTRAN only	PUTC
UNPOST ALL STRUCTURES	punpost_all_structs	PUPAST
UNPOST STRUCTURE	punpost_struct	PUPOST
UPDATE WORKSTATION	pupd_ws	PUWK
WRITE ITEM TO METAFILE	pwrite_item	PWITM

Appendix D

PHIGS and PHIGS PLUS Function List

The following is a complete list of all PHIGS and PHIGS PLUS functions grouped according to the type of functionality provided. All PHIGS PLUS functions are identified with a (+) following the function name.

Control functions:
    CLOSE PHIGS
    CLOSE WORKSTATION
    ESCAPE
    MESSAGE
    OPEN PHIGS
    OPEN WORKSTATION
    REDRAW ALL STRUCTURES
    SET DISPLAY UPDATE STATE
    UPDATE WORKSTATION

Output primitive functions:
    ANNOTATION TEXT RELATIVE
    ANNOTATION TEXT RELATIVE 3
    CELL ARRAY
    CELL ARRAY 3
    CELL ARRAY 3 PLUS (+)
    FILL AREA
    FILL AREA 3
    FILL AREA SET
    FILL AREA SET 3
    FILL AREA SET WITH DATA (+)
    FILL AREA SET 3 WITH DATA (+)
    GENERALIZED DRAWING PRIMITIVE
    GENERALIZED DRAWING PRIMITIVE 3
    NON-UNIFORM B-SPLINE CURVE (+)

NON-UNIFORM B-SPLINE CURVE WITH COLOUR (+)
NON-UNIFORM B-SPLINE SURFACE (+)
NON-UNIFORM B-SPLINE SURFACE WITH DATA (+)
POLYLINE
POLYLINE 3
POLYLINE SET 3 WITH DATA (+)
POLYMARKER
POLYMARKER 3
QUADRILATERAL MESH WITH DATA (+)
QUADRILATERAL MESH 3 WITH DATA (+)
SET OF FILL AREA SET WITH DATA (+)
SET OF FILL AREA SET 3 WITH DATA (+)
TEXT
TEXT 3
TRIANGLE SET WITH DATA (+)
TRIANGLE SET 3 WITH DATA (+)
TRIANGLE STRIP WITH DATA (+)
TRIANGLE STRIP 3 WITH DATA (+)

Bundled attribute selection:
SET BACK DATA MAPPING INDEX (+)
SET BACK INTERIOR INDEX (+)
SET BACK REFLECTANCE INDEX (+)
SET DATA MAPPING INDEX (+)
SET EDGE INDEX
SET INTERIOR INDEX
SET PARAMETRIC SURFACE INDEX (+)
SET POLYLINE INDEX
SET POLYMARKER INDEX
SET REFLECTANCE INDEX (+)
SET TEXT INDEX

Individual attribute selection:
ADD NAMES TO SET
REMOVE NAMES FROM SET
SET ANNOTATION STYLE
SET ANNOTATION TEXT ALIGNMENT
SET ANNOTATION TEXT CHARACTER HEIGHT
SET ANNOTATION TEXT CHARACTER UP VECTOR
SET ANNOTATION TEXT PATH
SET BACK DATA MAPPING METHOD (+)
SET BACK INTERIOR COLOUR (+)
SET BACK INTERIOR SHADING METHOD (+)
SET BACK INTERIOR STYLE (+)
SET BACK INTERIOR STYLE INDEX (+)
SET BACK REFLECTANCE MODEL (+)
SET BACK REFLECTANCE PROPERTIES (+)
SET CHARACTER EXPANSION FACTOR
SET CHARACTER HEIGHT
SET CHARACTER SPACING
SET CHARACTER UP VECTOR
SET COLOUR MAPPING INDEX (+)
SET CURVE APPROXIMATION CRITERIA (+)
SET DATA MAPPING METHOD (+)
SET DEPTH CUE INDEX (+)

SET EDGE COLOUR (+)
SET EDGE COLOUR INDEX
SET EDGE FLAG
SET EDGE TYPE
SET EDGEWIDTH SCALE FACTOR
SET FACE CULLING MODE (+)
SET FACE DISTINGUISH MODE (+)
SET HIGHLIGHT FILTER
SET INDIVIDUAL ASF
SET INTERIOR COLOUR (+)
SET INTERIOR COLOUR INDEX
SET INTERIOR SHADING METHOD (+)
SET INTERIOR STYLE
SET INTERIOR STYLE INDEX
SET INVISIBILITY FILTER
SET LIGHT SOURCE STATE (+)
SET LINETYPE
SET LINEWIDTH SCALE FACTOR
SET MARKER TYPE
SET MARKER SIZE SCALE FACTOR
SET PARAMETRIC SURFACE CHARACTERISTICS (+)
SET PATTERN SIZE
SET PATTERN REFERENCE POINT
SET PATTERN REFERENCE POINT AND VECTORS
SET POLYLINE COLOUR (+)
SET POLYLINE COLOUR INDEX
SET POLYLINE SHADING METHOD (+)
SET POLYMARKER COLOUR (+)
SET POLYMARKER COLOUR INDEX
SET REFLECTANCE MODEL (+)
SET REFLECTANCE PROPERTIES (+)
SET RENDERING COLOUR MODEL (+)
SET SURFACE APPROXIMATION CRITERIA (+)
SET TEXT ALIGNMENT
SET TEXT FONT
SET TEXT PATH
SET TEXT PRECISION
SET TEXT COLOUR (+)
SET TEXT COLOUR INDEX

Workstation attribute table specification:
SET COLOUR MAPPING REPRESENTATION (+)
SET COLOUR REPRESENTATION
SET DATA MAPPING REPRESENTATION (+)
SET DEPTH CUE REPRESENTATION (+)
SET EDGE REPRESENTATION
SET EDGE REPRESENTATION PLUS (+)
SET INTERIOR REPRESENTATION
SET INTERIOR REPRESENTATION PLUS (+)
SET LIGHT SOURCE REPRESENTATION (+)
SET PARAMETRIC SURFACE REPRESENTATION (+)
SET PATTERN REPRESENTATION
SET PATTERN REPRESENTATION PLUS (+)
SET POLYLINE REPRESENTATION
SET POLYLINE REPRESENTATION PLUS (+)

SET POLYMARKER REPRESENTATION
SET POLYMARKER REPRESENTATION PLUS (+)
SET REFLECTANCE REPRESENTATION (+)
SET TEXT REPRESENTATION
SET TEXT REPRESENTATION PLUS (+)

Colour model control:
SET COLOUR MODEL

Hidden line hidden surface
SET HLHSR IDENTIFIER
SET HLHSR MODE

Metafile functions:
GET ITEM TYPE FROM METAFILE
INTERPRET ITEM
GET ITEM TYPE FROM METAFILE
READ ITEM FROM METAFILE
WRITE ITEM TO METAFILE

Modelling transformations and clipping:
SET GLOBAL TRANSFORMATION
SET GLOBAL TRANSFORMATION 3
SET LOCAL TRANSFORMATION
SET LOCAL TRANSFORMATION 3
SET MODELLING CLIPPING INDICATOR
SET MODELLING CLIPPING VOLUME
SET MODELLING CLIPPING VOLUME 3
RESTORE MODELLING CLIPPING VOLUME

Viewing operations:
SET VIEW INDEX
SET VIEW REPRESENTATION
SET VIEW REPRESENTATION 3
SET VIEW TRANSFORMATION INPUT PRIORITY
SET WORKSTATION VIEWPORT
SET WORKSTATION VIEWPORT 3
SET WORKSTATION WINDOW
SET WORKSTATION WINDOW 3

Transformation utility functions:
BUILD TRANSFORMATION MATRIX
BUILD TRANSFORMATION MATRIX 3
COMPOSE MATRIX
COMPOSE MATRIX 3
COMPOSE TRANSFORMATION MATRIX
COMPOSE TRANSFORMATION MATRIX 3
EVALUATE VIEW MAPPING MATRIX
EVALUATE VIEW MAPPING MATRIX 3
EVALUATE VIEW ORIENTATION MATRIX
EVALUATE VIEW ORIENTATION MATRIX 3
ROTATE
ROTATE X
ROTATE Y

ROTATE Z
SCALE
SCALE 3
TRANSFORM POINT
TRANSFORM POINT 3
TRANSLATE
TRANSLATE 3

Output primitive utility function:
COMPUTE FILL AREA SET GEOMETRIC NORMAL (+)

Structure content and editing functions:
APPLICATION DATA
CLOSE STRUCTURE
COPY ALL ELEMENTS FROM STRUCTURE
DELETE ELEMENT
DELETE ELEMENTS BETWEEN LABELS
DELETE ELEMENT RANGE
EMPTY STRUCTURE
GENERALIZED STRUCTURE ELEMENT
LABEL
OFFSET ELEMENT POINTER
OPEN STRUCTURE
EXECUTE STRUCTURE
SET EDIT MODE
SET ELEMENT POINTER
SET ELEMENT POINTER AT LABEL

Structure manipulation functions:
CHANGE STRUCTURE IDENTIFIER
CHANGE STRUCTURE IDENTIFIER AND REFERENCES
CHANGE STRUCTURE REFERENCES
DELETE ALL STRUCTURES
DELETE STRUCTURE
DELETE STRUCTURE NETWORK

Structure display functions:
POST STRUCTURE
UNPOST ALL STRUCTURES
UNPOST STRUCTURE

Structure search and inquiry functions:
ELEMENT SEARCH
INCREMENTAL SPATIAL SEARCH
INCREMENTAL SPATIAL SEARCH 3
INQUIRE CURRENT ELEMENT CONTENT
INQUIRE CURRENT ELEMENT TYPE AND SIZE
INQUIRE ELEMENT CONTENT
INQUIRE ELEMENT POINTER
INQUIRE ELEMENT TYPE AND SIZE
INQUIRE OPEN STRUCTURE
INQUIRE PATHS TO ANCESTORS
INQUIRE PATHS TO DESCENDANTS
INQUIRE SET OF WORKSTATIONS TO WHICH POSTED
INQUIRE STRUCTURE STATUS

Archiving functions:
    ARCHIVE ALL STRUCTURES
    ARCHIVE STRUCTURE NETWORK
    ARCHIVE STRUCTURES
    CLOSE ARCHIVE FILE
    DELETE ALL STRUCTURES FROM ARCHIVE
    DELETE STRUCTURES FROM ARCHIVE
    DELETE STRUCTURE NETWORKS FROM ARCHIVE
    OPEN ARCHIVE FILE
    RETRIEVE ALL STRUCTURES
    RETRIEVE PATHS TO ANCESTORS
    RETRIEVE PATHS TO DESCENDANTS
    RETRIEVE STRUCTURE IDENTIFIERS
    RETRIEVE STRUCTURE NETWORKS
    RETRIEVE STRUCTURES
    SET CONFLICT RESOLUTION

Input device functions:
    AWAIT EVENT
    FLUSH DEVICE EVENTS
    GET CHOICE
    GET LOCATOR
    GET LOCATOR 3
    GET PICK
    GET STRING
    GET STROKE
    GET STROKE 3
    GET VALUATOR
    INITIALIZE CHOICE
    INITIALIZE CHOICE 3
    INITIALIZE LOCATOR
    INITIALIZE LOCATOR 3
    INITIALIZE PICK
    INITIALIZE PICK 3
    INITIALIZE STRING
    INITIALIZE STRING 3
    INITIALIZE STROKE
    INITIALIZE STROKE 3
    INITIALIZE VALUATOR
    INITIALIZE VALUATOR 3
    REQUEST CHOICE
    REQUEST LOCATOR
    REQUEST LOCATOR 3
    REQUEST PICK
    REQUEST STRING
    REQUEST STROKE
    REQUEST STROKE 3
    REQUEST VALUATOR
    SAMPLE CHOICE
    SAMPLE LOCATOR
    SAMPLE LOCATOR 3
    SAMPLE PICK
    SAMPLE STRING
    SAMPLE STROKE
    SAMPLE STROKE 3

SAMPLE VALUATOR
SET CHOICE MODE
SET LOCATOR MODE
SET PICK FILTER
SET PICK IDENTIFIER
SET PICK MODE
SET STRING MODE
SET STROKE MODE
SET VALUATOR MODE

Error handling functions:
EMERGENCY CLOSE PHIGS
ERROR HANDLING
ERROR LOGGING
SET ERROR HANDLING
SET ERROR HANDLING MODE

Error state list inquiry functions:
INQUIRE INPUT QUEUE OVERFLOW
INQUIRE ERROR HANDLING MODE

Operating state inquiry functions:
INQUIRE ARCHIVE STATE VALUE
INQUIRE STRUCTURE STATE VALUE
INQUIRE SYSTEM STATE VALUE
INQUIRE WORKSTATION STATE VALUE

PHIGS description table inquiry functions:
INQUIRE GENERALIZED STRUCTURE ELEMENT FACILITIES INQUIRE
LIST OF AVAILABLE WORKSTATION TYPES
INQUIRE MODELLING CLIPPING FACILITIES
INQUIRE PHIGS FACILITIES

PHIGS state list inquiry functions:
INQUIRE ARCHIVE FILES
INQUIRE ALL CONFLICTING STRUCTURES
INQUIRE CONFLICT RESOLUTION
INQUIRE CONFLICTING STRUCTURES IN NETWORK
INQUIRE EDIT MODE
INQUIRE SET OF OPEN WORKSTATIONS
INQUIRE STRUCTURE IDENTIFIERS
INQUIRE MORE SIMULTANEOUS EVENTS

Workstation description table inquiries:
INQUIRE ANNOTATION FACILITIES
INQUIRE COLOUR FACILITIES
INQUIRE COLOUR MAPPING FACILITIES (+)
INQUIRE COLOUR MAPPING METHOD FACILITIES (+)
INQUIRE COLOUR MODEL FACILITIES
INQUIRE CURVE AND SURFACE FACILITIES (+)
INQUIRE DATA MAPPING FACILITIES (+)
INQUIRE DEFAULT CHOICE DEVICE DATA
INQUIRE DEFAULT CHOICE DEVICE DATA 3
INQUIRE DEFAULT LOCATOR DEVICE DATA

INQUIRE DEFAULT LOCATOR DEVICE DATA 3
INQUIRE DEFAULT PICK DEVICE DATA
INQUIRE DEFAULT PICK DEVICE DATA 3
INQUIRE DEFAULT STRING DEVICE DATA
INQUIRE DEFAULT STRING DEVICE DATA 3
INQUIRE DEFAULT STROKE DEVICE DATA
INQUIRE DEFAULT STROKE DEVICE DATA 3
INQUIRE DEFAULT VALUATOR DEVICE DATA
INQUIRE DEFAULT VALUATOR DEVICE DATA 3
INQUIRE DEPTH CUE FACILITIES (+)
INQUIRE DIRECT COLOUR MODEL FACILITIES (+)
INQUIRE DISPLAY SPACE SIZE
INQUIRE DISPLAY SPACE SIZE 3
INQUIRE DYNAMICS OF STRUCTURES
INQUIRE DYNAMICS OF WORKSTATION ATTRIBUTES
INQUIRE DYNAMICS OF WORKSTATION PLUS (+)
INQUIRE EDGE FACILITIES
INQUIRE GENERALIZED DRAWING PRIMITIVE
INQUIRE GENERALIZED DRAWING PRIMITIVE 3
INQUIRE HLHSR IDENTIFIER FACILITIES
INQUIRE HLHSR MODE FACILITIES
INQUIRE INTERIOR FACILITIES
INQUIRE INTERIOR FACILITIES PLUS (+)
INQUIRE LIGHT SOURCE FACILITIES (+)
INQUIRE LIST OF AVAILABLE GDP's
INQUIRE LIST OF AVAILABLE GDP's 3
INQUIRE LIST OF AVAILABLE GSE's
INQUIRE NUMBER OF AVAILABLE LOGICAL INPUT DEVICES
INQUIRE NUMBER OF DISPLAY PRIORITIES SUPPORTED
INQUIRE PATTERN FACILITIES
INQUIRE POLYLINE FACILITIES
INQUIRE POLYLINE FACILITIES PLUS (+)
INQUIRE POLYMARKER FACILITIES
INQUIRE PREDEFINED COLOUR MAPPING REPRESENTATION (+)
INQUIRE PREDEFINED COLOUR REPRESENTATION
INQUIRE PREDEFINED DATA MAPPING REPRESENTATION (+)
INQUIRE PREDEFINED DEPTH CUE REPRESENTATION (+)
INQUIRE PREDEFINED EDGE REPRESENTATION
INQUIRE PREDEFINED EDGE REPRESENTATION PLUS (+)
INQUIRE PREDEFINED INTERIOR REPRESENTATION
INQUIRE PREDEFINED INTERIOR REPRESENTATION PLUS (+)
INQUIRE PREDEFINED LIGHT SOURCE REPRESENTATION (+)
INQUIRE PREDEFINED PARAMETRIC SURFACE REPRESENTATION (+)
INQUIRE PREDEFINED PATTERN REPRESENTATION
INQUIRE PREDEFINED PATTERN REPRESENTATION PLUS (+)
INQUIRE PREDEFINED POLYLINE REPRESENTATION
INQUIRE PREDEFINED POLYLINE REPRESENTATION PLUS (+)
INQUIRE PREDEFINED POLYMARKER REPRESENTATION
INQUIRE PREDEFINED POLYMARKER REPRESENTATION PLUS (+)
INQUIRE PREDEFINED REFLECTANCE REPRESENTATION (+)
INQUIRE PREDEFINED TEXT REPRESENTATION
INQUIRE PREDEFINED TEXT REPRESENTATION PLUS (+)
INQUIRE PREDEFINED VIEW REPRESENTATION
INQUIRE REFLECTANCE FACILITIES (+)
INQUIRE RENDERING COLOUR MODEL FACILITIES (+)
INQUIRE TEXT EXTENT

INQUIRE TEXT FACILITIES
INQUIRE VIEW FACILITIES
INQUIRE WORKSTATION CATEGORY
INQUIRE WORKSTATION CLASSIFICATION
INQUIRE WORKSTATION STATE TABLE LENGTHS
INQUIRE WORKSTATION STATE TABLE LENGTHS PLUS (+)

Workstation state list inquiries:
INQUIRE CHOICE DEVICE STATE
INQUIRE CHOICE DEVICE STATE 3
INQUIRE COLOUR MODEL
INQUIRE COLOUR MAPPING REPRESENTATION (+)
INQUIRE COLOUR MAPPING STATE (+)
INQUIRE COLOUR REPRESENTATION
INQUIRE DATA MAPPING REPRESENTATION (+)
INQUIRE DEPTH CUE REPRESENTATION (+)
INQUIRE DISPLAY UPDATE STATE
INQUIRE EDGE REPRESENTATION
INQUIRE EDGE REPRESENTATION PLUS (+)
INQUIRE HIGHLIGHTING FILTER
INQUIRE HLHSR MODE
INQUIRE INTERIOR REPRESENTATION
INQUIRE INTERIOR REPRESENTATION PLUS (+)
INQUIRE INVISIBILITY FILTER
INQUIRE LIGHT SOURCE REPRESENTATION (+)
INQUIRE LIST OF COLOUR INDICES
INQUIRE LIST OF COLOUR MAPPING INDICES (+)
INQUIRE LIST OF DATA MAPPING INDICES (+)
INQUIRE LIST OF DEPTH CUE INDICES (+)
INQUIRE LIST OF EDGE INDICES
INQUIRE LIST OF INTERIOR INDICES
INQUIRE LIST OF LIGHT SOURCE INDICES (+)
INQUIRE LIST OF PARAMETRIC SURFACE INDICES (+)
INQUIRE LIST OF PATTERN INDICES
INQUIRE LIST OF POLYLINE INDICES
INQUIRE LIST OF POLYMARKER INDICES
INQUIRE LIST OF REFLECTANCE INDICES (+)
INQUIRE LIST OF TEXT INDICES
INQUIRE LIST OF VIEW INDICES
INQUIRE LOCATOR DEVICE STATE
INQUIRE LOCATOR DEVICE STATE 3
INQUIRE PARAMETRIC SURFACE REPRESENTATION (+)
INQUIRE PATTERN REPRESENTATION
INQUIRE PATTERN REPRESENTATION PLUS (+)
INQUIRE PICK DEVICE STATE
INQUIRE PICK DEVICE STATE 3
INQUIRE POLYLINE REPRESENTATION
INQUIRE POLYLINE REPRESENTATION PLUS (+)
INQUIRE POLYMARKER REPRESENTATION
INQUIRE POLYMARKER REPRESENTATION PLUS (+)
INQUIRE POSTED STRUCTURES

INQUIRE REFLECTANCE REPRESENTATION (+)
INQUIRE STRING DEVICE STATE
INQUIRE STRING DEVICE STATE 3
INQUIRE STROKE DEVICE STATE
INQUIRE STROKE DEVICE STATE 3
INQUIRE TEXT REPRESENTATION
INQUIRE TEXT REPRESENTATION PLUS (+)
INQUIRE VALUATOR DEVICE STATE
INQUIRE VALUATOR DEVICE STATE 3
INQUIRE VIEW REPRESENTATION
INQUIRE WORKSTATION CONNECTION AND TYPE
INQUIRE WORKSTATION TRANSFORMATION
INQUIRE WORKSTATION TRANSFORMATION 3

Appendix E

List of PHIGS Attributes

This appendix contains a comprehensive list of all PHIGS and PHIGS PLUS primitives and the attributes that control their appearance. One can use this list to look up answers to questions such as: 1. Is the primitive cell array subject to being illuminated by light sources? or 2. Can one use the edge flag to display edges with fill area? The answer to the first question is 'yes', since the attribute LIGHT SOURCE STATE applies to CELL ARRAY; the second question's answer is 'no' since the attribute EDGE FLAG does not apply to FILL AREA.

The primitives are presented alphabetically followed by a list of their correponding attributes. All PHIGS PLUS primitives and attributes are identified by a (+).

Annotation text relative:
        ANNOTATION TEXT ALIGNMENT
        ANNOTATION TEXT CHARACTER HEIGHT
        ANNOTATION TEXT CHARACTER UP VECTOR
        ANNOTATION TEXT PATH
        ANNOTATION STYLE
        CHARACTER EXPANSION FACTOR
        CHARACTER EXPANSION FACTOR ASF
        CHARACTER SPACING
        CHARACTER SPACING ASF
        COLOUR MAPPING INDEX (+)
        DEPTH CUE INDEX (+)
        HLHSR IDENTIFIER

NAME SET
PICK IDENTIFIER
TEXT COLOUR (+)
TEXT COLOUR ASF (+)
TEXT COLOUR INDEX
TEXT COLOUR INDEX ASF
TEXT FONT
TEXT FONT ASF
TEXT INDEX
TEXT PRECISION
TEXT PRECISION ASF
VIEW INDEX

Cell array:
BACK REFLECTANCE INDEX (+)
BACK REFLECTANCE MODEL (+)
BACK REFLECTANCE MODEL ASF (+)
BACK REFLECTANCE PROPERTIES (+)
BACK REFLECTANCE PROPERTIES ASF (+)
COLOUR MAPPING INDEX (+)
DEPTH CUE INDEX (+)
FACE CULLING MODE (+)
FACE DISTINGUISH MODE (+)
HLHSR IDENTIFIER
LIGHT SOURCE STATE (+)
NAME SET
PICK IDENTIFIER
REFLECTANCE INDEX (+)
REFLECTANCE MODEL (+)
REFLECTANCE MODEL ASF (+)
REFLECTANCE PROPERTIES (+)
REFLECTANCE PROPERTIES ASF (+)
RENDERING COLOUR MODEL (+)
VIEW INDEX

Cell array plus (+):
All attributes specified for cell array.

Fill area:
BACK INTERIOR COLOUR (+)
BACK INTERIOR COLOUR ASF (+)
BACK INTERIOR INDEX (+)
BACK INTERIOR SHADING METHOD (+)
BACK INTERIOR SHADING METHOD ASF (+)
BACK INTERIOR STYLE (+)
BACK INTERIOR STYLE ASF (+)

BACK INTERIOR STYLE INDEX (+)
BACK INTERIOR STYLE INDEX ASF (+)
BACK REFLECTANCE INDEX (+)
BACK REFLECTANCE MODEL (+)
BACK REFLECTANCE MODEL ASF (+)
BACK REFLECTANCE PROPERTIES (+)
BACK REFLECTANCE PROPERTIES ASF (+)
COLOUR MAPPING INDEX (+)
DEPTH CUE INDEX (+)
FACE CULLING MODE (+)
FACE DISTINGUISH MODE (+)
HLHSR IDENTIFIER
INTERIOR COLOUR (+)
INTERIOR COLOUR ASF (+)
INTERIOR COLOUR INDEX
INTERIOR COLOUR INDEX ASF
INTERIOR INDEX
INTERIOR SHADING METHOD (+)
INTERIOR SHADING METHOD ASF (+)
INTERIOR STYLE
INTERIOR STYLE ASF
INTERIOR STYLE INDEX
INTERIOR STYLE INDEX ASF
LIGHT SOURCE STATE (+)
NAME SET
PATTERN SIZE
PATTERN REFERENCE POINT
PATTERN REFERENCE VECTORS
PICK IDENTIFIER
REFLECTANCE INDEX (+)
REFLECTANCE MODEL (+)
REFLECTANCE MODEL ASF (+)
REFLECTANCE PROPERTIES (+)
REFLECTANCE PROPERTIES ASF (+)
RENDERING COLOUR MODEL(+)
VIEW INDEX

Fill area set:
All attributes specified for fill area plus:
EDGE COLOUR (+)
EDGE COLOUR ASF (+)
EDGE COLOUR INDEX
EDGE COLOUR INDEX ASF
EDGE FLAG
EDGE FLAG ASF
EDGE INDEX

EDGETYPE
EDGETYPE ASF
EDGEWIDTH SCALE FACTOR
EDGEWIDTH SCALE FACTOR ASF

Fill area set with data (+)*:*
All attributes specified for fill area set plus:
DATA MAPPING INDEX (+)
BACK DATA MAPPING INDEX (+)
DATA MAPPING METHOD (+)
DATA MAPPING METHOD ASF (+)

Non-uniform B-spline curve (+)*:*
All attributes specified for polyline plus:
CURVE APPROXIMATION CRITERIA (+)
CURVE APPROXIMATION CRITERIA ASF (+)

Non-uniform B-spline curve with colour (+)*:*
All attributes specified for non-uniform B-spline curve plus:
POLYLINE SHADING METHOD (+)
POLYLINE SHADING METHOD ASF (+)
RENDERING COLOUR MODEL (+)

Non-uniform B-spline surface (+)*:*
All attributes specified for fill area set plus:
PARAMETRIC SURFACE CHARACTERISTICS (+)
PARAMETRIC SURFACE CHARACTERISTICS ASF (+)
PARAMETRIC SURFACE INDEX (+)
SURFACE APPROXIMATION CRITERIA (+)
SURFACE APPROXIMATION CRITERIA ASF (+)

Non-uniform B-spline surface with data (+)*:*
All attributes specified for non-uniform B-spline surface plus:
BACK DATA MAPPING INDEX (+)
BACK DATA MAPPING METHOD (+)
BACK DATA MAPPING METHOD ASF (+)
DATA MAPPING INDEX (+)
DATA MAPPING METHOD (+)
DATA MAPPING METHOD ASF (+)

Polyline:
COLOUR MAPPING INDEX (+)
DEPTH CUE INDEX (+)
HLHSR IDENTIFIER
LINETYPE
LINETYPE ASF

LINEWIDTH SCALE FACTOR
LINEWIDTH SCALE FACTOR   ASF
NAME SET
PICK IDENTIFIER
POLYLINE COLOUR (+)
POLYLINE COLOUR ASF (+)
POLYLINE COLOUR INDEX
POLYLINE COLOUR INDEX ASF
POLYLINE INDEX
VIEW INDEX

Polyline set with data:
All attributes specified for polyline plus:
POLYLINE SHADING METHOD (+)
POLYLINE SHADING METHOD ASF (+)
RENDERING COLOUR MODEL (+)

Polymarker:
COLOUR MAPPING INDEX (+)
DEPTH CUE INDEX (+)
HLHSR IDENTIFIER
MARKER SIZE SCALE FACTOR
MARKER SIZE SCALE FACTOR ASF
MARKER TYPE
MARKER TYPE ASF
NAME SET
PICK IDENTIFIER
POLYMARKER COLOUR (+)
POLYMARKER COLOUR ASF (+)
POLYMARKER COLOUR INDEX
POLYMARKER COLOUR INDEX ASF
POLYMARKER INDEX
VIEW INDEX

Quadrilateral mesh with data (+):
All attributes specified for fill area set with data.

Set of fill area set with data (+):
All attributes specified for fill area set with data.

Text:
CHARACTER EXPANSION FACTOR
CHARACTER EXPANSION FACTOR ASF
CHARACTER HEIGHT
CHARACTER SPACING
CHARACTER SPACING ASF

CHARACTER UP VECTOR
COLOUR MAPPING INDEX (+)
DEPTH CUE INDEX (+)
HLHSR IDENTIFIER
NAME SET
PICK IDENTIFIER
TEXT ALIGNMENT
TEXT COLOUR (+)
TEXT COLOUR ASF (+)
TEXT COLOUR INDEX
TEXT COLOUR INDEX ASF
TEXT FONT
TEXT FONT ASF
TEXT INDEX
TEXT PATH
TEXT PRECISION
TEXT PRECISION ASF
VIEW INDEX

Triangle set with data (+):
All attributes specified for fill area set with data.

Triangle strip with data (+):
All attributes specified for fill area set with data.

Appendix F

List of PHIGS Errors

PHIGS will generate errors if its functions are used incorrectly. This can be due to a function being called while PHIGS is in the wrong state, or being passed incorrect parameters. Most errors will result in the offending PHIGS function being ignored. Errors consist both of a number identifying the error and a text string describing the error. This Appendix lists the error numbers used by PHIGS and PHIGS PLUS and their corresponding description. PHIGS PLUS errors are written in *italics*. These errors have been sorted into groups of related functionality.

1. Implementation dependent errors

<0 Reserved for implementation dependent errors

2. State errors

001 Ignoring function, function requires state (PHCL,WSCL,STCL ARCL)
002 Ignoring function, function requires state (PHOP,*,*,*)
003 Ignoring function, function requires state (PHOP,WSOP,*,*)
004 Ignoring function, function requires state (PHOP,WSCL,STCL,ARCL)
005 Ignoring function, function requires state (PHOP,*,STOP,*)
006 Ignoring function, function requires state (PHOP,*,STCL,*)
007 Ignoring function, function requires state (PHOP,*,*,AROP)

3. Workstation errors

050 Ignoring function, connection identifier not recognized by the implementation
051 Ignoring function, this information is not yet available for this generic workstation type; open a workstation of this type and use the specific workstation type
052 Ignoring function, workstation type not recognized by the implementation
053 Ignoring function, workstation identifier already in use

054 Ignoring function, the specified workstation is not open
055 Ignoring function, workstation cannot be opened for an implementation dependent reason
056 Ignoring function, specified workstation is not of category MO
057 Ignoring function, specified workstation is of category MI
058 Ignoring function, specified workstation is not of category MI
059 Ignoring function, specified workstation does not have output capability (i.e., the workstation category is neither OUTPUT, OUTIN, nor MO)
060 Ignoring function, specified workstation is not of category OUTIN
061 Ignoring function, specified workstation is neither of category INPUT nor of category OUTIN
062 Ignoring function, this information is not available for this MO workstation type
063 Ignoring function, opening this workstation would exceed the maximum number of simultaneously open workstations
064 Ignoring function, the specified workstation type is not able to generate the specified generalized drawing primitive

4. Output attributes

100 Ignoring function, the bundle index value is less than one
101 Ignoring function, the specified representation has not been defined
102 Ignoring function, the specified representation has not been predefined on this workstation
103 Ignoring function, setting this bundle table entry would exceed the maximum number of entries allowed in the workstation bundle table
104 Ignoring function, the specified linetype is not available on the specified workstation
105 Ignoring function, the specified marker type is not available on the specified workstation
106 Ignoring function, the specified font is not available for the requested text precision on the specified workstation
107 Ignoring function, the specified edge type is not available on the specified workstation
108 Ignoring function, the specified interior style is not available on the specified workstation
109 Ignoring function, interior style PATTERN is not supported on the workstation
110 Ignoring function, the specified colour model is not available on the workstation
111 Ignoring function, the specified HLHSR mode is not available on the specified workstation
112 Ignoring function, the pattern index value is less than one
113 Ignoring function, the colour index value is less than zero
114 Ignoring function, the view index value is less than zero
115 Ignoring function, the view index value is less than one.
116 Ignoring function, one of the dimensions of the pattern colour index array is less than one
117 Ignoring function, one of the dimensions of the colour index array is less than zero
118 Ignoring function, one of the components of the colour specification is out of range. The valid range is dependent upon the current colour model
119 *Ignoring function, the specified depth cue mode is not available on the workstation*
120 *Ignoring function, the depth cue index is less than one*
121 *Ignoring function, the colour mapping index is less than one*
122 *Ignoring function, the specified polyline shading method is not available on the workstation*
123 *Ignoring function, the specified interior shading method is not available on the workstation*

124 *Ignoring function, the specified reflectance model is not available on the workstation*

125 *Ignoring function, the total of the colour range fields in all the table entries is too large*

126 *Ignoring function, the specified colour mapping method is not available on the specified workstation*

127 *Ignoring function, the specified approximation criteria type is not available on the specified workstation*

128 *Ignoring function, the specified parametric surface characteristics type is not available on the specified workstation*

129 *Ignoring function, the light source index is less than one*

130 *Ignoring function, invalid reference planes: DQMIN > DQMAX*

131 *Ignoring function, the specified light source type is not available on the workstation*

132 *Ignoring function, the specified spot light spread angle is out of range*

133 *Ignoring function, one of the entries in the activation list or deactivation list is less than one*

134 *Ignoring function, the requested entry contains a general colour specification with colour type other than INDIRECT*

135 *Ignoring function, the same entry exists in both the activation list and the deactivation list*

136 *Ignoring function, one of the components of the colour specification is out of range*

137 *Ignoring function, the specified data mapping method is not available on the specified workstation*

138 *Ignoring function, one or more of the fields in the specified data record is inconsistent with the specified type*

139 *Ignoring function, the specified reflectance property type is not available on the specified workstation*

140 *Ignoring function, one of the depth cue scale factors is not in the required range*

5. Transformations and viewing

150 Ignoring function, setting this view table entry would exceed the maximum number of entries allowed in the workstation's view table

151 Ignoring function, invalid window: XMIN >= XMAX, YMIN >= YMAX, ZMIN >= ZMAX, UMIN >= UMAX or VMIN >= VMAX

152 Ignoring function, invalid viewport: XMIN >= XMAX, YMIN >= YMAX or ZMIN >= ZMAX

153 Ignoring function, invalid view clipping limits: XMIN >= XMAX, YMIN >= YMAX or ZMIN >= ZMAX

154 Ignoring function, the view clipping limits are not within the NPC range

155 Ignoring function, the projection viewport limits are not within the NPC range

156 Ignoring function, the workstation window limits are not within the NPC range

157 Ignoring function, the workstation viewport is not within the display space

158 Ignoring function, front plane and back plane distances are equal when z-extent of the projection viewport is non-zero

159 Ignoring function, the view plane normal vector has length zero

160 Ignoring function, the view up vector has length zero

161 Ignoring function, the view up and view plane normal vectors are parallel; thus, the viewing coordinate system cannot be established

162 Ignoring function, the projection reference point is between the front and back planes

163 Ignoring function, the projection reference point cannot be positioned on the view plane

164 Ignoring function, the back plane is in front of the front plane

6. Structure errors

200 Warning, ignoring structures that do not exist
201 Ignoring function, the specified structure does not exist
202 Ignoring function, the specified element does not exist
203 Ignoring function, specified starting path not found in CSS
204 Ignoring function, specified search ceiling index out of range
205 Ignoring function, the label does not exist in the open structure between the element pointer and the end of the structure
206 Ignoring function, one or both of the labels do not exist in the open structure between the element pointer and the end of the structure
207 Ignoring function, the specified path depth is less than zero
208 Ignoring function, the display priority is out of range

7. Input

250 Ignoring function, the specified device is not available on the specified workstation
251 Ignoring function, the function requires the input device to be in REQUEST mode
252 Ignoring function, the function requires the input device to be in SAMPLE mode
253 Ignoring function, the specified prompt/echo type is not available on the specified workstation
254 Ignoring function, invalid echo area/volume: XMIN >= XMAX, YMIN >= YMAX or ZMIN >= ZMAX
255 Ignoring function, one of the echo area/volume boundary points is outside the range of the device
256 Warning, the input queue has overflowed
257 Ignoring function, input queue has not overflowed since OPEN PHIGS or last invocation of INQUIRE INPUT QUEUE OVERFLOW
258 Ignoring function, input queue has overflowed, but associated workstation has been closed
259 Ignoring function, the input device class of the current input report does not match the class being requested
260 Ignoring function, one of the fields within the input device data record is in error
261 Ignoring function, initial value is invalid
262 Ignoring function, number of points in the initial stroke is greater than the buffer size
263 Ignoring function, length of the initial string is greater than the buffer size

8. Metafile errors

300 Ignoring function, item type is not allowed for user items
301 Ignoring function, item length is invalid
302 Ignoring function, no item is left in metafile input
303 Ignoring function, metafile item is invalid
304 Ignoring function, item type is unknown
305 Ignoring function, content of item data record is invalid for the specified item type
306 Ignoring function, maximum item data record length is invalid
307 Ignoring function, user item cannot be interpreted

9. Escape errors

300 Warning, the specified escape is not available on one or more workstations in this

implementation. The escape will be processed by those workstations on which it is available

307 Ignoring function, one of the fields within the escape data record is in error

10 Archival / retrieval errors

400 Ignoring function, the archive file cannot be opened
401 Ignoring function, opening this archive file would exceed the maximum number of simultaneously open archive files
402 Ignoring function, archive file identifier already in use
403 Ignoring function, the archive file is not a PHIGS archive file
404 Ignoring function, the specified archive file is not open
405 Ignoring function, name conflict occurred while conflict resolution flag has value ABANDON
406 Warning, the archive file is full. Any structures that were archived were archived in total
407 Warning, some of the specified structures do not exist on the archive file
408 Warning, some of the specified structures do not exist on the archive file. PHIGS will create empty structures in their place

11. Miscellaneous errors

450 Ignoring function, the specified error file is invalid

12 PHIGS PLUS output primitive errors

500 Ignoring function, the specified order is less than one
501 Ignoring function, not enough control points for the specified order
502 Ignoring function, the specified order is inconsistent with number of knots and control points
503 Ignoring function, the knot sequence is not non-decreasing
504 Ignoring function, one or more of the vertex indices is out of range
505 Warning, the fill area is degenerate
506 Ignoring function, the parameter range is inconsistent with the knots
507 Ignoring function, the fourth coordinate of a rational control point is less than or equal to zero
508 Ignoring function, a trimming curve order is less than two
509 Ignoring function, a trimming curve does not contain enough control points for its specified order
510 Ignoring function, a trimming curve's order is inconsistent with the number of its knots and control points
511 Ignoring function, a trimming curve's knot sequence is not non-decreasing
512 Ignoring function, a trimming curve's parameter range is inconsistent with its knots
513 Ignoring function, inconsistent edge flag specification
514 Ignoring function, the data lists do not all contain the same number of entries
515 Ignoring function, the specified colour type is INDIRECT

13 System errors

900 Storage overflow has occurred in PHIGS
901 Storage overflow has occurred in CSS
902 Input/Output error has occurred while reading
903 Input/Output error has occurred while writing
904 Input/Output error has occurred while sending data to a workstation
905 Input/Output error has occurred receiving data from a workstation

906 Input/Output error has occurred during program library management
907 Input/Output error has occurred while reading workstation description table
908 Arithmetic error has occurred

14 FORTRAN binding errors

2000 Ignoring function, enumeration type out of range
2001 Ignoring function, output parameter size is insufficient. An array or string being passed as an output parameter is too small to contain the required data.
2002 Ignoring function, list or set element is not available. An index referencing an element in a list or a set is out of range.
2003 Ignoring function, invalid data record. Data record being passed to a PHIGS function cannot be decoded

15 C Language binding errors

2200 Ignoring function, start index is out of range
2201 Ignoring function, the length of the application's list is negative
2202 Ignoring function, enumeration type out of range
2203 Ignoring function, error while allocating a Store

2204 Ignoring function, error while allocating memory for a Store

Index

306